House of Lords

Poor Law Guardians (Ireland) Bill

House of Lords

Poor Law Guardians (Ireland) Bill

ISBN/EAN: 9783741104763

Manufactured in Europe, USA, Canada, Australia, Japa

Cover: Foto ©ninafisch / pixelio.de

Manufactured and distributed by brebook publishing software (www.brebook.com)

House of Lords

Poor Law Guardians (Ireland) Bill

Brought from the Lords, 27 July 1885.

REPORT

FROM THE

SELECT COMMITTEE OF THE HOUSE OF LORDS

ON THE

POOR LAW GUARDIANS (IRELAND) BILL;

TOGETHER WITH THE

PROCEEDINGS OF THE COMMITTEE,

AND

MINUTES OF EVIDENCE.

Ordered, by The House of Commons, *to be Printed*,
28 *July* 1885.

LONDON:
PRINTED BY HENRY HANSARD AND SON,
PRINTERS TO THE HOUSE OF COMMONS.

To be purchased, either directly or through any Bookseller, from any of the following Agents, viz.,
Messrs. HANSARD, 13, Great Queen-street, W.C., and 32, Abingdon-street, Westminster;
Messrs EYRE and SPOTTISWOODE, East Harding-street, Fleet-street, and
Sale Office, House of Lords;
Messrs. ADAM and CHARLES BLACK, of Edinburgh;
Messrs. ALEXANDER THOM and Co., or Messrs. HODGES, FIGGIS, and Co., of Dublin.

REPORT . . . . - p. iii
PROCEEDINGS OF THE COMMITTEE . . . - p. v
MINUTES OF EVIDENCE - . . . . . - p. 1

REPORT.

BY THE SELECT COMMITTEE appointed to consider the POOR LAW GUARDIANS (IRELAND) BILL, and to Report to the House :—

ORDERED TO REPORT,

THAT the Committee have met and considered the said Bill, and have examined several Witnesses, and have ordered the said Bill to be reported to your Lordships, with some Amendments.

And the Committee have directed the Minutes of Proceedings to be laid before your Lordships.

12th June 1885.

ORDER OF REFERENCE.

Die Jovis, 20° Novembris, 1884.

POOR LAW GUARDIANS (IRELAND) BILL.

Order of the Day for the Second Reading read: Moved that the Bill be now read 2ª; after debate, agreed to; Bill read 2ª accordingly, and committed to a Select Committee: the Committee to be named To-morrow.

Die Veneris, 21° Novembris, 1884.

Select Committee on: The Lords following were named of the Committee:

The Lord President [Lord Carlingford].
Viscount Powerscourt.
Viscount Hutchinson.
Lord Tyrone.
Lord Saltersford.
Lord Ker.
Lord Silchester.
Lord Shute.
Lord FitzGerald.
Lord Monk-Bretton.
Lord De Vesci.

The Committee to appoint their own Chairman.

Die Jovis, 19° Februarii, 1885.

Select Committee to meet To-morrow at Three o'clock.

Die Lunæ, 23° Februarii, 1885.

The Earl of Milltown added to the Select Committee.

Die Martis, 24° Februarii, 1885.

The Lord Sudley added to the Select Committee.

Die Veneris, 6° Martii, 1885.

The Evidence taken before the Select Committee from time to time to be printed, for the use of the Members of this House; but no copies thereof to be delivered, except to Members of the Committee, until further Order.

Die Veneris, 15° Maii, 1885.

The Lord Inchiquin added to the Select Committee in the place of the Lord Tyrone.

LORDS PRESENT, AND MINUTES OF PROCEEDINGS AT
EACH SITTING OF THE COMMITTEE.

Die Veneris, 20° *Februarii* 1885.

LORDS PRESENT:

Viscount Hutchinson.
Lord Tyrone.
Lord Saltersford.

Lord Shute.
Lord FitzGerald.
Lord De Vesci.

Order of Reference read.

It is moved that the Lord Tyrone do take the Chair.

The same is agreed to.

The course of Proceeding is considered.

Ordered, That the Committee be adjourned till Tuesday, the 3rd of March, at Twelve o'clock.

Die Martis, 3° *Martii* 1885.

LORDS PRESENT:

The Lord President.
Earl of Milltown.
Viscount Powerscourt.
Viscount Hutchinson.
Lord Tyrone.
Lord Saltersford.

Lord Ker.
Lord Silchester.
Lord Shute.
Lord Monk-Bretton.
Lord Sudley.
Lord De Vesci.

The Lord TYRONE in the Chair.

Order of adjournment read.

The Proceedings of the Committee of the 20th of February last are read.

Order of the House of the 23rd of February last, adding the Earl of Milltown to the Committee, read.

Order of the House of Tuesday last, adding the Lord Sudley to the Committee, read.

The following Witnesses are called in, and examined, viz.: Mr. *Henry Robinson,* C.B., and Mr. *Richard Bourke* (*vide* the Evidence).

Ordered, That the Committee be adjourned till Friday next, at Twelve o'clock.

Die Veneris, 6° Martii, 1885.

LORDS PRESENT:

The Lord President.
Earl of Milltown.
Viscount Powerscourt.
Lord Tyrone.
Lord Saltersford.

Lord Ker.
Lord Shute.
Lord Monk-Bretton.
Lord Sudley.

The Lord TYRONE, in the Chair.

Order of adjournment read.

The Proceedings of the Committee of Tuesday last are read.

The following Witnesses are called in, and examined, viz.: Mr. *George Morris* and Colonel *George Campbell Spaight* (*vide* the Evidence).

Ordered, That the Committee be adjourned till Friday, 8th of May, at Twelve o'clock.

Die Veneris, 8° Maii, 1885.

LORDS PRESENT:

The Lord President.
Earl of Milltown.
Viscount Powerscourt.
Viscount Hutchinson.
Lord Saltersford.

Lord Silchester.
Lord Shute.
Lord Monk-Bretton.
Lord Sudley.

The Earl of Milltown in the Chair in the absence of the Lord Tyrone.

Order of adjournment read.

The Proceedings of the Committee of Friday, the 6th of March last, are read.

The following Witnesses are called in, and examined, viz.: Mr. *Richard Bagwell,* Mr. *Garrett C. Tyrrell,* and Mr. *James Gray* (*vide* the Evidence).

Ordered, That the Committee be adjourned till Tuesday next, at Twelve o'clock.

Die Martis, 12° Maii, 1885.

LORDS PRESENT:

Earl of Milltown.
Viscount Powerscourt.
Viscount Hutchinson.
Lord Saltersford.

Lord Ker.
Lord Shute.
Lord Monk-Bretton.

The Earl of Milltown in the Chair in the absence of the Lord Tyrone.

Order of adjournment read.

The Proceedings of the Committee of Friday last are read.

The following Witnesses are called in, and examined, viz.: Mr. *Henry Smyth,* Mr. *John B. Hewson,* and Mr. *Henry Ringwood* (*vide* the Evidence).

Ordered, That the Committee be adjourned till Friday next, at Twelve o'clock.

Die Veneris, 15° Maii 1885.

LORDS PRESENT:

The Lord President.
Earl of Milltown.
Viscount Powerscourt.
Viscount Hutchinson.
Lord Saltersford.

Lord Ker.
Lord Shute.
Lord Monk-Bretton.
Lord Sudley.

The Earl of Milltown in the Chair in the absence of the Lord Tyrone.

Order of adjournment read.

The Proceedings of the Committee of Tuesday last are read.

The following Witnesses are called in, and examined, viz.: Mr. *Ebenezer Molloy*, Mr. *Harry M'Cann*, Mr. *Richard Edward Fox*, and Mr. *Peter Walsh* (vide the Evidence).

Ordered, That the Committee be adjourned till Tuesday the 9th of June next, at Twelve o'clock.

Die Martis, 9° Junii 1885.

LORDS PRESENT:

Earl of Milltown.
Viscount Powerscourt.
Lord Saltersford.
Lord Inchiquin.

Lord Silchester.
Lord Shute.
Lord Monk-Bretton.
Lord De Vesci.

Order of adjournment read.

The Proceedings of the Committee of Friday, the 15th of May last, are read.

Order of the House of the 15th of May last, adding the Lord Inchiquin to the Select Committee in the place of the Lord Tyrone, read.

It is moved that the Earl of Milltown do take the Chair in the place of the Lord Tyrone.

The same is agreed to.

The following Witnesses are called in, and examined, viz: Mr. *Patrick A. Meehan*, Mr. *Edward Fenelon*, and Colonel *H. D. Carden*.

Ordered, That the Committee be adjourned till Tuesday next, at Twelve o'clock.

Die Martis, 12° Junii 1885.

LORDS PRESENT:

The Lord President.
Earl of Milltown.
Viscount Powerscourt.
Viscount Hutchinson.
Lord Saltersford.
Lord Inchiquin.

Lord Ker.
Lord Silchester.
Lord Shute.
Lord Monk-Bretton.
Lord Sudley.

The Earl of MILLTOWN in the Chair.

The Title of the Bill is read, and postponed.

The Preamble of the Bill is read, and postponed.

Clauses 1 to 8 are agreed to.

Clause 9 is objected to.

On Question, That the Clause stand part of the Bill:

Contents, 2.	Not Contents, 7.
Viscount Powerscourt.	Earl of Milltown.
Lord Monk-Bretton.	Viscount Hutchinson.
	Lord Saltersford.
	Lord Inchiquin.
	Lord Ker.
	Lord Silchester.
	Lord Sudley.

A new Clause is then inserted.

Clause 10 is agreed to, with Amendments.

Clauses 11 and 12 are agreed to, with Amendments.

Clauses 13 and 14 are agreed to.

Clause 15 is agreed to, with an Amendment.

Clauses 16 to 20 are agreed to.

Clause 21 is agreed to, with an Amendment.

Clauses 22 to 24 are agreed to.

Clause 25 is read, and Amendments made therein.

It is moved to leave out Sub-Section 5.

Objected to: On Question, That the said Sub-Section stand part of the Clause:

Contents, 3.	Not Contents, 8.
The Lord President.	Earl of Milltown.
Viscount Powerscourt.	Viscount Hutchinson.
Lord Monk-Bretton.	Lord Saltersford.
	Lord Inchiquin.
	Lord Ker.
	Lord Silchester.
	Lord Shute.
	Lord Sudley.

It is then moved to insert the following new Sub-Section:

"In every case where the number of resident and non-resident justices qualified to be *ex-officio* guardians shall exceed the number of guardians to be elected by the ratepayers, the justices to serve as *ex-officio* guardians shall be selected from the said qualified justices in the manner following:

"At the prescribed time and place, after the passing of this Act, and in every third year subsequently, the justices so qualified shall assemble at a meeting to be specially held for the purpose, of which meeting the justice senior, by appointment, shall be the chairman, and thereupon the said justices shall by a majority of their number present and voting (the chairman, in case of an equality of votes in favour of two or more persons, to have a double or casting vote), appoint from the justices so qualified a number of persons equal to the number of guardians to be elected by the ratepayers, and the justices so appointed shall be entitled to act as *ex-officio* guardians of the poor for the term of three years. Provided always, that it may be competent for any justice to resign his office in the prescribed manner.

"Casual vacancies occurring among the *ex-officio* guardians, owing to resignations or otherwise, shall be filled up in the like manner at a meeting convened for the purpose in the prescribed manner."

Objected to: On Question:

Contents, 10.	Not Content, 1.
The Lord President.	Lord Silchester.
Earl of Milltown.	
Viscount Powerscourt.	
Viscount Hutchinson.	
Lord Saltersford.	
Lord Inchiquin.	
Lord Ker.	
Lord Shute.	
Lord Monk-Bretton.	
Lord Sudley.	

It is then moved to insert the following words at the end of the Clause:

"In any case where a ratepayer in any electoral division is rated as an occupier, and also as an immediate lessor, the valuations of these separate ratings shall be aggregated and votes allowed on their total according to the scale prescribed by the 1 & 2 Vict. c. 56, s. 81: Provided that in such case the said ratepayer may, by writing, elect to attribute the votes to which he is limited by this Act to such of the aforesaid qualifications as he thinks fit, but not so as to attribute to either of such qualifications a greater number of votes than he would by law be entitled to have in respect of that qualification if this Act had not passed.

"In case he does not elect, he shall be deemed to have elected to attribute his votes to these separate qualifications in the proportion of the two classes of property constituting such qualification."

Objected to: On Question:

Contents, 10.	Not Content, 1.
The Lord President.	Lord Silchester.
Earl of Miltown.	
Viscount Powerscourt.	
Viscount Hutchinson.	
Lord Salterford.	
Lord Inchiquin.	
Lord Ker.	
Lord Shute.	
Lord Monk-Bretton.	
Lord Sudley.	

The Clause, as amended, is then agreed to.

Clause 26 is agreed to.

Clause 27 is agreed to, with Amendments.

The Preamble of the Bill is again read, and agreed to.

The Title of the Bill is again read, and agreed to.

Ordered, That the Lord in the Chair do report the Bill, with Amendments, to the House.

MINUTES OF EVIDENCE.

LIST OF WITNESSES.

Die Martis, 3° Martii, 1885.

	PAGE.
Mr. Henry Robinson, c.b.	3
Mr. Richard Bourke	31

Die Veneris, 6° Martii, 1885.

Mr. George Morris	45
Colonel George Campbell Spaight	63

Die Veneris, 8° Maii, 1885.

Mr. Richard Bagwell	85
Mr. Garrett C. Tyrrell	96
Mr. James Gray	104

Die Martis, 12° Maii, 1885.

Mr. Henry Smyth	113
Mr. John B. Hewson	130
Mr. Henry Ringwood	143

Die Veneris, 15° Maii, 1885.

Mr. Ebenezer Molloy	151
Mr. Harry M'Cann	165
Mr. Richard Edward Fox	173
Mr. Peter Walsh	182

Die Martis, 9° Junii, 1885.

Mr. Patrick A. Meehan	189
Mr. Edward Fenelon	208
Colonel H. D. Carden	224

Die Martis, 3° Martii, 1885.

LORDS PRESENT:

The Lord President.	Lord Ker.
Earl of Milltown.	Lord Silchester.
Viscount Powerscourt.	Lord Shute.
Viscount Hutchinson.	Lord Monk-Bretton.
Lord Tyrone.	Lord Sudley.
Lord Saltersford.	Lord De Vesci.

THE LORD TYRONE, IN THE CHAIR.

MR. HENRY ROBINSON, c.b., called in; and Examined, as follows:

1. *Chairman.*] You are Vice-President of the Irish Local Government Board?
I am.

2. Had you previously been in any position under that Board?
I had previously been for many years an Inspector of the Board, and I was also Assistant Under Secretary for Ireland for a few years.

3. I suppose, therefore, you have a thorough knowledge of the whole working of every department of the Poor Law?
Yes.

4. Would you kindly state for the information of the Committee the present law in Ireland with regard to the formation of local poor law boards?
The election of guardians in Ireland is carried out by means of voting papers left at the houses of the voters; and the voters are ratepayers who comprise three classes: those who vote in respect of occupation, and who vote upon the valuation; the owners of property, who vote in respect of rents received; and the immediate lessors of holdings valued at and under 4 *l.*, who pay the whole of the rates. The occupiers, being the first class, must vote in person; the owners voting in respect of rents received, and the immediate lessors may vote by proxy. The following is the scale of votes laid down by the Irish Poor Relief Act of 1838: where the valuation does not amount to 20 *l.* there is one vote; where it amounts to 20 *l.*, and not to 50 *l.*, two votes; where it amounts to 50 *l.*, and not to 100 *l.*, three votes; where it amounts to 100 *l.*, and not to 150 *l.*, four votes; where it amounts to 150 *l.*, and not to 200 *l.*, five votes, and where it amounts to 200 *l.* and upwards, six votes. Where an occupier has a beneficial interest in his holding, that is to say, when his rent is below his valuation, he has an additional vote in respect of the holding; that is to say, if he holds the land in fee-simple he has a double number of votes. At present any man might have a maximum number of 30 votes; that is to say, he might have six votes as occupier, and six votes in respect of beneficial interest, six votes in respect of rent received, six votes in respect of the valuation of his immediate lessor property, and six votes in respect of beneficial interest out of that property.

5. Earl

3rd March 1885.] Mr. ROBINSON, C.B. [*Continued.*

5. Earl of *Milltown.*] In one electoral district, do you mean?
In one electoral division.

6. Up to last year it was held that the maximum number of votes could only be 18, but our decision upon the subject, which was based upon legal advice, was questioned in an election in the Shillelagh Union, and the Court of Queen's Bench, to whom the case was appealed, decided that we were right, but the case was carried into the Court of Appeal, and the Court of Appeal decided that the immediate lessor votes were to be given irrespective of the occupation votes, and in addition to them; and consequently at present, as the law stands, one person might have up to 30 votes. As I was saying, the elections are then carried on by voting papers. Notice of election is issued on the 25th of February, nominations are received on the 4th of March, voting papers are sent out on the 18th of March, and, if necessary, the 19th; they are collected on the 20th, and, if necessary, on the 21st; that is to say, the paper must remain one clear day at the house of the voter. The return is then made on the 25th of March to us, and the new Board is constituted. That is briefly the present state of the law of election.

7. *Chairman.*] The Board is at present composed half of elected guardians and half of *ex-officio* guardians, is it not?
Provided that the number of magistrates residing or having property in the union equals the number of elected guardians; but in some cases there are not a sufficient number.

8. Is that often the case?
Yes. There are several unions in which there are not a sufficient number of magistrates to equal the number of elected guardians; for instance, the elective guardians in Ireland are 3,894, and the *ex-officio* guardians only amount to 3,713; so that the difference between those two figures arises by reason of the number of the magistrates not being sufficient to equal the number of elected guardians.

9. Earl of *Milltown.*] The number of qualified magistrates you mean?
Qualified to be *ex-officio* guardians. Wherever the number is less than the elected guardians every magistrate is entitled to be an *ex-officio* guardian, supposing he has the qualification necessary under the Act.

10. *Chairman.*] *Ex-officio* guardians are made up of residents and non-residents, are they not?
Yes.

11. What is the qualification for a non-resident?
There is no qualification, except that he must be acting for the county in which he resides.

12. A non-resident I am asking about?
The magistrate, both resident and non-resident, must be qualified to act for the county in which he resides.

13. Lord *Skute.*] Are stipendiary magistrates included?
No.

14. *Chairman.*] Is there not some arrangement by which the non-resident magistrate's name should be on the rate book?
Provided the number exceeds the number of elected guardians, the highest rated are selected.

15. But is there not some rule by which an *ex-officio* guardian must have his name on the rate book?
It is not necessary that a resident *ex-officio* guardian should have his name upon the rate book.

16. I am now asking about the non-resident?
No, it is not necessary that he should have his name upon the rate book. The qualification is in Section 7 of the 12th & 13th Vict. c. 104, which provides that he "shall be seised, possessed, or entitled for his own use, and benefit, of or to any lands, tenements or hereditaments situate within such union, or in the
rents

rents and profits thereof, for any life or lives in being, or for any term of 21 years at the least, such estate being of the yearly value of 50 l. at the least "

17. But I will give you an example? Supposing a landlord is non resident, that he owns a large property in a union, but that he has no residence in the union, he would only pay one-half of his tenant's rates ; he would not pay any rates himself because he would have no occupation. Supposing that he had no tenants rated under 4 l., he would not appear upon the rate book, would he?
No.

18. I am informed that under those circumstances he could not be an *ex-officio* guardian. Has such a case ever arisen?
He can be an *ex-officio* guardian, but I think what your Lordship refers to is this: that provided the number of magistrates exceed the number of elected guardians, and that a selection has to be made, then the selection is made from those who appear upon the rate book ; that is to say, the highest rated are selected.

19. Viscount *Powerscourt*.] That is, that there never shall be more *ex-officio* than elective guardians?
Just so.

20. *Chairman*.] You have looked over the Bill which this Committee is appointed to inquire into?
Yes.

21. I should like to go through the Bill if you would kindly give us your opinion upon the different clauses in it. Page 1, I think, has mostly to do with definitions; I do not think I need ask you any questions about that part. On page 2, there is a proposal that the guardians for the future are to hold office for three years ; have you any objection to that?
No.

22. At present they are elected every year, I think?
At present they are elected every year.

23. Then the next three clauses, 5, 6, and 7, have to do with the election by ballot. Now, would there not be some difficulty in arranging for the election by ballot when there is a cumulative vote?
There is great difficulty in the matter, and I was going to bring the subject before the Committee. The Bill provides that our Board shall deal with that matter by an Order, and I think that that is much too important a matter to be decided by an Order, and I think it is a point upon which there should be legislation. We should not much like to incur the responsibility of deciding such an important point. There are only two ways in which it can be done. It can be done by giving each voter a separate ballot paper for each vote that he is entitled to give, or else the number of votes which each paper is to carry can be marked on the face of the paper. The polling clerk will have before him a list containing the names in the register in the particular district for which he sits; that list will contain the name of each voter, the number of the voter upon the register, and the number of votes such voter is entitled to give; and then, as I said before, suppose a man has six votes, the clerk would either have to give him six separate voting papers, or else to place on the face of the ballot paper the number " six," which would guide the returning officer in making up his poll. At present the polling clerk has to mark, that is to say under the Ballot Act he would have to mark, on the counterfoil of the ballot paper the number of the voter, so that the paper could be identified in the case of a scrutiny; and the counterfoil and the ballot paper bear corresponding printed numbers; so that no one knows, except in the event of a scrutiny, how each person votes. My suggestion would be that at the same time that the polling clerk marks upon the counterfoil the number of the voter he should also place upon the voting paper, either on the face or on the back, the number of votes that that paper is to carry. The first plan would be very cumbrous ; it would be very difficult indeed to carry on any election giving a separate voting paper for each vote, considering the number of persons who vote. I will give an instance. When the question of voting by ballot

was raised in the year 1877, I obtained a return of the number of persons who were entitled to vote, and I found that in one union alone, namely, in the North Dublin Union, there were about 9,300 occupiers and that there were over 2,400 proxies. Now, if the persons who had more than one vote each received a separate paper and voted upon it, the proceedings would be very much more protracted and very inconvenient.

24. I suppose that the difficulty of letting a man have one paper for the number of votes he was entitled to would be that it would be impossible then to preserve the secrecy of the ballot?
The secrecy of the ballot might be indirectly infringed in certain cases by the fact of its being known that in each electoral division there are perhaps only two or three persons having a very large number of votes, and when a ballot paper marked with "10," or "12," or "18 votes," is seen, it would be immediately known that that ballot paper must belong to the one of the two or three persons in the division who can give such a number of votes.

25. You consider that it would be cumbrous to give in a ballot paper for each vote?
I consider it would be.

26. And as far as I understand you, you think that the best system would be to give the voter a ballot paper for so many votes, let no ballot paper, say, carry more than six or four votes?
I think the polling clerk might mark upon the face or the back of the ballot paper the total number of votes that any one man was entitled to, so that there should be marked on the ballot paper the number of votes that the paper is to carry in order that only one paper should be given to each voter.

27. Would not that break up the secrecy of the ballot?
There would be no name on the ballot paper, but just on the face of it the number of votes it carried.

28. And it might carry six or four votes?
It might carry 18 or 30. The Bill limits the number to 18, but under the present system there might be 30 votes to one man.

29. *Lord President.*] Do you mean that you would have voting papers prepared for each of these numbers?
I think the simplest plan would be for the polling clerk to write upon the paper, before he issues it, the number of votes that the voter is entitled to give, and that will be a guide to the man counting the votes. There are difficulties both ways; but I am anxious that your Lordships should be good enough to consider the point in order that there may be legislation on the subject, and not leave it, as the Bill proposes, to our Board to decide it.

30. *Chairman.*] Would it be possible, as I suggested, to have no voting paper carrying more than six votes, to have voting papers for six votes, and four votes, and so on, down to one vote, so that a man who had 18 votes might use three of these papers; that would get rid of the cumbrous system?
Still there must be a mark put upon the voting paper, of the numbers under six.

31. But you would not object to that system?
No, if it were thought well to say that no voting paper shall carry more than six votes; and then, if a man is entitled to 30 votes, the polling clerk would give him five papers, and mark "six" on the front of each of them, which would prevent identifying any particular person; I do not see that there would be much difficulty in that.

32. I was thinking that that would be perhaps more secret than your proposal?
It might make it a little more secret.

33. Then I think that the following clauses have all to do with the Ballot Act.

Act. Have you any further remark to make about the Bill with reference to the ballot?

No, I have not. I think that it would be an improvement in the system of election.

34. *Lord De Vesci.*] Do you know whether cumulative voting prevails to any extent?

Just before I left Dublin I heard that cumulative voting is in force in Galway Town, but that is the only instance I ever heard of. I was about to say that it was proved clearly before the Committee that sat in 1878, that intimidation and undue influence existed to a very great extent, and I know from my own observation and knowledge of the working of the Poor Law every year, that intimidation and undue influence do exist to a very great extent, and I think that perhaps the ballot would remedy that evil.

35. *Lord President.*] What Bill was it of 1877 that you referred to?

When the question of voting by ballot was first considered, I do not know whether a Bill was actually prepared, but this matter has been under consideration for several years.

36. *Lord Monk-Bretton.*] That Committee that you speak of was a Committee of the House of Commons?

It was a Committee of the House of Commons.

37. *Chairman.*] I should like to ask you how it would be possible, if voting by ballot is adopted as proposed by this Bill, to have proxy votes given satisfactorily?

There would be no more difficulty than there is at present. The persons appointed proxies would make their claims within one month from the time of voting; and the persons appointing proxies must make the appointments within one month from the time of voting; and those names are entered in registers, and those registers would form the basis of the register so far as the votes of owners of property are concerned; and there would be no more difficulty in voting by proxies, by ballot, than there is in voting at present by papers.

38. *Lord President.*] Because the ballot would not apply in those cases?

The person would be allowed to vote by proxy or in person at an election by ballot.

39. But if he voted by proxy that would take the place of the ballot, would it not?

No, because the proxy might be allowed to attend at the ballotting place and give his vote for the owner who appointed him.

40. *Lord Shute.*] The proxy would know how the vote was given; it would not be secret from him?

Not from him, because he would give the vote.

41. *Lord Saltersford.*] A. B. is registered as holding so many proxy votes, and then he would return all those votes?

The list which the polling clerk would have before him would be the list of persons entitled to vote as occupiers, and the list of persons entitled to vote as proxies; then the proxy would appear before him and claim the voting paper, and receive it.

42. *Chairman.*] Clause 9 of this Bill proposes to do away with the proxy voting, and I should like to ask you some questions with regard to that. Do you think it would be possible for owners of property to attend and register their votes if the proxy vote was done away with?

No, I think it would be quite impossible. The owners of property possess property in many electoral divisions and unions, and I think that that clause would practically disfranchise them in every electoral division and union except the one in which they reside.

43. There was a proposal made that the Local Government Board might hold elections upon different days; what do you say to that suggestion?
I think it would be quite impracticable and very inconvenient, and I do not see how the Local Government Board could be guided in the matter; it could not meet the convenience of every landowner or owner of property.

44. You think it would be impossible to frame any scheme which would enable the owners to vote in person?
I think it would be almost impossible to frame any scheme which would do so.

45. I suppose, under those circumstances, you think that the proxy vote, or something analogous to it, should be retained?
That is my opinion. It is a question of policy; but I am clearly of opinion that owners ought to be allowed to vote by proxy. The owners of property pay more than half the poor rates in Ireland, directly or indirectly, and I do not think that they should be disfranchised in unions in which they do not reside.

46. Earl of *Milltown*.] They pay nearly five-eighths of the poor rates; is not that so?
I think that is a fair representation. I was reading the other day the report of Sir George Nicholls in 1835, showing the grounds upon which proxy voting was allowed in the first instance. Perhaps you would like me to read it to the Committee, as it is very short.

47. *Chairman*.] Will you please do so?
Sir George Nicholls was sent over, when the Irish Poor Relief Bill was under consideration, to report to the Home Secretary on the subject, and he says: "As regards the right of voting by proxy given to owners by the Bill, it may be observed that such a power is necessary for enabling the owner to protect his property, his interest in which is permanent, although he is not always present to represent it by his personal vote, and the Bill therefore provides for his doing so by proxy. The occupier is always present and may vote in person; not so the owner. He would very rarely be present, and his interest would be unprotected without this power of voting by proxy. That the owner's interest ought to be represented, I presume, will not be denied. The rate must be regarded as a charge upon the property, and as such it becomes a portion of the rent which, in the average of years would be increased by the amount of the rate, if this was not levied for Poor Law purposes; so that in reality it is the landlord, the permanent owner of the property, who finally bears the burthen of the rate, and not the tenant or temporary occupier; although this last is, as a matter of convenience, required to pay the rate in the first instance. It seems consonant with justice, therefore, that every facility should be afforded to the owner for protecting his interest by his vote." Those are the grounds upon which proxy voting was established in the first instance.

48. I suppose you see no reason to depart from those views at the present day?
No, I entirely concur in the opinions expressed in this report, and I do not think that any thing has occurred to make a change in that respect necessary.

49. Are you aware whether the proxy vote prevails in England?
Yes, it does in respect of rents received. An owner who votes on the strength of the rents he receives may vote by proxy in any parish in which he does not reside at the time of election.

50. Supposing that this clause was retained in the Bill, would it not be possible to enable owners to vote by registered letter?
I do not think that that could be done and the secresy of the ballot preserved; I do not see how it is to be carried out.

51. You think that if an owner could obtain his present number of forms, and forward

3rd March 1885.] Mr. ROBINSON, C.B. [Continued.

forward them to the returning officer by registered letter, the secrecy of the ballot would not be maintained?

He must sign the letter, otherwise how would the returning officer be able to identify the letter and he sure that it is a valid document.

52. Would you consider that if proxy voting was done away with it would produce a virtual disfranchisement of the owners of property?

Yes, in the unions in which they do not reside.

53. Earl of *Milltown*.] With regard to the registered letters, do you think that such owners of property as, under the suggestion of the noble Marquess, would vote by registered letter, are likely to require the protection of the ballot?

They may not always require it; but I think that if the ballot is established it should apply to all persons.

54. *Chairman*.] Have you any further suggestions to make about the Part I. of the Bill before we pass away from it?

Clause 8 provides that, "The Local Government Board may embody in any such order the second, third, fourth, sixth, ninth, twelfth, thirteenth, and twenty fourth sections of the Ballot Act, 1872," but the third, fourth, ninth, and twenty-fourth sections of the Ballot Act comprise a Penal Code, and we think it would be very desirable that they should, with certain modifications, be re-enacted or incorporated with the Bill, and that it should not be left to the Local Government Board to establish a Penal Code by means of an order.

55. Viscount *Powerscourt*.] The penal provisions should be in the Act, you think?

We think that they should be incorporated in the Act.

56. *Chairman*.] Would there be any inconvenience in the claims for the right to vote being lodged so short a time before the election takes place?

I was going to make a suggestion about that to the Committee. Clause 10 of the Bill provides that "At the prescribed time, before the day fixed for the polling at any poor law election, the returning officer shall prepare in the prescribed manner a list of the ratepayers;" and that precribed time means the time which may be prescribed by the Local Government Board; but under the existing Acts the returning officer must receive up to one month from voting the claims of persons to be registered in respect of property, and therefore he cannot prepare his lists until that day arrives. For instance, the 20th of February is the last day for receiving claims to vote, and the returning officer would not have time between that and the time of the election, the 25th of March, to carry out all the arrangements prescribed by the 10th and 11th clauses; and I would suggest therefore that Section 15 of the 25th & 26th Victoria, cap. 83, which provides that a ratepayer claiming to vote in respect of any property not in his actual occupation must lodge his claim at least one month before the day of voting, should be amended by substituting "two months" for "one month," and that will give the returning officer sufficient time to prepare his lists, hold his court of revision, and prepare the register.

57. Then as to the payments of rates, what do you say on that point?

The present Act provides that an occupier to qualify himself for voting may pay his poor rates up to the day of voting; so that on the day upon which the voting papers are sent out any person who has not paid his poor rates may come to the returning officer, pay his rates and receive a voting paper. Now, that would be impracticable under the Ballot Act, because there would be no finality in the lists, and no secrecy in regard to that voter's vote; and I would suggest that the same day, which is the last day fixed for the owner to make his claim, should be the last day for the payment of rates to qualify at the ensuing election; that is to say, that two months before the day of election, the right to vote should be completed by the service of the claim and the payment of rates.

(0.1.) B 58. *Lord*

58. *Lord President.*] Payment of rates, up to what date?
Of rates more than six months due; that is the present law.

59. Viscount *Hutchinson.*] You say that according to the present arrangements any ratepayer can go in and pay his rate to the returning officer on the day of the election, and then vote?
He can pay the rates on the day of voting.

60. But the returning officer is not qualified to give a receipt for the rates?
No; what I mean is that he may pay the rate to the rate collector, and take the receipt to the returning officer.

61. *Chairman.*] On Clause 11 have you anything to say?
Clause 11 provides that the returning officer shall sit on a certain day " to hear the claims of persons whose names have been omitted from any such lists;" and I think that when the returning officer, in pursuance of that clause, sits to hear the claims of persons whose names have been omitted from the list, he should also hear objections to the names of persons who have been put on. It is a very minor matter, but it is an omission from the clause.

62. What is the present system with regard to that; what is the present law as regards the returning officer sitting and receiving those objections?
That is entirely a new arrangement, a new clause.

63. There is no law about it at present?
No; as a matter of practice, in the two Dublin unions, the returning officer does sit to revise the claims, though there is no law upon the subject.

64. You propose that when he does sit he should deal with both matters?
That when he does sit to hear the claims of persons omitted he also should hear objections to names which have been put on the register, or to statements of claim. Then before we pass on there is another matter; Clause 10 only provides for the revision of the registries before every triennial election; but there may be supplemental elections during the three years that the guardians sit, and I think it would be very desirable that the registries should be amended and corrected in the manner prescribed by Clauses 10 and 11 every year, so that if a supplemental election takes place at the end of, say, two-and-a-half years, the election should not be held upon an inaccurate register. It would also facilitate the returning officer in carrying out his revision before the triennial election; he would have less to do.

65. Revision to take place every year is what you propose?
I think the revision should take place every year.

66. Earl of *Milltown.*] The Bill, as I understand it, contemplates the ballot taking place at the union workhouse; will it not be desirable in the case, particularly of large unions, that there should be several polling places?
That is provided by the Act. The returning officer is to sit at the union workhouse to count the votes; but the provisions of the Ballot Act enable us to make an order providing for the ballot being taken in different electoral divisions.

67. *Lord President.*] I think you said that the risk of the disclosure of the votes of a small number of those having the greatest number of votes to give, which seems to be inseparable from a system of voting by ballot, is not, in your view, a very important objection to it?
I think that the objection to that is not so great as the objection to giving a separate voting paper for every vote.

68. The risk would only arise in a small number of cases?
A very small number.

69. And, probably, in just those cases where the protection of the ballot is least required or desired?

I think,

I think, probably, it would be very well known how such persons would vote.

70. You think also that the suggestion made by the noble Marquess, of furnishing such persons with more than one voting paper, would diminish that risk?
I think it would; and I think it is possible, and that there is no difficulty about it.

71. Now, as to the suggestion that has been made, that it might be possible to hold Poor Law elections upon different days in different unions, in connection with the proposed abolition of proxy voting; would you explain a little more why you treat that as an impracticable proposal?
It would require a separate order for each union in place of a general order, that is a mere matter of detail which is very easily got over, but I do not see upon what data the Local Government Board could determine those dates. How could they ascertain in what way the convenience of the owners of property would be met or could be met; would they have to wait until the different owners tell them that they cannot vote in different places on the same day; we do not know what would suit the convenience of owners of property, and I do not quite see how we could make such an arrangement; and moreover, it would be very inconvenient if the time were to extend over 10 days or a fortnight or so: if the general election were going on for two or three months it would be extremely inconvenient.

72. You could prevent a great number of unions holding their elections upon the same day?
We could very easily do that. We could say that two adjoining unions should not hold an election upon the same day; but an owner of property in one union might not have property in the adjoining union, and might, without our knowing anything about it, have property in a union for which the election was fixed for the very day of the election in the union in which he did reside.

73. As to proxy voting, can you tell us what proportion or about what proportion of the votes given are given by way of proxy?
I cannot tell the Committee generally the number over Ireland. I can obtain a Return, if desired; but, as I said before, I obtained a Return from three unions in 1877, when this question was first mooted, and at that time I found that in one union, North Dublin, there were 9,307 occupiers entitled to vote; there were 1,693 proxies entitled to vote in respect of rents received, and 717 in respect of immediate lessor rating; so that there were over 2,400 proxies. In the South Dublin Union there were 16,574 occupiers, and there were over 1,700 proxies; but those are two metropolitan unions, and of course the number of proxies are not so great in the rural unions. In Rathdown Union I found that there were 5,130 occupiers entitled to vote, and 248 proxies.

74. Do those who vote in right of property make a very extensive use of this privilege of proxy voting?
It depends very much upon whether the divisions are keenly contested. In the North Dublin Union the electoral divisions are very keenly contested, and the election agents look out for the owners of property, and get them to sign claims to vote.

75. Taking the country generally, can you tell us what the state of the case is?
No; I am unable to give an approximate statement of the number who vote in that way; but there are in every union a considerable number on the register.

76. Cannot you tell us whether those who vote in right of property make a very extensive use of this privilege?
Yes, I think I may safely say that they do make an extensive use of it. I will obtain a Return, if the Committee wish it, from the clerks of unions, of the proxy votes in all Ireland.

3rd March 1885.]   Mr. ROBINSON, C.B.   [Continued.

77. Is there any restriction upon the right of proxy voting as to residence, or is it irrespective of residence?
Irrespective of residence.

78. I mean, if I am residing in a certain electoral division, can I vote in it by proxy if I choose?
Yes, in respect of rents received, or immediate lessor rating; but not as occupier.

79. I think you said that that is not the case in England?
I believe that is not the case in England; and that an owner may not appoint a proxy to vote in respect of his property in the parish in which he resides at the time of the election. It might be rather difficult to define always where a man resides; he might be away temporarily.

80. *Chairman.*] But in England the owner has not to pay half the rate?
Half the rate is not deducted from the owner, but still he votes in respect of the rent.

81. *Lord President.*] Is it not the case that the proxy lasts for a period of three years?
For five years.

82. What do you think of that; does it not appear to you to be an excessive duration?
It was unlimited formerly, and that was found inconvenient, and it was limited to five years. In view of the election being triennial, I should have no objection to seeing it reduced to three years.

83. That is to say, being *pro hac vice*, for the purposes of the coming election?
Then it would hold good for any supplemental election during the three years.

84. That is what you mean?
I should see no objection to that. At present one person may only hold 20 proxy appointments; he may only vote for 20 owners, unless he is the bailiff or agent of them.

85. Supposing that the system of proxy voting is to be retained, and not abolished, have you considered any points in which the working of it could be improved?
The only point which strikes me is that it would be convenient that an owner appointing a proxy in respect of rents received, and of his immediate lessor property, should appoint the same person for both; it would facilitate the proceedings for election. Instead of one man appointing two proxies, let him appoint one for both; that would not deprive him of any right, and it would facilitate our proceedings. One person only would have to attend the polling place instead of two. That is the only change.

86. Lord *Sudeley.*] If I understood you rightly, if the Bill is adopted as it is now framed, it would practically disfranchise the owners of property?
In unions in which they do not reside I think it would.

87. Lord *Monk-Bretton.*] When you said that a proxy lasted for so many years, the owner can withdraw the proxy?
Yes, he can withdraw it or appoint another person. The appointment of a second person is always looked upon as a revocation of the original appointment.

88. Have you had occasion to consider a system by which voting papers might be substituted for proxies?
Do you mean registered letters.

89. Voting papers in contradistinction to proxies. A voting paper is a paper by which a voter votes himself; a proxy is a system of voting by which he consigns himself into the hands of his proxy?
But as I said before, if votes were given by voting papers or registered letters

letters in any other way except at the polling places, and by ballot, the principle of the ballot would not be carried out.

90. I understood you to say that you considered that if voting papers were resorted to, the voting papers must be signed?
I said, that if a registered letter were sent to the returning officer it would be necessary for the person sending it to sign the letter, and therefore there would be no secrecy in regard to the votes.

91. But why might not a stamped and numbered ballot paper of the non-resident voter be sent to him by the returning officer?
The returning officer must satisfy himself that it comes from the person entitled to vote.

92. He would address it to the person entitled to vote, sending it by registered letter?
And then he would receive it back by registered letter, and he must know, therefore, who the voter is, and in what way he votes.

93. At present he knows who the voter is?
At present he does; but it is sought to abolish that knowledge by establishing secrecy in the voting.

94. But at present, under the system of the ballot, the returning officer knows who the voter is to whom he hands the paper?
He is not supposed to know how he votes; he might learn this by examining the counterfoil of the ballot papers.

95. But when I vote I go to the polling booth and I apply for a polling paper; the returning officer looks to my number on the register and gives me that numbered paper, therefore he knows the voter to whom he is delivering the paper?
He knows the voter to whom he is delivering the paper, and by comparing the number with the register the returning officer could ascertain how any particular person votes if he wished to do it; but I believe there is some provision made in the Ballot Act for sealing up these counterfoils, and not allowing them to be opened unless there is a scrutiny on an appeal.

96. If instead of walking into the office and applying personally for a paper, I apply for it to be sent to me by a registered letter, the returning officer would equally know, and know no more, who is the person who applies for the paper, and to whom he delivers it?
Quite so; if that system were established the returning officer would know how any person voted who applied to him for a voting paper by registered letter.

97. Why should he know more in the one case than in the other; if he knows who is the voter applying for the paper personally, where does the greater secrecy exist?
I think under the Ballot Act there is some provision made that the counterfoils are locked up; it is only by comparing the counterfoils that he can know how a person votes at present; I think there is some provision of that sort.

98. *Chairman.*] Under the Ballot Act when a man marks on his paper how he votes, he puts it into a receptacle?
Yes.

99. But you consider that the difficulty is, that in the other case it would be the returning officer who would put it into the receptacle, and therefore he could look at it first?
It would never go into the receptacle at all. The returning officer sits at the head-quarters of the union, he appoints polling clerks, and the persons who attend at the polling places receive the ballot papers, which they put into this receptacle, and the box is locked up and sent to the returning officer at head-quarters, who counts the votes, and it is only by comparing the lists of the polling clerks with the register of the votes and the counterfoils of the books kept

kept by the polling clerks, that he could ascertain how any person votes; and such a scrutiny is only held in the event of an appeal against the election. But in this case to which Lord Monk-Bretton alludes, the voter would not have to attend at the polling place in the division at all; he would give his vote by a registered letter, if I understand it.

100. Lord *Monk-Bretton*.] He would apply for his numbered voting paper, and would receive it by registered letter, and would return it by registered letter; where is that less secret than the system of his going and asking for the paper himself?
It is directly brought under the returning officer's notice by means of the correspondence, whereas the other can only be ascertained by means of an examination of the paper.

101. But before he delivers to any voter a voting paper he must know who the person is?
The polling clerk would do that, and he would know. The correspondence could not take place with the polling clerk.

102. May I take it that you have not carefully considered whether a system of voting papers could be substituted consistently with the secrecy of the ballot for proxy voting?
I think that the returning officer would be obliged to make himself aware directly of the way that each of the persons applying for a paper or a registered letter voted; and further, there would be some difficulty in carrying on the election, because with a very great number of proxies appointed there would be a very large correspondence. If, for instance, the returning officer, say in the South Dublin Union, received over 2,000 proxy votes by post, that would involve a large correspondence.

103. But you have not had occasion to consider whether such a system of voting papers could be devised?
I have not given it sufficient consideration to give any further evidence on the point.

104. Lord *Silchester*.] Is it probable that any different class of guardians would be elected by ballot than otherwise?
I do not think that it would affect the class of persons elected if proxy voting is maintained.

105. Lord *De Vesci*.] Can you see any objection to the right of voting by proxy being extended to the occupier?
I do not see any cause for that.

106. Viscount *Hutchinson*.] I think you answered Lord Carlingford just now that proxy votes were largely availed of in severe contests?
More largely used then.

107. You have no statistics, have you, on the point?
No; none beyond those three unions that I have mentioned.

108. Would it be possible to secure any statistics of the general use of proxy votes in Ireland for the last three or four years?
We might obtain a return of the number of occupation votes and proxy votes given in Ireland at any one election.

109. Could you obtain a return which would show the increase or decrease in the use of proxy votes; a comparative return?
That would take a longer time to prepare.

110. Have they been much used in the last two years?
I think they have in some cases, especially in towns; in Dublin, for instance.

111. You have no statistics to give us at present?
No, not on that point.

112. Lord

112. Lord *Shute*.] How is the area of unions settled in Ireland; by Act of Parliament?
The area originally was settled by the Poor Law Commissioners, and it is now determined by the Local Government Board, who may alter any area if they think fit.

113. The same as in England, in fact?
I suppose so. That is the law in Ireland.

114. The rates, of course, vary in different districts; can you tell me what the average rate in the pound is?
The average expenditure last year was 1s. 5½d. in the pound for poor relief, and 1s. 10d. for all purposes.

115. Do you think that under the ballot owners of property would be likely to elect guardians, supposing this Bill were passed?
I do not think it would make any difference, provided proxy voting is maintained.

116. Lord *Monk-Bretton*.] Is it not the fact that in Ireland the owners pay the poor rates for the occupiers whose occupation is under the value of 4l. a year?
At and under, yes.

117. And that, taking into account that fact and the fact that they pay half the rates in the case of all other occupiers, it is estimated that, on the whole, the owners pay five-eighths of the rates?
I think that that is an approximate statement of what the owners bear now.

118. *Chairman*.] Would you not have to add to what Lord Monk-Bretton has put to you, as to the payment of rates by the owner of property, that he has, in addition to paying the whole of the rate for his tenants at and under 4l. and half the rate of the rest of his tenants, to pay the full rate on land in his own occupation?
He pays the rate on land in his own occupation in the same way as any other occupier. If he holds property in fee simple and occupies it, he pays the whole rate upon it. If he pays a head rent, he deducts from that the proportion of the rate.

119. Earl of *Milltown*.] Would it not be true also to say that indirectly the owner pays the other three-eighths, because if it were not for the poor rate being deducted his rent would be proportionately higher?
That is a question which I could not well answer.

120. You said that elections were keenly contested: has that been different recently; were they formerly keenly contested?
In some cases they always were keenly contested, but I think the contests have been very numerous of late.

121. Do those contests notoriously arise, not so much from a desire for selecting efficient guardians for the poor, as from political reasons?
Political and religious reasons influence the voters very much in the nomination of candidates. I was going to state to the Committee the number of contests. There are 3,289 electoral divisions and wards in Ireland, and in the March election there were 557 contests. That will give an idea of the extent to which they prevail.

122. As far as my experience goes, proxy votes had not been extensively used until the political element was so strongly brought into the Poor Law elections; is that your experience?
I cannot well answer that; I cannot well say whether proxy voting has increased by reason of that cause of late.

123. Lord *Monk-Bretton*.] In reference to Clause 4, have the Local Government Board in Ireland any power to extend the time for which any particular Board of Guardians shall be elected to serve?
No.

(0.1.) B 4 124. They

124. They do not possess the same power as the English Local Government Board in that respect?
No; the Board of Guardians must go out on the 25th of March in every year.

125. Lord *Saltersford*.] But I think I am right in saying that if there is no opposition to a guardian he remains in?
Yes, that individual; if there is no nomination for an electoral division the guardian of the former year is returned again.

126. Viscount *Hutchinson*.] Practically the Board is recast every year?
Yes.

127. Lord *Saltersford*.] Of course you are aware that the proxy vote is more availed of in some unions than in others?
Yes.

128. Could you at all say whether the Poor Law is better administered in unions where the proxy vote is made use of than in others?
I should not like to express an opinion upon that point with the information I have.

129. *Chairman*.] I will now pass to Part II. of the Bill. Clause 14 provides that election petitions shall be tried in a different form from what they are at present; would you state what the present system is?
Under the present system an objection to the right of a person to act as a guardian may be lodged with the Local Government Board, who may enquire into the matter and make such order as they see fit. The appeal, practically, therefore, is to the Local Government Board at present.

130. Do you find that there are a great number of petitions that come in?
A very great number, and many of them on very frivolous and insufficient grounds. I mentioned just now that there were 557 electoral divisions or wards contested at the March election of last year; there were no less than 109 returned guardians objected to, and the Committee may judge of the very slight grounds upon which these appeals were made to us from the fact that we only found it necessary to unseat 21 of the guardians; therefore four-fifths of the appeals to us were groundless.

131. Might I ask what line the general objection takes?
Informality in the nomination, the right of the person who nominates, the qualification of the person appointed, and in the majority of cases the objections are made on the ground of the invalidity of votes given for the persons returned.

132. Do you consider that the proposal in this Bill would be an improvement on the present system?
I consider that it would be a very great improvement, because now persons appeal to us, knowing that it costs them nothing; but if they appeal to the Court of Quarter Sessions they know that if the appeal is groundless they will have to pay the costs, and then they will only lodge appeals when they know that they have good grounds for them.

133. Is the register of voters as returned by the returning officer deemed final at present?
No, certainly not; an appeal may be lodged with us on the ground that persons have been improperly registered or improperly omitted.

134. With regard to the list handed in by the clerk, of the names of the voters, is there any appeal from that?
An objection may be made to the return of a guardian on any of the grounds I have named.

135. Might it not be possible under Clause 15 that frivolous objections might be made, thereby putting the returning officer to very large costs, and that that might be done by men of straw, who would not be able to pay the costs if it went against them?
No, I do not think that that is likely; I think that persons who are entitled

to

3rd March 1885.]   Mr. ROBINSON, C.B.   [*Continued.*

to appeal under this Bill would be persons who would be able probably to pay the costs, and that the fear of having to pay the costs would prevent their making frivolous objections. It would be quite impossible, I think, to have an appeal without including in the appeal the question of the correctness of the register.

136. You do not consider that it would be necessary to have some security for the costs?
That is a matter of detail; it might be, perhaps, advisable to have some security if there is any doubt about it.

137. The returning officer's expenses, if it went against him, appear by this Bill to be paid out of the poor rate?
Yes, it is so; but Clause 21 says that, "where a returning officer is made respondent to a petition, he shall not be ordered to pay the petitioner's costs, except the Court shall be of opinion that he was guilty of negligence or improper conduct in the matter of the election or petition;" consequently, if he was merely guilty of an error of judgment, he would not be mulcted in costs.

138. Do not you think that it would be very unfair that the costs of the respondent should come out of the poor rate?
There would be no objection at all to the person petitioning being obliged to give security for the costs if necessary.

139. If the returning officer had misconducted himself in any way, of course he ought to be personally liable; but if he had not, and the costs were thrown on him, do not you think it would be wrong to place that extra expense on the rates?
I think, if the returning officer were proved to have been guilty of actual misconduct, or wilful default, he would not be fit to hold the office of returning officer, and would be dealt with otherwise.

140. I am speaking now of a case in which it was not so; supposing a case turned up such as I suggested just now; supposing that men of straw were to bring an objection, and then the costs were given against them, and they were not able to pay the costs, the returning officer would have to pay the costs, and it would fall upon the rates?
But I do not see any objection to their being required to give security for the costs before the appeal is entertained.

141. Do you think that would be an improvement?
Yes; I think it would be an improvement.

142. There is no proposal of that sort in the Bill?
No, and I think it would be an improvement.

143. Viscount *Hutchinson*.] Would it not be done on the application of one party to the County Court Judge?
I do not know whether it is a practice; there can be no objection to its being defined in the Bill, that that shall be the case.

144. *Chairman*.] Clauses 17, 18, 19, and 20, have all to do with this system of trying cases before a County Court Judge, and Clause 21 is the one I have just referred to; have you any further remark to make about those clauses?
No.

145. Have you any objection to any of them?
I have no objection to them. I think that the reasons given on which an appeal may be lodged are quite right, that, if the registers are found to be incorrect it should be a ground of appeal. I have heard it urged that the returning officer's registers should be final when he prepares them; but that, I think, could not be admitted for a minute. There should be an appeal to the County Court Judge in the same manner as there is an appeal to our Board at present.

(0.1.)   C   146. Lord

3rd *March* 1885.] Mr. ROBINSON, C.B. [*Continued*.

146. Lord *Saltersford*.] With regard to the costs of contested elections at present, are they charged on the union or on the electoral division concerned?
The returning officer's salary and the publication of the notices are charged upon the union at large, the other expenses upon the divisions concerned; where there is a contest it is on the division concerned.

147. Then do not you think that in the same way the costs of contested petitions, where they are put on the poor rates, should be charged on the poor rates of the electoral division concerned?
Yes; I think that that would follow as a matter of course.

148. Viscount *Powerscourt*.] May I ask how you read sub-section (*e*) of Clause 14, " Provided that the court shall not avoid any election on the grounds of any such error, inclusion, or omission, unless satisfied that the result of the election might have been effected thereby," what does that mean?
I think it means that unless a sufficient number of votes are struck off the register by reason of being void to affect the election, the proceedings are not to be affected.

149. *Chairman*.] Passing now to Part III., Clause 25, sub-section (1.), " No person under the age of 21 years shall be permitted to vote at any poor law election;" would you allow, if the case occurred, his guardian or trustee to vote for him?
Yes, I think the trustee of a minor should be allowed to vote; in fact he is allowed at present to vote.

150. He is under the present law, but he would not if this became law?
I think there should be something added to that to say, Provided that in the case of property in trust the trustee should be allowed to vote, to make it quite clear.

151. *Lord President*.] Do you think the words of this sub-section would have the effect of repealing the present law?
I do not think there is anything in the law with respect to trustees; it is a matter of practice that we allow trustees of minors to vote if they are in receipt of the rents.

152. Not under any statute?
No. We have got advice, according to which, under the terms of the present law, the trustees may vote in respect of the rents received.

153. Earl of *Milltown*.] Supposing that to be the case, this sub-section would not affect them; it merely says that the minor himself may not vote?
It might be well to make it clear. At present there is no such provision in reference to occupation, and a minor is allowed to vote if he is in occupation of property; he is allowed to vote as an occupier, and there is a great deal of difficulty sometimes in deciding whether he is of an age to vote, and I think it would be better to define the age, and that a person of 14 or 15 or 16 should not be allowed to vote.

154. *Chairman*.] Sub-section (2) of Clause 25 directs that the Local Government Board shall have an election within a reasonable time if vacancies should occur on the board; would you propose any improvement on that?
Yes, I would, certainly; I would suggest that it should be altered in this way: that the word " shall " should be taken out, and the word " may " substituted, except in a case in which the board of guardians apply to have the vacancy filled; I mean that in the event of a vacancy by death taking place within four or five months of the triennial election, the board of guardians and our board might consider it quite unnecessary to put the electoral division to the expense of an election, the triennial election coming on in so short a time; I think if the board of guardians wish it, then we should be compelled to order an election, but that if they and we agree that it is unnecessary, the division should not be put to the expense. I would suggest that it should be amended

by

3rd March 1885.]   Mr. ROBINSON, C.B.   [Continued.

by substituting the word "may" for "shall," except in a case mentioned in Clauses 16 and 20, and inserting after the word "may," the words, "and shall if requested by the board of guardians." Under the former clauses it provides that if the election is set aside by the County Court Judge then we shall order a new election; and that is quite reasonable and right, because the appeal must take place within a very short time after the return, and the division should not go unrepresented for three years; but I think in the case of a casual vacancy we should have power with the board of guardians to determine whether an election is necessary or not.

155. But supposing that the time was just running out, that it was nearly the end of the three years, it would not be necessary to have a fresh election, would it?
That is just what I say; that we ought to have the power of ordering it or not, as we see fit, provided the board of guardians agree with us that it is unnecessary.

156. Sub-section (3) says that a justice of the peace is not qualified to be an *ex-officio* guardian of any poor law union, unless he is a ratepayer of such union; what is the law at present about that?
A resident justice of the peace does not require the qualification of being a ratepayer; a non-resident justice of the peace requires the qualification I read before of being a ratepayer in respect of property of the annual value of 50 *l*. at the least.

157. Do you think that there would be some difficulty created by that section?
No, I do not think so; I think it is very fair. I do not see why a person should be on the board who has no interest in the expenditure of the rates.

158. You stated just now that it was difficult to find *ex-officio* guardians in many unions?
Not exactly that; I said that the number was less in some unions than the elected guardians.

159. Then sub-section (4) is a proposal for the reduction of the qualification of voters. I think at the present time the Local Government Board have the power of reducing the qualification in different unions?
Yes, we have; we have power to fix it at anything below 30 *l.*; 30 *l.* is the maximum.

160. Do you think that the power that you possess now ought to be regarded as sufficient?
Yes, I think so. I do not see any necessity whatever for the change. There are many cases in which it would be difficult to find men qualified at 12 *l.*, and we are obliged to fix the qualification at 10 *l.*, and sometimes even lower; this would make a uniform qualification of 12 *l.*, which I think would be objectionable, and I think a scale according to the necessities of each case would be the best.

161. The average throughout Ireland is at present what?
I cannot say the exact average. The maximum is 30 *l*; there are several at 25 *l.*, several at 20 *l.*, some at 15 *l.*, some at 10 *l*, and there is one union where I think the qualification in one electoral division is as low as 6 *l.* There are a great number at 10 *l.*

162. Then sub-section (5) proposes to reduce the number of *ex-officio* guardians on the board; do you think that that would be injurious?
I think it would be objectionable. I do not see any cause whatsoever to alter the number of *ex-officio* guardians. The grounds on which they were placed on the board in the first instance are contained in the same report of Sir George Nicholls, which I mentioned before. He says, "There are many reasons why magistrates should form a portion of every board of guardians. The elected guardians will probably, for the most part, consist of occupiers or renters, not the owners of property; and their interest will consequently be temporary, and may end with the current or any future year; but the interest of the owner is permanent and embraces all times. Some union of these two interests seems

(O.1.)   c 2   necessary

necessary towards the complete organisation of a board of guardians; and as the magistrates collectively may fairly be regarded as comprising the great landed proprietors of the country, the Bill proposes to accomplish this object by creating them *ex-officio* members of the board. The elected guardians, moreover, are subject to be changed every year, and it is not improbable that their proceedings might be changeable, and perhaps contradictory, and mischief and confusion might be caused by the opposite view of successive boards. The *ex-officio* guardians will serve as a corrective to this evil. Their position as magistrates, their information and general character, and their large stake as owners of property, will necessarily give them much weight; whilst the proposed limitation of their number to that of one-third of the elected guardians will prevent their having an undue preponderance. The elected and the *ex-officio* members of the Board will probably each improve the other, and important benefits may be expected to ensue from their frequent mingling, and from the necessity for mutual concession and forbearance which such mingling cannot fail to teach. Each individual member will feel that his influence depends upon the opinion which his colleagues entertain of him, or upon the respect or regard which they feel towards him; and hence will arise an interchange of good offices and a cultivation of mutual goodwill, beginning with the members of the board of guardians, but extending to every class throughout the union, and eventually, it may be hoped, throughout the country; and thus the union system may become the means of healing dissensions and reconciling jarring interests in Ireland." Then upon that report the number of *ex-officio* guardians was fixed at one-third the number elected. When the Irish Poor Relief Extension Act was brought in in 1847, Sir George Grey, who was the Secretary of the Home Office at that time, explained the reasons in his speech why he proposed that the numbers should be more equal; and this is an extract from his speech:—
"In England it was quite true that all justices resident in any union became *ex-officio* guardians; and it was thought that when it was proposed to add a great burden to property in Ireland there should also be an increase in the representation of the property in the boards of guardians. That was the motive with which this clause was proposed; and he must remind the House that a much larger portion of the rate fell upon property in Ireland than was the case in England. In England the occupier paid the whole of the rate, though there was not much difference in the end, because, by arrangement, it came ultimately to be paid by the landlord. But in Ireland the liability was, in the first instance, thrown exclusively upon the landlords in the case of tenements rated under 4 *l.* per annum; and in all cases above 4 *l.* the landlord was, in the first instance, in some cases liable to half, and in many cases to considerably more. Now, looking to the increased amount of the rate likely to be paid by the operation of this Bill, it was thought proper that there should be an increased representation of property in the boards of guardians." It was then provided that the magistrates resident in the union should be *ex-officio* guardians if they did not exceed the number of elected guardians.

163. Do you, after reading that report, see any reason to change your opinion?
No; I see no reason whatever to make a change in the system which has existed so long.

164. And do you consider that the system has worked well?
I think that the *ex-officio* guardians attend very badly; I think that their attendance is not at all satisfactory; but I do not see for that reason that they should be deprived of the power of attending.

165. Do you find that where the *ex-officio* guardians do attend, the rates are kept down more than in unions where they do not attend?
I do not wish to reflect upon the administration of the elected members of the board, but I think that as a general rule, where there is a constant attendance of both classes, the administration is conducted upon more economical principles.

166. Since the agitation has there been out-door relief given to families of evicted tenants, and suspects, and for political reasons?

A great

A great deal of out-door relief was given in the south and the west; very freely indeed to those classes, at one time. It is not carried on to so great an extent at present.

167. Out-door relief to the extent of a large sum of money a week, do you mean?
I have known as much as 1 *l*. a week voted.

168. What is the usual out-door relief?
It varies very much indeed in the different unions, but it is 2 *s.*, or 3 *s.*, or 4 *s.*, or 5 *s.* The relief I speak of was very much in excess of the ordinary amount.

169. Do you consider that the *ex-officio* members, being one-half of the board, have that representation in consideration of paying half the tenant's rates?
The *ex-officio* guardians I consider, to a great extent, represent the interests of the owners of property upon the board, and that the owners not only can vote for the elected guardians, but they also represent property for which they cannot vote. For instance, they have a much greater interest in their properties than the number of votes they can give by the cumulative votes. Six is the maximum; but if they were allowed to go on voting in respect of the amount of their property, they would give a much larger number of votes. The consequence is, that their interest is not quite represented by the voting for the elected guardians.

170. Under the present law you consider that their interest is not adequately represented?
No, they can only give six votes in respect of rents received; that is to say, they can only vote in respect of 200 *l.* received; and, therefore, they have a very much larger interest in the expenditure of the union than is represented by 200 *l.*

171. This Bill would materially diminish their voting power?
If that clause reducing the number of *ex-officio* guardians is adopted it certainly would.

172. You said just now that the attendance of *ex officio* guardians was not very good; are there any particular reasons that have occurred to you why they do not attend?
I have heard various reasons assigned; and they say that they have not weight upon the board. I think that arises very much from not attending sufficiently. I think that in those places where they do attend regularly they do carry weight, and I think it is very unfortunate that they do not attend more frequently.

173. Might not the fact of many of them being non-resident account for their not attending?
That prevents a portion of them from attending; but those who are resident and can attend do not attend in the way I think they ought to.

174. Since the agitation in Ireland, has it not come before you that some *ex-officio* guardians have complained that they have not been treated with much respect on the board?
I have heard that stated.

175. And is it not the case that they have given that as a reason to you for not attending?
I think that is a question that would be answered better by the local inspectors who are attending boards, and some of them are present.

176. The *ex-officios* have been charged occasionally with swamping the elected guardians; have you ever seen a Return which I think was got by Lord Ventry with regard to the attendance of *ex-officios*?
I have got a Return submitted to the House of Commons in 1884, "of the number of attendances of Poor Law Guardians at the Board Meetings of each Poor Law Union in Ireland, in the year ended the 25th day of March 1884."

177. That is not the one I mean, but this Return (*handing a Return to the witness*)?
I have not seen that Return, and I have not got it here. That is a Return of the *ex-officios* and elected guardians in each union, but it does not give the attendances. The Return that I mentioned of 1884, which was submitted to the House, gives the attendances.

178. And that Return you have got?
Yes.

179. Does it show that the *ex-officios* attend more largely than the elected guardians on the days of electing chairmen and officers?
There is no doubt that both classes attend in much larger numbers on days of election: that is not confined to the *ex officio* guardians. The elected guardians, many of them, do not attend on ordinary days, and yet attend always on an election. The whole strength of the elected and *ex-officio* guardians generally attend on the election of a chairman or clerk of the union or important officer. Therefore the *ex-officios* do not attend any more than the elected guardians do themselves on those days; that is to say, all flock in for an election.

180. The appointment of the chairman of a board is a very important one, is it not?
Very important.

181. Do not the *ex-officio* guardians look to that appointment for the purpose of making sure that the board will be properly carried on during the year?
I think so, certainly. It think it depends very much upon the person holding the position of chairman whether the affairs of the union are carefully and properly administered or not.

182. If the proposal in this Bill was carried out for the reduction of the *ex-officio* guardians, do you think it likely that the rates would increase?
I think if it were carried out, and the *ex-officio* guardians were selected by their brother magistrates instead of by valuation, the general attendance would probably be improved; but it would, of course, deprive some of the *ex-officios*, or rather some of the magistrates, of the power of attending on the occasions you have just mentioned of elections. I do not think, however, that the ordinary attendance would be impaired, but I think it would be rather improved, provided that the system of election was that established under the original Poor Law Relief Act; that is to say, that these guardians were selected by election and not by valuation. In the Act of 1838, when the magistrates were one-third of the elected guardians upon the Board, they were selected by their brother magistrates; that is to say, they were elected; and I look upon that as a much better system than selecting the men by valuation, because the men of the highest valuation might not be able to attend, whereas those elected would make it their business to attend.

183. My question was, whether you consider that if the number of *ex-officio* guardians on the board were reduced, that would tend to make the rates higher?
I do not think it would tend to make the rates higher, provided, as I say, that the number entitled to act as *ex-officios* on the board were selected as fit persons for the office; but if they are merely taken by the valuation, I think the probability is that it might have that tendency.

184. But if the voting power of the *ex-officio* guardians was very largely reduced, would they have the power of keeping down extravagant out-door relief?
They do not attend at present and exercise their powers at all in that respect; the attendance is very bad indeed; and the question of expenditure on out-door relief is one which is decided at every meeting of the guardians, and nothing but a constant attendance will provide for the due administration of out door relief. Even if the numbers were maintained as they are at present, I think it would be very desirable that, wherever the number of magistrates

3rd *March* 1885.] Mr. ROBINSON, C.B. [*Continued.*

trates is in excess of those entitled to be placed on the Board, the magistrates themselves should select the magistrates who are to comprise the *ex-officio* guardians, instead of having them selected, as at present, by valuation.

185. Lord *Monk-Bretton*.] Would you look at Sub-Section 4 of Clause 25; do you read that as fixing the elected guardians' qualification at a maximum of 12 *l.*, or as stereotyping the amount at 12 *l.*?
I had read it as fixing the qualification of 12 *l.*, but now that your Lordship draws my attention to it, I do not know whether it is intended by that sub-section that we may fix the qualification, provided that it does not exceed 12 *l.*, or whether it maintains the original law, which enables us to vary the qualification in different unions. I think if that is the intention, it should be more clearly expressed.

186. You think, on looking at it again, that may be the intention?
I really do not know what is the intention of the drawers of the Bill, I cannot say what they meant, whether that was intended or not.

187. You think the construction is very doubtful?
I think the construction is very doubtful.

188. Earl of *Milltown*.] To carry out their intention it should be " rated at 12 *l.* or over," I presume?
No, " or under." I took it to be that it was to be a fixed qualification of 12 *l.* Lord Monk-Bretton seems to think that it fixes the maximum at 12 *l.* I think it would be desirable to make that quite clear.

189. It seems on first sight desirable that it should be uniform; why should it be varied?
The circumstances of different unions vary, and there are many unions in which, if the maximum were fixed at 30 *l.*, you could not get a number of qualified ratepayers to act as guardians.

190. *Lord President.*] Some questions have been asked you as to evicted tenants; what is the duty of a board of guardians as to evicted tenants?
Under the Act 11th & 12th Vict. c. 47, called " An Act for the protection and relief of the destitute poor evicted from their dwellings in Ireland," a person evicted may apply to the relieving officer and may immediately get relief, and then the board of guardians in that case may give out-door relief for one month to the evicted tenant, although he may be an able-bodied man, and thereby under the ordinary Poor Law disqualified from receiving any such relief.

191. Then by a former answer of yours you meant that boards of guardians have been very ready of late to use that power?
In some cases; but it is not so much being very ready, as that they gave very large sums to persons evicted, sometimes three or four times as large as they would allow in cases of ordinary destitution; 1 *l.* a week, for instance.

192. And they made a distinction between an evicted family and any other family?
Precisely so.

193. Although they did not exceed their legal powers?
They did not exceed their legal powers. In some cases I may say they did exceed their legal powers, but those were disallowed by the auditors; but in the exercise of their legal powers they gave very large relief.

194. As to the number of elective and *ex-officio* guardians the proposal of the Bill is, is it not, to return to the proportion under the original Poor Law Act?
No; the original proportion was one-third of the elected guardians; the Bill proposes one-half of the number of elected guardians.

195. That is to say, one-third of the whole?
One-third of the whole. Before it was one-fourth of the whole.

(O.1.) c 4 196. Therefore

3rd *March* 1885.] Mr. ROBINSON, C.B. [*Continued.*

196. Therefore the number under the Bill would be one between the original and the present number?
Exactly.

197. You were asked by a noble Lord whether you thought that the introduction of vote by ballot would make any difference in the constitution of boards of guardians, as to the class of persons elected and so on; do you think that the change which the Bill proposes by these two means, by the abolition of proxy voting, and by the diminution of the number of *ex-officio* guardians, would make much difference in the constitution or action of the boards?
I think that the abolition of proxy voting would make a serious difference in the constitution of the boards, that it would place the elections much more in the hands of the occupiers than it is at present.

198. That is just what I want to know. These provisions of the present law are intended as a protection to property?
A protection to the voter, is it not? The ballot is a protection to the voter.

199. I do not mean that: I mean that proxy voting and the large proportion of non-elective guardians are intended as means of protecting the interests of property in Ireland?
Certainly.

200. I want to know in what way you think that the changes proposed by the Bill would affect the interests of property. It could only be by a change in the character of the persons elected to the Board. In what way do you think that the future boards of guardians, supposing this Bill were to become law, would differ from the existing boards of guardians?
In regard to the election by ballot, I do not think that that will affect the class of persons elected; but I think that if the right of voting is taken away from the owners of property, the right of voting will rest entirely, or to a much greater extent than at present, with the occupiers; and I think that a class will be elected as guardians who have less regard for the rights of property; I mean to say that they will have less interest in economical and careful administration.

201. That, I suppose, is the point; the danger to the rights of property would lie in an extravagant Poor Law administration?
Yes.

202. And unduly heavy rates?
Yes.

203. Do you believe that, supposing the changes proposed by the Bill to have taken place, the future boards of guardians would be less economical, more extravagant, than the present?
It is only a surmise; but my impression is that a class of persons would be returned who would have less interest in the economical administration of the rates than the guardians have at present when the owners of property have so much power in voting. That, however, is only a surmise.

204. Of course, what are called the "interests of property" is a very vague term, but for our purpose, dealing with this Bill, property could only be injured by extravagance in the administration of the Poor Law?
Yes.

205. By excessive rates.
Yes.

206. Do you believe that the Poor Law constituencies, even supposing this Bill to become law as it stands, will allow their guardians to rate them extravagantly?
I think that if the elective guardians were merely returned by the occupiers,

or

or much more by the interest of the occupiers than they are at present, a class of persons would be returned who would not be so economical in the administration of relief as those returned by the owners of property.

207. Do the occupiers like heavy rates?
No, they do not; but they have not as much interest as the owners in keeping down rates. The principal item in which careful or careless expenditure consists, is the administration of out-door relief, and I think that careless expenditure there would be encouraged by the class of persons who would be returned if the owners of property had less power in the elections.

208. They could not go beyond the law?
They could not go beyond the law.

209. And the law strictly limits the power of giving out-door relief?
It does, it is true; but the numbers in receipt of out-door relief are increasing every year, and I think they have been in the last 10 years nearly doubled.

210. They were almost *nil* at one time, were they not?
At one time they were almost *nil*.

211. Viscount *Powerscourt.*] Under the existing system, do you mean?
The number of persons in receipt of out-door relief 10 years ago in Ireland was 30,319, and last year it was 60,384; so that you may say that in 10 years it has doubled. That is the average daily number of persons receiving out-door relief.

212. Lord *President.*] It is quite insignificant, as you know, compared with the out-door relief in this country?
Yes.

213. But starting from almost nothing it has increased to something?
Yes.

214. Is it increasing now?
It has increased in the last year, but the two years previously were very bad years, 1880 and 1881, and I do not think very much of the increase in those years; but if we take the last four years, in 1877-78, 33,517 was the average daily number relieved; in the following year the average daily number relieved was 36,274; in the following year it was 39,629; then came two bad years, and they got up at once to over 60,000 in number.

215. That increase was accounted for by exceptional distress?
In the two years 1880-81 and 1881-82; but I am not taking those years into comparison, but I am comparing last year with 10 years ago.

216. But when once the amount had so increased from the cause we all recognise, you would not expect it to come down again very rapidly, would you?
No, not very rapidly; but I should consider that there ought to have been a greater decrease than has occurred.

217. Has it been stationary of late?
Last year the number was 60,384, and the year before it was 58,835; so that there was an increase in 1883-84 as compared with 1882-83 by nearly 2,000.

218. How has it been during this winter?
Rather lower than last year.

219. That is so far encouraging?
It is; it has been a good year as far as pauperism is concerned.

220. Is it your belief that these changes, especially the abolition of proxy voting, would lead to any considerable increase of the rates in Ireland?
I think it would.

(O.1.)   D   221. Viscount

3rd March 1885.] Mr. ROBINSON, C B. [Continued.

221. Viscount *Powerscourt*.] In what way?
In the way which I have already mentioned, namely, in bringing in a class of persons as guardians who would have less interest in the careful administration of outdoor relief.

222. *Lord President*.] And you think that the ratepayers would allow that to happen?
I think that after a time the ratepayers, if they found it getting too far, might object to it, but still I think it would, no doubt, cause an increase. But that is, as I say, merely a surmise.

223. Lord *Monk-Bretton*.] Have you any observation to make on the 6th Sub-section of Clause 25, limiting the number of votes that a ratepayer may give to 18?
No, I have not. That was the practice since the establishment of the Poor Law up to last year, when the Court of Appeal altered it, and I do not see any objection to that sub-section. But before I finish I may make a suggestion with reference to that; I do not know whether now is the proper time to do so.

224. *Lord President*.] The limitation to 18 would be merely leaving things as they are now?
As they were before up to six months ago.

225. But it would leave them as they have been in practice?
As they have been in practice. It was about five or six months ago that the appeal was in the court.

226. Earl of *Milltown*.] No alteration was made in the law then?
It was simply a declaration of what the opinion of the Court of Appeal was as to the law.

227. The Court of Appeal simply declared what the law was; it did not make any alteration in the law?
That is so.

228. *Lord President*.] If the decision given a few months ago were acted upon, it would create a large increase in the number of property votes over and above the number that have ever been used in Ireland.
Certainly; we have felt it necessary to make the decision of the Court of Appeal known to all the returning officers; the consequence is, that now, unless this clause in the Bill before the Committee becomes law, a person may give as many as 30 votes.

229. And in practice that decision, if that provision of this Bill did not become law, would raise the maximum number of votes from 18 to 30.
Yes. With regard to that point, as I mentioned before, an occupier may give as many as 12 votes; a person in receipt of rents may give six, and an immediate lessor may give 12, making 30. This Bill proposes to cut the number down to 18, but it does not say how that is to be apportioned among the different votes; that is to say, suppose a man is entitled to 30 votes, there is no provision made as to what description of property the 12 is to come off, and a difficulty may arise in this way: We will suppose that proxy voting is allowed; a man would find that he holds a proxy power to vote for 18, and reserves 12 for himself; and the returning officer would not know how he is to apportion those votes. The way I would suggest to meet that defect would be that when a person appoints a proxy (if he is to appoint a proxy), he should declare to the returning officer, providing that his votes given separately would exceed 18, in what way he would like them apportioned; and in the event of his not giving such instructions to the returning officer, that the returning officer should take the number off according to the net annual value of the different properties. Suppose that an occupier has a right to give 12 votes himself, and that according to separate voting he would give 18 by a proxy, that would be 30; the returning officer must reduce that to 18 under this Bill; the returning officer would be in a difficulty to know whether he was to deprive
the

the occupier of the whole of the 12, and leave the 18 to the proxy, or whether he should take 12 off the proxy, and leave the proxy six, and the occupier 12.

230. *Lord President.*] But what would have happened before this decision of the Court of Appeal ?
Before the decision of the Court of Appeal we were of opinion, and the Court of Queen's Bench was of opinion, that the immediate lessor votes had to be aggregated with the occupation votes; that the valuation of the immediate lessor voting was to be aggregated with that of the occupation voting, and that the beneficial interest of the occupier was to be aggregated with the beneficial interest of the immediate lessor. The consequence was that putting the two together he could only have a maximum of 12 votes in regard to occupation and immediate lessor voting, and six as in receipt of rent.

231. But does not this provision of the Bill restore things to what they were before that decision of the Court of Appeal?
It restores the state of things as to the number of votes, but it does not say how it is to be restored. The Act 1 & 2. Victoria, Chapter 56, provides by Clause 81 that " the aggregate amount of the valuation under this Act for the time being of the property in respect of which the ratepayer claims to vote shall be taken to be the annual value;" that is, that the aggregate value of the man's interest in any one electoral division is to be taken together; and the Act authorising immediate lessor voting provides as follows: " Be it enacted, that it shall be lawful for owners or immediate lessors who are so rated as aforesaid to vote, in person or by proxy, in the election of guardians in respect of the property or rent for which they are so rated in the same manner as occupiers paying no rent or paying rent less than the net annual value of the rateable property, as the case may be" (that is Section 17 of the 25 & 26 Victoria, Chapter 83), so that we held, and the Court of Queen's Bench held, that the immediate lessor's voting and the occupier's voting must be aggregated. Therefore it reduced the two down to 12 votes as the maximum, and that 12, added to the six which an owner could give in respect of his rents, brought the maximum only to 18.

232. Would your difficulties under this Bill be any greater than they were before?
If it were not for this Bill there would be no difficulty, for one person might have 30 votes. It is reducing the number to 18, without saying how it is to be done; that will place the returning officer in difficulty.

233. But you think that could be got over?
It could be got over if the Committee will decide to recommend how it should be got over. One way of doing that would be to declare the law to be such as we originally held it, that these votes are to be aggregated, or else that they are to be apportioned according to the value of the property in respect of which the votes are given.

234. *Lord Monk-Bretton.*] Which course do you suggest?
I think the best course is what I suggested first; to allow the person appointing a proxy to determine in respect of what interest he would have his votes reduced, and if he does not do so, to let the returning officer reduce them according to the value.

235. You would prefer that to returning to the system of aggregating votes, which you acted upon before?
I think it would be preferable. The matter is so very complicated that I asked the draftsman of Irish Bills to draft a clause which would carry out that arrangement. Perhaps it would explain it better if I read it. This is the draft clause: " In any case in which a person would but for this Act be entitled to more than 18 votes, by reason of his having (in addition to the qualifications created by the Act 1 & 2 Vict. c. 56, ss. 80 and 81, also the qualification created by the Act 25 & 26 Vict c. 83, s. 17), he may by writing elect to attribute the votes to which he is limited by this Act to such of the aforesaid qualifications as he thinks fit, but not so as to attribute to any of such qualifications a greater number

number of votes than he would by law be entitled to have in respect of that qualification if this Act had not been passed. In case he does not elect he shall be deemed to have elected to attribute his votes to the several qualifications which he has, in the proportion of the valuations of the different classes of property constituting such qualifications."

236. *Lord President.*] Would that be a troublesome process for the returning officer?
No.

237. *Lord De Vesci.*] In Sub-section 1 of Clause 25, would you think it visable to add that in all cases of minors and lunatics the guardians and trustees should exercise the right of voting?
I should see no objection to treating lunatics in the same way as minors in that respect.

238. *Viscount Hutchinson.*] You said just now that if sub-section 5 was adopted the effect would be to arrive at a certain compromise between the old system established in 1838, and the system inaugurated in 1847; that whereas the proportion of *ex-officio* guardians was a fourth then it would be a third now.
Yes.

239. But I understood from your extract from Sir George Grey's speech in 1847, which you read, that the number of *ex-officio* guardians was increased at that time, because greater burdens were put upon the land, and because it was considered right that the taxation paid by property owners should be properly represented?
Yes.

240. And the state of things is precisely the same now as it was in 1847, so far as the amount of taxation paid by the owners of property is concerned?
Yes.

241. And, according to all the ordinary principles of taxation and representation, the owners of property are entitled to that proportion?
I did not advocate the alteration of the present system.

242. Then a question was asked about the attendance of the *ex officio* guardians, and you said that they did not attend very regularly; do you not think that that has something to do with the way they are appointed; that they are not actually representative?
As I said before, I think that wherever a selection is to be made it would be very much better that the selection should be made by the magistrates themselves.

243. As it was done in 1838?
Yes.

244. Have you ever considered whether it would be possible to devise any scheme by which the owners of property could be represented otherwise than by the appointment of *ex-officio* guardians?
I have not considered that. I have heard plans suggested, but I am not prepared to give evidence upon them; they are not mentioned in the Bill, and it is only in casual conversation that I have heard the scheme mooted of having persons elected to represent owners of property; but I do not know what the scheme is exactly, and I should not like to express an opinion upon it.

245. *Lord Salteraford.*] You said that you saw no objection to the 3rd sub-section, that " No justice of the peace shall be qualified to be an *ex-officio* guardian of any Poor Law union unless he is a ratepayer of such union." I suppose that is not likely to happen often?
Very seldom.

246. But still it might happen in the case of agents of large non-resident proprietors?

I think

I think it is very seldom that the agent of a non-resident proprietor is not rated for something.

247. The Shillelagh Union is nearly all the property of one individual, and the agent is a magistrate, but I doubt very much whether he is a ratepayer; under such circumstances should he be a guardian?
That would be a very exceptional case, I think.

248. With reference to the proportion which the *ex-officio* guardians bear to the elected guardians, though it is theoretically equal to the number of elected guardians, is it not often the case that they are not really so on account of their not being able to attend that, owing to their not residing in or near the union, they cannot attend?
No doubt many of them are unable to attend.

249. There is no necessity for the *ex-officio* guardian being a magistrate of the county in which the union is situated?
He must be acting for the county in which he resides; but he may reside in one county, and he may have property in another county, in another union, and if he acts as a magistrate for the county in which he does reside, and is thus a resident *ex-officio* guardian of his own union, he is also qualified then to be a non-resident guardian of any union in which he has property.

250. A magistrate, for instance, of County Kerry, may have property in a union of County Wexford, and, therefore, be an *ex-officio* guardian?
Yes, exactly.

251. But it would be extremely improbable that he should be able to attend?
Yes.

252. Lord *Ker*.] I understood you to say that even supposing the proportion of *ex-officio* guardians is not altered, as suggested by this Bill, you are of opinion that it would be advisable that the *ex-officio* guardians should be elected by the magistrates?
There are some unions in Ireland in which the numbers do not equal those of the elective guardians, and in those unions no change would be requisite; but there are some unions in which the magistrates qualified to be *ex-officio* guardians are in excess of the elected guardians. The selection in those cases is now made by valuation, and I should prefer it made by election.

253. Even in the case of the proportion not being altered?
Yes.

254. Lord *Shute*.] Has the law always been the same in Ireland with regard to all justices of the peace being *ex-officio* guardians?
The law was altered in 1847.

255. But before that time were all justices of the peace *ex-officio* guardians?
No, the resident magistrates were qualified to be *ex-officio* guardians, and the numbers almost always did exceed one-third of the elected guardians, and they were selected then by election of the magistrates.

256. With regard to the attendance of the *ex-officio* guardians, I understood you to say that many of them did not attend in consequence of their residing a long distance from the union, from the place where the board was held; but is there any other reason why they should not attend?
I think there is not a sufficiently good attendance of those who are able to attend. There are many who are able to attend who do not in many cases.

257. Do you think they have any particular reasons for not attending?
Reasons have been suggested here.

258. You know nothing personally of that, intimidation or violence?
No.

259. Then about the election of chairmen; are the elective guardians generally in favour of having an *ex-officio* guardian as chairman or not?
I think that up to the last few years there was almost always an *ex-officio* guardian elected as chairman. Some changes have been made in that respect in some unions of late years.

260. Is any reason assigned for that?
I have reason to think it is for political reasons.

261. *Earl of Milltown.*] Considering the immense importance of the office of chairman, and that in fact it depends upon him whether totally extraneous matter should be brought before the board, have you ever considered the desirability of having a magistrate always chosen for that position?
I do not think that has ever been entertained.

262. Do you think it would be desirable?
I do not think that the mere fact of a man being a magistrate would make him better qualified to preside over a board of guardians.

263. Is it the fact that now a right to vote lapses after five years unless it is re-registered?
A right to vote as an owner lapses after five years, not a right in respect of occupation; an occupier's vote is not dependent upon that.

264. Do you think that that is a fair and desirable thing?
I have mentioned before that I do not think there would be any objection, as they are to be triennial elections, that the number of years should be reduced to three. I think it is very convenient that they should be renewed from time to time. Whether the owner appoints a proxy or not, he must make his claim every five years to vote. If he even wants to vote in person he must make a claim.

265. I asked the question in consequence of a resolution which I have before me, passed by a Limerick association calling attention to it. It says that it would be desirable that no claim to vote should lapse for want of re-registration after five years, as at present?
That is the case at present; a statement of claim to vote in respect of rents received must be renewed every five years whether the owner intends to vote in person or by proxy.

266. *Chairman.*] But the occupier is put upon the register without making any application?
The occupier's list is formed from the rate-books of each year.

267. Therefore the occupier has to make no application?
He has to make no application.

268. *Lord President.*] But the question I asked was in substance this: whether you thought it right that when one person tendered a vote for another, that person's statement of claim might be five years old; that the authority derived from his principal, the person he represents, might be five years old. I asked you whether you did not think it was an extravagant and objectionable provision of the law?
I intended to say that I thought that both the claim to vote, and the appointment of proxy, should expire at the end of three years instead of five.

The Witness is directed to withdraw.

3rd March 1885.

Mr. RICHARD BOURKE, having been called in; is Examined, as follows:

269. *Chairman.*] I BELIEVE you are an Inspector under the Poor Law?
Yes.

270. How long have you held that appointment?
I was appointed in 1847, before the Irish Administration Bill was passed. I was appointed to the English Commission.

271. You were appointed, you say, before the Irish Bill was passed?
Yes; the Bill was passed the same year, but I was sworn in on the English Commission.

272. Were you one of the first Inspectors that were appointed?
No; there were others appointed under the English Commission before me, who acted in Ireland.

273. Do you mean to say that there was one Poor Law then for the two countries?
There was one Poor Law administration, and in Ireland it was managed by an Assistant Commissioner of the English body, and the Inspectors were appointed by the Poor Law Commission. Then in 1847 there came the new administration Act.

274. Were they English Inspectors up to that time?
Yes, Inspectors belonging to the English Commission.

275. Then you have a very long experience of the working of the Poor Law in Ireland?
Yes, very long.

276. Where have you been located during the greater part of your experience?
On my first appointment I was located in the west of Ireland, in the County Mayo, at Ballina, and I remained in charge of districts in that part of Ireland up to 1860, when I was transferred to the district in which I now act, which is Limerick and Clare.

277. Was that first position you held in the poorest part of Ireland?
Yes, I think it was.

278. What did it comprise besides Mayo?
Galway, and some parts of Roscommon and Sligo; it varied at different times, but Mayo and the greater part of Galway remained always part of my district, increased at times by unions in Roscommon or Sligo, or some of the adjoining counties.

279. In 1860 you were transferred to the south?
Yes, to County Limerick.

280. And what is your charge now?
It is, roughly speaking, the whole of the County Clare, half of the County Limerick, and about half of the County Tipperary, the North Riding.

281. You have read over the Bill which is before this Select Committee?
Yes.

282. Do you consider that a system of triennial elections would be an improvement on the present system?
Certainly.

283. Have you any objection to the principle of vote by ballot?
On the contrary.

284. You consider that it would be an improvement?
I do.

285. Then I will pass on to the question of proxy voting. There is a proposal in this Bill to do away with the proxy vote; do you consider that that would be injurious to the owners of property?
I think it would be opposed to the principle of the law giving representation to property, because, practically, it would not operate to represent it.

286. Do you consider from your experience that it would be impossible for any rules to be framed by which owners in different unions should give their votes?
I think it would be so extremely difficult as to render it practically impossible to frame an Order which would meet the varying circumstances.

287. In your experience, have you ever known a case, or has any case ever come to your knowledge, in which the proxy votes have swamped the occupation votes in the district?
No, never; it is impossible. In most of the unions with which I am acquainted, those property votes do not amount to more than about one-third of the occupation votes, and, in point of fact, are not claimed to anything like that proportion.

288. Would you agree with this statement, which was made in the House of Commons by Mr. Trevelyan, that "the proportion of votes in the hands of owners was small as compared with that in the hands of occupiers"?
Certainly.

289. "Even in very rich unions in Ireland the proportion of votes in the hands of occupiers were seven or eight times that which was in the hands of owners;"
Yes.

290. "While in the poor districts the owners' proportion was infinitesimal;" you would agree with that statement?
Yes, I would agree with the statement so far as the proportion between property votes and occupation votes is concerned. I do not know that I should agree with the part of the statement that referred to poor unions, because there generally the landlord represents almost the whole, the tenements for the most part being rated at and under 4 *l.*, in which cases he pays the whole rates, and represents the whole thing.

291. But as he is limited by the Bill to 18 votes, would not the voting power in the hands of the occupiers be enormously in excess of what he himself holds?
Yes, there might be a large proportion of resident occupiers over 4 *l.*; but I thought that the assumption was that there were very few, and that in the very poor unions the property was chiefly in the landlords' hands, as far as voting is concerned, by reason of their being chiefly 4 *l.* tenements.

292. But have you ever come across a union so very poor that there was nothing but 4 *l.* occupiers in it?
No, I would not say entirely 4 *l.* occupiers.

293. I will put it to you in this way; have you ever come across a union where the representation of occupiers over 4 *l.* would be limited by 18 votes?
No, I think the landlord's voting power is diminished of course by this limitation.

294. Therefore it might occur, as Mr. Trevelyan stated, that the voting power of an owner might be infinitesimal if he owned the whole of a poor union, because he would only have 18 votes, whereas the occupiers might have 100 votes, or 200 votes?
Certainly.

295. Have

3rd March 1885] Mr. BOURKE. [Continued.

295. Have you ever heard any objection taken to the principle of proxy voting until very recently?
No, not till very recently.

296. In fact, I suppose since the agitation begun in Ireland?
Yes, I think it is chiefly from political motives.

297. Have you considered the question of the system of trying election petitions before the county court judges?
Yes, I have read the provisions of the Bill on the subject.

298. Do you think it would be an improvement?
Yes, a decided improvement, I think.

299. There is a proposal, I believe, that the poor rate should bear a portion of the costs of petitions; do you think that that would be unfair or fair?
I think it would be unfair. I do not see any reason why the costs of the returning officer, who is brought in by virtue of his office, should be thrown upon the union at large, or upon the electoral division, as the case might be, and paid by the public; I think they ought to be paid by the persons who failed in their suit, like any other costs.

300. Would you think it would be necessary to have security before one of these objections was lodged?
I think it would be desirable, certainly, that security should be given in many cases; at the same time I do not much think that there would be an election petition brought unless the man was aware of his responsibilities, and was prepared to undertake them.

301. I suppose you have had a great deal of experience in inquiring into these objections?
I have had some, but the Local Government Board, as a rule, have not directed many inquiries; they have limited inquiries under Inspectors, in reference to election matters, as closely as they could, and have decided them all in the office themselves.

302. In regard to Part III., Sub-section 1, would you approve of a guardian or trustee having the right to vote for a minor?
I certainly should, upon the principle that it is not a personal right that is conferred upon the owner of property; it is a right in respect of the property he holds, and if he is incapacitated by being a minor, or not being of sound mind, it is only fair that the property should still have its representation; and that should be by the guardian or trustee, as the case may be.

303. Then as to the qualification for the right to elect a guardian, it is here limited to 12 *l.* ?
Yes.

304. Do you think that that would be an improvement?
I do not think it would be an improvement to fix a definite sum, because I happen to know of some electoral divisions where there is not a single occupier rated at 12 *l.* I can give an instance in the Glenties Union, where there is no such thing as a 12 *l.* occupier.

305. The present system, you consider, works well?
I have never heard it objected to.

306. The Local Government Board have the power of reducing the qualification as they find it necessary?
Yes, they have in two or three Unions fixed it at 6. *l*

307. Then as to Sub-section 5, the proposal there is to reduce the number of *ex-officios*, that it is not to exceed one-half of the elected guardians; do you consider that that would be an improvement, or the reverse?
If some other method were found of choosing the *ex-officio* guardians, with a view to securing better attendance on their part, I should see no objection to it at all.

308. You would see no objection to the reduction of the numbers?
No; if some different qualification than that of merely being a magistrate residing in the union, or the highest rated of non-residents, were taken, and if the selection was made elective in some way or another, with a view of securing due attendance. The present system does not secure attendance; on the contrary, the attendance of *ex-officio* guardians is exceedingly bad.

309. But is it not an arrangement that the *ex-officios* should represent on the board the half of the rates which they pay for their tenants?
I think that the creation of *ex-officio* guardians was a form of representing ownership of land and payment of rates.

310. What is the proportion of rates that the owners pay at present?
I should say it was over two-thirds, or two-thirds at least; I have heard it put at five-eighths.

311. Do you consider that it would be fair that the number of *ex-officio* guardians who represent property should be reduced on the board, when such a very large proportion of the rates are paid by the owners of property?
In the abstract, I should say that perhaps it would be right to represent them fully; but I was rather viewing the case by the list of circumstances as they exist at present, and considering whether the present mode of appointing *ex-officio* guardians secures an equable and fair representation of property upon the Poor Law Boards, and according to my experience it does not.

312. Then would you decrease that representation by reducing the numbers?
I think that if you had a different mode of selection you might arrive at the end desired. I think that the mere property or residence selection has not succeeded in giving you a fair and good attendance of *ex-officio* guardians.

313. But if you have so bad an attendance with the present number of *ex-officio* guardians, would you not be likely to have even a worse attendance, at least, in proportion, when the number was reduced?
I should hope not. Perhaps bad attendance may arise from the principle of every man's business being no man's business; but if you could get the prescribed number selected, I think they would feel the responsibilities upon them, and that knowing they numbered but one-half of the Board, they would give more regular attendance.

314. But supposing that you are correct in stating that the owners of property pay two-thirds of the rates, do not you think that it would be very unfair, even if you had the guardians elected on a different system, to reduce their number on the board; what chance could they have of looking after the rights of property on the board if they were reduced to, say, one-half of the elected guardians, even in any form in which they might be elected?
As I said before, in the abstract that may appear to be true; but looking at things as they really are, I find that the attendance of the officers has been generally so very defective that they do not seem to be quite alive to their responsibilities in the way of protecting property, and that a change of system might ensure their being more so.

315. You think it might?
It might.

316. But with regard to the men that would represent property under the proposal you have made, what guarantee have you that they would attend better than the old *ex-officio* guardians?
No guarantee. There are a certain number of *ex-officio* guardians in every union who attend with regularity and with great advantage. The larger number of them absent themselves.

317. I do not understand your argument, which goes to show that by reducing the number you get more to attend.
I qualified that by saying if you had a different way of selecting them; and if the selection was made from the body of magistrates themselves they would undoubtedly

undoubtedly select men who would attend; and in that way I think the security would be more complete and effective.

318. Have you come across any reasons why the *ex-officio* guardians have not attended more regularly?
Of late years no doubt there have been political reasons which have caused them to absent themselves; but long before political feeling was as violent and vehement as it now is, the attendance of *ex-officio* guardians was very irregular.

319. Earl of *Milltown*.] What do you mean by political reasons?
Political questions being raised and discussed at boards, and persons of very strong political opinions being returned as elected members, who rendered the proceedings disagreeable.

320. *Chairman*.] There might be also another reason, might there not. According to a Return I have here of Lord Ventry's, one-third of the *ex officio* guardians in Ireland are non-resident in their unions?
That is a misfortune which cannot be prevented.

321. That might prevent their attending, might it not?
Certainly. My observations do not apply to that class exclusively.

322. If a good chairman is appointed on a board, is it not much more likely, and do not you find as a rule, that the work of the board will be more economically and, in fact, better carried out in every way?
Much more satisfactorily carried out, and upon sounder economical views generally.

323. Would there be much chance of a good chairman being appointed in many districts in Ireland if the *ex-officio* element was largely reduced on the board?
I think there are a great many unions where an *ex-officio* guardian would be retained as chairman of the board if he had shown himself a good practical guardian.

324. But there are many others which you have come across where they have already been put on one side?
There are several unions that I know where they have been put aside.

325. Have there been any grounds given for putting them aside?
No; no practical grounds; only the preference given by the majority of the board to elected members.

326. Do you know of any unions in your district where elected guardians and *ex-officio* guardians have worked satisfactorily together, even in these times?
Yes, I do.

327. And where it is not so, what reason do you put it down to?
There are several reasons.

328. Is it in consequence of the agitated state of the country?
Yes; and perhaps the *ex-officio* guardians have absented themselves rather more readily than they might have done.

329. I suppose that the great thing upon boards is to try and keep the rates down, is it not; that is the great wish of owners of property?
Yes.

330. If the *ex-officio* guardians were reduced upon the board, do you think that the rates would generally be increased or not?
I think that there would be a probability of a worse administration, and that might lead very likely to an increase of rates. I think that business would be more capriciously and ignorantly managed if there were not the attendance of *ex-officio* guardians who, from their habits of thought and education, are better qualified to deal with large public subjects.

331. In your experience, where the *ex-officio* guardians do not attend on boards, as a rule, are the rates higher than on boards where they do attend?
Yes,

Yes, I think, as a rule, perhaps they are. There is a great desire upon the part of the majority of elected guardians to be economical; but I think they do not know how to set about it. They save money upon some things where they should spend it, and spend it lavishly very often where they should save it, it is their ignorance chiefly, I think, of public affairs which leads to that.

332. Since the late political agitation, have you come across cases of the expenditure on outdoor relief for political purposes being done very lavishly by some of these boards?
To evicted tenants you mean? Yes, I have indeed.

333. And suspects?
I do not at present remember a case in which the family of a suspect in any union of mine has received relief, but I do remember cases where evicted tenants received very unusually large amounts of relief, and where their destitution was by no means apparent or proved.

334. Have you come across any boards where the finances of the union were badly managed in consequence of the *ex-officio* guardians not attending?
I dare say it may have been attributed in part to that cause; but in one union that I have in my eye where that lavish relief was given in the case of evicted tenants, the finances had not been badly managed.

335. I think there is a union which has come before the public lately, of which you are Inspector, the Tulla Union, in County Clare?
Yes.

336. Will you give us a little information about that union; do the *ex-officio* guardians attend?
No; as a rule, unfortunately, they do not.

337. Was there a case in February of Major Molony evicting a large number of tenants in that union?
Yes.

338. Is Major Molony owner of a great portion of the division?
He has the greater part of the electoral division of Kiltannon, in which his residence is. February 1883, I think you mean, not last February.

339. Did the guardians give these tenants outdoor relief?
Yes, and prolonged it beyond the time limited by law.

340. What sort of relief did they give?
About 1 *l.*, in some cases 25 *s.* a week; indeed, I think in some cases even more than that. There was a great deal of scandal in connection with that union.

341. Were the rates very much increased?
On that electoral division enormously.

342. Could you tell us to what extent; have you any recollection?
I think that the rate was 6 *s.* in the pound for the half-year, if I do not mistake, whereas the normal rate was from 10 *d.* to 1 *s.* 2 *d.*

343. And upon whom did that rate mostly fall?
Its incidence, of course, was regulated by law. I cannot at once say whether there were very many 4 *l.* holders there, in which case Major Molony would pay for all; but his demesne, of course, would pay full rates, and he paid half the tenants' rates. The charge, however, fell heavily upon a good many of the tenants occupying farms rated over 4 *l.*

344. But the great proportion would fall upon the landlord who had ejected the tenants?
Yes, clearly.

345. And did it come under your notice whether those tenants were well off?
I can

I can say this, that their destitution was certainly not proved.

346. Were they put back into their holdings?
I think so, upon payment of the full rent; but there were scandals connected with that case.

347. Was there an objection raised upon this point before the auditor?
Yes.

348. And was it demanded that the guardians who signed the cheque should be surcharged?
It was demanded that the expense should be surcharged upon those who signed the cheque.

349. You were beginning to say something about the books?
The auditor required the production of the books, showing by whom the expenditure was authorised. There is a book called the Application and Report Book, and when any particular sum is given as outdoor relief, the chairman of the day initials it; and the auditor called for that book in order to ascertain by whom the expenditure was authorised in the first instance; and the book was produced, but with all the leaves having reference to that subject cut out, and therefore he was unable to determine the party whom he should surcharge for the illegal relief.

350. What was done then?
I was directed to go down and hold an inquiry to ascertain if possible by what means this destruction of the books had been brought about, or by whom it was done. I was only able to discover how it took place, but there was nothing but a strong case of suspicion as to the guardian (it must have been a guardian) who actually committed the offence. The book had been put into a particular room; the clerk of the union had given the key to one or two guardians, and the book was found destroyed there.

351. Was the result that you could not surcharge the drawer of the cheque?
Ultimately the surcharge was paid by some arrangement amongst the guardians themselves.

352. It was an arrangement made?
It was some private arrangement made.

353. Was that on proceedings being threatened by the landlord of the district?
I really do not know what motive there was. I rather think that it was done more to save the clerk from the dismissal which was impending over him for carelessness in guarding the books.

354. Have you known cases where men were appointed as rate collectors, who had been charged with political offences?
In that union I have known an instance of a man so appointed who was charged with being concerned in a criminal conspiracy.

355. Was that a man called Loughery?
Yes.

356. Was he elected?
Yes, he was.

357. As rate collector?
As rate collector.

358. And was he allowed to hold the appointment?
Yes; he held the appointment. He was never convicted of crime; he was only accused of it.

359. Are the finances of that union in a very bankrupt condition?
They are in a very embarrassed condition; but I do not think that the amount of rate required to clear their embarrassments will be unusually heavy; but there has been a delay in striking it, which has produced financial embarrassment.

3rd March 1885.] Mr. BOURKE. [*Continued.*

360. Have the Local Government Board ever threatened to send down vice-guardians?
Yes; they have intimated that if things continue in so unsatisfactory a state it will become their duty so to do.

361. Has the bank ever refused to cash their cheques?
Yes, on two or three occasions; they continued to refuse cashing them for a period.

362. Do you think that they will be able to tide over their difficulty?
I have no doubt they will.

363. But they are in a very bad way at present?
Very much embarrassed.

364. Do you consider that if there had been a better attendance of gentlemen interested in property these things might have been obviated?
Certainly; because rates would have been struck in due time.

365. *Lord President.*] Do you think that the choice of a magistrate, of an *ex-officio* guardian as chairman of a union, depends much upon the number of *ex-officio* guardians on the board?
I should say not. Just at the present moment when political opinions run very high, there may be a disinclination upon the part of certain politicians on the board to elect a magistrate; but that used not to be the case.

366. Is it not generally dependent upon the esteem felt for the gentleman in question by the board as a whole?
Very much indeed.

367. Have you ever known a case in which such an election of a chairman was secured by the *ex-officio* guardians, by the mere fact of their voting power?
Certainly not. I do not think that they would have been able to affect the election without the assistance of a certain number of the elective guardians.

368. Although they might turn the scale?
They might turn the scale.

369. I should like to know a little more what you think of the actual value and effect of the system of property voting, voting in right of property by means of proxies. I think you said that the changes proposed by the Bill would be injurious to the owners of property; but could any such change be injurious to the owners of property without being injurious to the ratepayers?
I think I must have been a little misunderstood. What I meant to say was, that it was rather opposed, as it appeared to me, to the principle of the representation of property; that if it was considered desirable that property should be represented in the election of guardians as the law now directs, you would throw an additional impediment in the way, requiring personal attendance and personal voting, and you would *pro tanto* injure the holders of property; but I think that the proportion in which they vote, and the limit which is fixed upon their votes, really makes their vote, as far as the election of the elective guardians is concerned, of hardly any value; I do not know of any election that would be turned by the number of proxies; the occupation votes would always swamp them.

370. You said it was impossible that the proxy votes should swamp the occupation votes?
Quite so.

371. Then I want to know what the actual effect of the system of proxy voting is upon the constitution of the board of guardians?
I do not think it has any practical effect, but it goes towards the establishment

hlishment of the principle that property should be represented in the election of guardians for any electoral division.

372. Do you see any use in that principle unless it keeps down the rates; does it keep down the rates?
No, I do not think it does.

373. Does the system of proxy voting produce economy and lower rates, in your belief and experience?
I was confining my answer to the effect that voting had upon the election of guardians.

374. I am talking now about the system of proxy voting?
In the election of guardians, I really think it is of no importance at all. In one union where I happened to be when I got the summons to your Lordships' Committee, I inquired how that matter stood, and I found that in the electoral division of Rathkeale (and it is really a fair representative of the other electoral divisions of that union and of other unions), there were 70 property or beneficial votes to 360 tenants' or occupying votes, and that the whole of the number, if they had all been claimed and all proxied, would have been only 90. I do not think that that proportion is really of any great importance; it has a certain weight, of course, as 70 is to 360, but it cannot be supposed to swamp the 360.

375. Then you do not believe that the abolition of the system of proxy voting would tend to increase the burden of the rates in Ireland?
No, indeed I do not.

376. *Chairman.*] You said just now that you did not think that property was adequately represented at the present time; in fact, that this proxy vote did not give the representatives of property the representation they were entitled to according to the rates they paid?
I did not say "what they were entitled to;" but I think that the limitation which has been placed upon it so far diminishes it as to destroy much of that practical effect, that limiting it to six votes under every head, is such a limitation as merely represents a fractional part of the property, and not the property itself.

377–8. But if that is the case, what would be the argument that it should be still further reduced?
I say that it is of very little value as it is.

379. Earl of *Milltown.*] As I understood you, you said that the abolition of proxy voting would not tend to increase the rates; that was the answer you gave to the noble Lord; on the other hand, I understood you to say that it would absolutely disfranchise non-resident owners?
A good many of them.

380. Entirely, unless they were able to attend personally?
Unless they were able to attend personally; and so many of them would not be, that it would disfranchise a good many.

381. And therefore it would be a complete example of taxation without representation?
I think that the representation of property is two-fold; it is in the number of votes it gives to an elected guardian, and it is also in the *ex-officio* guardians. I do not think that the proportion of voting power that it gives in the representation is of very much importance in one way or another, but I hold that the representation of property by members of a Board of Guardians is of great importance.

382. *Lord*

3rd *March* 1885.]   Mr. BOURKE.   [*Continued.*

382. *Lord President.*] But is there not a much more important protection of the interests of property in this fact, that the owners and occupiers have alike an interest in keeping down the rates?
I think that ought to be so, arguing from general principles.

383. But speaking generally, is it not so?
I think that in Ireland, with regard to Poor Law matters, you must look at it with reference to the intelligence with which the desire for economy is acted on. I think that elected guardians are much more susceptible of local influence, and much more imperfectly acquainted with economic science, and therefore are much more likely to act foolishly in the administration of the law, and to run up the rates, even though they have a great desire to keep them down; and that the more sense and intelligence you put into the board, the more chance there is of having a good administration, and an economical one.

384. But do you think that a board of guardians is likely for any length of time to be permitted by its constituents to burden them with extravagant rates?
I think the vote by ballot will have a strong bearing on that.

385. You think that capable men who would study economy of the rates would be much more likely to be chosen?
I think so.

386. You mean that persons would be more likely to be chosen on good grounds like those, rather than on the ground of mere popularity?
Yes, precisely.

387. You have been asked a good deal about the amount of representation given to property under the present system; of course it does not pretend for a moment, in spite of the limited plurality of votes, to adapt the voting power to the extent of the property?
No.

388. Otherwise many persons would have an enormous number of votes?
Clearly they would.

389. Of course the same thing happens in the case of the occupiers?
He has a limit put to his votes; he has not an unlimited power of voting.

390. I mean that the same principle is applied in the case of the occupiers?
To a certain degree, yes, but of course it has not so large an operation.

391. You told us that in some of the poor western unions that you have been familiar with, where the number of very small tenants is very great (as of course is the case), the owners pay a large proportion of the whole rate of the union?
Yes.

392. And those, of course, are the unions in Ireland where the occupiers have least interest in economy?
Yes.

393. Because they do not, at all events, feel the immediate pressure of the rates?
No, not in any large degree; the few that there are feel it.

394. They probably feel it very acutely?
Yes.

395. Have you found that that condition of things has produced any marked effect; have you found that the elected guardians in such unions as those have been inclined to be extravagant, knowing that so great a part of the rate will fall upon their landlords and not upon themselves?

I could

3rd March 1885.] Mr. BOURKE. [Continued.

I could not say that I have not seen instances of that kind, but I do not think they are the general rule.

396. It is a singular condition of things; I wanted to know what your experience about it was?
I have not seen it in any very marked way. I have heard it said in boards of guardians, "Oh it does not signify; the landlord pays all those rates;" but I think that case exceptional.

397. Do you think the tenants have felt that if the rates were very high it would affect the rent?
I do not think they considered the one to be dependent in any way upon the other. I do not think they would ever expect to get an abatement on account of high rates; certainly they could not be made to expect an increase of rent because the rates were high.

398. Lord *Monk-Bretton*.] Is not part of the objection that is made to the system of proxies due to a great many proxies being sometimes in the hands of one agent?
I think so.

399. Would it diminish the unpopularity of proxies if you limited the number of persons for whom one man might act as proxy?
I think it would to a certain extent.

400. It is limited in the case of a man who is not an agent for the person whose proxy he holds?
Yes.

401. Would there be any objection to applying to such an agent the same limit to the number of proxies in one hand, which is now placed upon proxies in the hands of a man other than an agent of those for whom he holds proxies?
No, I do not see that there would be any objection to that, though upon principle there seems to be no objection to a man who has considerable property making his agent his general proxy; but, undoubtedly, that has added to the unpopularity of proxies?

402. I am speaking of the case of one agent who has proxies for a great many different owners?
I do not see why there should not be a limit placed to that.

403. Do you know of any instances in which one agent holds the proxies for a very large number of owners?
I can only speak from hearsay; I am not absolutely concerned in elections; it is no part of our duty as inspectors to deal much with elections; but I believe that it is the case. I have heard of it in Kerry.

404. What is the greatest number you have heard?
I should hardly like to fix the number. I think I have heard of a man holding proxies upon 15 or 20 properties.

405. Did I understand you to say that in the case of that particular union, Tulla, concerning which you were examined, its finances would not have become so much embarrassed if the *ex-officio* guardians had attended better?
Yes.

406. They being the persons interested in defending other owners of property and their own property, can you account for their neglecting to attend?
I could only account for it on the ground which I believe to be the only and the real one, that political excitement ran very high in the union, and that they feared that they would expose themselves to disrespect, or perhaps to insult, if they attended at all.

407. And therefore they preferred to neglect their attendance and let the owners of property take their chance?
The greater number did; it is very much to be deplored.

408. *Chairman*.] In the case put by Lord Monk-Bretton, might it not be the fact

fact that the *ex-officio* guardians were in such a minority that they found it was useless to attend?

In that particular case, I do not think they tried the experiment; they might have thought it would have been useless, and perhaps it would. I do not say that it would not.

409. *Lord President.*] But if such a motive as that deterred them, it cuts at the root of the whole system, does it not. The *ex officio* voters cannot expect to be in the majority under a representative system?

No, but this was a very exceptional state of circumstances. Under ordinary circumstances their influence was sufficient to guide and rule the action of the board.

410. But do not you think that *ex-officio* guardians must trust more to their personal influence upon the board than to their mere voting members?

Yes; and their personal influence it is which tells. The numbers are casual, and only happen every now and then, but the presence of an *ex-officio* guardian who attends his board regularly cannot fail to be felt, and is so in many unions at the present moment.

411. *Chairman.*] You stated, in answer to the noble Lord, that you considered that the proxy vote was so small that it was not of very much use; then would you see any reason why, if that is the case, there would be any hardship in retaining it?

Not the least hardship. I think it would be perfectly impossible that it should operate in the way of swamping occupation votes; the numbers would not admit of it; it would be arithmetically impossible.

412. I would ask you the same question about *ex-officio* guardians; if they do not attend can there be any hardship to the elected guardians in retaining them as they are?

I was not looking upon it in the nature of a hardship towards any particular persons; I was looking upon it as a mode of representation.

413. Quite so; but as this Bill is proposed with the view of remedying a hardship in the law I asked you the question whether there could be any hardship in retaining *ex-officio* guardians at the numbers they are at now, as according to your evidence they have not attended regularly?

I do not think any hardship whatever; because if the argument was that they, by whipping up all their numbers, could carry any particular point, the same argument applies, but with greater force, to the elected guardians; they can whip up, and they do whip up, and as their body are all resident on the spot, they whip up more successfully. Therefore I do not think that the numbers of the *ex-officio* guardians act as a hardship towards the occupiers or elected guardians.

414. *Lord Ker.*] Did I rightly understand you to say that you were in favour rather of the clause in the Bill; that is to say, reducing the number of *ex-officio* guardians on the understanding that the system of election was different.

Yes; that I was not opposed to it.

415. But supposing this clause came into effect, the result would be that the *ex-officio* guardians would be one-third of the board, and yet they would represent property to the amount of two-thirds of the board?

Yes.

416. Do you consider that that would be a fair representation?

No, I do not consider that it would be a fair carrying out of the abstract principle upon which this whole system has been framed; but I think that practically, if you could get one-third or one-half of the *ex-officio* members to attend, that would produce much more good than would be gained by having a larger number if the attendance was imperfect.

417. Then with reference to another point, is it not the practice that on special occasions the election of a chairman, or any special occasion of that sort,

sort, the *ex-officio* members do attend in larger numbers now, in the present state of the law?
They do so.

418. If the number was reduced they would not have that power?
No.

419. That would add still more to the unfairness of the proposal to reduce their numbers?
That is an inference. I do not know whether I should be prepared to say that bringing up the whole body for a particular purpose was a perfectly fair and legitimate exercise of that power. I should prefer to see them in constant attendance and discharging the general duty of guardians.

420. But the elected guardians would whip up, and therefore I suppose there would be no objection to the *ex-officio* guardians doing so?
Yes; but two wrongs do not make one right.

421. I think you said that the proxy votes are unpopular?
In the hands by which they are used; where there are a great number of them placed in the hands of one agency, I believe they are unpopular.

422. Do you think it would add to the practical popularity of the working of the whole system if the proxy voting were done away with?
I do not think it is considered of sufficient moment or importance by the public to render its abolition effectual in popularising a system.

423. It has no practical effect, therefore, in your opinion?
No.

424. Lord *De Vesci*.] Do you consider that elected guardians are more subject than *ex-officio* guardians to coercion from outside the board in matters of granting out-door relief, or dealing with contracts for supplies?
To "influence" I should rather put it than coercion; certainly much more.

425. Lord *Saltersford*.] Corrupt influence?
Generally speaking, it is more or less corrupt; in the case of contracts it is corrupt.

426. It has been stated that in some wards the granting of contracts is notoriously corrupt; do you think that is the case?
Yes; I am sorry to say that there are cases in which I think that the granting of contracts has been improperly managed. I would not say that it has been "notoriously corrupt," meaning personal corruption, but it has been done through favour.

427. The granting of a contract to a relation, for instance?
Very often.

428. I think I understood you to say that the proxy votes had not much effect on the election of guardians?
I do not think they have.

429. Are they very largely used, do you know, in your district?
No, they are not largely used.

430. Is it not the case that, I think it was last year or the year before, there was a great increase in the number of the proxy votes in the Limerick union?
I think it was so.

431. And were there many changes, do you know, in the personality of the guardians, in the elected guardians, in consequence of that increase of proxy votes?
None whatever that I have been able to perceive. On the contrary, the

Limerick board is much more constituted from the National side than it was before.

432. Earl of *Milltown*] Do not you think that it would tend very much to ncrease the attendances of *ex-officio* guardians if some stringent qualification could be enforced for the prevention of political or seditious matters being brought before the board?

I dare say it might. The prevalence of those discussions is so distasteful to a number of *ex-officio* guardians, that I believe it accounts for a great deal of the absence that has taken place.

433. Do you believe that the people at large consider that there is any hardship in the existing number of *ex-officio* guardians?

No, I do not.

The Witness is directed to withdraw.

Ordered, That this Committee be adjourned to Friday next, at Twelve o'clock.

Die Veneris, 6° Martii, 1885.

LORDS PRESENT:

The Lord President.
Earl of Milltown.
Viscount Powerscourt.
Lord Tyrone.
Lord Saltersford.

Lord Ker.
Lord Shute.
Lord Monk-Bretton.
Lord Sudley.

The LORD TYRONE, in the Chair.

Mr. GEORGE MORRIS, called in; and Examined, as follows:

434. *Chairman.*] I believe you are a Commissioner of the Local Government Board?
Yes.

435. And prior to your appointment were you not a poor law guardian?
Yes, I was guardian for three unions in the West of Ireland for many years, and I was Vice-Chairman of the Galway Union for a great number of years.

436. As an *ex-officio* guardian?
Both elected and *ex officio*.

437. You were an elected guardian as well?
Yes, for many years.

438. Then you have naturally a thorough knowledge of the working of the Poor Law in Ireland?
A fair knowledge.

439. You have seen the Bill which is before this Committee?
Yes, I have got a copy of the Bill with me.

440. I will begin with Section 4. Have you any objection to the provision in that Section which makes the elections take place every three years?
I should be rather in favour of that.

441. Sections 6, 7, and 8 have to do with the ballot; have you any objection to that system being extended to poor law elections?
I have no particular objection to it. When it has been extended to all the other elected bodies, to corporations, and town commissioners, I, of course, have no objection to offer to the ballot for the election of poor law guardians.

442. Do you think that it might put down intimidation?
I think that of the two it would be more useful than the present system.

443. We had some evidence on Tuesday as to the difficulty of the electors voting by ballot?
Principally caused by the cumulative vote, I think.

444. Yes, it was so represented to us. Have you any suggestion to make as to the best means of enabling the cumulative vote to be given under the ballot?
Under the Local Act for Galway, there is a cumulative vote for the town commissioners (I believe they are the only body of town commissioners in Ireland

Ireland for which there is a cumulative vote) and it is pretty much I think upon the same line as this scale of voting for poor law guardians; and that has been in existence for a great number of years in the town of Galway for the town commissioners; and when residing in Galway I was for some years chairman of that body, and therefore I know the way in which the election was conducted there.

445. Was that by ballot?
The time when I was chairman was before the ballot; but the election now, since the passing of the Ballot Act, is held by ballot; and I am aware of the mode of voting in Galway with the cumulative vote. An elector who has six votes comes up and he gets six voting papers, and he goes behind a screen and marks his voting papers, and they are counted singly. Where he has three votes he gets three voting papers.

446. Then would you be in favour of giving a voting paper for each vote.
I would be in favour of a separate paper being given for each vote, except that since I became Commissioner of the Local Government Board, I am aware that in very large constituencies, such as Dublin, Cork and Belfast, there are electors who hold proxies, who have 18 votes, and now, under the law as it has been lately laid down, 30 votes; and of course in such cases it might lead to some complication and a great deal of extra expense for voting booths.

447. Might there not be some system, such as letting no voting paper carry more than six votes, which would get rid of the difficulty?
Yes, I am inclined now to think that that would be the better way; but previous to considering the matter, my knowledge being confined to the elections that I have spoken of, I was in favour of the single paper for each vote.

448. I will pass now to Clause 9, which deals with the proxy voting; do you think it would be possible for the owners of property to vote in the different unions in which they held property if the proxy vote was abolished?
In my opinion, it would be impossible to carry it out, because, as your Lordships are aware, many large proprietors hold property in different parts of Ireland, in different counties, and different provinces; and I think it would be, I should not like to use the word "impossible," but almost impossible, to arrange the elections so that an owner of property could exercise the right in person.

449. In answer to a question of a noble Lord, the Lord President, one of the witnesses on Tuesday stated that he did not consider that the proxy vote was of very much use; do you consider that it is of any use?
Yes, I do consider it of very great use.

450. Do you consider that it ever turns the scale at an election?
I think it does at many elections; and I think it sometimes prevents contests where it is calculated and known that there are a great many proxies in the electoral division, and that the candidates would not be likely to get the support of those proxies.

451. If the proxy vote was done away with, would you not consider that owners of property would be disfranchised in unions where they could not attend?
Yes, certainly, to a large extent. Of course, some of them, being more energetic than others, might exert themselves to attend at some of the elections; others could not possibly do it for various reasons. I also have considered the question from the fact of my having been myself for over 20 years very extensively engaged, both in farming as a large ratepayer, and also as agent representing about 25,000 *l*. a year, in the West of Ireland; and judging from my experience at that time, I think that to abolish the proxy vote would not result in a fair representation, considering the amount of poor rate that is paid by the owners. I have heard it stated that they contribute

tribute five-eighths, taking it over the whole; there are electoral divisions in which they pay three-fourths.

452. Then if they were prevented from voting by proxy, they would pay that amount of the rates without having any representation?
It would come out of their income, because though it might be paid by the occupier in the first instance, half of it would be deducted by him when paying his rent; and the owner would pay all where he was the occupier, and he would pay all for tenements rated at and under 4 *l*. I have had considerable experience of that kind of property in my time.

453. Not only does he pay the whole of the rates in the case of property rated at and under 4 *l*, but he has to pay for the land in his own occupation?
He has to pay for the land which he occupies himself.

454. With regard to the cases of banks and railway companies, do they at present vote by proxy?
I think not; I do not think that they exercise the power very much.

455. But my question is pointed to this: Are they able so to vote?
I think so.

456. If this Bill were to pass, as they could not vote by proxy, I suppose they would be disfranchised altogether?
In some cases the manager of a bank is personally rated in the district and not the bank; in other cases the bank is rated.

457. Viscount *Powerscourt*.] Shareholders in railway companies vote by proxy?
Yes.

458. *Chairman*.] There was, I think, a suggestion made to the Committee the other day that all voting claims should be lodged some time before the election; what is your view on that subject?
I should be inclined to extend it to a period somewhat longer than that proposed by the Bill, which is one month.

459. How long would you make it?
I should suggest two months; I think that would be an improvement.

460. As to the payment of rates I understand that at present the ratepayers are able to get their votes by paying their rates upon the day of election. Would you allow that to continue if this Bill became law, or would you make them pay some days before the election?
I should be inclined to make them pay some days before. I should be inclined to have them pay the rate before the list was made out by the clerk of the union.

461. Does the proposal in this Bill to have election petitions tried before the county court judge instead of your Board, meet with your approval?
I think it would be a very great improvement. At present it is not a very satisfactory mode that we have of trying the petitions. I made out a short return from my office, and I find that last year in the elections of guardians, there were about 550 contests, and there were about 109 petitions lodged; that is to say, that in about one-fifth of the number of contests there was a petition lodged; and out of those 109, I believe I am accurate in stating there were only 21 set aside.

462. Were many of those petitions frivolous?
Several of them were frivolous. I think that when the defeated and disappointed candidate has got merely to write up and lodge a complaint to the Local Government Board it is a very great encouragement to him to do so.

463. Do you think it would be necessary to make the petitioners give security for costs?
I should be in favour of it.

6th March 1885.] Mr. MORRIS. [Continued

464. Do you think there would be any danger of their lodging petitions, and then, if the petitions were dismissed, the costs falling upon the union?
I think that up to the last few years there were very few petitions; not near so many contests; but the matter in the last few years has assumed rather an angry character sometimes, and therefore I think it would be better if there were security given by the defeated candidate to some small amount when lodging his petition. And I should also be in favour of the county court judge awarding costs in the case, just in the same way as the High Court of Justice in Dublin now award costs in the election of town commissioners The petition is lodged before a judge in Dublin, and he awards costs either way.

465. There is a proposal that if the costs should fall on the officer of the Board, it should be placed upon the rates; do you think that that would be fair?
I do not object very much to that. The officer is very much under the control, both of the board of guardians and of the Local Government Board, and if he wilfully misbehaved, I think he might be dealt with in another way.

466. That might be the case; but supposing the case of the defeated party not being able to meet the costs, then would it be fair that the costs of the returning officer should fall upon the rates?
I should say that the county court judge should have full power to deal with cases like that. I should be quite willing to leave a great deal of the power of awarding costs to the county court judge who hears the case.

467. Earl of *Milltown*.] But supposing the petitioner was a man of straw and could not pay the costs?
Then if he gave security for costs, the costs could be recovered.

468. *Chairman*.] Do you think that if the system of proxies were abolished it would be possible for owners to vote by registered letters?
I am not in favour of the registered-letter principle.

469. Why not?
I think there would be a great deal of difficulty about it, and it would be very difficult to keep it secret. I have not quite turned the thing over in my mind. It does not strike me at present, any way, by which, with a registered letter, and the clerk receiving the letter, there could be any secrecy about it.

470. No plan occurs to you by which votes sent by a registered letter could be kept secret?
No, not at present.

471. In regard to Part 3 of the Bill, we had evidence that it would be advisable that if a person under 21 years of age is not permitted to vote, his guardian or trustee should be permitted to vote for him; is that your view?
Certainly.

472. Would you say the same with regard to lunatics?
Certainly.

473. Then as to Sub-section 2, of Clause 25, the Local Government Board by this sub-section is obliged to order an election within three months; would you be in favour of that as it stands, or would you rather give the Local Government Board more discretion?
I should give the Local Government Board and the board of guardians discretion. If the board of guardians asked for an election, I think then the Local Government Board should issue an order to hold one. If the board of guardians did not ask for a new election, I should leave it with the Local Government Board to issue the order or not. I think that that is very much the practice at present, and I have found for the last few years that it has worked very well. We have never had any misunderstanding on that point with any board of guardians.

474. Sub-

8th March 1885.] Mr. MORRIS. [*Continued.*

474. Sub-section (4) deals with a reduction of the qualification for an elected guardian to 12 *l.*; would you be in favour of that, or would you be in favour of retaining a sliding scale in the hands of the Local Government Board, as at present?
I should be in favour of leaving the qualification as it is at present. No doubt at present it varies very much, but in many unions in Ireland, where the Local Government Board have reduced the qualification, that has been principally done, because it was impossible to get higher qualified men to fill the place in the electoral division; and also, I think, that with regard to guardians rated very low, it is not alone the fact that they have not very much interest in the expenditure, but many live at a distance from the workhouse, 20 or 15 Irish miles; and it is hardly to be expected that a man rated at 12 *l.* or 10 *l.* or 6 *l.*, could afford to come into the board every week. Some of them may not have a horse to ride, and I think it would be very hard to expect that men would walk in.

475. Do you consider that the expense would disqualify these lower rated men, even if they were disqualified for no other reason?
I think that a man very low rated might be under a temptation to make something of the office in some other way.

476. Earl of *Milltown.*] Is the qualification altogether discretionary now?
It is discretionary now; I think the lowest is 6 *l.*, but that is only in one or two electoral divisions.

477. *Chairman.*] You can make it as high or as low as you like?
£. 30 is the limit of the amount that we can make it.

478. Do you see any reason at all why the present system should be altered on this point?
I think the present system is as good a system as any that could possibly be substituted for it. If I saw any reason for it I should be very glad indeed to agree with the proposition in the Bill.

479. Sub-section No. (5) deals with the reduction of *ex-officio* guardians to one-half of the number of elective guardians; do you think that that would be an improvement, or the reverse?
I do not think it would be an improvement. I, for many years had experience as a poor law guardian myself, both elected and *ex-officio*, and I always found that a mixed element was very much the best for conducting the business. Where the *ex-officio* guardians attended, I think it was always followed by less discussion, and more business was transacted; and I also think that the *ex-officio* guardians, as a rule, are more capable of withstanding pressure to give out-door relief, what I would take the liberty of calling extravagant out-door relief.

480. The number of *ex-officio* guardians was fixed, I believe, at one-half the number of the board, in consequence of the very large proportion of the rates which owners of property had to contribute?
Yes, it was so changed in 1847; previous to that I think they were one-third, but in 1847 I believe they were made equal in number. But out of the 163 unions in Ireland there are some few unions where the *ex-officio* guardians, both resident and non-resident, having property in the union, do not equal in number the elected guardians.

481. We have had evidence of that before; but what I intended to ask you was, whether there was any reason why the number of the *ex-officios* should be reduced now, more than at the time when they were first placed in the position which they occupy at present?
I can see no reason.

482. They still pay the same proportion of rates?
Giving my own individual opinion, I must say that I can see no reason for such a reduction, but it is a matter for the Imperial Parliament altogether.

(0.1.)   G   483. Do

483. Do you consider that if the number of *ex-officio* were reduced, the probability would be that the rates in different unions would rise?
I think it would be likely to have that effect.

484. Where the *ex-officio* do not attend the boards, has it come under your notice whether the rates there are generally higher in proportion than in cases where they do attend?
That is my experience. I think most of the elected guardians are thoroughly honest, thoroughly straight; but occasionally there are disturbances in the country, when out-door relief is demanded for evicted families, as it was during the time that a number of people were in prison as suspects. There was a clause, I think, in that Act that enabled the guardians to give out-door relief to families of men who were put in prison.

485. Earl of *Milltown*.] Was there such a clause in the Act. They made the clause for themselves, did they not?
I think there was some clause under which the families of suspects were given out-door relief. If I do not mistake that was so, but I shall refer to the matter.

486. *Chairman*.] I fancy that the families of suspects would be give out-door relief in the same way that any other distressed person might be given it?
Well, some were given it, who I think were not entitled to out-door relief; and, even if they were, they received a much larger proportion of out-door relief as a weekly allowance than poor people did who were deserving of it.

487. In fact, I understand you that the power of the boards to grant out-door relief was used for political purposes?
I think in some cases it may.

488. What amount of out-door relief have you known granted to the families of suspects and evicted tenants?
I am quite certain of a pound a week, but I think there was even something over that.

489. What is the usual amount granted to ordinary families?
It varies from 1 s. 6 d. to 10 s. as the highest I almost ever knew until within the last three or four years.

490. In cases where tenants have been evicted, the extra rate would fall in a great measure upon the owners of property in the district, would it not?
Yes, of course in the same proportion, except in some electoral divisions where there would be a larger proportion of people rated at and under 4 l., and there of course a larger proportion would fall upon the owner.

491. It has been stated that *ex-officio* guardians are in the habit of attending largely on election days; have you noticed whether elected guardians also attend very largely on those days?
I think they are about equal on that score.

492. Is it not very important for the proper working of the board that good officers such as the chairman and vice-chairman should be chosen?
I have scarcely ever known a union in which there was a good chairman, a gentleman who was fairly popular, and knew how to manage the people, but that the affairs of that union were much better managed.

493. If that is the case the *ex-officios* naturally attend largely on the days of the election of the chairman?
They do.

494. For the purpose of seeing that the board is properly carried on during the year?
Yes; I believe they very often do that.

495. And

495. And if their number were largely reduced they would not have the power, at any rate, of turning the scale in favour of a good chairman at these times?
I think in many unions they would not.

496. I suppose that before this agitation began in Ireland there were no great difficulties in regard to electing the chairman of poor-law boards?
There was hardly ever a contest, and I think that most of the contests that have taken place latterly have been in cases in which the chairman, who, perhaps, had been many years chairman, tried to prevent the board discussing other subjects.

497. Political subjects, do you mean?
Extraneous subjects, matters not in any way connected with the administration of the poor law or the sanitary law, or any of the duties which ought properly to bring them there.

498. We were told by Mr. Robinson that at present 30 votes were the maximum number of votes that might be given by one person?
Yes, that is owing to a recent decision of the High Court of Appeal in Ireland.

499. But up to six months ago, 18 was what was allowed?
Yes.

500. This Bill proposes to reduce it to the old figure; do you see any objection to that?
I should be in favour of that change; that is to say, leaving the proxy votes to the owners of property, and also leaving the *ex-officio* guardians as they are at present, I should be in favour of curtailing the number of votes to 18.

501. *Lord President.*] You are aware, of course, that in the case of municipal elections all voting is purely personal?
Yes.

502. Votes of the individuals voting in person, as rated occupiers?
Yes.

503. And that it is not thought necessary to provide any special representation of property as distinct from occupation?
I believe not.

504. I take it that this system of proxy voting, which the Bill proposes to abolish, is only important as a machinery to provide for a complete exercise in all cases of the right of property voting?
Yes; but if your Lordship would allow me to illustrate the difference of taxation by my own case in Dublin; I pay between 40 *l.* and 42 *l.* a-year as taxes for my house in Dublin, and the amount of the poor rate is about 9 *l.* of that. The whole consolidated tax comes to about 40 *l.*; the amount of the poor rate is, as I say, about 9 *l.*, and I deduct half that from the landlord; but out of all the rest I only get 1 *l.* 2 *s.* allowed from the landlord. Therefore if you take 9 *l.* from 40 *l.* it leaves 31 *l.* Then I get an allowance out of that 31 *l.* of about 1 *l.* 2 *s.* or 1 *l.* 10 *s.*

505. I do not quite understand the point?
It is, that so much more of the poor rate is paid by the landlord than of any other tax.

506. Has your landlord in Dublin the power of voting as a landlord, as an owner?
For the poor law guardians he has. He has no power to vote in respect of the house which I occupy in an election for a town councillor; but, if he has no right to vote, it must be borne in mind that he pays, as I have mentioned already, only about 30 *s.* of taxes out of about 30 *l.*

507. You mean in the case of the municipal taxes?
Yes; so that his interest in the municipal vote would be very small indeed.

6th March 1885.] Mr. MORRIS. [Continued.

508. You consider this machinery of proxy voting to be very important as a means of using property votes?
I consider it a fair representation according to taxation.

509. And is it largely used within your knowledge?
It is increasing, I think. In some places it is, and in many places it is not. In the union in which I was vice-chairman there were scarcely ever any proxy votes used; but in those days there were very few contests indeed.

510. What is the limit within which one person can give proxies for others; that is to say, what number of proxies can any one individual hold?
I am not aware that there is a limit.

511. May not that give an amount of power and influence over the elections to an individual, which is invidious?
I do not think it would have that effect, but it is a matter, I think, that any two men might differ upon in opinion.

512. The case is, therefore, that that one individual may hold a large number of votes, and may hold them for years together, without any renewed authority from the persons he represents?
I should be in favour of limiting the time, decidedly. If the guardians were elected for three years, I should have the proxies renewed every three years, or allowed to drop.

513. *Chairman.*] At present they have to be renewed, when?
Every five years, I think.

514. *Lord President.*] Would you see any objection to the proxy being given, *ad hoc*, for the occasion of the election, and only so?
If the poor-law guardians were elected for three years, I should be in favour of the proxy being given for that particular election, and any vacancy that occurred during the three years.

515. Why should there not be fresh proxies for any election occurring during the three years?
It might be very inconvenient. It is a matter very much of detail, and I have not got a very strong opinion upon it.

516. Lord *Saltersford.*] Would it not cause a delay in the election; of course a sufficient time must be given for the proxies to be got in?
Yes; it would create some difficulty in that way.

517. *Lord President.*] You did not give a positive opinion; I think you said you had not thoroughly considered the point as to the possibility of substituting voting by registered letter for the present system of proxy voting?
As well as I can form an opinion on the subject, I think a registered letter would be objectionable.

518. Because, as I understand you, you think that it would not, or that it might not, secure absolute secrecy to the use of the vote?
Not, it would not secure secrecy to the vote.

519. But is not the right of proxy voting, for which this would be a substitute, supposing it were approved of, in the nature of a privilege attaching to property voting?
Yes.

520. It does not attach to the occupier's vote?
No.

521. The non-resident occupier has no such privilege?
No.

522. Therefore, even supposing that it were not in every case to confer the most absolute security for secrecy, might not that be endured in consideration of the privilege which the property vote enjoys?

I think

6th March 1885.] Mr. MORRIS. [Continued.

I think I have already stated that, as far as my opinion goes, I should prefer the proxy vote.

523. You disapprove of the proposal to decrease the number of *ex-officio* guardians?
Yes; and in case they were reduced, I certainly would suggest that the *ex-officio* guardians should be elected; because at present they are taken from the highest rated, and a great many of the *ex officios* taken in that way never attend, and never can attend.

524. You would prefer a choice by the whole body of magistrates?
Yes, by the body of magistrates interested in the union, should Parliament think it wise to reduce the number of *ex-officio* guardians.

525. Earl of *Milltown*.] Even if the number remains as it is, do not you think that that would be an advisable alteration?
Does the point arise?

526. I will explain my meaning. You say that it would be advisable that the magistrates should elect their representatives, supposing the number to be reduced. My question is, supposing the number to remain as it is now, would it not still be advisable that in that case also they should elect their representatives, instead of the highest rated being chosen?
I think there are very few unions, if any, in which the number exceeds the number of elected guardians.

527. Where they do, would you think it advisable that the magistrates should elect their representatives?
Where they do, I certainly would be in favour of that; I think it would be a very much better plan, and perhaps lead to a better attendance of *ex officios*.

528. Lord *President*.] Do you think it would improve the attendance of *ex-officio* guardians if they had been chosen by the body of magistrates?
I do not think it would make very much change.

529. But do you think it would make some change?
I think it might, a slight one.

530. In the direction of better attendance?
Yes, very slight indeed.

531. Is it not necessary to remember, in dealing with the question of the proportion of *ex-officio* guardians, that under the present poor law system in Ireland, property, as distinct from occupation, is represented twice over, directly and indirectly?
Not to the extent of twice, I think.

532. When I say "twice over," I mean by two different methods; directly through the *ex-officio* guardians, and indirectly through the influence conferred upon property in the election of ordinary guardians?
In most of the electoral divisions of which I have experience, the number of occupiers in the electoral divisions are so much more numerous than the number of votes that the landlord would have that it would be a very small increase indeed.

533. What do you mean by "a small increase"?
A landowner in an electoral division, we will say, can have 30 votes; that is the most he can have in any electoral division; and in that same electoral division there would probably be 60 or 100 resident occupiers who would have votes.

534. *Chairman*.] Taking the resident occupiers in an average union, how many votes, supposing there were 100 occupiers, would they have?
You could scarcely strike an average, I think.

535. But, supposing that they were rated, we will say at an average of 40 *l.*?
I do

6th March 1885.]   Mr. MORRIS.   [Continued.

I do not think there is any electoral division where the owner could have near the number of votes as owner that the occupiers would have.

536. Viscount *Powerscourt*.] That is under the present system?
Under the present system.

537. Lord *Sudley*.] Not enough votes materially to affect the result of an election?
I would say not. They might turn an election; supposing the occupiers all went one side, and the owners of property went another, I do not think that the owners of property could return anyone in any electoral division.

538. Viscount *Powerscourt*] Do you think it is an almost impossible case that the occupiers should all go one way?
I do not think that the case is likely to happen.

539. *Lord President*.] I am not sure that I quite understood the argument that you drew from the occasional excessive grant of outdoor relief, which happened especially, you said, in the cases of evicted tenants, or what were called political suspects. You mean, I understand, that the facts show the danger of making any such change or changes as those proposed by the Bill; but the present provisions of the law evidently have not prevented those abuses, if they were abuses?
Not entirely. I mean to convey this, that a guardian, rated say at 10*l.* or at 15*l.*, and living in a thatched house in a country district, would be certainly more likely, no matter how honest and straight he was, to be afraid to refuse outdoor relief than another higher class guardian; and I quite sympathise with his feelings. I know one or two cases myself where that has occurred.

540. Of course if we pushed that argument too far, we should have no electoral system at all in Ireland; but I want to know the degree of importance that you attach to this system of proxy voting, and to the existing proportion of *ex-officio* guardians for the purpose of preventing occasional abuses of that kind?
I think it strengthens the board to have the *ex-officio* guardians attending; it strengthens the proper administration of the poor law, I think.

541. Viscount *Powerscourt*] You said that the election of *ex-officio* guardians by their brother magistrates would secure a better attendance, and then afterwards, I understood you to say that you did not think it would make much difference in the attendance?
I said it might. I do not think it would make much difference, but I said I thought it might make some.

542. Lord *Monk-Bretton*.] You said that you had acted as vice-chairman of the Galway Union, and that for a long time you had served on a union in the West of Ireland; is that another union?
Yes.

543. What union is that?
Lough Rea Union. I had property in Lough Rea Union, and was an *ex-officio* guardian of it; but it was 20 miles from my residence, and I do not think I ever attended more than twice.

544. Were you an *ex-officio* guardian in Galway too?
I was both *ex-officio* guardian and elected. I was an elected guardian because the ratepayers wished me to be one, and I wished it myself.

545-6. How many years altogether did you act in the Galway Union?
I should say that I was guardian for over 20 years, and vice-chairman for a considerable part of that time.

547. Could you give me the name of the case in which it was recently decided that one individual could have 30 votes, and the reference to the report of it?
Yes. The Local Government Board *ex parte* Byrne and James; Earl Fitz-William. The Law Reports (Ireland), Part 9, pp. 395 to 407.

548. Did

6th March 1885.]   Mr. MORRIS.   [Continued.

548. Did I understand you correctly to say that the voting of corporations depended upon the law permitting voting by proxy?
I stated that the only corporation (and it is not a corporation, it is a body of town commissioners, and it is under a local Act) that I am aware of in Ireland, that are elected with the cumulative vote, are the Town Commissioners of Galway.

549. That was not my point. I thought I understood you to say, in answer to a question from the Chairman, that the power of a corporation to vote at the election of guardians would stand or fall with the system of proxy voting; but the principle of the law which allows one individual to appoint another to vote for him is a different principle, is it not, from that which allows a corporation to act by one of its officers?
Yes.

550. And, therefore, the power of a corporation to vote at the election of guardians would not depend upon the system of proxy voting?
I should not consider that it entirely depends upon proxy voting.

551. Whether proxy voting were abolished or not, that would not affect the right of a corporation to act as an elector through its appointed officer?
The only case in point that I am aware of is that of a railway company; and there I think the secretary of the railway company is rated in the rate books. That is my impression, but I should not wish to put it forward as being quite certain of it. In that case the secretary of the railway company would proceed to the place and vote; but if he was to proceed to all the unions through which the line of the railway company goes, he would be travelling for a very long time.

552. *Lord President.*] A railway company does not vote in respect of its property, does it?
Yes; the part which goes through each electoral division is rated in that electoral division, and pays all the county taxes and the poor rate.

553. But that would be an occupation vote. Has it a right of voting in respect of its ownership of the land?
I am not aware that it has.

554. Earl of *Milltown.*] A railway company would have exactly the same difficulty in voting without proxy voting as any other non-resident proprietor?
Yes.

555. Lord *Monk-Bretton.*] I will ask you to look at Clause 11, which says that the returning officer shall appoint a day to hear the claims of persons whose names have been omitted from the list; are you of opinion that he should at the same time hear objections to persons who have been put on?
I am, certainly.

556. If that were provided, would you be satisfied to allow the register as settled by the returning officer to be conclusive proof of the right of a person to vote?
No, I should leave that to the county court judge.

557. You would have an appeal to the county court judge?
Yes.

558. And, subject to that appeal, would you have the register conclusive as to the right to vote?
I would.

559. Earl of *Milltown.*] I see it says in that Clause that "the returning officer shall appoint a day or days, within prescribed limits of time, before the day fixed for the polling." What are the "prescribed limits of time"?
That would be regulated, I suppose, by the regulations for the election.

560. There is nothing in the Bill to regulate it?
There is nothing in the Bill to do so. I might point out that in Clause 8 of this

6th March 1885.] Mr. MORRIS. [Continued.

this Bill, where it says that the Local Government Board shall make rules and regulations, the words being "The Local Government Board may embody in any such order the second, third, fourth, sixth, ninth, twelfth, thirteenth, and twenty-fourth sections of the Ballot Act, 1872," the word used is "may;" and I think that where it is enacting penal enactments, that should form part of the Bill itself, and not be left to the regulation of the Local Government Board, and that by the word "may," a discretionary power should not be left with them to do it or not.

561. Line 25, clause 10, enacts that "At any time prior to, but not after the signing of the register of voters by him as hereinafter mentioned, the returning officer may add to, excise from, alter, or amend the list of voters, and may add thereto the name of any ratepayer originally omitted therefrom, because of the non-payment of any poor rate, on being satisfied that such poor rate has since been paid;" have you noticed that?
Yes.

562. Then if the time for signing the register was fixed by statute at some considerable time antecedent to the day of the polling, the difficulty to which you just now alluded would be got rid of?
Yes. I fancy that the motive of putting in that part of the clause was, that the clerk might be making out his list, and the man might pay his poor rate to the poor-rate collector, and then the poor rate collector might come in just at the last moment and say, "This man paid me the poor rates this day week, or four days ago."

563. Lord *Saltersford*.] Have you reason to believe that there is corruption in boards of guardians in the granting of contracts, that contracts have been granted from corrupt or political motives?
I think there may be some such cases, but I have not much complaint on that head made to me.

564. But such complaints do reach you?
Yes; I have had letters myself from persons tendering from the West of Ireland, addressed to me, simply because they knew me, but which I have dealt with, of course, officially, complaining of not getting a contract, because they were not, as they expressed it in the letter, "of the right sort."

565. I presume you would say that *ex-officio* guardians are less open to imputations of that sort than elected guardians?
I think they are less open to them.

566. Complaints have been made of the non-attendance of *ex-officio* guardians at boards; have you reason to believe that that has been partly caused by the way in which they have been treated by the elective guardians, by insults directed against them, for the express purpose of making it disagreeable to them to attend.
Yes; I think some *ex-officio* guardians have given up attending in consequence of that, although I must say that my own sympathy is not with them; I think it would be much better for them to attend.

567. Then do not you think that their want of attendance has been sometimes from their being engaged in other occupations?
Certainly.

568. An *ex-officio* guardian, of course, must be a magistrate?
Yes.

569. And a grand juror; and he may be an agent?
Yes.

570. So that he is not able to give the same attendance as an elected guardian who has no other occupation?
All that explanation applies, certainly.

571. Do not you think that, under those circumstances, an *ex-officio* guardian,
not

6th *March* 1885.]   Mr. MORRIS.   [*Continued.*

not being able to give a regular attendance at the board, is perfectly justified in attending the board when important offices are to be filled up ?

I do, particularly at the election of a chairman. I consider that the election of a good chairman practically keeps the union straight.

572. *Lord President.*] Do you mean that you think an elected guardian, who is probably a farmer, is a less busy man than an *ex-officio* guardian ?
Certainly not.

573. Or that the latter is less able to attend ?
Certainly not.

574. Provided, of course, that he is resident within a reasonable distance ?
I have already expressed the difficulty that many guardians find in attending, owing to the distance and to their position. Many of the elected guardians may not have a horse, and they cannot walk 20 miles once a week.

575. Is it not the fact that the *ex-officio* guardians, if they are resident within a reasonable distance, can attend with much greater ease than the ordinary farmer?
I think not with much greater ease.

576. More easily, I will say ?
A great number of the meetings of boards of guardians are held on market days, it must be remembered.

577. *Chairman.*] That enables the farmers to be on the spot ?
Yes.

578. And the *ex-officio* guardians may have business in other parts of the country ?
I do not suggest any excuse on behalf of the *ex-officio* guardians for not attending.

579. The question I would ask on the point about the *ex-officios* is, whether the fact of many of them being non-resident prevents them attending ?
Yes.

580. *Lord President.*] Have you found that *ex-officios* have often been deterred from attending because they have found themselves outvoted upon occasions in which they were anxious to carry a point or to carry a candidate ?
I think that that is one element. I think that another element in the falling off of the attendance of the *ex-officio* guardians is, that for the last three or four years, at a great number of the meetings of boards of guardians, a large proportion of the time has been taken up in discussing matters that have nothing to say to the administration of the Poor Law, or of the sanitary law ; and the Local Government Board about a year, and a half ago, I think, issued a general circular to the boards of guardians in Ireland, calling their attention to the discharge of their duties, and making a regulation upon the matter, that the business of the board should be first transacted. The issuing of that circular was, I think, owing to what I have stated, that the time of the boards was very largely given to discussing other questions.

581. Lord *Saltersford.*] Do you think that that circular produced any effect ?
I think it had some slight effect, but not much.

582. *Lord President.*] But if the *ex-officio* guardians attach so much importance to their rights under the Poor Law, and so much dislike the idea of their numbers being at all diminished, is it not somewhat strange that they do not take the trouble of attending, or make whatever effort is required for that purpose?
I could only answer that question by saying that I have some slight hopes that things may settle down, and then both parties would be better able to pull together.

(0.1.)   H   583. But

583. But did the *ex-officio* guardians attend much better than they do now before this Nationalist agitation began?

I think very much better. I have no statistics to offer, but from observing local newspapers, of which I read a great many, considering that it is my duty to see what is going on in those different unions, I think that I have observed a decided falling off, a large falling off, in the attendance of *ex-officio* guardians during the last two or three years.

584. Lord *Monk-Bretton*.] How long is it since you were a guardian in Galway?

I was obliged to resign when I got my present appointment five years ago. Under the Act of Parliament I was obliged to resign being a Poor Law guardian, or having any connection with a board of guardians.

585. What was the proportion of *ex-officio* guardians to elected guardians on that Galway Board?

I think they were very nearly half-and-half; they used to attend in my time very nearly in equal numbers; but there were a great many of the borough magistrates in Galway, or rather I should say of the county magistrates, because Galway is a county of a town; who resided near the town, and therefore probably there was a larger attendance in the Galway Union of *ex-officio* guardians.

586. Galway is a county of a town?
Yes.

587. And, on the strength of that, the magistrates of Galway are *ex-officio* guardians?
Yes.

588. A borough magistrate is not an *ex-officio* guardian?
No.

589. And the number of elected guardians, if I understand you rightly, and that of the *ex-officio* guardians on the board of the Galway Union, are about equal?
They are equal on the list.

590. And the attendance was practically about equal, as I understand you?
Speaking, of course, only from recollection, I should say that it was very close.

591. Lord *Shute*.] And is the attendance of ordinary guardians large, according to your experience, at ordinary meetings, generally in Ireland; in what sort of numbers do they attend?
About a third, I should say.

592. We have had it in evidence that the number of elected guardians, and that of *ex-officio* guardians, are about equal; but what is the number that attend?
There is a very much larger number of elected guardians that attend than of *ex-officio* guardians.

593. Then when there is any special business, I suppose you issue a special notice, before elections of officers, or anything of that kind?
Yes.

594. And then you say the attendance of the *ex-officio* guardians is larger than at other times?
I think it is, and also the attendance of the elected guardians is larger on a special occasion.

595. So that there can be no suspicion of the gentlemen who act *ex-officio* as guardians, wishing to commit any job in the case of the election of any officer?
Well, I have heard many stories, and I should rather not say anything as to that.

596. Have you heard of such a thing happening as a job being perpetrated by the elective guardians, or a desire to perpetrate one?
I have heard it, but I have not known any of my own knowledge.

597. Under the present system they are half-and-half?
Yes.

598. And you told the Lord President that you were against any decrease; what objection is there to an increase; what objection is there to assimilating the law to that in England, that all justices of the peace should be *ex-officio* guardians?
I think there is an objection to that.

599. Has it anything to do with the payment of half the rates?
I think that if the *ex-officio* guardians are left as they are, all things considered, they ought to be very well satisfied.

600. What is your reason for stating that; why should they be very well satisfied?
I think, giving the *ex-officio* guardians equal numbers with the elected guardians, and giving them also the proxy votes, and giving them the cumulative vote, their representation is then quite equal to the proportion which they pay.

601. But that is what they have in England; they have the proxy vote in England also; and as far as the payment of rates goes, I suppose it cannot be very much disputed that the owners of property pay a very large proportion of the rates, and the farmer does not take a farm without ascertaining beforehand what he is going to pay in the shape of rent?
I can only give my own opinion.

602. Earl of *Milltown*.] Do you see any objection to proxy voting as it now exists?
No.

603. You are well acquainted with the people of Ireland and their opinions on most of these subjects; have you ever heard them express any objection prior to the recent seditious agitation?
I have always for some years heard a discussion about it; but I cannot say that I have heard of any downright dissatisfaction and agitation upon the question until recent years.

604. Does the objection to it now arise, do you think, from political reasons, or simply from a desire that guardians more suited to the purposes of the administration of the poor law should be elected?
I think it arises from a desire that the people have to have more control and exercise more authority in the country.

605. Politically, you mean?
Not politically exactly; but it gives them patronage. They have the appointment of the dispensary doctor very often; they have the appointment of poor rate collectors; they have the appointment of relieving officers; and many of those small elections I can assure your Lordship give as much trouble and cause as much excitement almost as an election for a Member of Parliament.

606. But then you think it is for purposes of patronage and for political reasons?
I think it is in a great measure for the exercise of patronage in the country.

607. Now I want to ask you a question on another point; at present trustees of minors and lunatics are allowed to vote?
Yes; I think they are.

608. Do you know whether that is by statute?
I think not; not that I am aware of.

609. Simply

609. Simply by a regulation of the Local Government Board?
Yes.

610. Then this Bill does not affect that?
No; but I should like to see a special enactment, settling exactly what is right.

611. The Lord President has alluded to the proxy voting as a privilege appertaining to property; should you not rather describe it as a necessity for the owners of property, if they are to exercise their votes?
Of course I desire to be somewhat reserved as an official; but giving my own individual opinion, I must say that I consider it but just.

612. Then, further, it was put to you by the Lord President that property was twice represented under the existing circumstances; do you think that, taking into consideration the admitted fact that owners of property pay five-eighths of the poor rate, even with half the number of the guardians being *ex-officio*, and with the proxy vote which they now possess, property has a greater influence with regard to the administration of the poor rate than it is fairly entitled to?
I do not.

613. Lord *Monk-Bretton*.] Are you aware whether, when the Poor Law was first established in Ireland, the Poor Law Commissioners assigned as a reason for recommending a limit to the number of *ex-officio* guardians in Ireland, that the proportion of magistrates in Irish counties was much larger than in English counties?
I have heard that.

614. *Lord President*.] Let me ask one question about your own Galway board which you know so well or used to know so well. First of all you told us that one-half of it consisted of non-elected *ex-officio* guardians, who generally attended; can you tell us from your knowledge how the elected half was elected; in fact, how far was the elected half of the board elected by the occupation votes, and how far was it elected by the influence of the property votes?
In the times that I speak of it was nearly all by the occupiers' votes; there were very few proxies indeed used in the Galway union.

615. Apart from proxies, can you give us any idea as to what amount of influence the property vote had upon the election of the elected guardians?
I cannot give you any accurate account.

616. Were the elected half of the number of guardians to any considerable extent elected under landlord influence?
No, not to a large extent.

617. I wanted to ascertain how the fact was in your experience of that particular board?
Not to a large extent.

618. But to some extent?
To some extent, but not by the power of proxy votes.

619. I am not speaking now about proxy votes at all. I am taking the fact that first of all half of this body is non-elected, consisting of magistrates directly representing property, and the other half is elected; and I want you to tell us in what degree, within your knowledge, the elected guardians were elected by the influence of the owners of property?
I could not form an opinion at present.

620. Earl of *Milltown*.] I suppose under the ballot, whatever influence the Land Act has left them, they could not possibly exercise it?
Well, in most unions now I do not think that occupiers, as a rule, are much led by either the landlord's or the agent's opinion.

621. Even were the agent or the landlord desirous of influencing their votes
with

with the protection of the ballot, they could not possibly give effect to that desire?
Of course not.

622. *Lord President.*] Were any of the elected guardians on your board themselves owners?
I was an owner myself.

623. Lord *Monk-Bretton.*] Were many of them?
No.

624. About how many elected guardians were there?
I can find the exact number I think. I think it but right to mention that the late Mr. Joyce was chairman of that board of guardians. He was an *ex-officio* member of the board also, and he exercised very great influence over the board, an influence personal to himself. He only died last year. There never was a move to put him out; although, upon some occasions, he was obliged to withstand a good deal. He exercised a very great deal of personal influence with the board, and I think they followed his advice very much.

625. *Lord President.*] A very beneficial influence?
Certainly beneficial. I am afraid I have not got the number here, but my recollection is that about 30 or 32 were elected, and the same number *ex-officio* guardians.

626. Lord *Monk-Bretton.*] Out of the 32 elected guardians how many might be owners?
Owners in fee?

627. Owners, not merely rated occupiers?
I should say about a fourth at the time I speak of.

628. *Chairman.*] Do you consider that it would be possible that the proxy votes could ever swamp the occupier's vote?
I do not. I have heard it stated that they can, but I can only give my own opinion.

629. There was a point raised by the Lord President in a former examination that the occupiers in the union would have the same interest in keeping the rates down as the owners; is that your belief?
No, it is not quite my belief. While certainly not wishing to insinuate that the occupiers are not very good guardians, an occupier is only rated for a small amount, whereas the owner has to pay on a very large amount. The owner of an entire electoral division would have to pay certainly half the entire poor rate, five-eighths as a rule, and there will be probably 100 occupiers who will be only paying one-hundredth part each of the remaining three-eighths.

630. But the proportion paid by the owner, taking into account the fact that he pays half the poor-rate, and even the whole in certain instances, would be much larger than the proportion paid by the occupier?
Larger even than the proportion paid by all the occupiers.

631. Lord *Sudley.*] Therefore you think there is a temptation on the part of elected guardians to be somewhat generous with other people's money?
They have so much smaller an interest in it that there is the temptation.

632. *Lord President.*] But does not the ordinary ratepayer in Ireland consider the amount of the rate which he will have to pay very important?
Yes.

633. Considering that, as a rule, he is a man of very small means, to whom a small sum is a matter of great consequence?
Yes. I think I have already said that on ordinary occasions I consider that the ratepayer and occupier, who is an elected guardian, is a very good guardian.

634. I mean

6th March 1885.]   Mr. MORRIS.   [Continued.

634. I mean this, as a rule, and speaking generally, apart from special cases, and special temptations, do you think that the Irish ratepayers would allow their guardians to burden them with extravagant rates?
No, I do not think they would burden them with extravagant rates; I think they might be in some instances perhaps a little too stingy, and in others a little too liberal.

635. Earl of *Milltown*.] As a matter of fact, they have so burdened themselves in several unions, have they not?
Yes, the rates have increased.

636. In the Dungarvan Union, I believe, they have raised the rates to such an immense sum that it is a question whether the union must not become bankrupt?
Yes.

637. And the Local Government Board were on the point of sending down vice-guardians to do the business for them?
We had written the letter, and should have been obliged to send down vice-guardians if they had not at last struck a rate.

638. *Chairman*.] When you have sent down paid guardians, have you found generally that the rates have been reduced?
The paid guardians are never sent down until the union is in a dreadful state of embarrassment, and then the paid guardians remain on some time. Generally their duty is to strike a pretty good high rate to get the union out of debt, which the elected guardians are more or less afraid to do; because sometimes when the elected guardians find themselves getting into difficulties, they dislike striking a sufficient rate, because when they went back to their constituents of course they would not be at all popular. I think that the elected guardians are a little open to that; they are fond of borrowing money from the bank or whoever is their treasurer, and fonder, I think, of staving off the evil day, and not wishing to strike a sufficient rate very often.

639. *Lord President*] I presume you do not mean to say anything which would condemn the representative system in local matters either in town or country, because the highest standard of virtue and wisdom is not always maintained?
I consider, in answering that question, that it is an invidious question for me. I am endeavouring to convey my views to your Lordships.

640. 'I only wish to do you justice; I mean that I presumed by your criticisms (which may be very just), you do not mean to condemn the representative system generally in local matters?
I think in some boards of guardians the elected guardians are quite as good as the *ex-officio* guardians.

641. Earl of *Milltown*.] But, as a rule, you think that men of intelligence, education, and independence, are more likely to make good and efficient guardians than those who are uneducated, and subject to every kind of pressure from without?
If the union is getting embarrassed, getting into debt for want of striking a sufficient rate, or from striking a low rate for two or three years in succession not adequate to meet their engagements, I think that the *ex-officio* class of guardians is more likely to face a thing like that than an elected guardian. I do not wish to convey anything in the way of condemnation. I think if I were in the same position myself I should very likely do just the same.

642. *Lord President*.] But you do not propose to reform the Poor Law system in Ireland by diminishing the number of elected guardians?
No.

The Witness is directed to withdraw.

6th March 1885.

Colonel GEORGE CAMPBELL SPAIGHT, having been called in; is Examined, as follows:

643. *Chairman.*] You are an Inspector of the Local Government Board, are you not?
Yes.

644. I think your districts have been changed lately?
Yes; for two years I have had Kerry and the West Riding of Cork; and before that I had three whole counties in Connaught, and parts of three others.

645. Will you mention what they were?
I had Sligo, Leitrim, and Roscommon (except part of one union), and half Mayo, parts of Donegal and Fermanagh.

646. Would you tell the Committee what your duties mostly are.
A general supervision of the administration of the Poor Law. We attend meetings of boards of guardians where we think it is necessary, and that we can advise and assist them in any way; and we have to make half-yearly inspections of the unions, and report upon the state of the workhouses, and the financial condition of the unions, and their general management.

647. If a new clerk of a union was selected by the board of guardians, would you have to put him through any examination.
I always do. There is no regular rule for it; but of course you have to recommend his sanction by the Local Government Board, and you cannot do that unless you satisfy yourself that he is competent.

648. I should like to ask you to give us your opinion upon the Bill which is before the Committee. Do you approve of the principle of triennial elections?
I do. I think that it will be a very great improvement.

649. Do you approve of the system of vote by ballot?
Yes, I think that will also be a vast improvement, and do away with a great many abuses in the present system.

650. What is your opinion about proxy voting, which is dealt with by Section 9 of Part 1.?
I am afraid that the effect of that clause would be a very bad one.

651. Why?
Because it would practically disfranchise owners altogether.

652. Do you consider that there is no arrangement by which owners could vote in different unions?
It would be a physical impossibility. Where a landowner owns property in several electoral divisions, he could not possibly attend in person, and vote at the different polling places at the same time.

653. Do you consider that the proxy vote is useful, as it is at present?—I think very useful.

654. Does it often turn the scale?
In unions, where parties are evenly divided, it may often have a very great influence in returning a practical, useful, good guardian, who would otherwise be excluded, and in this way is of the utmost importance.

655. I will pass to Clause 11, by which it is provided that the claim to vote should be lodged before an election; have you anything to say about that?
I think the time is too short a great deal. It would be utterly impossible for the returning officer to make out the register if the claims are not lodged at least two months before the time of election. One month is too short a time.

656. With

6th March 1885.]   Colonel SPAIGHT.   [Continued.

656. With regard to the system enacted in Part II., which proposes to transfer the trial of election petitions to the county court judge, does that meet with your approval?
I think so. It would be a very great improvement upon the old system.

657. Were many of the petitions frivolous and vexatious?
Yes. I have known them brought without any real valid reasons at all, for one purpose and another. After a very careful investigation, sworn inquiries which I have held, they have turned out to be wholly frivolous.

658. Do you think that security should be given for the costs?
I would suggest that the costs under no circumstances should be put upon the rates of the union. I think, of course, that where it arises through any error of the clerk, he should be personally charged with it, as there appears to be provision made in the Bill; but in other cases I think that the costs should be borne by the defeated party in the action, whoever he may be, before the county court judge.

659. In the Bill there is a proposal that the costs of the Returning Officer should be thrown on the rates, is there not?
There is a proposal in the Bill that they should be borne by the rates, excepting the case in which some error or neglect has been committed by the clerk of the union; and in a case of that sort I think it is very fair that the clerk should be mulcted in the costs; but otherwise I would strongly recommend that they should be borne by the parties themselves.

660. My former question was more with regard to the necessity for security for costs; might it not be possible that if a frivolous petition was brought forward, the persons bringing it forward might not be able to find the money to pay the costs, and then they might be thrown on the rates?
Tried in that way before the county court judge, I do not think that the costs would be anything very serious, or such that they could not be met by a man, who at any rate would be able to give security. I think that it would do away with a great many frivolous objections, and a great deal of unnecessary trouble, if some provision was made to have a named sum lodged in the court as is done in Parliamentary elections. I think it would have a very wholesome effect in checking objections which were made without any grounds.

661. Passing now to Part III., Sub-section I. of Clause 25, I suppose you would be in favour, as the other witnesses have been, of a minor being allowed to vote through his guardian?
There are very often cases in which minors and lunatics own property, and I think that in those cases the trustees ought to be allowed to represent them.

662. I believe that at present a minor is in certain instances allowed to vote?
At present he is, I think, but I am not quite sure about that.

663. In Sub-section No. 2 it seems to be laid down that the Local Government Board are, in case of a vacancy, obliged to order a fresh election; would you leave them an option about that?
I think that the present system works very well, and cases may arise in which it would be well to avoid having a fresh election close upon the expiration of the term; and I would suggest that that should be left as it is.

664. Then passing to Sub-section 4, the qualification for elected guardians is proposed to be reduced by that section to 12 l.; are you of opinion that such a reduction is necessary?
I do not think it is. I think that the Local Government Board having the power at present to reduce the qualification, if any valid reasons are given, always do so; and I do not see any object in changing it now.

665. You would prefer leaving it as it is at present?
I would prefer leaving the law as it stands.

666. I have

666. I have heard it mentioned that it is unfortunate that publicans should be eligible as guardians; is that your experience?
If I had a voice in framing the measure, I should disqualify them, certainly, because there is hardly a case in the country districts in which the publicans are not creditors to a very great extent of a number of ratepayers, and I think that in that way they would exercise a very undue influence, and I should certainly disqualify all publicans from acting as guardians.

667. Are publicans often elected at present?
They are in some instances. Where they choose to go in for it they exercise a good deal of influence, and I think that it would be better if they were disqualified.

668. Sub-section 5 reduces the number of *ex-officio* guardians to half the number of the elected guardians of the board; do you think that would be an improvement?
I am very much afraid that in many unions it would have a very bad effect; indeed I am sure of it.

669. In what way?
Where there are a sufficient number of them to be at all equal to the number of elected guardians, and to work the affairs of the board, if they were reduced to half, as proposed in the Bill, they would be utterly swamped; they would have no voice in the matter at all.

670. They would be utterly swamped, you say?
They would, in most instances.

671. Do you consider that they are of use upon the boards?
I can only judge from my experience in attending meetings of boards of guardians and watching the working of them; and in cases where *ex-officios* have retained control, to a certain extent, of matters, and worked with the others, the unions are sensibly and practically managed; where the *ex-officios* have for different reasons ceased to attend, just the reverse is the case; and one can only argue from that, that they are of very great benefit in the administration of the Poor Law.

672. Would you state to the Committee what are the reasons why the *ex-officios* have ceased to attend?
Since I came over to London it struck me that it might be useful to you to have some information with regard to the difference in the management of these unions, and I took the county of Kerry, and have brought a map with me to make it clearer. There are six unions in Kerry. Three of them are, to a certain extent, under the control of *ex-officio* guardians, and three of them are under the control of elected guardians; and thinking that perhaps the statistics as to the relief administered in those unions may be of some use to you, I telegraphed to the clerks of the six unions yesterday, asking them to give me the amount of out-door relief administered in the year 1879–80, and the amount of the same relief administered in the year 1884.

673. *Lord President.*] In what sense do you mean that three of them are "under the control of *ex-officio* guardians"?
There are certain unions where for some reasons the *ex-officios* have ceased attending, and then the whole control of the union is left in the hands of the elected guardians.

674. When you describe three of the boards in Kerry as being under the control of the *ex-officio* guardians, do you mean that they are cases where the chairman is an *ex-officio* guardian?
Yes, where the chairman is an *ex-officio* guardian.

675. Or where some influential *ex-officio* members of the board are in the habit of attending?
Yes; particularly where the chairman is an *ex-officio* guardian. That has a vital influence on the affairs of the union, and having things kept straight.

6th March 1885.] Colonel SPAIGHT. [*Continued.*

676. *Chairman.*] In the cases to which you are now alluding, a fair share of *ex-officio* guardians attend, as I understand you, whereas in the cases of the other unions none attend?
They do not attend on ordinary occasions because, as they say (and I have often asked them), "There is no use in our attending; we are swamped; we have no voice in the matter whatever." But when an occasion arises of permanent importance to the union, such as the election of an officer, a clerk, or master, or matron, then they endeavour to attend, and come from long distances to attend, because I think they feel that it may have a very serious permanent effect upon the management of the union if they do not. On these occasions, therefore, they do make an effort to attend, and they sometimes have succeeded in appointing a good officer.

677. Would you state, for the information of the Committee, the facts which you have received from the clerks as to these six different unions, of which you began to speak just now?
I was saying that I got the statistics from the clerks showing you exactly the amount of relief administered in a bad year, such as 1879–80 was (a very bad season, bad crops, bad weather, everything in a very bad state), and the amount so administered in 1884, in which matters were just reversed. I thought it would be an interesting matter for you to have before you, and I got that information from the clerks of the unions by telegraph yesterday. If the Committee would allow me, I would show them how the unions in question lie. The unions are contiguous; they join each other. This (*producing a map*) is the Ordnance map for the county of Kerry, in which there are three unions in a great degree entirely controlled by elected guardians, and three unions which are in a great degree controlled by *ex-officio* guardians. There is the union of Listowel, to begin with, to the north (*pointing it out*).

678. With regard to the union of Listowel, is that well attended by *ex-officio* guardians?
No, that is one in which the others have the principal management of affairs. The next is Tralee; that is one of the same class; and the third is the union of Killarney.

679. Earl of *Milltown*.] In all three of those, as I understand you, the elected guardians have it pretty much their own way?
They have.

680. Lord *Sudley*.] May we take it for granted that the circumstances of the six unions are more or less identical?
I cannot say that.

681. I mean for the purposes of comparison?
Yes, for the purposes of comparison. Some of the unions that are managed at present principally by *ex-officio* guardians are even, if possible, poorer than those that are in the hands of the others. Of the other three unions, the first is the union of Dingle, the second, that of Cahirciveen, and the third is Kenmare.

682. *Chairman.*] Those three unions are unions where the *ex-officio* element attends, as I understand you?
Yes, at least there is an *ex-officio* chairman. Really, not very many *ex-officio* guardians attend in the union of Cahirciveen, but there is a competent *ex-officio* chairman.

683. Earl of *Milltown*.] Is an elected guardian chairman in the first three unions that you mentioned?
There is an *ex-officio* guardian in Killarney, but in Listowel and Tralee there is an elected guardian chairman.

684. *Chairman.*] Will you state to the Committee the comparative out-door relief granted in the three unions, separately, in which the elected guardians have the preponderance, and that granted in the three unions in which they have not?

'I will

6th March 1885.]   Colonel SPAIGHT.   [*Continued.*

I will begin with Listowel, which is one of the unions in the hands of elected guardians. In the whole year ended 29th September 1880, the out-door relief in Listowel Union was administered to 258 persons at a cost of 65 *l.*

685. And what was it per head?
It would be an average of about 5 *s.* per head. In the year ended 29th September 1884, relief was administered to 2,187 persons.

686. Viscount *Powerscourt.*] And that is a good year?
That is a year in which the crops were exceptionally good, and provisions very cheap. That was at a cost of 1,638 *l.* 9 *d.* 3 *d.*, being an average of 14 *s.* 11¾ *d.*

687. *Chairman.*] That was much higher per head than the former average?
That would be very nearly three times as much per head as what was administered four years before.

688. Was this union of Listowel, before the agitation, a well-managed union?
One of the best in Ireland, I have always heard. It did not come into my charge until February 1883

689. Would you now tell us about the next union?
Tralee would be the next union, and in 1879, which was there and everywhere else a particularly hard and bad year, there were 87 persons who received out-door relief at a cost of 30 *l.* 17 *s.* 11 *d.*, making an average of 7 *s.* 1 *d.* per head; and in the year 1884 there were 3,434 people that received out-door relief at a cost of 2,534 *l.* 13 *s.* 10 *d.*, making an average of 14 *s.* 9 *d.*

690. Therefore not only the numbers who received relief were increased, but the expenses for them were very much larger?
The average per head increased considerably In Killarney Union, which is the next, in 1880 there were 2,107 persons that received relief at a cost of 1,752 *l.*, making an average of 16 *s.* 7¼ *d.*; in 1884, there were 2,867 persons that received relief at a cost of 3,617 *l.*, making an average of 25 *s.* 2 *d.*

691. Now what would be the highest amount of relief that a man would receive in the year; have you anything to enable you to tell us that?
I have not got any papers giving that information, but it is usual in these unions that I have just been giving you statistics of, to give evicted tenants considerably more than they do to ordinary recipients of relief; they have given them up to 20 *s.* and 25 *s.* a week.

692. Have you ever known men who received relief of that description to have sufficient money to get back into their farms again afterwards, or has that never come to your notice?
I do not think they husband the relief. I have known them receive sufficient money when they came for relief to get very drunk; but I do not think they husband it.

693. You misunderstood my question; what I meant to ask was this, whether after a man had been receiving out-door relief, you have known him to have sufficient money put away to enable him to pay up his arrears of rent?
I have not.

694. Now would you tell us about the unions that I might call non-political unions?
The first of those, which adjoins Tralee Union, is Dingle; the land in that union is very poor, and the people are poor.

695. Viscount *Powerscourt.*] Who is the chairman of that union?
Lord Ventry. It is a very well-managed union, a well-conducted board altogether; they do things very sensibly and very well. In 1880 the number of persons on out-door relief was two, and the cost was 9 *l.* 2 *s.* And I may tell you that I know what those cases were, they were cases of hopeless idiots who

(O.1.)   I 2   could

could not well be looked after in the workhouse, as it would cause a good deal of trouble, and the sum given them would only amount to about 1 s. 6 d. a week; the guardians thought therefore that it would be better to allow their own people to take care of them rather than bring them into the house, where they would be a nuisance to everybody; and they were well and comfortably taken care of. In 1884 (to draw the same contrast that one has done with the other unions) the number of persons relieved was three, and they cost 13 l. 10 s. 4 d.

696. *Chairman.*] That is in the same year when the very large rise took place in the three unions which you first gave us?
Yes.

697. There was only a rise of one in the Dingle Union in that year?
Only a rise of one; and those three are of exactly the same class; they are all people whom it would only cost 1 s. 6 d. a week to keep out, and they must have come into the house otherwise, and then it would have cost at least 3 s. 10 d. to have kept them in the house.

698. Will you tell us next about Cahirciveen?
In 1880 there were 561 persons on out-door relief at a cost of 717 l.

699. What does that average?
That averages 25 s. 6 d.

700. Viscount *Powerscourt.*] Who was the chairman of that union?
Mr. Butler of Waterville an *ex-officio* guardian.

701. *Chairman.*] And in 1884 what were the numbers?
The clerk made a mistake in sending it to me; he gave me these for 83 instead of for 84 for this union; but for the purpose of the contrast they show much the same thing. In 1883 there were 1,070 in receipt of out-door relief, at a cost of 903 l.

702. Making an average of what?
Sixteen shillings and tenpence halfpenny.

703. Therefore the average per head was reduced in that union, whereas it increased in all the others except the one you mentioned just now, Dingle?
Yes.

704. Will you tell us now about Kenmare?
In 1880 there were 519 persons in receipt of out-door relief at a cost of 890 l., making an average of 34 s. 3 d.; and in 1884 the number of persons was reduced to 513, at a cost of 870 l., making an average of 33 s. 4 d.

705. Who is the chairman there?
Mr. Townsend Trench, Lord Lansdowne's agent in Kerry.

706. *Chairman.*] I suppose it is this out-door relief which causes the great increase in the rates?
That is the main and principal cause of it.

707. And do you consider that a great deal of this out-door relief is given for political reasons?
There is no question about it, that, as a rule, they propose a larger amount to be given to a man because he is evicted, than they would if that man was entitled to relief as an ordinary case.

708. Do you consider that if the number of the *ex-officio* guardians were reduced the rates would be likely to rise?
I have no doubt whatever of it. The *ex-officio* guardians try to control things. In my experience I have never known them refuse relief where it was really wanted, but at the same time they administer it carefully, and they take care that they only give it where it is wanted.

709. I suppose

709. I suppose you consider that it is a misfortune that the *ex-officio* guardians are not able to attend more than they do?
I think it is a very great pity.

710. Would you suggest any improvement in the method by which they are placed upon the list?
At present the *ex officio* guardians are taken from the highest rated magistrates in the union, and I think that it would be a much better plan if the magistrates of the union were allowed to elect the *ex-officio* guardians. Then instead of men who are absentees, and who are chosen because they are the highest rated magistrates in the union, you would have men elected who would be most likely to attend and able to give their attention to the business of the union. I think it would also act as an incentive to many to attend if they were elected by their brother magistrates, instead of being put on as a matter of course.

711. But is it not the case that in many unions in Ireland there are not sufficient *ex-officios* even to make up half the number?
There are some instances where that occurs.

712. How would you arrange for a selection under those circumstances?
In all probability in such cases they would be all on the board, so that it does not matter with regard to them; it is only in cases where the number of *ex officio* guardians exceeds the number of elected guardians at present, that it would be absolutely necessary to have a selection; but under any circumstances I think it would be well that the magistrates should be asked to elect or appoint the *ex-officio* guardians.

713. If that were the case would you keep the number up to what it is at present?
I would certainly. In some unions, of course, it would not make any difference; in others it would make a very great difference.

714. Do you consider that the *ex-officio* is one of the great representatives of the proportion of rates which property contributes?
He is about the only representative of property. The owners pay a much larger proportion of the rates than the occupiers. In one of those unions that we were speaking of just now, Listowel, I heard that the chairman, who is an elected guardian, said that the landlords were paying 14 s. out of every pound of rates paid; and of course the only people to represent the owners of land are the *ex-officios*.

715. Even in a case where proxies are used, do not the votes in the hands of the occupiers very largely out-number the votes in the hands of the owners?
The voting power of the landowners is very trivial compared with that of the occupiers.

716. It has been stated that *ex-officios* attend largely on election days; is it your opinion that the elective guardians also attend equally largely on those days?
Yes, they do certainly; they all attend; and (I can only speak from my own experience) it becomes a struggle between the appointment of a good and qualified man, and the appointment of some friend or relation of some of the elected guardians.

717. Do politics enter into the appointment of officials to boards of guardians?
Where relationship or personal connection does not exist, then politics would come in as a matter of course. I may mention what has happened in the union of Listowel since it fell into the management of elected guardians. I found the house in a dreadful state there, and everything in a very discreditable condition. Two members of the same family had been elected one after

after the other, as masters of the house, which accounted in a great degree for the bad state that the house was in; then there was a necessity for another election, and they elected a third member of the same family, and he proved unfitted for his post; I was obliged to report so strongly upon his mismanagement and neglect of duty, that he was called upon to resign, and the matron at the same time; and the result of it was that the elected guardians, who were in a majority, re-elected the master, who was called upon to resign; and they elected the wife of a broken-down wretched poor little public-house keeper in Listowel as matron of the workhouse, who never had had any experience in any public institution, and had no qualification whatever for the post. The papers in the usual official routine came to me, and before I could recommend the sanction of the Local Government Board, I went and visited this woman in the wretched little place that she was living in; she told me that she had never had any experience of any kind, but she hoped that they would elect her, and when they did they might elect her husband, the owner of the public-house, as master, and that it would be a very comfortable thing for them. They were related to two or three of the guardians.

718. You stated just now that this was a well-managed union some years ago?
Yes, a Mr. Sandes, a large agent in the union, was chairman of the union; and up to that time it was a very well-managed union indeed, and the rates were very considerably less than they are at the present time.

719. How long is it since things began to go down in this union?
I think Mr. Sandes gave up the chairmanship and gave up attending. I am not quite sure as to the time; it was before I took over that district.

720. Was he defeated at an election of a chairman, or did he resign?
He told me himself that he found such a want of courtesy, and the system so much changed in the board there, that he would not attend any longer. He is an *ex-officio* guardian, and was a very good chairman.

721. Practically he considered, if I understand you rightly, that he might be insulted if he did attend?
He did not say that; but it was made so disagreeable for him, that he gave up attending. I have never seen him in the board-room since, but once.

722. Have you ever heard of circulars being sent round by the Land League to make the guardians vote for any particular persons as masters and matrons, or officers?
On the occasion of an election in Killarney Union lately, in which I had recommended that a relieving officer's district should be divided, and the Local Government Board had asked the guardians to do it, the guardians refused at first, and it appears that they were anxious to elect an evicted tenant of Lord Kenmare's. A circular was handed to me at the meeting (I only looked at it for a moment), emanating from somebody at Castle Island, which called upon the guardians to support "the victim of landlord tyranny," and the usual powerful motives were urged.

723. *Lord President.*] Was he elected?
He was elected.

724. Is he in office now?
He is not. I recommended the Local Government Board to divide the district, and they acted upon their powers and divided it, which they have the power to do, and the election is to take place, I think, this week for the divided district. But the guardians, as far as they went, elected him, and they were very wroth indeed that the Local Government Board did not sanction it.

725. *Chairman.*] Do you consider that the occupiers are as interested in keeping down the rates as the owners of property?

Some

Some of them do try to keep them down; in cases, for instance, of out-door relief, the guardian of an electoral division may possibly object to the relief being given, because it becomes a charge upon his electoral division, but he is only one out of about 20 or 25 men who think that this recipient ought to get out-door relief, and who have not got personally to pay, because it will be charged to the electoral division to which the recipient is legally chargeable; and then they are all aware that the landlord pays at least five-eighths to three-fourths of the rates; so that it is a small thing to them in comparison to what it is to the owner of the property.

726. Have you ever known a guardian put in an application for out-door relief?
Yes; I was present at a meeting of the Cahirciveen Board of Guardians, with Mr. Butler in the chair, on one occasion; he was going over the applications for out-door relief, and a guardian was standing close by him watching the administration of relief, and Mr. Butler read out his name (which I do not know that it is necessary for me to give), and looked up at him and said, "Surely this is not your name?" he said, "Yes, it is, Sir; and I want relief as much as anybody in the union."

727. Lord *Monk-Bretton*.] What is the qualification for a guardian in that union?
£. 15 rated value.

728. Earl of *Milltown*.] Then was this person not really in want of out-door relief?
He had been evicted; but of course I do not believe that he was in any want.

729. *Chairman*.] Was his application refused?
Certainly, his application was at once refused.

730. In consequence of the action of the elected guardians or the *ex-officios*?
Mr. Butler, the chairman, at once laughed at it; he did not entertain it at all.

731. Do you think that there is any feeling among the occupiers that if local taxation is increased there may be a chance that their rents may be still further reduced?
I think that a very great number of the occupiers imagine that if local taxation is increased, eventually it will make a better case for them for a further reduction of rent.

732. Do you think that they consider it is likely eventually all to fall upon the landlord?
Where a landlord pays such a large proportion of the rates, of course they are aware that it will fall upon him; but they all complain very much about the increase of rates, and a feeling may actuate them, that the circumstance of the increase of local taxation may give them a better claim for a further reduction of rent. There is a feeling through the country that they will look for that before very long.

733. I think you were in charge of Swineford Union at one time?
I was.

734. Will you tell us some of the circumstances of that union?
I got the charge of the Swineford Union, and found it in a dreadful state through the maladministration of the guardians, and I recommended the dissolution of the board, and it was dissolved within a very short time after I took charge of the district.

735. *Lord President*.] In what year was that?
One thousand eight hundred and eighty.

736. *Chairman*.] Was it in a bankrupt condition?
I may say that it was. The guardians had gone in for a very large supply of seed, under the Seeds Supply Act, though it is one of the poorest unions in Ireland;

Ireland; they obtained a loan of 28,747 *l.* for supply of seed, and on looking into matters, I ascertained that men who had been absent for 10 or 12 years in America, were returned as recipients of seed, also men who had been dead for a great number of years, and women who never had had a bit of land in their lives. The seed used to be issued by verbal orders, so that there was no documentary evidence; but, on questioning the seed distributors, I ascertained that in one instance a guardian had ordered seed potatoes and oats for a woman who was living as a prostitute, and had never had any land.

737. Then I may take it, I suppose, that you consider it would be the very greatest injury possible to the management of the poor rates in Ireland, if the *ex-officio* element was reduced.
There cannot be a doubt about it in the mind of anybody who has ever watched the working of those boards; they could not doubt it for a moment.

738. *Lord President.*] When you describe those three unions in Kerry, which you contrasted with the other three as being controlled by the *ex-officio* guardians, I do not understand you to mean that on those boards the elected guardians were outvoted by the *ex-officio* guardians?
No.

739. Or that the *ex-officio* influence had anything whatever to do with the numbers of the *ex-officio* guardians?
Are you alluding to the last three unions?

740. Of course I am alluding to the three unions which you describe as being in the hands of the *ex-officio* guardians, or controlled by the *ex-officio* guardians; I want to see exactly what you mean by that?
I thought I explained it when I said that the chairman was an *ex-officio* guardian, and that he exercised an influence over the board.

741. That is what you meant?
Yes.

742. You did not mean that it had anything to do with the numbers of the *ex-officio* guardians?
By no means.

743. But in these three cases the chairman was an *ex-officio* guardian, and his influence was of great value?
Yes; In the management of the affairs of the union and controlling the expenditure.

744. Then those cases, which are so interesting, had nothing to do with the numbers of the *ex-officios*; it was not a question of voting power?
Not in those unions.

745. It was not a case of one set of guardians outvoting the other set?
No, it was not.

746. I think you said that if the proportion of *ex-officio* guardians were to be diminished, as the Bill proposes, they would be swamped by the elected guardians?
In unions where parties are at all evenly balanced they would.

747. And I think you said even that their presence would be therefore of no use; but is that consistent with the great use which you have shown us that the presence of even a single *ex-officio* guardian may have?
I did not myself say that their presence would be of no use; I said that that was what they gave as an excuse for not attending.

748. But do I rightly understand you that your view is that the great and valuable influence which they may exercise depends upon individual influence and action, and not upon the mere number of their votes on the board?
I do not say that at all; I think that, as a rule, in the case of an appointment when it comes to a vote; it is a case of numbers then, not only individual influence. I speak from what I have seen myself, and I have never known

an

an instance of *ex-officio* guardians coming to an election, except with the object of getting the best officer appointed. Generally, in my official capacity, I have taken the trouble to ascertain what are the qualifications of the candidates, and I have never known the *ex-officios* come with any other object than that of trying to get the best officers they can.

749. But the excellent results which you have shown in those three unions where an *ex-officio* guardian was the chairman, depended upon individual influence, and not upon mere voting power; that is so, is it not?
There is no doubt that at a board of guardians when these questions arise the influence of a firm and intelligent chairman is very great. If there is a weak man in the chair and a man who is not so well educated or has not so much independence of judgment, he is very easily influenced by anybody; but there cannot be a doubt that when there is a gentleman in the chair who knows his work the elected guardians are greatly influenced by him.

750. You said, in one answer, that you thought the voting power of landowners was very trivial; do you mean that the property votes have very little influence upon the election of guardians?
I have not got any papers with me such as I could have picked out if I had had the slightest idea that they would be of any interest; but take the case of a landowner having the maximum number, which is 30 votes, and take the occupiers on his property, they have a very much larger number of votes. That is what I say, that the number of votes possessed by the owner is very trivial compared with the voting power possessed by the occupiers.

751. Do you think that, as a fact, the property votes have much influence upon the elections to the board?
I think in a very great many instances they have in an electoral division, where there may be a great many practical good farmers. It is not for a moment to be supposed that elected guardians are all one way. There are a great many of them who have every wish to act rightly, and there may be such a close balance that the proxy votes of the landlords might make all the difference in an electoral division between getting a good practical sensible guardian and getting one that was not; it might make a very great difference in many electoral divisions.

752. I suppose the greater number of the property votes are given in person, and not by proxy; is that so?
I cannot say that the greater number are. I think that in many cases the greater number would be given by proxy; but that I am hardly in a position to say, because except when they come before us on inquiry on petition, we have not got much to say to the elections; they are worked by the returning officers. As an illustration to show you how things are sometimes managed by the elected guardians, I remember a case in Leitrim, in the Mohill Union; an application was made for relief by a letter written, or rather supposed to be written, by the wife of a suspect, and the guardians were about ordering the relief, but the matter stood over, and Lord Granard called the attention of the Local Government Board to the matter. I believe the man was a tenant of his, and had been evicted off one farm. The guardians ordered a pound a-week out-door relief to the family of this suspect, which they were empowered to do under the Act. I went to Mohill and made some inquiries, first of all as to how the application was made, and I found that it was by letter, and on making inquiries in the workhouse I found that the application had been written by a guardian, and that the master of the workhouse had been asked to sign the name of the woman, who was the wife of the suspect, to the application for relief. The master of the workhouse very properly refused to do it, but somebody else was found outside who signed the application of the woman for relief; and on inquiry I found that the woman was very well off indeed, and had two other farms besides the one they were evicted out of, and denied all knowledge whatever of any application for relief. It was done simply from political motives upon the board; the application was made there and then without the knowledge either of the husband in prison or of the wife out of it.

6th March 1885.] Colonel SPAIGHT. [*Continued.*

753. *Of course an evicted family may be, and very often is, in real need of relief, and the law intends that they should have it. You mean that it has been given in excess of the necessity of the case?*
With regard to evicted tenants, I think that in many cases larger sums than were absolutely necessary have been given; take a man with a wife and a certain family, if they were recipients of relief under the ordinary system which has existed, they would get very much less than the pound which they might get as evicted tenants. That is what I mean, that as a rule the guardians give more to evicted tenants than they do to any other of the recipients of relief.

754. *The great contrast between the unions which you compared with one another just now, lay in the increased amount of out-door relief given in three of them?*
Yes.

755. *Does that go on increasing, or has it gone back, or is it stationary?*
I can only speak from the papers that I have got; I do not know exactly what they are doing now but I think it remains very much the same; I do not think there is any palpable difference whatever.

756. *In one of your answers you used the expression, "that they all complained of the increase of rates, which is very natural;" do you think that the ratepayers will be content for any length of time to permit their elected guardians to impose excessive rates upon them?*
It is very hard to say what may occur in the future.

757. *You used the expression that all complained of excessive rates?*
You hear complaints everywhere of the enormous increase of rates lately.

758. *Enormous comparative increase in these cases of outdoor relief; it was almost nil a few years ago, was it not?*
Almost *nil*. If I had gone back, perhaps, two or three years before, for instance in Listowel, I think it was *nil* there.

759. *And it has now in some unions increased to an amount which would be thought very small in this country, but you regret that it should have increased to that figure?*
I regret it. Personally I am not at all interested in the matter, but of course I regret that there should be such a heavy burden thrown upon the ratepayers.

760. *You think that outdoor relief has been given in some cases beyond the necessities of the case, and in an extravagant spirit?*
I think that the very fact that one man, say with a wife and three children, gets a pound a week, and another man with the same family only 3 s. or 4 s., explains it. If; that the guardians think in one case he ought to get more. What the reason is may be inferred; I am only stating facts.

761. *I was not referring to any special popular feeling in favour of evicted tenants and so on, but to the tendency to give outdoor relief in general in too easy and too extravagant a spirit?*
My own opinion is that giving out-door relief has a most demoralising effect everywhere where it is done, and that when it is once begun it is very hard to stop or to check it. Take a union like Dingle, and then take a union like Bantry, in County Cork, where out-door relief is seldom given; the people to all intents and purposes, as far as I can see, are just as poor there, and yet they get on as well without it; but when once the thin end of the wedge is let in and they give out-door relief to one they give out-door relief to all; and one guardian says to another, "I got relief for So-and-so for you, and you must get it for So-and-so for me;" and they manage things in that way, and then it is very hard to limit it. Of course when those guardians are living in the country in far removed isolated places, it is very hard to place them in a position of that kind, and expect them, unless they are thoroughly independent, to refuse outdoor relief; pressure is brought to bear upon them; they are asked and are

pressed

6th March 1885.]   Colonel SPAIGHT.   Continued.

pressed to give relief, and they have not got the strength of mind or independence to refuse.

762. The law as to out-door relief has not been relaxed for many years, has it?
Except under the Relief of Distress Act in 1880.

763. Which has expired?
That has expired.

764. Is the law as to out-door relief the same now as it has been for many years?
Yes, it is.

765. But the guardians in some unions are using their discretion more freely in that direction than they used to do?
They are giving a very much greater amount of out-door relief than they ever used to do before.

766. Do you think that that is on the increase?
I cannot say what has been the case very lately; it was on the increase up to this year in 1884, certainly.

767. I suppose that it began to increase in the bad years when there was great distress?
No, not quite then. I think that it would be rather later than that. I think the increase began within the last three years, almost after the cessation of the late distress.

768. Do you mean that you think it had no connection with the exceptional distress in certain parts of the country?
In my district I cannot think that it had if you take the statistics that I have given you; 1879 and 1880 were the worst years that have come for perhaps the last 25 years in Ireland, and the out-door relief given then was very small indeed in proportion to the out-door relief given last year. That is what I endeavoured by getting these returns yesterday to show you. You cannot account for it in that way.

769. What is the extent of the power of a board of guardians in the matter of out-door relief; in what cases can they give it?
There are certain classes that are legally entitled to out-door relief, and the guardians are empowered to give it to them, provided that they are not able-bodied people, and that they are not holders of more than a quarter of an acre of land. They are ineligible if they hold more than a quarter of an acre of land, and able-bodied men are also ineligible; but that difficulty is sometimes got over by a certificate from a doctor stating that the man is unable to work.

770. What are the classes that are legally entitled to it?
  I. Persons permanently disabled from labour by reason of old age, infirmity, or bodily or mental defect.
  II. Persons disabled from labour by reason of severe sickness, or serious accident, &c.
  III. Widows having two or more legitimate children dependent on them.

771. Lord *Monk-Bretton*.] And the old?
Age and infirmity entitle people to it.

772. Lord *Saltersford*.] And the blind?
And the blind. The inmates of the workhouse in my district mainly consists of the aged and infirm, mothers of illegitimate children and young children. It is only legal to give an evicted tenant relief for one month, and after that he has to return to his own resources; but in some cases which I have known myself, it has been continued even till now, going on for nearly three years on the certificate of a doctor that the man is unable to work.

773. Lord *President*.] Has the lawfulness of this out-door relief ever been contested; has the Local Government Board interfered?
Yes,

Yes, it has, through the auditors. The union auditors check it where it is palpably illegal, and surcharge the chairman or gentleman who initialed the amount.

774. Have you known of such cases?
A great many.

775. Then would you desire to see no outdoor relief given.
I think there may be cases where it is necessary, but it requires the very greatest caution and discretion in the administration of it. It is much easier to go on when you have once begun, I found, in unions than to check it or control it when you once have the system established.

776. Viscount *Powerscourt*.] You say that mismanagement is due to *ex-officio* guardians not attending. I suppose it is quite in their power to attend if they choose?
In some cases it is. There are a great many who are resident and others who are non-resident.

777. I mean the resident *ex-officio* guardians?
In cases where they are in a minority they give me as an excuse for not attending the reason that it is useless their going there; their advice is not taken, and they are swamped in those cases.

778. They are assisting to swamp themselves really?
I do not say that it is right; because I have always tried to urge them to go, and it is their duty to go and watch things, and do what they can; but that is the excuse they give, that it is useless their going there, because their voice is not heard and their advice is not followed.

779. You said that the influence of an *ex-officio* chairman or any *ex-officio* guardian upon a board had a great effect with the elected guardians. If the *ex-officio* guardians had attended, they might possibly have kept down all this enormous outdoor relief, and it might have had a very good effect in that way.
It might; but where they are in a very small minority they think it is of no use. I have always urged them to attend, and I believe that if they did attend it would do good eventually; but men get tired and sick of attending where their influence is reduced to nothing at all.

780. Lord *Sudley*.] Should you say in the unions with which you are acquainted that the guardians, either elected or *ex-officio*, generally speaking, are satisfied with the present incidence of the rates?
I do not exactly understand the question.

781. I understand that your experience leads you to suppose that the occupiers pay about one-fourth, and the owners of property pay about three-fourths of the poor rates?
With regard to the owners of property, it is hardly, perhaps, always three-fourths, but in a great many instances in poor unions it is; they pay half upon all the tenements valued at over 4 *l.*; they pay the whole upon all the tenements valued at and under 4 *l.*, and they pay all upon what is in their own occupation. In that way I calculate that they pay always five-eighths of the rates, and very often considerably more.

782. But have you ever known in your experience that resolutions have been passed in boards of guardians to throw the whole incidence of the tax upon the owners?
No, not in my district.

783. Lord *Monk-Bretton*.] In the three unions that were mentioned, Listowel, Tralee, and Killarney, in which the advantage of the presence of *ex-officio* guardians would have been most felt, they are in a very decided minority?
A very decided minority.

784. More so than in the other three unions?
Except when the non-residents come long distances for an election. The
resident

resident *ex-officios* who could possibly attend the weekly meetings of the board are in a very small minority indeed.

785. They are in a much smaller minority in the three unions which you have instanced as mismanaged, than in the three unions you have instanced as better managed?
I do not know as to that exactly. In the three unions of Dingle, Cahirciveen, and Kenmare, which I have given you the statistics of, where the rates have not increased, the board is controlled by an *ex-officio* chairman, and, in fact, they are remote unions, and politics and other matters have not got in there, and they all pull and work well together; they are not what one might call political unions.

786. Then that advantage which they possess is due to the general circumstances of the union rather than to the circumstance of their having a much larger number of *ex-officio* guardians than the other three unions.
I think it is due to their attending to the business which brings them together, attending to poor law business instead of attending to extraneous matters. I think that is mainly what the good management is attributable to.

787. I think you said that you would disqualify publicans from being guardians?
I did, most decidedly.

788. Owing to the fact that the publican may be the creditor of a large number of ratepayers?
I think that even in the elections as they stand at present it leads to a great deal of drinking and expenditure, and I think that if publicans were qualified to act as guardians it would lead to more; and for that reason I should recommend their disqualification.

789. But they are qualified now?
Yes.

790. Do you think it would be practically possible to disqualify them. I suppose the village shopkeeper also is the creditor of a great many ratepayers?
In all villages in Ireland; in a country district the publican is also a shopkeeper for everything; you hardly ever hear of a public-house alone; it is a general store, and they sell all sorts of things. It would be quite practicable to disqualify them, because now in the case of all officers we do not allow them to live in a public-house. Relieving officers, and poor rate collectors, and men of that class, are always prevented from having any connection whatever with public-houses.

791. Supposing proxy-voting were abolished, could the voting by owners of property be facilitated under the proposal, which no doubt you are aware has been made to the Local Government Board should have power to fix the elections on different days?
I think it would be utterly impossible; it would take such an enormous time to complete. A man may have property not only in one electoral division, but in different unions and different parts of the country altogether, and unless you allow him to vote by proxy you practically disfranchise him.

792. Lord *Ker*.] I have not been present during the whole of your examination, but from what I have heard of the evidence you have given I gather that from your experience you would be in favour of continuing the present system of proxies, and be against the diminution of the number of *ex-officio* members of the board of guardians?
I would be against the diminution of the number of *ex-officio*, certainly.

793. And, therefore, you are against the diminution of the voting power representing property upon the boards of guardians?
Yes.

794. I should

6th *March* 1885.]   Colonel SPAIGHT.   [*Continued.*

794. I should like to ask you whether apart from the question of the representation of property upon the board, which is a separate question, perhaps; in your opinion it would therefore be detrimental to the interests of the whole body of ratepayers in Ireland that the voting power of property should be in any way diminished on the boards of guardians?
I have no doubt whatever that the ratepayers would suffer in the end.

795. That is to say that the Poor Law would not be so efficiently administered for the benefit of the whole body of ratepayers if there were any diminution in the voting power which now represents property. If that voting power was diminished it would be detrimental to the interest of the whole body of ratepayers, in your opinion?
Certainly, because the *ex-officio* element on the board represents a much greater amount of rate paid than the elective guardians.

796. That is not the point I wished to ask so much as this: Whether even the administration of the Poor Law as affecting tenants, not the owners but the holders of property, would be affected by the diminution of the number of *ex-officios* on boards of guardians?
It would; and the general well-being would be affected if the *ex-officio* element was diminished or withdrawn; there is no doubt of that whatever.

797. Lord *Saltersford*.] With regard to those unions in Kerry in which so little out-door relief has been given, have there been any deaths attributable to starvation or great destitution in those unions?
I have never heard a single complaint. I always take the trouble to make myself intimately acquainted with my district through the parish priest and others, and I should be certain to hear if there were any complaints, and I have never heard of an instance of any kind.

798. Perhaps you can inform the Committee as to a certain case which appeared in a newspaper, and as to which I would ask whether it has come within your knowledge. It was stated that in a union, I think, not far from your district, there was great complaint about the amount of out-door relief, and on investigation it was discovered that in one particular instance a large sum, apparently, was given to a voter, but on inquiry it turned out that it was divided between the individual, the guardian of the electoral division, and the relieving officer, has that come within your knowledge?
That is not in my district.

799. Have you heard of such a case?
I have not heard of it.

800. It would appear, I think, from what you stated, that the Local Government Board is able to exercise a considerable amount of control over boards of guardians in the conduct of their business?
In the matter of appointments. The Local Government are prohibited by law from interfering in cases of individual relief, and that is never done; but they exercise a certain amount of control in the matter of the appointments of officers of the unions, from clerks of unions down to relieving officers, poorrate collectors, masters and matrons; all officers of the union must be sanctioned by the Local Government Board before any payment to them becomes legal.

801. But is it the case that you cannot control in any way the dishonest granting of contracts, for instance?
If a guardian of a union takes a contract in any way any individual can prosecute him. Of course if it came to the ears of the Local Government Board they would take action in the matter; but it is open to any individual to prosecute a guardian who in anyway becomes connected with a contract for the union?

802. But if the guardians, for political or for private reasons, chose to give a contract to one individual rather than to another, you have no control over that?
No, that is a matter left to them.

803. There

6th March 1885.]   Colonel SPAIGHT.   [Continued.

803. There is a small matter with reference to the costs of elections, on which I want to put a question; you said that you thought that in no case they should be charged upon the rates; but I see in a Sub-section of the 14th section it says that an election shall be void in case " the provisions of this Act, or of any Order of the Local Government Board for the time being in force relating to Poor Law elections were violated, or were not observed in some material particular;" do you not think that it might be rather hard on the clerk of a union on some occasions if costs were incurred possibly by an oversight on his part?
I took the trouble to speak to one or two clerks before I came over on that subject, and I think they seemed quite satisfied, and thought that it was perfectly fair that if any neglect or negligence occurred on their part they should be held responsible. They are generally very intelligent men, and know their work well, and I do not think there is any objection to that.

804. Lord *Skate*.] You made a statement just now (which was confirmed by the last Witness) to Lord Monk-Bretton to the effect that, when the Poor Law was established in Ireland it was taken into consideration that there were a very much larger number of magistrates, comparatively speaking, in Ireland than in England, and that was the reason why the *ex-officio* guardians were diminished in number?
You are alluding to the Act of 1838, if I understand you.

805. You are aware, of course, that in England all justices of the peace are *ex-officio* guardians; in Ireland they are only in equal numbers to the elected guardians; but the reason for that hinted at by Lord Monk-Bretton was, that in Ireland there were a very much larger number of magistrates proportionally than there were in England; does that still continue to be the case?
I think the number of magistrates resident in the country is now very much less than it used to be.

806. Then that would tend to diminishing the force of the reasons against all the magistrates being *ex-officio* guardians?
Yes; no doubt many of the magistrates who were resident in the country have, since the late agitation left the country.

807. But do you see any objection to all magistrates being *ex-officio* guardians?
I see no objection; but I made a suggestion that the *ex-officios* should be elected by the whole body.

808. Amongst themselves?
Yes. I think they know the circumstances of every justice, and would select those who could attend; it would be much better to have men elected and eligible to attend than to have men chosen, simply because they were the highest rate-payers, who never could attend, and never did.

809. Better to do that, you think, than to leave it to their discretion?
Yes.

810. In England they do not all attend; it is left entirely to the discretion of the magistrate whether he attends or not; and, as a rule, I suppose in a division not above three or four magistrates do attend regularly?
Very seldom more than that, as a rule.

811. Are there many friendly or benefit societies in Ireland?
No.

812. Are you aware that out-door relief has sensibly diminished in England in consequence of the action of friendly and benefit societies?
I know nothing of the working of the Poor Law in England.

813. Do

813. Do you think that the establishment of friendly and benefit societies in Ireland would be a good thing?
It might be a good thing if it were possible; but I do not think it is practicable.

814. They devote their spare money, I suppose, to other purposes?
I am afraid it is not practicable.

815. But you think it would be a good thing if it could be carried out?
I have no doubt it would.

816. Earl of *Milltown*.] Do you see any objection to the present system of proxy voting?
I do not.

817. Are you aware of any hardship that it imposes on any class of the community?
I am not.

818. I understood you to say that for the purpose of selecting good and efficient guardians of the poor, it is highly desirable that owners of property should be enabled to exercise their votes?
I think that, certainly.

819. Are you aware of any way in which they could do so without either the proxy system, or something closely approximating to it?
I am not aware of any other way in which they could exercise their voting power, except by proxy. There are others besides ordinary landowners; banks must exercise their voting powers by proxy, so must incorporated societies; all that must be done by proxy, as far as I can see. I do not know any other way of doing it.

820. Have you ever heard any advantage suggested as likely to arise from diminishing the existing number of *ex-officio* guardians, any advantage I mean to the whole community?
I think it would be a very great disadvantage to the community generally.

821. So I understand you to say, but have you ever heard any reason given for diminishing the existing number of *ex-officio* guardians?
I have never heard any reason except political reasons.

822. And in fact until political matters were allowed to invade the Poor Law Boards as they have done of late years, was any agitation ever originated in Ireland, so far as you know, for the purpose of diminishing the number of *ex-officio* guardians; before political matters were allowed to take the place which they unfortunately now do in Poor Law Boards was any such agitation ever started?
Not that I am aware of.

823. *Chairman*.] In the unions that you have had to do with, have not some of those gentlemen, who were chairmen before the agitation, in some cases for a long while, been displaced?
In two of the unions that I quoted as having very largely increased their rates they have. In the Union of Listowel and in the Union of Tralee they were *ex-officio* chairmen in both cases, until the late change came over affairs.

824. Until the agitation began, in fact?
Yes. There was a Colonel Rowan who was Chairman of Tralee Union, and a Mr. Sandes was Chairman of Listowel.

825. Have you heard throughout the country generally (it has come under my own notice) of the old chairmen of boards, who were mostly *ex officio*, being replaced by elected guardians in many instances?

In

6th March 1885.] Colonel SPAIGHT. [Continued.

In my district they have not, with those two exceptions. There were very strong efforts made at the election last year to oust the chairman of the Bantry Union, and it led to complaints being made, and on my holding a sworn inquiry afterwards, I told you they turned out frivolous and invalid. But there was very great pressure indeed put upon the people with the object of ousting the chairman; that is the main object avowed by the agitators.

826. And in two of the cases which you have mentioned the chairmen have been displaced?
In Listowel and in Tralee the *ex-officio* chairmen were put out and replaced by elected guardians.

827. My question arises out of a question of the Lord President's. You had stated what it was in consequence of the Board having a good chairman that the rates were kept down, and the question which the Lord President asked you upon that seemed to imply that the chairman by himself was a great power upon the Board and was thus able to keep the rates down. Now I would put it to you whether it is possible to retain these good chairmen unless the *ex-officio* element is kept up?
You would have no possible chance of having a good chairman elected if the numbers of *ex-officio* guardians were reduced, because the first action of a board of guardians after the annual election, or triennial, as it will be, under the new Act, is to elect a chairman, and that is the first trial of strength. The *ex-officios*, as a rule, try to put in some practical good chairman; the others try to put in somebody else, perhaps not always studying his qualifications as a chairman; and there the first trial of strength always occurs; and the result to the union is of the most vital importance, because where a good and practical chairman is in the chair, for that year matters are bound to be well regulated and successful to a certain degree; and where there is a chairman who is not up to the mark they invariably go wrong.

828. Lord *Monk-Bretton*.] Mr. Sandes, as I understand you, retired from the chairmanship?
Yes, at Listowel.

829. And did Colonel Rowan retire?
Colonel Rowan was forced to retire; on an election he was defeated.

830. *Lord President*.] Can you tell me about what numbers of resident *ex-officio* guardians there are in the unions that you know of; I put aside altogether the non-resident; but what proportion would the resident *ex-officio* guardians bear to the elected?
It is very hard to make a general rule about it. For instance, in a union like Killarney the number would be small in proportion. In a union like Dingle there are two or three or say four *ex-officio* guardians that attend, and there would not be in the ordinary course of things more than four elected guardians that attend; there they would be about equal therefore.

831. I am not speaking of whether they attend or not, but I am asking what the proportion of resident *ex-officio* guardians would be; I am not talking of attendance?
I do not think that in proportion there would be more than one-third absolutely resident in the union.

832. Viscount *Powerscourt*.] Under present circumstances?
Under present circumstances.

833. *Lord President*.] All the others would be non-resident?
I do not mean permanently non-resident, but they would not be residing within sufficient distance to attend the meetings of the board every time. Taking the unions in general (of course I am only speaking without paper;

(0.1.) L and

6th *March* 1885.] Colonel SPAIGHT. [*Continued.*

and speaking I may say by guesswork), I should say that where there are 40 elected guardians there would not now be more than about 10 or 12 *ex-officio* guardians resident; but as I have said, it is entirely guesswork.

834. Earl of *Milltown*.] You are speaking of the south and west of Ireland?
Yes.

835. Lord *Monk-Bretton*.] Did I rightly understand you to say just now that the average attendance in Dingle Union would be about four *ex-officio* and four elected guardians?
I have never on any occasion at Dingle met more than four elected guardians.

836. And that is one of the mismanaged unions, if I remember rightly?
No, one of the well-managed unions.

837. Lord *Saltersford*.] It is a very mountainous country there?
Very mountainous wild country.

838. And probably difficult of access?
Yes, it is shut out from any agitation of any kind.

839. Earl of *Milltown*.] You do not know the number of *ex-officio* guardians, I suppose, in the other more inhabited parts of Ireland?
I do not know the absolute number, but of course in the better class of districts, in richer districts, there are large numbers.

840. Lord *Sudley*.] In Swineford, for instance, you would not have as many as 10, would you?
In the Union of Swineford there was only one resident *ex-officio* guardian.

841.] Viscount *Powerscourt*.] Did he attend?
In the time of the distress it was utterly impossible to get a magistrate to sign a warrant for the removal of the fever patients, and I strongly called attention to the want of this, and the misery it led to. The poor people were spreading the fever about, and I suggested that one of the vice guardians should be given a commission of the peace, which he was. There there is only one magistrate residing in the whole union, with a population of 58,000.

842. What do you mean by "one of the vice guardians"?
The board in that case was dissolved, and vice guardians were appointed.

843. *Chairman*.] What you refer to in answer to that question takes place in the very poor districts in the west?
I am only referring to the very poor districts in the West.

844. And it is not the case in the rest of Ireland?
No, not at all.

845. *Lord President*.] Take the Union of Listowel; how would it be there?
Do you want to know the number of magistrates residing in the union, in comparison with the number not so residing?

846. I mean residing in the same sense in which the elected guardians reside in it?
There the number of magistrates actually residing in the union is 18, and the number of elected guardians is 32.

847. Lord *Monk-Bretton*] I suppose that a certain number of the elected guardians are owners of property in most cases?
I do not think they are.

848. None

848. None of them?
Very few indeed, if any.

849. Earl of *Milltown*] Are landlords likely to be elected under the present state of circumstances in Ireland?
Very unlikely indeed.

The Witness is directed to withdraw.

Ordered, That this Committee be adjourned.

(84)

Die Veneris, 8° Maii, 1885.

LORDS PRESENT:

Lord PRESIDENT.
Earl of MILLTOWN.
Viscount POWERSCOURT.
Viscount HUTCHINSON.
Lord TYRONE.

Lord SALTERSFORD.
Lord SILCHESTER.
Lord SHUTE.
Lord MONK-BRETTON.
Lord SUDLEY.

THE EARL OF MILLTOWN, IN THE CHAIR.

MR. RICHARD BAGWELL, having been called in; is Examined, as follows:

850. *Chairman.*] You are a Deputy Lieutenant and Magistrate of the County of Tipperary?
Yes.

851. And an *ex-officio* guardian of Clonmel and Clogheen?
Yes.

852. Has your attention been called to the Bill now before their Lordships?
Yes, I read it when it was in the House of Commons.

853. Which is the first clause to which you wish to direct our attention?
Clause 4.

854. That is the clause which enacts that poor law guardians shall hold office for three years instead of for one?
I think that would be an improvement, and on that I should like to say that I think renewals by one-third at a time would be better than that It is frequently done in public bodies, and the object gained by that would be that a political issue which happened to be before the people at the time would not be the only question asked them, because there would be another issue next year; so that instead of the entire elective portion of the board being elected under the pressure of a political cry, you would only have one third elected under the pressure of that cry, and the following year there would be a totally different cry; and by that means you would get something like impartiality.

855. The next clause relates to voting by ballot; have you anything to say on that?
That is an improvement, I think.

856. What is the next clause on which you have any observation to make; the one which provides for the abolition of proxy voting, I think?
Yes; that is Clause 9, "Voters to vote in person." I think that is right for people who are voting as occupiers, but that is all. I do not approve of it so far as it abolishes proxies for those who vote as owners. It says here: "After the commencement of this Act no ratepayer shall have power to appoint any person to vote as his proxy at any poor law election." As the law stands now I distinctly disapprove of that; I think it is the only real protection that property has, and as the Irish Poor Law is a thing of recent introduction only, a thing of the last 50 years, and as the incidence of the tax was from the first divided

8th May 1885.] Mr. BAGWELL. [Continued.

divided between landlord and tenant, I think that the landlord should certainly have a very considerable representation. It is different entirely from the English Poor Law. The English Poor Law has been in existence since the 43rd of Queen Elizabeth, and the tax has during the whole of that time been paid by the occupier, and of course it has long since been allowed for in adjustment of rents and other matters.

857. Do you suggest any alteration in the present system of proxy voting?
If the law is to stand in the main as it does now, I do not think that the present system of proxy voting can be very much improved.

858. You do not see any objection to it?
I think proxies are bad things always, if you could find any other means of representing property; but as the law stands now, unless there is a radical change made in the poor law, I am not prepared to say that there is any better way of doing it. I think if property were directly represented it would be better still.

859. Viscount *Powerscourt*.] Is there any way you could suggest in which property could be directly represented?
I have proposed this elsewhere, and am ready to abide by it; I think one-half of the board ought to be directly elected by the immediate lessors; that is to say, by the landlords practically, by those who pay half the rate; and then I should be prepared to abolish proxies if that were done, but not till then.

860. *Chairman*.] Perhaps you would explain a little more fully what your suggestion is?
I do not think it requires a great deal of explanation, but of course the point of the thing is this, that a landlord may have property in a great many different places; that is no fault of his; and he may have no residence in any one of the places; that may be no fault of his either. In many of those cases personal voting is impossible, and he cannot have any voice in the thing at all for the half rate which he pays. I should propose that the ballot having been allowed as the system of election where occupancy is the qualification, where the landlord's paying half the rate is the qualification, then in those cases there should be a system of voting papers which should be sent by post, and which could be made as secret as was desired. I do not think landlords would care about secrecy, but if it were desired, there might be safeguards easily invented for it, and that has been done in other cases. A man would then have a vote according to the rate which he paid; and I would make it cumulative, as it is already by the present poor law. I would say that a man who pays a certain amount shall have a certain amount of voting power, and so on, up to a certain point, and it would be for your Lordships and not for me (who have not the whole facts before me) to decide what, in a case of that kind, should be the exact amount of property which it would be necessary to put as a maximum. Two hundred pounds is the maximum for occupancy. I should think probably for property it would be better to put the maximum somewhat higher, so as to give the people having a large stake some more power; but I would not arrange it so as to make it possible for any one owner, or even two or three, to sweep the election of that half of the board; that would be very invidious.

861. Do I rightly understand you that the occupier is to have one class of representatives at the Poor Law Board, and the owner of property another?
That is the plan that is put forward.

862. Where the owner of property is himself an occupier, how would he vote?
He would have to elect either one thing or the other. Either he would have to vote on the double (which some people think would not be unfair) or else to give up one of the two; and if the landlords of Ireland as a rule had half the power in the board, that is if they had power to elect half the board, and had to choose between voting for elective guardians and voting for the guardians representing property, they would infinitely prefer to waive the vote for electing occupancy guardians; because as a general rule the landlord class could have

very

very little weight in the election of elected guardians in the part of Ireland which I am acquainted with. I will call one class of guardians occupancy guardians, if I may. Supposing proxies were abolished, and there was direct voting, the landlords voting for occupancy guardians would have little power, because their numbers would be very small.

863. *Lord President.*] Do you mean that these property guardians would be in addition to the *ex-officio* guardians?
I would have them instead of the *ex-officio* guardians; and I am prepared to give reasons for that, if required.

864. That is an essential part of your scheme?
My scheme is this: that if the *ex officio* guardians are retained, they ought to be at least one-half of the board; but I should prefer to abolish the *ex-officios*, and have property directly represented by election instead, for half the board.

865. *Chairman.*] With regard to the proposal of the Bill to reduce the number of *ex-officios*, what do you say to that?
As the law now stands, I think it would be quite wrong, and I cannot see any reason for it at all. I hope I am not travelling out of my province in saying that I have taken some trouble to understand the history of the question, and it appears to me that something of this sort happened; I speak with great diffidence, because some of your Lordships are much better acquainted with it than I can be; but when the law was first brought in, in 1838, one-third was the number chosen for *ex-officio* guardians, and that poor law was brought in very much against the weight of Irish landlord opinion; it was brought in by Mr. Poulett Thompson and his school, who were very hostile to Irish landlords; and it was thought that one-third would be quite enough to give them.

866. I may tell you that we have had evidence on this point already?
Then I will not take up your time by going into it further. Then afterwards the proportion was changed to one-half; and I think for very good reasons. It was changed in the year 1847 to one-half, and I think the reasons that were good in 1847 are quite as good now, if not better.

867. *Viscount Hutchinson.*] The alteration was made to one-half about the year 1846, was it not?
1847.

868. When that change was made was it not on the ground that the proportion of rates borne by the landlords at that time justified the increase in the number of their representatives?
The Bill of 1843, which passed into an Act, was brought in by Lord Eliot; and Lord Eliot proposed in that Bill, in 1843, to make the *ex-officios* one-half. That was the Act which rated the landlord for holdings valued at 4 *l.* and under; and it was thought then that a certain proportion of the rate having been transferred from the tenant to the landlord, the landlord should have higher representation. That was dropped out in Committee, I suppose owing to certain pressure; and the Government of 1847 (it was Lord John Russell who made the speeches on that occasion) restored on that occasion what had been lost in the Bill of 1843, to the Bill of 1847; and the principal question before the House of Commons in 1847, so far as I understand it, was out-door relief; but the original object of increasing the number of *ex-officio* guardians was to meet the transfer of rates in the case of the very small holdings. That was the original object of introducing it on the part of the Government.

869. *Chairman.*] Supposing that your suggestion is not adopted, but the *ex officio* system is retained, have you any suggestions to make with reference to the existing system?
Yes. I think that there should be a power of resignation; that is perhaps the most important of any.

870. Is it the case now that an *ex-officio* guardian cannot resign?
That is the law now. There is this difficulty, that at present a magistrate is made an *ex-officio* guardian without his own consent; he cannot help being made

made an *ex-officio* guardian, except in the unions where the number of magistrates qualified exceeds one-half of the number of the board; in those cases option is allowed. It is the case in the Carlow Union, and it may be the case in a few others, that the number of magistrates resident within the union is greater than one-half of the Board; in those cases some option is allowed; a man will have to say that he will serve. In the case, which is the general case throughout the south of Ireland, where the number of magistrates qualified under the first qualification are considerably less than half the board, in those cases a magistrate has no power to refuse being put on; he must be put on, and when he is on he cannot resign.

871. What object would be gained by his having the power to resign?
You might get a useful man instead of a useless one.

872. But if you have not enough magistrates to fill up vacancies, what then?
In any case, even where there was double the number of magistrates, one would like a man to be able to resign.

873. But take the case where there are not as many magistrates qualified as there are elected guardians in the district, what object would be gained there by the power of resignation?
There would be this object gained: a magistrate resident in the union is primarily qualified, but he might not be a man willing to act; and it he resigned there would then be a place, perhaps, for a gentleman having property in the union, but not having a residence within it, but who might, nevertheless, be able to act occasionally. Where counties are conterminous that frequently occurs. In order to qualify him he must be acting for the county in which he lives; and there are very many cases in which a resident in a conterminous county might prove a better guardian than a resident within the county where the workhouse is situate.

874. That would be altering the qualification?
Yes.

875. Lord *Saltersford*.] Am I right in thinking that magistrates living outside the union are put on in proportion to the rateability of their property?
That is so.

876. So that a person having a large qualification might be put on with no sort of probability of his attending, whereas a man with a smaller qualification might be able to attend?
That is so.

877. Lord *Shute*.] What objection do you see to all magistrates resident in the union being *ex-officio* guardians?
As a representation of property it might be excessive, or, on the other hand, it might be no representation at all. The conferring of the honour of becoming a magistrate, a place in the commission of the peace is becoming less and less connected with property every year. I know a case in which a magistrate, who is a magistrate of the county in which he lives, is not a proprietor in the county; he is not even a ratepayer; he lives in lodgings and pays no rates, and he attends every board or very nearly every board throughout the year. Now he represents nobody. I know one such case, and there may be others.

878. Lord *President*.] What is his qualification?
He was a resident magistrate originally, and when he retired from that they made him a magistrate, and he remains living on there, but he has absolutely no interest in the rates; and such cases may happen not at all unfrequently. In cases where a man has been a justice of the peace and has ceased to be interested in property, he may remain on in a lodging or may remain on living about in hotels and that kind of thing; and, I think, I could point to instances very nearly like that.

879. Lord *Shute*.] I suppose the appointment of magistrates is entirely in the hands of the Lord Lieutenant of counties?
Not entirely. The Lord Chancellor can overrule them, and has in some
cases

cases overruled them. There have been cases in which the lord lieutenant of a county (or rather the lieutenant of a county as we call him in Ireland) has been refused his nomination. There have been such cases within my knowledge. There have also been cases in which nominations have been made over his head. There are few such, but there are some; and there are cases in which considerable pressure has been put on the lieutenant of a county to reconsider his decision.

880. *Chairman*.] Is the attendance of the *ex-officio* guardians in your judgment advantageous to the ratepayers, and to the union generally?
I could not say how highly I value the attendance of *ex-officio* guardians. Even when there are only one or two of them I think they are of the very greatest possible value.

881. I think you can give the Committee your experience of a union where the *ex-officios* do attend in some numbers, and of another where they do not?
I can mention such instances in my own county; but perhaps it would be better that I should not mention particular unions, because it is a little invidious; but I have no hesitation in saying that the unions where the *ex-officio* guardians have been in the habit of attending in some numbers conduct their business better, and are on the whole more financially sound than those which are entirely left to the elective guardians.

882. What is the cause of the non-attendance of the *ex-officios* in those cases where they do not attend?
It is very disagreeable; that is the principal reason I think.

883. I do not quite understand that answer; will you explain it a little further?
They are generally in a minority, and political feeling runs high in Ireland; and it is very often attempted by the local demagogues to make it disagreeable to a magistrate who attends; that is the truth of the matter. Personally, I do not care how disagreeable it is, but some do. That is one reason. Another reason is that men who are not elected as a general rule do not feel any very strong obligation to attend. A man would say, "I am put upon this board in virtue of an Act of Parliament, in virtue of a General Order; I do not wish to be on it; I will not attend." That is said, and frequently said.

884. The introduction of political matters into the discussions of the boards is of somewhat recent occurrence, is it not?
It has been going on ever since I became a guardian, and for much longer, but it has got worse lately; and in these days of political organisations, which are not confined to Irish electors, for there are political organisations everywhere, there is a tendency to make a thing run through the whole country which makes it more disagreeable. Formerly a question was more truly local; now frequently a sort of kite is flown, and some resolution, which is very often very absurd (though sometimes not so), is sent from one union to another, and it is not poor law business, and gentlemen find a difficulty in allowing such a thing to pass unobserved, and if they happen to be in a great minority they do not like being out-voted on a matter of that kind; and that makes the thing disagreeable.

885. In your judgment would it be very desirable that it should be rendered absolutely impossible that extraneous matters should be brought before the poor law boards?
It would be a good thing if it did not introduce evils on the other side; and it could have been done long ago if the Local Government Board had chosen to stop that practice before it became confirmed.

886. How could they stop it?
They have issued new general rules, but rules that can be evaded to a very considerable extent. If the chairman of the board is determined not to allow the introduction of extraneous matter, he undoubtedly has the power of excluding it; but, on the other hand, the majority of the guardians have the power of adjourning the board without the business being done; and even supposing that the chairman may be as unwilling as possible to introduce extraneous

8th May 1883.] Mr. BAGWELL. [Continued.

extraneous matter, &c, as a practical man, and a man having the interests of the poor at heart, will be very slow, merely for the sake of his own feelings, or of his own ideas on the subject, to obstruct the business which he is there for, which is the relief of the poor; and the effect of a chairman adopting such a course, if it comes to an adjournment of the board, is that the business of the board is adjourned for a week at least. Then the thing is repeated next week, and it either goes on being repeated or else the Local Government Board have to dissolve that board.

887. Lord *Saltersford.*] That has taken place, has it not?
In one place it has; and a chairman of a union, wishing to live on friendly terms with his neighbours, and not anxious to see paid officials put in the place of a board, will be very slow to force the thing to its bitter end. I should be very slow myself to do so. I should dislike these resolutions to which I have alluded, but I should attribute very little importance to such resolutions, and I should prefer to get the business done somehow myself. That is my own feeling.

888. *Chairman.*] Do you suggest any mode by which the Local Government Board could put an end to the introduction of these extraneous topics?
I see no means, except by categorically forbidding them; and they have not done that.

889. How could they enforce such an order?
It would be very difficult, no doubt. I suppose the *ultima ratio* would be the dissolution of the board. If a sealed order is disobeyed, the *ultima ratio* is the dissolution of the board, but I think that would be very difficult.

890. Lord *Monk-Bretton.*] Does an inspector of the Local Government Board attend the meetings?
Occasionally; he has a considerable number of unions to visit. And my experience of the poor law inspectors is that they are men who are very earnest and anxious to do what is right, and who do, as much as possible, attend the boards; in the nature of things they can only do it occasionally, but they attend each board several times in the year; they are very ready to come if they are asked to come, it they can possibly make a day. If I may give my own experience, I may say that I have generally observed that on the days when the inspector is present there is a great improvement in the way that business is done by the guardians; they seem to be acting under the official eye, and they do it much better. I have observed that.

891. The extraneous matter is not then introduced?
Not to the same extent at all. I think that they respect the inspector, as a rule, and are anxious to carry on things square when he is there.

892. *Chairman.*] Is it your experience that the elective guardians are more or less economical in spending the rates than the *ex-officio* guardians?
I think on the question of out-door relief, which is the great point where there is waste, the *ex-officio* guardians, as a class, are far more aware of the economic objections to out-door relief than the elective guardians. The elective guardians, many of them, do not understand the great objection to it. That is not by any means universal; some of them are as sound as possible; but as a general and very frequent rule, they do not understand what, of course, is a common place to those who have studied it, that out-door relief is the most extravagant thing in the world. They see an immediate saving, and that is all.

893. Lord *Saltersford.*] I daresay you are aware, even though it may not have come under your actual notice, that in some unions there is a great deal of jobbing in the matter of contracts?
I am afraid it is so.

894. Which class of guardian would you say were most liable to be guilty of that?
Whatever the magistrates in Ireland may have been in past times, they are not jobbers now.

895. The

895. The presence of an *ex-officio* guardian is a certain safeguard against jobbing, you think?
I think certainly that may be said without any danger of overstepping the mark.

896. *Chairman.*] Do the *ex-officio* guardians as a rule attend well in your district?
A few attend. In my own union there are three or four who give very fair attendance, and there are three or four more who give occasional attendance; but, as a body, I cannot say that they attend well in any union I am aware of, except the Carlow Union. I know they attend well there, but the only union I know anything about where the attendance is really good, is the Carlow Union.

897. I suppose you attribute considerable importance to the election of a good chairman?
A good chairman can do a great deal in everything; but the chairman must always be elected by the Board, and it will depend upon the goodness of the Board what sort of chairman they will choose.

898. Do you think that diminishing the number of *ex-officio* guardians is likely to diminish the chance of a good chairman being elected?
I think that a strong body of *ex-officio* guardians are much more likely to secure a good man in the chair than a small body.

899. Lord *Salteresford.*] You said just now that the attendance of *ex-officio* guardians was larger in Carlow than in other unions?
Much larger than the average, as far as I am aware.

900. You also said that there was a larger number of resident magistrates in the Carlow Union than the number entitled to be *ex-officio* guardians?
Yes, I think so.

901. Therefore, to some extent the non-attendance of *ex-officio* guardians in other unions would be in consequence of their not being within the unions one may suppose?
Partially so, and also partially that where the number of magistrates is comparatively limited you have to go through the whole gamut and get down to a rather low note, get down to lazy men, and men not willing to do any work; whereas in such cases as Carlow you are able to choose from a larger number of men, and by having a hundred men to choose from you get them better men than where you have only 10 to choose from.

902. *Chairman.*] Where there is a large number of men to choose from, I suppose you think the elective principle might be adopted with advantage?
Wherever you see your way to adopting the elective principle, or something approaching to election, it would be an advantage, I think. Wherever there are means of securing active guardians, it should be done.

903. Passing now to Part III. of the Bill, I suppose you see no objection to Sub-section (3). which says: " No justice of the peace shall be qualified to be an *ex-officio* guardian of any poor law union unless he is a ratepayer of such union;" or do you see any objection to it. In the case of an agent, it has been suggested that might be rather harsh?
I have great doubts about agents; I am aware that that subject has been before Parliament more than once, and I have great doubts whether it is desirable that agents should be guardians. I would really rather not give a very distinct opinion, because it seems invidious to do so; but I have great doubt whether it is for the real interest of owners that their agents should be *ex-officio* guardians.

904. What do you say to lowering the qualification for a guardian to 12 *l.*, as proposed by the Bill?
I think that is bad; the present law is 30 *l.* as a maximum, and I do not see why it should be reduced. The Local Government Board can put it as low as 10 *l.*,

8th May 1885.] Mr. BAGWELL. [Continued.

10 l., and have done so in some cases; they can put it lower if they like; and I do not see that there is any real reason to question the way in which the thing has been done. I have seen nothing to call for such a change, and it is merely an attempt at swamping; the effect would be to swamp the substantial men; and in a money question I see no reason why the people who pay the rates should be entirely swamped; 30 l. is the maximum, and 20 l. or 25 l. has been the usual thing fixed. The Local Government Board have the power of fixing the amount. I think there is only one union fixed at 30 l.; 20 l. and 25 l. are usual, and frequently it is fixed at less than that; and I do not see any reason to restrict the discretion of the Local Government Board further than it has been restricted.

905. The Local Government Board practically now can lower it as much as they like?
They can lower it as much as they like, but they cannot put it higher than 30 l.

906. Is there any desire amongst the ratepayers to have it lowered?
Not the slightest, as far as my knowledge goes, among the real public; I do not mean to say that there are not people who are managers who desire to see it lowered; but speaking of the real public, such as the farmers, whom one would meet with in the course of one's day's work or day's walk, I believe there is no desire at all; I have not met any instance of it whatever.

907. Is there any other suggestion you would like to make with reference to the Bill?
On the point of the appeal, there is I believe an arrangement for a cheap appeal in the Bill; I have not gone much into that, but I think it is a very good thing that there should be a cheap appeal; but I do not think that the costs should come out of the rates. If that is not provided for, it should be provided for in my opinion.

908. *Lord President.*] Why do you think the costs should not come out of the rates?
I think it would lead to an enormous number of absolutely fictitious appeals.

909. *Lord Saltersford.*] Who would have to pay the costs in your view?
The petitioners, as they do in every other case. If the thing is of sufficient interest let them club their money; if it is not of sufficient interest let it go as it is. The beaten party should pay the costs.

910. *Viscount Powerscourt.*] You did not mean that the costs should fall upon the Consolidated Fund?
Certainly not; I am always against putting things on the Consolidated Fund if it can be helped, for a great many reasons; but I do not think that the ratepayers should be called upon to pay for what may only be the act of one or two. I think that people in all branches of public life have to bear their own costs.

911. The parties you think should bear these costs?
The party beaten.

912. *Chairman.*] You think it would lead to a great number of frivolous objections if it did not cost them anything?
I do, certainly.

913. *Lord Saltersford.*] You are supposing that the petitioner is the person to pay the costs?
If he is beaten.

914. The Bill runs in this way: "Where a returning officer is made respondent to a petition he shall not be ordered to pay the petitioner's costs, except the court shall be of opinion that he was guilty of negligence or improper conduct in the matter of the election or petition"?
That I think is right, because a mistake might possibly arise from an ambiguity in the law, and it would be unfair to make the returning officer suffer. It is a principle

a principle in all things that the official man, if he acts *bonâ fide*, should be held blameless by the State.

915. *Chairman.*] Still if the mistake has arisen through his default, it would be rather hard on either party to make them pay the costs, would it not?
I do not see how that can be avoided. I think it might be wise to provide that where a petition is lodged some security for costs should be given. I think, perhaps, that would be the best safeguard of all against frivolous petitions.

916. Do you think that under the present system property is sufficiently represented?
No, I cannot say that I think it is. In case the *ex-officio* guardians are retained, it would be hopeless to attempt to fully represent property; but I cannot think that property is really fully represented; because the proprietors really pay five-eighths of the rates, and they certainly have not got five-eighths of the power. But it is better to have it as it is than to reduce the representation still further.

917. So that in your judgment, even under the existing system, property is not sufficiently represented?
I do not think it ever has been since the Irish Poor Law was invented.

918. And I suppose if this proposal to further reduce the number of *ex-officio* guardians were adopted, that would tend to its being still less represented?
Certainly it would.

919. *Lord President.*] Do you mean that you would wish for a system under which the majority of the inhabitants of the union, and their wishes and ideas, would be completely overridden by the small minority, consisting of owners of property?
No, I have not at any time proposed that the owners should have more than half the board; and in the nature of the case they wou'd never have half, because they always have gentlemen of property representing them on the board who are frequently absentees, and even those who are not absentees are frequently away, and therefore I do not think there would be any danger of the kind which you have suggested. I think in Ireland the danger is all the other way. If I thought that there would be any danger of the board falling entirely into the hands of the landlords I should wish to guard against that danger. I should be very sorry indeed if that were to happen; but I do not think it could happen under any circumstances, unless you gave the landlords a majority of the board. If you gave them an absolute majority of the board it might happen; but that is not proposed under any system.

920. I suppose you would treat that as an impossible idea; a thing not to be thought of?
A thing not within the range of anything like practicability.

921. It would turn the elective system into a farce?
It would have that tendency; but finding that property is, under the present system, inadequately represented, I should be opposed to seeing the representation of it still further reduced.

922. Would you hold it to be inadequately represented, supposing the *ex-officio* guardians chose to make use of their rights and to take the trouble of attending?
It would then be much better. I feel as strongly as any one can feel the great *lâches* of which the magistrates have, in many cases, been guilty. I have felt that, and suffered from it as much as anybody; but it must not be forgotten that there are a vast number of cases in which the magistrates cannot attend. I have a friend in the county of Cork, an *ex-officio* guardian in four or five unions; I myself am an *ex-officio* guardian in two; and it is almost impossible to attend two boards; it is quite impossible to attend four.

923. I do not understand that you have suggested any remedy for that state of things; I mean supposing the *ex officio* system to be maintained?
I do not see that there is much that can be suggested.

924. Except a greater public spirit on the part of the *ex-officio* themselves?
I only see this remedy. As the Chairman has said, in the cases where the magistrates resident within the union are smaller in number than one-half of the board, there would be no point at which it could be remedied, except by letting the second class come in instead of them in cases where they were willing to resign. A magistrate having a residence within the union, and who was unwilling to act as an *ex-officio* guardian, might resign in favour of a gentleman not resident in the union, but still near enough to act. In a great many unions that would bring in an active man here and there, instead of an inactive man. That would certainly be the case, and I think it would be a great improvement.

925. Do I understand you to attach great importance to the system of proxy voting, although you say that you dislike it upon its merits?
I think proxies are always bad things, I think there is a danger in all proxies that a local manager or a local busybody may ho'd a lot of proxies, and may have a great deal more power than he ought to have. That occurs in every case where proxies are used. In all public companies proxies are very frequently worked not at all for the benefit of the shareholders; and in the same way proxies may be worked not at all for the benefit of the ratepayers. That is the danger. But there is a limit now to the number of proxies that one person may hold; one person cannot hold a vast number; so that I do not think there is practically very much abuse of that sort. But I do object, on general grounds, to proxies, if property could be fairly represented in any other way.

926. Lord *Monk-Bretton*.] I suppose the proxy holder is, generally speaking, the agent of the owner?
I have held proxies for a person not as an agent; small proprietors who are resident elsewhere, and have a few acres of land, or a few hundreds a year, have sent me proxies. There have been cases of that sort, but I should think very often it is the agent who holds the proxies; and, as I said before, putting too much power in the hands of an agent is not for the interest of his principal. Very often, I think, it would be well if the principal were forced to face things a little closer himself, even if he were not there; a great deal can be done by the landlord, and it would be much better than leaving so much to the agent. I have seen much harm done by that.

927. Lord *President*.] Would you object to the proxy being made valid only for the election for which it is given?
I am not quite aware how long it lasts now. It lasts five years, I believe; I think five is perhaps too long. It would be a little harassing perhaps to make it last one year only. I do not see that there is any objection to it in principle; it would only give more trouble.

928. Do you see any objection to its being valid only for the election in question, that it should be issued expressly for the purpose of an election?
I would not insist upon any objection to that; I do not think there would be any real objection to it. The only objection that could be made to it would be that it would give a little more trouble.

929. Do you not think that if this privilege is to be maintained, people may be expected to take some little trouble in using it?
I think so; I do not at all object to trouble, but there are men who do. I do not at all object to having any public work put upon me, and what I am asked to do I try to do it as well as I can; but a good many people living in the country are constitutionally lazy; and it might have the effect perhaps of making them a little more sharp, and that would be no harm.

930. This privilege of proxy voting is perhaps just a case in which the plea of trouble ought not to be used?
I have no personal objection whatever to making it valid for just the one election; and if that were to be the condition of retaining the proxy system, I should very willingly retain it on that condition.

931. Viscount

8th May 1885.]   Mr. BAGWELL.   [Continued.

931. Viscount *Hutchinson*.] There is precedent for adopting that plan?
I think it is so in all public companies.

932. Lord *Shute*.] It is proposed in this Bill that the elections of guardians should be triennial?
I think that is right, but I should have preferred that one-third should be elected each year.

933. If the proxies are given for each election, and the election is triennial, it would not make much difference as compared with the present system?
No.

934. *Chairman*.] Do you see any advantage to be derived from making proxies only available for one election?
No, not much real advantage. It would make it a little less invidious; perhaps that would be an advantage in a thing of this sort, because it is a thing that arouses some animosity. It is also very conceivable that a question may arise during the existence of a proxy in which the person who originally gave the proxy may find it used for a purpose he did not contemplate, and perhaps would not like. I think that is quite conceivable, and I think it is an argument that might be used with force.

935. Suppose it were given for three years only, and this Bill was to pass which makes the time of office three years instead of one, practically that would mean only for one election, unless there happened to be an accidental vacancy during the time?
That is so.

936. *Lord President*.] In making my supposition, I do not mean that it should be given three years beforehand or 12 months beforehand, but that it should be granted within a short time before the election for which it is intended to be used?
I have no objection to what you suggest.

937. And with a definite view to that election?
It would certainly be logically better; I do not know that it would make much practical difference.

938. Lord *Shute*.] The present system of electing ordinary guardians is by voting papers left at the houses; do you think that the voters generally are able to act according to their individual will?
No.

939. Do you think very much intimidation takes place?
I think there has been intimidation in many ways and from many quarters.

940. In what way does it generally take place?
I am very unwilling to say anything of a class character, but it is within all your Lordships' knowledge that there have been times when the Irish gentry were a little bit oppressive sometimes; I do not think they are so now, in any case hardly; but there have been such cases; and I believe there have been cases in which agents have had more power put in their hands than they ought to have; I do not know any recent case, and I do not say that that goes on much now; but other classes have come in who use their power quite as unscrupulously, I think, as ever the agents did. I know cases of house-to-house visits by managers connected with local organisations; and it is intimidation whoever does it; I do not care what class does it. I have known cases in which guardians who had influence with small people, have habitually insisted on seeing the paper filled up. That is not freedom of election.

941. I will first read you a statement taken from a newspaper of Monday, 23rd March, and ask you if you think it is likely to be correct: "A party of men visited the house of a farmer named Moriarty, at Barlymount, at a late hour on Thursday night. One of them entered with a loaded gun and demanded the voting paper, which was issued last week for the coming election of poor law guardians for the Killarney Union, there being two candidates, a

(O.1.)   M 4   Conservative

Conservative and a Nationalist, for the Aghadoe division. The farmer's wife hesitated, when one of the party threatened to blow her brains out if she did not show them the paper. The woman then produced the document, which had not been filled up, and she was warned that if the Nationalist was not voted for they would return and carry out their threat. Four men named Cronin, Kennedy, Moriarty, and Sullivan have been arrested on suspicion." Is that the sort of intimidation you know of?

That is a very aggravated case; but I have no doubt whatever that such cases might happen. I have no reason to believe, *primâ facie*, that that paragraph is not true, though I know nothing of that particular case.

942. *Lord President.*] A great deal may be done short of that?
A great deal may be done short of that, and has been, within my knowledge.

943. *Lord Shute.*] There is no way you can suggest, I suppose, for remedying such a state of things?
The ballot is the only remedy; even that is not perfect; but that is the only thing to be done.

944. *Viscount Hutchinson.*] You were saying that the board might be renewed to the extent of one-third every year?
I think there would be great advantages in that.

945. How would you propose to do it; would it not come to an annual election, one-third of the board retiring yearly?
They would retire by rotation every year, as is done by club committees. In a club committee, a committee of nine, three retire each year; and that would be the plan. My object is, of course, entirely to prevent a whole board being elected under a cry.

946. *Viscount Powerscourt.*] They would all be elected triennially?
Each individual guardian would sit for three years, but I think it would be certainly better in Ireland; and I think it is a principle of very general application, that a partial election is better.

947. *Chairman.*] I suppose the retiring members of the board should be eligible for re-election?
I see no objection to that; I think it very important that the guardians should not be constantly changed. I would rather have the same man guardian, even though not a very good man, than have frequent changes. Men get to know something about the work. As a rule, the men elected guardians do not study books, and they only learn the administration of the Poor Law by the rule of thumb, and it takes a long time to learn; and I think that the retiring by rotation bears upon that point, because you would always have two-thirds of the elected portion of the board consisting of seasoned guardians; and I think that would be very much for the benefit of the public.

The Witness is directed to withdraw.

Mr. GARRETT C. TYRRELL, having been called in; is Examined, as follows:

948. *Chairman.*] I BELIEVE you are a magistrate for the county of Kildare?
Yes.

949. And *ex officio* guardian of the Edenderry Union?
Yes.

950. And you have been for three years deputy vice chairman of the board of guardians?
Yes.

951. Have you considered the Bill now before the Committee?
I have.

952. What

8th May 1885.]   Mr. Tyrrell.   [Continued.

952. What do you say with regard to triennial elections?
I approve of the triennial elections.

953. As proposed in the Bill?
Yes.

954. And with regard to the voting by ballot, what do you say?
I approve of that also, as tending to do away with some of the intimidation and undue influence brought to bear on electors at present.

955. Have you any suggestion to make with regard to the mode of carrying out the ballot?
I think that a voting paper should be issued for each vote to which the elector is entitled.

956. What would be your object in that?
I think if voting papers were not issued for each vote, the secrecy of the ballot would not be preserved.

957. Perhaps you will explain your meaning a little further?
In any electoral division there would not be perhaps more than four or five, or perhaps not so many, occupiers entitled to six votes; that is to say the others would not be paying sufficient rates to get six votes; then there would only be four or five voting papers issued for six votes each, and it could be easily traced then how the parties voted.

958. What do you say with regard to the proposal to abolish the proxy vote by Clause 9 of this Bill?
I think the proxy is the only method by which you can get the landlord vote at present; I do not think there is any other method by which it could be as efficiently given.

959. Do you see any objection to it as it now exists?
I do not.

960. Is there any great complaint, as far as you know, among the people at large, of the proxy vote?
Among a certain class there have been complaints.

961. I said "among the people at large"?
No, not among the people at large.

962. With regard to those who do object to it, what objection do they state?
I have heard it stated, and I have seen it in print, that the proxy vote swamped the occupier vote at elections.

963. In your experience is that the case?
It is not.

964. Would it be possible, so far as you know?
It would be quite impossible for the landlord vote to swamp the occupier vote.

965. What is about the relative proportion so far as you know?
The proportion of proxy votes to occupiers' votes would be very small; I should not think it could be a fourth, even when all such votes have been registered.

966. Do you attribute importance to the proxy vote?
I do.

967. On what ground?
The proxy vote, although it is small in itself, is able to turn the scale at a contested election.

968. Are the elections sometimes rather close?
They are very close sometimes.

969. And what proportion does the power, as voters, of those who possess these proxy votes, bear to the amount they contribute towards the rates?
It is not at all in proportion to the amount contributed by them towards the rate; it is very much less in proportion.

970. I believe

8th May 1885.] Mr. Tyrrell. [*Continued.*

970. I believe you have some statistics with regard to the electoral division of Ballaghassan and Esker?
Yes.

971. Where there was a close contest, I believe, between a Loyalist candidate and a candidate of the National League?
Yes.

972. I use those terms because I believe that was what they called themselves?
The National League candidate called himself the National League candidate; but the other, the man I call a Loyalist, was really elected simply as an opponent of the National League Candidate, and was not a political candidate at all.

973. Can you tell us now how the votes went on that occasion?
Yes. There were 259 votes altogether in the electoral division. Of these 15 were not used at all, and 13, that is to say, eight landlord and five occupier, votes, were disallowed to the Nationalist at the scrutiny, and three occupier votes and six landlord votes were disallowed to the Loyalist. There were therefore 222 votes left; and of these the National League candidate got 105, made up of 82 occupier votes, 20 profit rent (that is rent paid less than the valuation), and three immediate lessors. The Loyalist candidate received 117 votes, made up of 42 occupiers, 24 on account of profit rent, 16 immediate lessors, and 35 proxies. The supporters of the National League candidate contributed to the rates about 27 *l.* 12 *s.* 3 *d.*; the supporters of the Loyalist contributed 88 *l.* 4 *s.* 11 *d.*

974. And yet they only won the election by 12?
By 12. Then there were some ratepayers who did not vote; they contributed in all 9 *l.* 7 *s.* 6 *d.* to the rate.

975. Then I believe you have with you the statistics of another election which took place, where, notwithstanding the proxy vote, the Loyalist candidate was defeated?
Yes, that is the Clonbullogue electoral division in the Edenderry Union, in King's County. At that election the Nationalist got 148 votes, made up thus: occupiers, 94; profit rent, 39; rated lessors, 13, and landlord votes, 2. The supporters of the Loyalist were allowed 128 votes; 43, as occupiers; 18, profit rent; 9, as rated lessors, and 58 proxies. The Loyalist supporters contributed 122 *l.* 13 *s.* to the rates, and the Nationalist 42 *l.* 15 *s.*

976. That is to say, the Loyalists contributed nearly three times as much as the Nationalists, and yet they were defeated!
Yes. I speak, of course, in round numbers, because I cannot be certain that that is exactly the amount of rate contributed by each, but it is as close as I could calculate it; it is practically correct.

977. Is there any division in your union where a Loyalist candidate could be returned without the proxy vote?
There is one.

978. What is that?
Ballyburly.

979. How does that stand?
He could be returned by allowing the property vote without the proxy vote.

980. Perhaps you would just tell the Committee how much of the rates in that instance are paid by Loyalists and how much by the Parnellites?
The supporters of the Loyalist at the election paid 109 *l.* 11 *s.* 5 *d.*, and the supporters of the Nationalist paid 14 *l.* 6 *s.* 2 *d.*

981. Viscount *Hutchinson.*] And by what was the election won?
One hundred and five votes the Loyalist got including proxies, and the Nationalist, 51.

982. Lord

982. *Lord President.*] Are poor law elections, in your experience, often fought upon these political grounds?
Recently, I think, they have been; almost always so within the last three or four years.

983. *Chairman.*] So that, as I understand you, the result of abolishing the proxy vote in your union would be that the seditious candidate would be returned in every electoral division, with the exception of Ballyburly?
Yes.

984. Notwithstanding that the amount of rates paid by his supporters is much less than the amount paid by the supporters of the Loyalist?
Yes.

985. *Lord President.*] You did not use the term "seditious;" the term you used was "National League Candidate"?
National League Candidates; this is what they term themselves.

986. The candidates supported by the influence of the National League?
They are chosen, as a rule, by the local branches of the National League, and supported by them on political grounds.

987. That is what you mean definitely?
Yes.

988. *Chairman.*] Can you tell us something about the attendance of the National League guardians and the Loyalist guardians at your board?
I find that from March 1884 to March 1885 there were 52 board days; the National League guardians attended on an average 12·7 days; the non-political elected guardians attended on an average 17·6 days.

989. Therefore their attendance was considerably better than that of the National League guardians?
Considerably better.

990. I believe you approve of the suggestion in Clause 10 of the Bill that a claim to vote should be sent in two months before the election?
Yes, I think it would be a good provision.

991. You think that that is desirable, judging from your experience?
I do; so that then a complete list of owners as well as of the occupying voters, should be made out, and open to criticism.

992. Lord *Saltersford.*] Do you think it desirable or not that the rate should be paid before the claim to vote is put in?
I do.

993. It is not the case at present?
It is not the case at present.

994. I think the rates may be paid up to the very last moment?
Yes, that is the present practice; but I think it is desirable that before the claim is registered, that is two months before the election, all rates due should be paid to enable the ratepayer to vote.

995. *Lord President.*] On what ground do you give that opinion?
At present the payment of the rates is very often put off to the last moment. I think, as a financial matter, it would be better to have the rates paid before these claims are lodged; and I think the register would then be less likely to be disturbed.

996. *Chairman.*] What do you say about Part II. of the Bill with regard to Election Petitions?
I think the suggestion made in the Bill for petitions to be tried before the county court judge is a good one; but I think that the petition should only be presented by the candidate or his nominators, and that they should give security for costs before presenting the petition. I think otherwise you will have a number of frivolous petitions presented.

8th May 1885.] Mr. TYRRELL. [Continued.

997. What do you say with regard to payment of the costs out of the rates?
I think that the costs should be paid by the petitioner if his case is found to be frivolous.

998. But not otherwise?
I think he cannot be made to pay them otherwise, but the respondent may.

999. Viscount *Powerscourt*.] That is to say, that in all cases the parties should pay their own costs?
No; I think the petitioner should pay all the costs, if the case is found to be frivolous, out of the money he has lodged; and if the returning officer is found to have acted improperly, he should be made to pay the costs too.

1000. *Chairman*.] But in case of the returning officer having made default through an accident for which he was not very blameable, it would be rather hard to call upon either party to bear the costs?
Yes, I think in that case the rates would have to bear the costs.

1001. Turning to Part III. of the Bill, what do you say to Section 25, and the provisions in it, that no person under 21 years of age should be permitted to vote at any poor law election?
I think that minors should vote by their guardian or trustee, on their guardian or trustee lodging a claim.

1002. At present how is that?
In the case of occupiers the practice is, I believe, to allow no vote.

1003. And in the case of a landlord?
In the case of a landlord, I believe, proxy votes are allowed to the trustees.

1004. But, as I understand, you cannot see any objection to the guardian of a minor being allowed to vote for the minor?
No, I think it would be fair whether occupier or owner.

1005. Viscount *Hutchinson*.] Supposing a case where there is a minor, and his mother is left sole guardian?
At present there is nothing to disqualify a woman from voting under the Poor Law Acts.

1006. *Chairman*.] What do you say to the reduction proposed in the Bill of the qualification for elected guardians to 12 *l.*?
I think it would have a bad effect; I consider that it is low enough now.

1007. What is the qualification in your own union?
£. 25.

1008. Have you ever heard any complaints of its being too high?
No.

1009. What do you say to the proposal to reduce the number of *ex-officio* guardians?
I think it would be a great mistake to reduce the number.

1010. In your judgment, is property under the existing system sufficiently represented?
It is not, even with the *ex-officio* guardians.

1011. In your union, what proportion of the rates do the owners pay?
About five-eighths.

1012. And taking the Loyalist occupiers, what proportion do they pay amongst them?
I have not calculated that, but they pay a very considerable portion of the rate. If you add what the Loyalist occupiers pay to what the landlords pay, I should think that they pay over three-fourths of the rate.

1013. *Lord President*.] What do you mean by "Loyalist occupiers"?
The supporters of the Loyalist candidate at elections. There are also a number of people, not actually owners but practically owners, who hold under very long leases,

8th May 1885.] Mr. TYRRELL. [Continued.

leases, leases for ever perhaps, but they are not returned on the valuation books as owners; they are holders of large property in the union very often.

1014. Is "Loyalist" an ordinary description, a proper technical term?
I do not know that it is, but I do not know how better to describe them; at all events the voters opposed to the National League candidate are popularly termed "Loyalists."

1015. *Chairman.*] It means those who are not National Leaguers?
Yes.

1016. What is the proportion of *ex-officio* guardians and elective guardians in your union?
They are equal.

1017. Are they practically?
There was one vacancy at the time I made up the return, thus leaving 30 elected guardians and 29 *ex-officios*.

1018. I believe some of your *ex-officio* guardians are non-resident?
Yes.

1019. How many?
There are nine non-resident.

1020. *Lord President.*] Do the non-resident guardians ever attend?
Yes, occasionally; some of them do.

1021. *Chairman.*] What is the state of things with regard to the general attendance of the *ex-officio* guardians?
Some of them never attend; for instance, the Duke of Leinster never attends the Board; nor the Earl of Rosse, who is chairman of another Board, and resides 40 miles away; and there are other cases of *ex-officio* guardians similarly circumstanced. But I find that taking the whole number of *ex-officio* guardians they attended on an average 9·4 days last year; the elected guardians altogether attended 14·5 days last year on an average. Then if you take the resident *ex-officios*, they attended 14·1 days; so that their average attendance is almost identical with that of the elected guardians.

1022. And I believe you have also before you the average attendance of the National League guardians?
Yes, it is 12·7 days.

1023. That is considerably less than the attendance of the *ex-officios*?
Yes.

1024. Who is the chairman of your union?
Captain Longworth Dames, D.L.

1025. I believe, in 1882, he was not the chairman?
No.

1026. Who was the chairman then?
Mr. Paterson, an "ex-suspect."

1027. I presume as he was an "ex-suspect" he was a National League candidate?
Yes.

1028. From that fact I suppose we may take for granted that the majority of the board were then National Leaguers?
They were.

1029. What was the state of things under those circumstances?
The attendance of *ex-officios* was very bad; I attended and one or two others, but their attendance generally was very bad.

1030. Viscount *Powerscourt.*] Why would not the *ex-officios* attend?
The action of the National League guardians made it very disagreeable for them to do so.

1031. Lord

1031. *Lord President.*] Could they have prevented the election of Mr. Paterson?
No, they could not have prevented his election at the time.

1032. If they had come and voted, I mean, could they have prevented it?
If all the non-residents, such as the Duke of Leinster, and the Earl of Rosse, had attended, they might have been able to do so; but those who ordinarily attended that year could not have prevented it.

1033. *Chairman.*] What was the result upon the rates, or was there any result upon the rates, from the fact that the board was in the hands of National Leaguers?
The rates have been better administered since.

1034. But what was the state of things in 1882?
At the end of 1882 the union was considerably in debt.

1035. Was it the case that they had struck an insufficient rate?
Yes. They had struck about the same rate, as well as I can remember, as the year before, but it had not carried them through.

1036. I believe you got back Loyalists to the board in 1883?
Yes.

1037. And the majority is now the other way?
Yes, the Loyalists have now a small working majority.

1038. And what has been the result of that?
A considerable decrease in the rates, and a very much better financial state of the union.

1039. *Lord President.*] How do you explain the change that took place at the last election; how do you account for it?
To a certain extent in this way; Mr. Paterson's nomination as chairman took the Board by surprise; the ratepayers did not anticipate that an "ex-suspect" would have been put forward for the chair, and they were not prepared for it; they were rather negligent up to that time in registering their votes; the management of the union had for 25 years been in the hands of another chairman, and they did not anticipate that this Mr. Paterson would have been elected, and they did not perhaps look after the election as well as they might have done.

1040. Viscount *Powerscourt.*] It was their own fault, in fact?
Yes, it was their own fault; they had the same power then as now, if they had exercised it.

1041. *Chairman.*] When there was a return to a better state of things, was the result, to a considerable degree, owing to the use of the proxy vote?
To a certain extent it was, but not entirely.

1042. Have you had any experience of any jobbery in regard to contracts that took place during the time that the National Leaguers held the board?
I do not remember any jobbery with regard to contracts during that year; but, as a rule, the National League party are rather inclined to assist their political friends at the expense of the rates.

1043. With regard to the giving of contracts to the highest bidder, I mean?
I have known a number of cases in which contracts were given to the highest contractor, though the other was a properly qualified person.

1044. And on what grounds were they given?
Simply on political grounds.

1045. Have you heard Mr. Bagwell state his scheme as regards electing property guardians?
I have.

1046. What do you think of it?
I think that so far as our union is concerned you would have an equal number returned from each side, and I think it would end in a deadlock.

1047. Viscount

8th *May* 1885.]   Mr. TYRRELL.   [*Continued.*

1047. Viscount *Powerscourt.*] But the chairman would have the casting vote if an equal number were returned?
I do not know. At present at the board of guardians the chairman has no casting vote.

1048. *Chairman.*] He has a vote, has he not?
He has a vote at present, but not a casting vote.

1049. Do you think that six votes is enough for persons who are rated at more than 200 *l.*; that is the maximum, no matter what the rating is?
I do not. I do not see why you should stop at 200 *l.* There are many occupiers rated at over 200 *l.*, and they are not sufficiently represented by having six votes.

1050. A rating of 2 *s.* 6 *d.*, I believe, gives a vote?
Yes; I know a Nationalist was allowed one vote for a profit rent of 10 *d.*

1051. What do you say to the number of votes which under a recent decision one person can give; it is now, I believe, held to be 30?
Yes.

1052. It was formerly supposed to be only 18?
Yes.

1053. What do you say about it?
I see no objection to return to the old ruling of 18.

1054. *Lord President.*] Which the Bill does?
Yes; but I would do it by aggregating the rated lessor rating with the occupancy rating.

1055. *Chairman.*] Perhaps you would explain that, as it is rather complicated?
Under the present ruling, if a person is occupying a farm, say rated at 90 *l,* he gets three votes; if he is rated as immediate lessor of a cabin on that same farm, rated at 5 *s.*, he is allowed an additional vote upon that, while an occupier rated at 90 *l* 5 *s.* has only three votes allowed him, though he pays the same rates as in the first case, where the ratepayer is allowed four votes.

1056. That is owing to this recent decision?
Owing to the recent decision. I think that the 5 *s.* rating for the cabin should be added to the 90 *l.* occupation rating, and the number of votes calculated on the aggregate valuation.

1057. As a whole?
Yes, the separate valuations aggregated together. This was the practice before the recent decision of the Court of Appeal.

1058. Have you anything else you would like to say with regard to this Bill?
I think that the suggestion that the *ex-officio* guardians should be allowed to resign if they do not wish to act, is a good suggestion. Some of the *ex-officios* on the list at present are physically unable to attend. One I know in the Edenderry Union is a very old gentleman; another *ex-officio* guardian is paralysed, and cannot attend except with very great difficulty; and if these had the power of resigning, others might be put on in their place who would attend.

1059. Viscount *Hutchinson.*] Have you more magistrates than you want to fill up all your seats on the board?
No, at present there are not more, only just the number; but it is different in other unions.

1060. *Chairman.*] How do you propose to fill the places of those who resign?
It might happen that another qualified person would come forward. At present a resident magistrate must go on as an *ex-officio* guardian, whether he likes it or not; then the highest rated non-residents are put on, if there are not sufficient residents to make up the required number. If the power was given for a resident to resign, one of the non-residents might be elected in place of him, and might be able to attend better.

8th May 1885.] Mr. TYRRELL. [Continued.

1061. But how do you explain your remark that the non-residents are more likely to attend than the resident?
In the case of a very old gentleman who cannot come out, or in the case of a paralysed person, it is possible that that may happen; because "non-resident" may mean that the person lives really within a very short distance of the workhouse, although in a different county.

1062. Viscount *Powerscourt*.] It sounds rather curious that a man who is not there attends better than a man who is there?
He may live in the union, but he is not deemed a resident if he does not reside in the county for which he acts as a magistrate; I am myself a "non-resident" *ex-officio* of Edenderry Union, because, though I reside only half a mile from the workhouse, my residence is in the King's County, while I hold the commission of the peace for the County Kildare. Though I am a "non-resident" my attendance last year at the board was the second highest out of all the guardians elected or *ex-officios*.

1063. Lord *Saltersford*.] There was a question which Mr. Bagwell could not answer, but which perhaps you could answer, with regard to the present law; do you recollect how many proxies one individual can hold as the maximum?
He can hold proxies for 20 landowners.

1064. *Chairman*.] How long does it last?
For five years, unless revoked in the meantime. The person appointing the proxy can revoke it at any time.

1065. But it dies of itself in five years?
Yes, it must be renewed in five years. I think it might be a good plan to have it renewed every third year, so as to come in every election.

1066. On the eve of the election, I presume?
Yes; two months before it is the suggestion here.

The Witness is directed to withdraw.

MR. JAMES GRAY, having been called in; is Examined, as follows:

1067. *Chairman*.] I BELIEVE you are Clerk of the Roscrea Union?
Yes.

1068. How many years have you held that post?
Thirty-six.

1069. You have then very great experience with regard to the Poor Law?
Yes.

1070. You have considered this Bill, I believe, now before the Committee?
I have looked carefully through it.

1071. What do you say to Clause 9, which proposes to abolish the proxy vote?
I should say that the proxy vote should by all means be retained; otherwise you disfranchise a very large proportion of property.

1072. Do you see any objection to it as it now exists?
No, I do not see any objection to it; in fact, I would rather go further; I would give proxies to a class that do not at present enjoy the privilege of proxy voting.

1073. Viscount *Powerscourt*.] What class?
The class of occupiers.

1074. *Chairman*.] What reason do you give for that suggestion?
I would say that it would be quite essential in view of the ballot, if adopted.

1075. Why; will you explain that?

In

8th May 1885.]   Mr. GRAY.   [Continued.

In case of the ballot I think it should be extended to property in the owner's hands as well as to property that is not in the owner's occupation. The present system of allowing proxies is as regards property not in the owner's occupation. The same reason as applies for allowing it to property not in the owner's occupation, that is, to landlords who may be absent, would apply with more force to property in his own hands, and where he may be absent, or with fully as much force.

1076. I suppose in the case of aged persons, or infirm persons or women, it might be a great advantage?
Yes, with a view to the ballot I think it would be absolutely essential, because many of those persons would be otherwise disfranchised if the proposal in the Bill were carried out.

1077. Perhaps you would just explain that a little more clearly; why do you say that they would be disfranchised?
The Bill proposes that they should be required to vote in person. Sick persons or persons at a distance could not, of course, vote in person; on the other hand, there would be need of caution lest persons should come in and take up a lot of votes for proxies and so make invalid votes.

1078. Viscount *Hutchinson*] Are you speaking now of the occupier?
Yes, I am speaking of the occupier.

1079. That would have to be guarded against?
It is with regard to occupiers the matter would be practised more. From experience, I think, that there would be more of that kind of work practised with regard to occupiers than there is at present in proxies.

1079*. *Chairman*] Have you heard any complaint amongst the people at large as regards the proxy vote, whether they object to it?
No; on the contrary, the parties on both sides very freely register both their proxy and their property votes; as, for instance, previous to the last election, which was very fully contested in the Roscrea division, the property was all fully registered; everything was done in the fullest possible way on both sides.

1080. Can you suggest any other means by which absent owners of property would not be disfranchised?
I have heard some doubt about allowing absent owners to vote by post, on the ground that that would invalidate the secrecy of the ballot, because the returning officer without some complicated machinery would know something himself about how a party voted.

1081. On the whole, you know of no system so fair and against which so little complaint could be made as the proxy?
No, I think it is very fair.

1082. Now with regard to Part II. of this Bill, which speaks of the election petitions; what do you say about it?
I would say, with regard to the petitions, that in order that there might not be captious objections taken and points raised on one thing or another (because I know it to be the case that there are very frivolous and very vexatious questions raised at elections), I would have it provided that at least there should be a recognisance entered into to prosecute the petition, and for costs against the petitioner if it were given against him.

1083. Have you anything more to say upon that point; what about its being brought before the county court judge?
I was thinking of it in this way: Cases are brought before the county court judge where the defendant resides. Then if an electoral division be, say, in the King's County (as with us we have King's, Queen's, and Tipperary), I was thinking that if the contest and the petition arose out of a matter in the King's County it should come before the county court judge of the King's County; if, on the contrary, in Tipperary, then before the county court judge of Tipperary, and so on. I think that, when speaking to one chairman, he said perhaps

(O.I.)   O   the

8th May 1883.] Mr. GRAY. [*Continued.*

the best thing would be to have all appeals tried in the county where the union workhouse is situated.

1084. What do you say about compelling the petitioner to lodge a security for costs; do you think that that is a good suggestion?
In ordinary appeals there is a recognizance entered into that the appeal will be prosecuted.

1085. And you think that that should be the case in regard to these petitions?
Yes, I do; to prevent frivolous and vexatious appeals.

1086. Do you wish to say anything more on that head of the Bill?
No.

1087. *Lord President.*] Do you mean that you would give the costs against the petitioner, even if the appeal were not frivolous and vexatious?
No, I would let it come against the union; because, in fact, the respondent in that petition is the union, the electoral division, say; because the expenses incurred in elections belong to the electoral division. There are general expenses regarding the elections, but the special expenses belong to the electoral divisions. Therefore I would say the ratepayers, who are really the respondents, should pay.

1088. *Chairman.*] What do you say to Part III. of the Bill in regard to the proposed lowering of the qualification of the guardians to 12 *l.*: Part III., Clause 25, Sub-section (4) is: "Any ratepayer in a poor law union rated at or exceeding 12 *l.* shall be qualified to be elected as guardian for any electoral division in such union"?
I think that would be very wrong. Our qualification is 20 *l.*, and I think it is quite low enough.

1089. I believe the qualification for common jurors was lowered?
Very much, and it had to be raised; it was found to be productive of a great deal of dissatisfaction, an immense deal of dissatisfaction in the administration of justice; I mean the law at first providing for the selection of jurors; and the qualification had to be raised.

1090. What is it now?
£. 40 occupation, and 20 *l.* leasehold, and 10 *l.* household.

1091. Do you think it right that a guardian, who is charged with an important public trust, should have a lower rating than a common juror?
I think he ought to have at least as much; I would rather propose raising the qualification.

1092. What is the qualification for the dispensary committee?
£. 30.

1093. The Bill does not propose to alter that?
No, because that is under a different Act of Parliament, the Medical Charities Act.

1094. The result would be that the qualification for the Board would be less than that for the Board's committee?
As at present, our guardians' qualification is 20 *l.*, and in order to make up the number for a dispensary committee you must select a 30 *l.* ratepayer.

1095. Viscount *Hutchinson.*] And under your present system it is possible, I suppose, that no 30 *l.* ratepayer might be there to be elected?
That would be so in very rare cases in Ireland. For that same reason the Local Government Board have power to lower the qualification for guardians, and they do so in order to enable them to get guardians in the remote districts in the west and south.

1096. *Chairman.*] And, in fact, they do lower the qualification?
For different counties there is a special qualification for jurors, both for common jurors and for special jurors; they are classified.

1097. Viscount

8th May 1885.]   Mr. GRAY.   [Continued.

1097. Viscount *Hutchinson.*] But with regard to guardians, how does the matter stand?

I think for the two Dublin unions the qualification is 30 l., and then the Local Government Board have power to fix, and they have fixed, the scale for other unions down to 10 l., and 15 l.; and we have 20 l.

1098. You do not happen to know what the lowest qualification in Ireland is?
No.

1099. Lord *Monk Bretton.*] The Local Government Board have power to vary the qualification not only in different unions but in different electoral divisions of the same union, have they not?

I cannot say; but I know that they have generally fixed the scale of the union.

1100. Is the qualification for a member of the dispensary committee fixed by Act of Parliament at 30 l.?
I think it is.

1101. The Local Government Board have no power to vary that?
No, I think not. I am not quite certain about that, but I know it is fixed at 30 l.

1102. *Chairman.*] What do you say about the proposed reduction of the number of *ex-officios*?
I think it would work badly.

1103. What objection do you see to it?
We can have a selection from a larger number, and so it is very likely that in that case we may have better men. The fact of the matter is that my opinion about that is founded very much upon a fact, and a curious fact it is, if you will allow me to state what it is. I may say, and it will be borne out by figures, that our union has been working remarkably well since the year 1849, and it was in 1847 the number of *ex-officios* was increased. Previous to that date I have laid my hand upon some minutes of the Board, which show a very unsatisfactory state of things indeed, and it was in the year 1846, just about the very time the increase was being contemplated.

1104. You have had, in fact, experience of the state of things when the *ex-officios* were less in number, and also the state of things since they were increased to their present number in 1847?

Yes; the unsatisfactory condition to which I refer occurred before my entering the service of the Roscrea Union; but I have extracts taken from the minutes, which will show that things were in an unsatisfactory state under the other system.

1105. *Lord President.*] In what respect unsatisfactory?
As to the money matters, very unsatisfactory; as to the appointment of officers, rate collectors, for instance.

1106. *Chairman.*] What was the state of money matters; was the union bankrupt?

It was practically. It appears by a minute of the board that a cheque for 25 l. was dishonoured, and at the same time there were 50 poor men looking for payment of their turf contract; and you may think how poor these men were when the whole contracts, 50 of them, only amounted to about 6 l. a piece, or say 315 l.; and money could not be procured for them until the clerk and a guardian went security to the bank for part of it, namely, for 100 l., and two guardians went security for 200 l.

1107. So that the bank preferred the security of private individuals to that of the union?
Yes.

1108. Lord *Sudley.*] Was not that the time when the country was impoverished by famine?

(O.1.)   O 2   It

8th May 1885.]   Mr. GRAY.   [*Continued.*

It was about becoming so; but it was in the year 1846; the worst of the famine had hardly come at that time.

1109. *Chairman.*] I believe the board were unable to take advantage of low contracts if they were required to pay cash?
Yes, I found in connection with the same minutes, and at about the same time, that is in September 1846, that a party tendered for oatmeal at 22 *l.* 10 *s.* per ton for six months contract, or he would give three tons at 19 *l.* 10 *s.* cash payment. On the following board day I found that the clerk reported that the contract for the three tons at 19 *l.* 10 *s.* had not been supplied; and I found on subsequent board days that the guardians had to advertise for oatmeal and Indian meal in consequence of that man not supplying.

1110. What was the proportion at that time of *ex-officios* to elected guardians?
There have been 23 of each, since 1847 to the present time.

1111. But before that; in 1846, what was the proportion?
Before that it was nine *ex-officios* to 28 elected, one-third.

1112. And this was the result which you have described?
It was a fact which occurred there at all events.

1113. *Lord President.*] Do you account for the improvement by the fact of the increased number of *ex officios* since 1847?
Yes; you may take it as an inference; but it is a fact that the union has been going on remarkably well ever since.

1114. Viscount *Powerscourt.*] But every union in Ireland was in the same state at that time, was it not?
I cannot say; I can say for myself what the fact was in this case, because I have taken it from the records.

1115. *Lord President.*] Have you the actual number of *ex-officios* who attend; do the *ex-officio* guardians of the Roscrea Union attend in large numbers?
No, not in very large numbers; not more than say one to four; but before I came away I looked to see what was their attendance upon the election of the officers at present in the service of the guardians, and I find that taking the whole of them, there was an average of 17 elected and eight *ex-officio*. The day I was appointed myself I found 16 elected and 14 *ex-officios*. So in the case of the master, 18 elected and 13 *ex-officio*; he has been a long time in their service too; he has been 34 years in their service.

1116. *Chairman.*] What is the condition of your union now?
A very good condition; very fair. Our average rating is exactly half the average of all Munster, and it is not above two-thirds the average of all Ireland.

1117. To what do you attribute that?
To very close attention on the part of the guardians; and there is one element in the management of our board, and that is we exclude all politics whatever.

1118. You do succeed in excluding them?
We do.

1119. Then I presume what has been called the National League element is not in the ascendant in your union?
It may be there, and, of course, I, as the officer of the board, can see it, but we never mention those things. We can see, perhaps, indications of it which of course I am not at liberty to say anything about; but the fact is that it is practically excluded. The guardians would not even allow me to read for them circulars coming from other unions bearing upon political questions.

1120. Viscount *Hutchinson.*] I suppose you get a number of those?
We do, a great many.

1121. *Chairman.*] You are quite the exception in Munster; is that so?
I think it is.

1122. And,

8th *May* 1885.]   Mr. Gray.   [*Continued.*

1122. And, as a matter of fact, your rates are on the average about one-half the average for all Munster?
Precisely one-half the average of all Munster.

1123. Viscount *Powerscourt*.] Who is your chairman?
Mr. William Peisley H. L. Vaughan, of Golden Grove, Deputy Lieutenant of King's County.

1124. *Lord President*.] I suppose your out-door relief is very moderate in amount?
Yes; in point of numbers our out and our in-door relief are about the same; but our out-door relief is about 2¼ d. in the £. Our guardians, especially the *ex-officio* guardians, offer a good deal of resistance to the out-door relief; but there is no deserving case that is absolutely refused; not one. For instance, for last year, the year ending 29th September 1884, the out-door relief cost 666 l.; that is over 2¼ d. in the £. It decreased, strange to say, from the famine year, 1849. The next period that I took, after an interval of five years, was in 1853, when it was 4 l.; after the next five years, say, to the 29th September 1858, for the entire year, there was only 1 s. in out-door relief; 1 s. altogether, and now it is 2¼ d. in the £.

1125. When did it begin again to be given?
From that shilling, which was in the year ending 29th September 1858, it rose to 42 l., 176 l., 448 l., 515 l., 633 l., and 666 l. You see there is a gradual increase, a tendency to increase; but there has been a proportionate resistance to the extension of the out-door relief. And there is one thing that the guardians do very carefully; every four weeks they revise the entire list of out-door relief.

1126. *Chairman*] Is that an unusual thing to do?
It is.

1127. Lord *Salterford*] Do changes frequently occur at the revision of the out-door relief list; are there frequent reductions made at the revision of the list on the fourth week?
Yes; sometimes cases are added to, sometimes decreased; but the increases generally come between the four weeks, and then we have a complete revision every fourth week.

1128. *Chairman*.] What proportion of the rates is paid in your union by the owners?
The proportion of property is as 64 per cent. to 36 per cent.

1129. That is to say, the owners pay 64 per cent., as I understand you?
Yes; the property contributes at the rate of 64 per cent., and the occupying ratepayers at the rate of 36 per cent.

1130. That is to say, the owners of property contribute 64 per cent.?
Yes.

1131. Have they any direct representatives on your Board except the *ex-officios*?
No, I may say not: we have one, perhaps.

1132. Could they return an elected guardian with their own unaided votes?
There is only one division where they could.

1133. And there you think they could?
Yes, I think they could; I am sure they could.

1134. And in all the others, nothwithstanding the enormous proportion they pay of the rates, they could not turn the election?
No, they could not. Perhaps you will allow me to refer to an allusion I made before. I said that in the Roscrea electoral division we have had a contest; we have had several, but this last year was an open contest. I, myself, acting on a prerogative that I have as returning officer, have never allowed either the general public, the candidates, or anybody to be present; in fact, I have practically acted upon the ballot all the time, till last year. Pressure was then put on, so that

8th May 1885.] Mr. GRAY. [Continued.

that I found it expedient and right to allow the parties all to be present, that is the candidates and their proposers.

1135. Viscount *Hutchinson*.] At the scrutiny you mean?
At the examination, the making up of the votes; and the thing was done you may say in a very public way, and it was done in a most complete way, and so that nobody could make any complaint regarding it. I found that the property votes represented 479 and the occupiers votes 540, although in that same electoral division the property contributes on 8,508 *l.*, and the occupation votes represent 4,002 *l.*

1136. Lord *Monk-Bretton*.] When you give the number 479, those are property votes?
Yes.

1137. How many persons do those votes represent?
I issued 700 voting papers; 1,011 votes represented 700 persons; there was plurality of votes.

1138. Then were there 700 voters altogether?
Yes.

1139. Taking owners and occupiers, altogether?
Yes.

1140. Now, I ask, how many owners' votes were given?
Four hundred and seventy-nine.

1141. And how many persons gave those votes?
I did not make any such calculation; but it must must be comparatively few, because the owners have a great plurality of votes.

1142. How many occupiers' votes were there?
Five hundred and forty.

1143. Could you tell how many persons those were given by?
No, I did not make that up.

1144. Have you any doubt that the number of persons in the case of the occupiers were very much larger in proportion to the number of votes than in the case of the owners?
The number of occupiers was larger in proportion to the number of votes. The way I take it is this: each property owner represents a greater number of votes than the occupiers would represent.

1145. Lord *Silchester*.] Is this Bill required at all by way of improving the administration of the poor law?
I should say better leave things as they are. Perhaps there might be one or two alterations that I might suggest.

1146. Viscount *Hutchinson*.] What are they?
One is in regard to adding proxies for the occupiers; that is for the owners when their holdings are in their own possession.

1147. Lord *President*.] Do you mean that you believe there would be no advantage in introducing a system of vote by ballot for the poor law elections?
Yes, I do think there would be an advantage in it.

1148. But that is a principal provision of the Bill?
But that is the principle upon which I have been acting, and therefore I say that the vote by ballot would be an advantage; I have been acting on it myself practically.

1149. You were asked whether you thought it would be better to have no Bill at all, and you said you did think so?
I did not think of the vote by ballot when I gave that reply.

1150. Lord *Silchester*.] I did not quite complete my former question; would a different class of guardians be in all probability elected or would they perform their duties in any different way, as the result of this Bill?
I should

I should say they would hardly act as well if this Bill be passed, for it would lower the standard of qualification, and it might take away some of the advantages that property ought really to derive; I mean if it passes in its present shape.

1151. *Lord President.*] Do you think that under the system of the ballot there would be some prospect of elections not depending as much upon politics and agitation as they do now?

There would be considerable protection, and parties would be freer to vote according to their own conscience and their own will. I may say that the reason why I acted as I have stated I have done, was because of my seeing that there was a great deal of pressure put upon the ratepayers. There is a discretion left with the returning officer whether he will allow these things to be published or not by admitting the parties to be present at the scrutiny; and I thought it would be most injudicious to allow the voting papers to be published, that is to say how the parties voted; and therefore I kept the thing quite secret.

1152. Do you think, under the ballot, there would be more chance of a person being elected, because he would make a good guardian, than because he was a political character?

I should think so.

1153. Viscount *Powerscourt.*] Do not you think that it would be better if you have a scrutiny of papers that you should have it public, so that (I do not say there is any suspicion) it should be impossible that there should be any suspicion?

The scrutiny, as at present authorised, requires that the returning officer and the rate collector should conduct it themselves. It is optional with the returning officer to allow the candidates and their proposers to be present; but if he refuses to allow them, he should give a good reason for it; and I have always had what I considered a valid reason, in the feeling that prevailed through the union or through the electoral division, and the pressure that was put upon the voters; in fact it was more for their protection than for mine, because it was rather a ticklish thing for me to do.

1154. I should think it was very ticklish; I do not mean to say that the papers should be published, or the public informed who the votes are by; but I mean to put to you that the actual scrutiny itself ought to be public?

But you cannot have a scrutiny of the papers without making it known.

1155. There should be witnesses?

Witnesses; but in this recent case they took notice how every man voted, and it was a matter of threat that how every man voted would be known on this occasion.

1156. Lord *Shute.*] Then I think we may gather that although from your own experience you think that things might be left as they have been hitherto, you are decidedly in favour of the ballot being introduced into elections for guardians, as a matter of protection for voters?

I think it is better to introduce it as a matter of protection, because you see my own conduct has been to carry it out as far as I could in that way.

1157. Lord *Monk-Bretton.*] Are you in favour of having guardians elected for three years?

I think it would be a very good thing. There is always more or less of a little ferment in our little communities you know; and to stave the election off for three years I think would not be at all a bad thing.

1158. *Chairman.*] You would make the ferment less, if possible, instead of more?

Yes.

1159. Lord *Shute.*] Do you think that the plan suggested by Mr. Bagwell, with regard to the election of guardians, that it should not be entirely triennial, but that one-third of them should be elected every year, would be a good plan? It

8th May 1885.] Mr. GRAY. [Continued.

It would be keeping up chronic irritation. I think I would rather have it all together once in the three years.

1160. Lord *Saltersford.*] Has your attention been called to the Tenth Clause, the provision for making the list: "At the prescribed time before the day fixed for the polling at any poor law election, the returning officer shall prepare in the prescribed manner a list of the ratepayers entitled to vote at such election, and shall sign the same, and shall publish in the prescribed manner a notice stating that such list has been prepared, and when and where it may be inspected by any ratepayer. Every such list shall state the number of votes to which each voter is entitled"; and so forth?

It would be quite necessary in view of the introduction of the ballot. At present there is a discretion, in fact I can scarcely say a discretion, left to the returning officer as to the claims to vote. Once they are registered with him, having been signed in the presence of a magistrate, he takes them as a *primâ facie* evidence of the fact; and he must not allow anyone to have access to these; and there is a difficulty then in anyone objecting to them; and that process of having a day upon which all the claims could be examined previous to the election, I think, would not be a bad idea; I think it would be absolutely necessary in view of the ballot.

1161. And do you think it desirable that the rate should be paid as at present up to the very last, or at the time of making the claim?

At the time of the making out of that list, say, some definite time.

1162. You think the rates ought to have been paid then?

Yes. At present there is sometimes confusion as to the payment of rates, and it is by all means desirable that the rate should be paid before.

The Witness is directed to withdraw.

Ordered, That this Committee be adjourned to Tuesday next, at Twelve o'clock.

Die Martis, 12° Maii, 1885.

LORDS PRESENT:

Earl of MILLTOWN.
Viscount POWERSCOURT.
Viscount HUTCHINSON.
Lord SALTERSFORD.

Lord KER.
Lord SHUTE.
Lord MONK-BRETTON.

The EARL OF MILLTOWN, IN THE CHAIR.

MR. HENRY SMYTH, having been called in; is Examined, as follows:

1163. *Chairman.*] I BELIEVE you are a magistrate for the county of Roscommon?
Yes.

1164. I do not know whether it is an invidious question to ask, but are you classed as a landlord or as a tenant farmer?
I am a tenant farmer.

1165. What we call a gentleman tenant farmer?
In Ireland we call it so; I call myself a farmer.

1166. You have had a great many years' experience, I believe, as guardian?
Something over 30 years.

1167. During part of that time you were an elective guardian?
Yes.

1168. And 22 years an *ex-officio* guardian?
Yes.

1169. I believe at one time you were vice-chairman of the union?
Yes, for some years.

1170. When was that?
For five or six or seven years prior to April 1882, when I became temporary resident magistrate in the County Tipperary.

1171. Who was elected in your place?
A gentleman who at that time was, I think, in gaol; a merchant; he was a Land Leaguer. He was in gaol as a suspect.

1172. What do you mean by the term "a merchant"?
He was a shopkeeper.

1173. Now, have you looked at the Bill at present before this House?
Yes, I have read it carefully.

1174. I believe you approve of the clause providing for triennial elections?
Yes, generally, if proper precautions be taken to prevent greater expense, and to put the expense on the contesting parties, not on the rates. I greatly dread that a great deal of the expense may be made by mutual consent to fall on the boards of guardians, if some safeguards be not introduced.

(O.1.)   P   1175. How

12th May 1885.]　　　　　Mr. SMYTH.　　　　　[Continued.

1175. How is that at present; there is at present hardly any expense on the rates?
There is none at all.

1176. But you anticipate that, should the ballot become the law, there will be very considerable expense owing to the polling booths that will have to be established in the various electoral districts?
Yes.

1177. And you think that expense ought to be borne by the candidates?
A considerable portion of it should be borne by the candidates certainly, as in Parliamentary elections. Take the election for an electoral division, under the ballot, in which the clerk of the union will be, I presume, the returning officer; he will have to go out with a paid staff to the scene of the election, and he must employ paid assessors; be will have to pay all those out of the rates of the division, which will be a very considerable expense; also the ballot boxes and renting a house; all those expenses will be incurred if the ballot be accepted, and I think no reasonable man can contend that the ballot is not required now.

1178. With regard to the expense, you said something about the rent of a house; do not you think that the petty sessions court of the district could be utilised for the purpose of taking the ballot?
In the electoral divisions, petty sessions courts are sparse, and, therefore, that could rarely be done.

1179. Are there a great many electoral divisions that have none?
Yes.

1180. And you think, in those cases, a room would have to be provided for the purpose of the ballot?
Exactly so.

1181. And you think that the expense of that ought to be paid by the candidates?
If my own opinion were of any value, I should prefer the election taking place at the workhouse, which would save expense.

1182. It would save expense to the rates, but it would entail considerable inconvenience on the electors, would it not?
They would have to walk 8 or 9 or 10 or 12 miles.

1183. Lord *Monk-Bretton*.] Could the school-rooms be used for the purpose?
It is doubtful whether the National Board would allow it.

1184. *Chairman*.] Do not you think it would be rather a hardship on the candidates for the office of poor law guardians that they should be put to a large expense which would have to be incurred solely in consequence of a proposed alteration of the law?
A small ratepayer thinks it no expense to walk 8 or 10 or 12 miles.

1185. But is there any suggestion that they should be called upon to contribute towards the expenses supposing the electoral district system be established?
Practically, if he is to get a list of voters; at present he has to pay for it.

1186. How much?
A few shillings; whatever the clerk may choose to charge him for it.

1187. May the clerk charge him anything he pleases?
There would be a row if he charged too much, but I have known him to charge so much for a list of voters.

1188. How much has he a right to charge?
I do not think any scale is laid down.

1189. It seems a great hardship, does it not, that he should charge anything?
It is a long thing. He gives the book to any ratepayer, and he allows the

ratepayers,

ratepayers, if they like, to make the extract. Every man is not quite competent to do it.

1190. There is no printed list?
No printed list.

1191. Then what is your suggestion with regard to the deputies whom the returning officer must have for the purposes of carrying out the ballot?
Supposing it to be adopted, I would suggest that he should have either the head constable of the district or of some neighbouring district appointed by the county inspector as his assessor, with some number of constables of some literary capacity; they would be free.

1192. Would they be entitled to make any charge for that?
No, they do not charge.

1193. So that would get rid of a considerable item of expense?
Yes, or if a local magistrate was appointed not connected with the division, it might do equally well; but there would be objections to that.

1194. At the same time they would of course be more trustworthy persons, more impartial persons than anyone selected at random from the neighbourhood?
Yes. Then in the ballot some precautions would require to be taken for the larger votes, which could easily be identified.

1195. I will ask you about that in a minute; but on what ground chiefly do you think it would be desirable that you should have the ballot substituted for the present mode of election?
It is so in Parliamentary elections, and I believe in municipal elections; and I am sorry to say that there is a good deal of intimidation at present on the popular side, and it would modify that.

1196. There is a good deal of intimidation, is there, to your knowledge?
To my knowledge. Might I quote an instance?

1197. Will you please do so?
At a recent election contest between two guardians in the Roscommon Union, in the largest division of the union, one man was a pretty extensive farmer, and he calls himself a Nationalist, but he has the misfortune to have taken land, which gives him the name of being what is popularly called a land grabber; and the other was a man who was already elected for a division, but he opposed the former on the principle that it was his duty to oppose any man who was not a practical Leaguer; and the large man, who was the land grabber, as they said, was returned. One of the local papers, the organ of the party, immediately published a full list of every person who voted for that man, in order to show the country people who were the people who voted against what is called the National cause. Side by side in the same paper appeared resolutions from the local Land League boards denouncing these people, and calling upon the country ratepayers not to buy from or sell to those people in the future, and saying that they would know who were their friends. I take it that although that could have no bearing on the past election, it will have a very distinct bearing on the election which will and must take place against the same man next year; and it appears to me so boycotting, that it makes me, although not loving the ballot individually, think that it is wanted.

1198. Viscount *Hutchinson*.] It makes you think that some protection is wanted?
Some protection is required, in my opinion.

1199. *Chairman*.] With regard to the mode of conducting the ballot, what suggestion have you to make?
I think that the ballot should have all the precautions of the Parliamentary ballot at as little expense as possible, with an extra precaution which is rendered necessary through the number of votes. A large ratepayer having six votes, and there being only two or three of those voters perhaps in a division, they could easily be identified by the clerk and other people when the votes were gone into.

into. There are not very many in some of the rural divisions who would have that number of votes.

1200. Your suggestion is, I suppose, that separate voting papers should be issued, one for each vote?
Exactly so.

1201. Viscount *Hutchinson.*] You suggest that separate voting papers should be issued, one for each vote; would not that entail a great deal more labour, and considerably more expense?
Mere penmanship or printing.

1202. That means expense, does it not?
Printing is nothing, absolutely nothing as far as expense goes.

1203. Lord *Shute.*] What objection would there be to conducting the election in the same way as the ordinary Parliamentary election; there are no voting papers there?
But a rated elector may have from one to six votes, and it might so happen that in a particular electoral division (I have my eye on one such) there is only one having six votes; then it would be known to the clerk and other people, when examining the votes, how that particular voter voted; there being only one man having six votes in the constituency, perhaps only two or three having five, and so on. The present system would be quite efficient for one vote.

1204. Viscount *Powerscourt.*] That would do away with the secrecy of the ballot altogether?
It would, certainly.

1205. Lord *Shute.*] Would you do away with the six votes?
No, I would give the voter all his votes, but let him give six separate voting papers; instead of voting in one, I would let him vote in six.

1206. Do you think there would be any danger of a voter entitled to a large number of votes being mobbed outside?
Well, it has been done.

1207. And there are no means of preventing that except by the police, I suppose?
It is very hard for the police to prevent mobbing in Ireland in times of excitement.

1208. *Chairman.*] I suppose if he did escape mobbing, he would stand a very good chance of being boycotted?
That would be so, if such a thing ever gets strong again.

1209. That, hitherto, the police have been unable to prevent?
The police, individually, could not prevent boycotting.

1210. Lord *Saltersford.*] You think that a person known to give a particular vote might be exposed to odium?
Yes. A large proportion of the voters in my part of the world are Roman Catholics, and at the chapel on Sunday a voter would be exposed to taunts and unpleasantness, which he could escape by saying that he did not give his vote in the way supposed.

1211. He might express an opinion one way, and vote another, you mean?
Yes.

1212. And so avail himself of the secret vote?
Yes, and help to return the man he considered the best man.

1213. Lord *Ker.*] Is it the case that it is generally known beforehand which way a voter will vote?
Well, it is now.

1214. *Chairman.*] Is it your opinion that men who would probably otherwise vote for the Loyalist candidate are coerced by intimidation at present to vote for the League candidate?
Quite so.

1215. And

1215. And you think that if they had the protection of the ballot they might be enabled to give an independent vote for the men they think best qualified to sit on the Poor Law Board?
That is exactly my present idea. I have always been a non-ballot man till lately.

1216. At present they are compelled to give a vote, through intimidation in many cases, on solely political grounds?
On political grounds.

1217. Have you considered the question of the abolition of the proxy vote, as proposed in this Bill?
Yes.

1218. What do you say to that?
I say that if you strike out proxy votes you strike out the voting power of at least three-fifths of the parties who pay or allow rates in my part of the world. In other parts the proportion is very much larger. You are aware that the landlord at present allows one-half of the poor rates paid by his tenants; he pays directly for the holders of 4*l*. and under the whole rate; and he pays for all land, demesnes, and farms in his own possession the full rate.

1219. How much, in your opinion, do the landlords pay, either by allowances to their tenants or directly; what proportion?
About three-fifths the landlords pay or allow. They pay as 3,619*l*. is to 2,823*l*.; those figures are roughly made out by myself from the rate book.

1220. How many elective guardians have you in your union?
Nineteen.

1221. How many of those are returned by the League vote?
I think there are 14 or 15 that are what are called "advanced men." A recent division shows that to be the number of very advanced men who adopt every shibboleth of the League.

1222. So that out of the 19 elective guardians the landlords either return, or aid in returning, only four or five?
That is so.

1223. And yet they pay, as you tell us, three-fifths of the entire amount of the rates?
Yes; my contention is that the landlord proxy vote so influences the four or five Loyal divisions that it gets in a moderate representative.

1224. Supposing the proxy vote to be abolished, would the Loyalists still retain the four or five seats out of the 19 elective guardians on the board?
No, I think they would not retain one.

1225. Then the proxies turn the scale at these four or five elections?
Yes.

1226. Are they used in the other electoral districts?
Proxy votes in my union have not been extensively used at all. I have never seen them used in more than five or six electoral divisions in an experience of 33 years.

1227. What do you attribute that to?
The landlords are largely absentees, and they do not take the trouble to issue the proxies. Some are in London, and some are in France, and some are in other parts of the world; and some do not take any interest in local affairs.

1228. But supposing they did make use of their proxy votes, would that be sufficient to turn the scale in the 14 cases out of 19 where the League candidates are now returned?
It would exercise a very great influence if they did, but not sufficient. I could quote the numbers of a couple of rural divisions if you pleased. I will take a division in which I have resided myself for over 30 years. The valuation is 3,374*l*. There are 170 rated voters. We have only five owners of property in

12th May 1885.] Mr SMYTH. [Continued.

in that division, and those five owners can only, at the outside, poll 28 proxy votes; 28 proxy votes, in a constituency of 170, making 198 in all, could have only a turning influence.

1229. Have you ever heard any complaint amongst the people at large against the proxy vote?
No, I have never heard any complaint at all against it.

1230. Do you consider that the number of votes now allowed to the landlord for tenants rated at 4 l. and under (in which cases, as you know, he pays the whole of the rate), is sufficient?
I think the proxy vote requires some modification; my own idea is that it looks an anomaly that a man with perhaps 300 l. or 400 l. or 500 l. a year should have the same number of proxy votes as a man who may have so many thousands, because the man with so many thousands allows half of the rate; each man allows half of the rate in his electoral division; and I have seen the case of a small landlord who polled as many as 20 votes because he was resident, while the very largest proprietor could not poll more than six votes; and my suggestion, if I might presume to offer one, would be, that after the first six votes for 200 l. there should be two proxy votes added for each 100 l. up to some limit, 20 or 25 votes.

1231. Now passing on to Part II. of the Bill, what do you say to the provisions with regard to election petitions?
No doubt the chairman of the county would be a more competent person to decide difficult questions of election practice than a poor law inspector, who has no training of that sort, generally speaking.

1232. By "the chairman of the county," you mean the county court judge?
Yes.

1233. Therefore, you approve of that so far?
Yes, providing there is no expense for costs put on the ratepayers.

1234. A suggestion has been made that the petitioner should lodge security for costs; do you think that that is a good idea?
I think so; and then the costs might abide the decision as in ordinary cases, to be paid by the party who had failed.

1235. Under no circumstances, you think, ought they to be put upon the rates?
I think not.

1236. Because you think that the effect of doing that would be to increase the risk of frivolous petitions being lodged?
No doubt; anything that goes on the rates does not create much dissatisfaction amongst some of the guardians.

1237. Have you any other observation you would like to make on the subject of election petitions?
No, I am in favour of the provision that the tenure of office should be for three years.

1238. That we have passed from; but I am asking now on the question of election petitions in Part II. in regard to poor law elections?
No.

1239. Coming now to Part III.; what do you say to the clause which prohibits persons under 21 years of age from voting?
I should imagine that could be got over by their guardians voting for them.

1240. No doubt it can be got over, but do you think it is desirable that it should be so got over?
I think so.

1241. You see no reason why the guardian or trustee should not be entitled to vote for the minor?
No; the property being there, and paying the rate.

1242. What

1242. What do you say to the proposal that every *ex-officio* guardian should be a ratepayer of the union?
I am quite with that; I have seen some scandals through *ex-officios* having no qualification whatever.

1243. And that, I daresay, was naturally thought a hardship by the elective guardians?
Yes.

1244. And, to a certain extent, by the other *ex-officios*?
Yes. A man who had never had any property might be the chairman of the board, and might be very profuse and liberal with the rates, which is just the way to get popular.

1245. What do you say to the proposed reduction of the qualification for a poor law guardian?
I am against that. I think it is as low as it possibly could be.

1246. What is it in your union?
£. 20.

1247. We have heard that the Local Government Board can practically fix it at any amount they please?
In some parts of Ireland, where valuations are very low, in Mayo, for instance, and places like that, it is often hard to get a man who will take the office at all, and 20 *l.* would be too high there; but in the south of Ireland that is very low indeed.

1248. And considering that the Local Government Board already possesses that power of fixing the amount lower; you think it unnecessary and undesirable that it should be arbitrarily fixed in this manner by an Act of Parliament?
I think so; it would have the result of pitchforking a lot of mere nominees without any interest in the rates into the board to oust well-qualified men. I have known the seat of a Member of your Lordships' House taken by a very petty shopkeeper indeed; the seat of a man who had always been a resident, and owning three-fourths of the division, was taken by a petty shopkeeper, who had his name on the rate book, but was not actually a ratepayer.

1249. And seeing that the chief business of the poor law guardian is to look after the rates and the expenditure, there is not much analogy between the election of a poor law guardian and the election of a Member of Parliament, whose duties are totally dissimilar?
Quite so. The poor law guardian deals with money expended before everything else. He should represent rates if he represents anything.

1250. Now passing to the proposed reduction of the number of *ex-officio* guardians, what do you say to that proposal?
It would not be of a great deal of consequence if they were made resident, because in practice it is a small portion of them who attend; but the great advantage to my mind of the *ex-officio* element is, that it leavens the board; it gets us a set of men who have some educational training, who are gentlemen, and who know something of accounts and take large views, and who will influence even a very advanced board. I think a reduction to one-third would not be very serious, but we rarely get a third.

1251. Do you see any reason why it should be done?
I see no reason, except that there is a doubt in many cases whether, through having no qualification, they are ratepayers at all; that is the cry against them.

1252. Lord *Shute.*] It is your opinion that the non-attendance of the *ex-officio* guardians is due to idleness on their part, or to want of care, or is it because their position is made disagreeable to them by the elective guardians?
During the last three years that was so; they practically ceased attendance, save at the election of the chairman; generally speaking, there was a muster for the chairman's election, and the *ex-officios* attended then in a body, to try and get in a chairman; but they were liable, in many cases, to very gross insults, you

you know, and they did not attend; and as a consequence the rates went up, I think.

1253. *Chairman.*] We will come to that in a moment; you attach considerable importance to the election of a good chairman, I think?
Yes, every importance.

1254. Supposing the number of *ex-officios* were reduced, as proposed in this Bill, the chances of the selection of a good chairman would, I presume, in your opinion, be diminished?
Yes.

1255. And the election of a bad chairman would tend still further to decrease the attendance of the *ex officio* guardians?
No doubt.

1256. And, therefore, on that ground you see no reason why the reduction should be made?
No.

1257. What do you think would be the result of the non-attendance of the *ex-officios*?
The result would be, I believe, primarily, a very large increase of rates.

1258. On what do you ground that statement?
Up to about 1879 our gross rate never went beyond 5,000 *l.* in my union, but from one cause or another, the year after, our so called famine year, in 1881–82, our rate was 6,377 *l*, while in 1884–85 it had sprung up to 7,506 *l*, being an increase of 1,125 *l.*; that is nearly 20 per cent.; while the numbers relieved are about the same, and our contracts are very materially lower. The out-door relief has gradually increased from 500 *l.* to 900 *l.* and 1,000 *l.* yearly. This increase of out-door relief has arisen altogether in the year when the *ex-officios* did not attend, and could not attend; at a time when many people would say it was unsafe for them to attend.

1259. Do you mean by "unsafe," that they ran personal danger?
Unpleasant questions were raised, and outside a man incurred great odium. In 1880 our out-door relief was 730 *l.*; in 1881 it was 936 *l.* Then the *ex-officios* ceased to attend, and those who could attend were afraid to do anything; it rose then, until it amounted in 1883 to 1,072 *l.* From that day the *ex-officios* have been attending, four or five of us regularly, and now we have reduced it down to 900 *l.* a year, and I hope we will reduce it further.

1260. I believe you can give some instances to the Committee, cannot you, of excessive out-door relief having been given during this period?
Yes. In 1881–82 some men were arrested as what were called suspects, being suspected of a crime, and it was at once proposed to give them out-door relief in the division that they come from, of Drumdaff, to the amount of 1 *l.* a week in each case.

1261. To give their families, you mean?
Yes, to give their families 1 *l.* a week. I could not get anyone to support me in opposing it. The elective guardian for the division was afraid; he was an advanced Land Leaguer, and would not take any step. It was useless to divide the board; I would have had no supporter except Lord Crofton, who was then an elected guardian. Things were bad enough, and I did not wish to make anyone unpopular. I drew up a protest against the allocation of the out-door relief, and got it on the minutes; and the Local Government Board wrote down calling attention to the fact that the out-door relief in the form of 1 *l.* a week in cash was illegal, because it should, under the Poor Law Act, be in food and fuel, and they disallowed it so far. The next board day, the board of guardians continued the 1 *l.* a week, charging it in food and fuel, and went through the farce of buying so much meal and so much flour and so much sugar, and everything else in that way, on Saturday at a favoured guardian's establishment; and the men got their pound a week. I then drew up another protest on the ground that these men were not what are described as poor persons within the meaning

of

of the Poor Law Act, and that the out-door relief was altogether excessive; that they had cows, sheep, cattle, land which was of value under the Land Act; and I stated that I protested (although not paying rates in the division, I was then vice chairman of the union) against the rates being so applied. The Local Government Board took no action on that. They were a little inclined to go with the times at that time, and they let it be, went to sleep. I was under police protection at the time, and I was sent away as a resident magistrate to Carrick-on-Suir The auditor came down, and he disallowed the out-door relief on the grounds which I stated in my protest. The guardians then went before the magistrates, and procured the magistrates to decline to surcharge the chairman. The auditor took it before the Queen's Bench, and the Queen's Bench had a great case on it, and a great deal of costs were incurred; and I believe there was a division on the ground that the Local Government Board had committed what is called in law a *laches*, in not taking any notice of the protest which came before them, and no Rule was made; the result being that this unfortunate division had to pay the whole of the costs. The chairman got out of it, and the division had to pay it; and I believe we owe the costs to our solicitor of the appeal and all; yet of course it will have to be paid in the future; and that never could have taken place if we had not been afraid. There were men on that board as inclined, and far more inclined to do what was right, probably, than I was, but they did not dare to support the right course.

1262. Viscount *Hutchinson*.] Do you mean to say that if these gentlemen who you say were afraid, had come forward and voted, they would have turned the scale?
I do believe there were men enough at that time to have done so; there are not now. I looked round the room, and I could not count on anyone that I could say would have supported me (and I had a great many personal friends there) save Lord Crofton. He would, but I felt it would be doing wrong to ask anybody. The times were very bad.

1263. The feeling was so bad that you believe yourself that it would have been absolutely dangerous to these gentlemen to come forward and vote that way?
I believe that it was so then.

1264. *Chairman*.] With the present formation of the board, formed as it now is, do you think there would be a majority of that way of thinking, and that a similar resolution might be passed under similar circumstances?
It would. I read a case reported in the papers within the last three weeks, in the south of Ireland.

1265. Lord *Shute*.] Lord Monk-Bretton and myself are the only two English Members of this Committee now present, and I have no doubt that he will agree with me that such a state of things as you have related would be perfectly incredible if it did not come from your mouth to us, as Englishmen, who have to do with boards of guardians; but do I really understand you to say with regard to these suspects, that although they had land and cattle, and all that kind of thing, their families were given indiscriminately 1 *l*. a week?
Yes.

1266. Irrespective of the number of their families?
Probably the number of children may have been considered; but the normal rate of relief in our union at that time never went beyond 3 *s*.

1267. For each individual, do you mean?
No, for the family.

1268. And in the case you have related they put it at 1 *l*. ?
Yes.

1269. But these were people who had got property?
They did not own those properties; they were ratepayers having a limited interest.

(O.1.)   Q   1270. But

1270. But I suppose they did not pay any rent?
I know as a matter of fact that they were not paying rent.

1271. *Chairman.*] I believe you can corroborate the statement of what happened there, which I will just now read out to you: "When the head of a family was arrested as a suspect the Land League guardians proposed and carried that 1 *l.* per week be given. This illegal relief was continued for four weeks, when the Local Government Board sent down a sealed Order empowering the guardians to give the families of suspects food and fuel to such amount as the guardians might think necessary. Relief was then given in fuel, meat, tea, milk, &c. The auditor disallowed all the relief given, and the chairman who signed the relief orders was proceeded against at petty sessions"?
Yes.

1272. "His solicitor admitted that the 4 *l.* given before the Order of the Local Government Board, was illegal, but argued that as the sealed Order did not specify any certain sum for each family, the board had felt justified in giving the relief. The result was that the magistrates gave a decree for the 4 *l.*, and dismissed the further claim. The auditor, Mr. Jephson, was not represented by counsel, but conducted his own case. It is the opinion of many that were this otherwise a decree for the full amount would be given. I do not know that there were worse cases than this, but I think there were. Although not a ratepayer in the division, I think it was a gross injustice that the poor ratepayers as well as the rich should be saddled with the large sum of 44 *l.* for the benefit of a well-to-do farmer having crops, cows, sheep, and horses of his own"?
Yes.

1273. That is your opinion, and you can corroborate that statement?
Yes. The case is reported in Ireland. I think my Lord FitzGerald was on the Queen's Bench at the time the case was tried.

1274. Lord *Monk-Bretton.*] You corroborate that statement?
Yes, that is a correct statement.

1275. That is, I presume, the very same case to which you referred just now in your own evidence?
Exactly.

1276. Do you accept that statement which has just been read out as a strictly correct statement of the case?
That is a correct statement of it; that was probably copied from the law papers.

1277. Because, if I understood that statement, and caught the words of it correctly, it is there said that the Local Government Board sanctioned the payment of a pound a week to suspects?
Yes.

1278. I apprehend that that was not the Order of the Local Government Board?
To the families of suspects; the suspects were in gaol.

1279. Were those the terms of the Order of the Local Government Board?
I could not tell you exactly what the terms were. They do not quite state that they are suspects; but it was on the ground that they were arrested as suspects that their wives and families got the pound a week. The reason they got that amount was that the Land League Organisation used to give a pound a week from their head-quarters in Dublin to the families of all the people who were arrested under Mr. Forster's Act as suspects; and in order to save the Land League funds the money was got from the board of guardians, if practicable, in order to make the landlords, as they said, pay, forgetting that the unfortunate tenants equally paid. That is the *rationale* of the whole proceeding. It looks very ridiculous now after two or three years' time, but still there are similar cases.

1280. *Chairman.*]

12th May 1885.] Mr Smith. [*Continued.*

1280. *Chairman.*] It was no joke to those who had to pay for it?
No joke. I know ladies in the place who were going to petition about it, but they got afraid.

1281. Lord *Monk-Bretton.*] Then that statement is one which we may take as an *ex-parte* statement of the case which you yourself have given evidence about just now?
Yes; I take it that it is in substance my evidence. The subsequent events happened after I had left the union, and I was engaged in very hard work in Tipperary, and had a lot of business to do, and I was merely kept *au fait* of the business in that union by correspondence and reading the local papers which were sent to me. But that statement is perfectly accurate.

1282. *Chairman.*] What I have just read, you say, is a perfectly accurate statement of what occurred?
Yes.

1283. Besides these cases of excessive out-door relief to those persons called suspects, of which you have given us information, are there other instances, to your knowledge, of excessive out-door relief given to evicted tenants?
They always get more than any others.

1284. What is the ordinary amount given?
We give from 1 *s.* 6 *d.* to 2 *s.* in ordinary cases.

1285. And what has the evicted tenant got?
The evicted tenant, even now, thinks anything less than 6 *s.* a week very wrong, and he will not work at all if he can get the out-door relief; 6 *s.* or 7 *s.* a week is about their normal rate of wages.

1286. Is that done with a view to punish the landlord who has evicted them?
That is the intention.

1287. Now, have there been any instances of jobbery lately in your union?
In what way?

1288. In any way; in regard to contracts, for instance?
I think it is not easy to job in contracts if you have anyone to watch you, even if it is only one in a large number, and the chairman is an honourable man.

1289. Lord *Saltersford.*] Have you never heard of a contract being given to an individual for political reasons?
Not in my union. Even one man on a board can prevent that from being successfully carried out.

1290. Lord *Monk-Bretton.*] But I think you told us that when the Local Government Board prohibited the payment of relief in money to the families of these ex-suspects at the rate of 1 *l.* a week, it was given in kind from the shop of a political supporter of the majority on the board of guardians?
What the Local Government Board did was this: on receiving my first protest against the 1 *l.* a week in cash, they sent down a circular calling attention to the clause under which it could be given, and they said if it was given under that clause it should be given in food and fuel; and it was given in food and fuel; and they said they would send down a sealed order authorising the grant for one month; the Act said it should be for a month only, and it was then that the sealed Order came down, and it was given. I then changed my ground of protest, and protested on the ground of the amount being excessive; and the articles were bought at the house, of course, of one of the guardians.

1291. Who was of the same political opinions as the majority?
To a great extent. He was a respectable man, of a better class than the ordinary Land Leaguer.

1292. *Chairman.*] You said just now that the present chairman was an honourable man, in whom you reposed confidence?
Yes.

1293. Supposing

12th May 1885.]　　　　　　　Mr. SMYTH.　　　　　　　[Continued.

1293. Supposing the Bill now before their Lordships' House were to pass in its entirety, and this reduction in the number of the *ex-officios* were to be made, do you think it probable that that chairman would be re-elected?
I greatly fear that he would go.

1294. Viscount *Powerscourt*.] You said that there were 19 elective guardians in your union, of whom 14 were Land Leaguers; how many *ex-officios* are there?
Nineteen; an equal number.

1295. How many of those attend, more or less, regularly?
Since I returned, four or five support me regularly. Quite lately, under the new regulation, some extra *ex-officios* have been appointed, and there is going to be a better attendance of *ex-officios* coming from another class.

1296. *Chairman*.] How many attend when the election of chairman takes place?
About 12 or 14 *ex-officios* is the most that have attended.

1297. Viscount *Powerscourt*.] But there are only four or five who attend regularly?
Only four or five who attend regularly.

1298. Lord *Saltersford*.] Are there more than that, or a considerable number more than that, who could attend regularly, who live within a reasonable distance of the workhouse?
There are not so many now as there used to be; so many resident gentlemen have left. I think 12 is about the most we could count upon. In the old days we used to be able to whip up a great many more; but now I think 12 would be the very outside.

1299. Lord *Monk-Bretton*.] If all the *ex-officio* guardians attended there would be a majority on the board against the Leaguers, I gather from your evidence?
Yes.

1300. How many electors of the guardians are there in your union?
I could not tell you in the whole union. I picked out a few divisions with which I was personally familiar, but did not go through the whole. The largest constituency is the Town of Roscommon; that returns two guardians, and that has about 450, I think, roughly.

1301. Of those 450, do you know what proportion are owners, and what proportion are occupiers?
There were 72 proxy votes cast at the election, which is just over 55 on the Loyalist's side and 17 on the Land League's side, and some did not vote.

1302. But my question had reference, not to the number of votes, but to the number of voters?
We cannot quite distinguish. You know one man may have anything, from one to 24 votes.

1303. But you told me that there were so many voters in the electoral union of Roscommon?
Yes.

1304. Upon that I asked the question, how many of those voters were owners, and how many were occupiers?
I must correct that by saying "votes" instead of "voters." The actual voters are there (*producing a list*), but it would be a long task to count them up.

1305. Could you tell, by an examination of them, how many of the total number of voters were owners and how many were occupiers?
I could, but it would take some time, I am afraid. A farmer may have a rented farm of 100 acres of land, for which he pays, near a town, 50 *l*., or 60 *l*., or 70 *l*., to an absentee landlord. He may have that actually let to a man for 200 *l*. a year, and that man would vote as a property owner for the difference
　　　　　　　　　　　　　　　　　　　　　　　　　　　　　　　between

between the rent that he paid his own landlord and the rent that he received, and then he claims to be an owner; and it would not be very easy to get at those men.

1306. You are not prepared to answer my question?
No, I could not, as to the exact number.

1307. *Chairman.*] But perhaps after your examination is over you could make the calculation for the noble Lord?
Yes, I could tot it up and tell exactly the number of voters that went to the poll.

1308. Lord *Monk-Bretton.*] The number that are on the rate book and could vote?
A great number did not, or would not, vote at all.

1309. That list you have got is a list of the men who did vote?
Yes.

1310. Not of the men who might vote?
It says, "the following were handed in blank, and are not returned."

1311. Viscount *Powerscourt.*] You said that the rates had increased largely in 1881-82?
Yes.

1312. And then still more in 1884-85?
No, they have decreased in 1884-85.

1313. Had the contracts of the union been raised at all in those years?
No, the tendency has been decidedly the other way.

1314. Then how do you account for it; is it mostly in out-door relief?
I account for it by the extravagance of the new class of men, who have not as great a stake as the guardians we used to have.

1315. For what purpose do you think the out-door relief in cash was used?
They spent it; an Irish small tenant farmer would take anything.

1316. *Chairman.*] He is not very singular in that respect, is he?
He has rarely so much that he would not be very glad to take anything that was offered to him.

1317. Lord *Skute.*] With regard to these insults that you said the *ex-officio* guardians were subjected to, do they take place outside the board-room or in the board-room?
In the board-room there would be very rough language used, but the more unpleasant business was outside. If, for instance, a man was driving, on the roadside, a band would get up and play a "O'Donnell abo," or a dead march, and everyone would commence spitting. I, myself, at the railway station, seeing off a lady member of my family, have been hooted and hustled, and got her across under a railway engine; and there are a lot of little things like that make life very difficult.

1318. You naturally said that you attached great importance to the election of the chairman, to the chairman being a proper person for the post?
Yes.

1319. I am speaking of what takes place in the board-room; an insult is directed by one guardian against another; would it not be the duty of the chairman to call the insulting guardian to order?
It is very difficult with the class of men that come in now; many of them are very rough, and do not understand any of the amenities of gentlemen at all.

1320. They would not understand being called to order, you think?
They would think it humbug.

1321. Lord *Saltersford.*] Has the chairman of a poor law board any power of enforcing order?
I do

I do not know. When I was chairman I used to say sometimes, "You may talk till evening, gentlemen, we cannot help it."

1322. Lord *Shute.*] The only way you would have of enforcing order would be to leave the chair, I suppose?
Yes.

1323. Now the evidence that is brought before this Committee is not published; therefore, it is to be hoped it will not get to Ireland; supposing it did, should you think that you would get badly treated in consequence of the evidence you have given?
I think not in that way now; I would get what is vulgarly called in Ireland, cross-hackled at the board of guardians, and be told I did not represent the ratepayers, and that I maligned them, and that I was a Rossmorite; that is a gentleman that supported the petition condemning the late Lord Chancellor. Those expressions were used quite recently in that board.

1324. Viscount *Hutchinson.*] I suppose you agree with one previous witness, that the position of a chairman in a case like that is extremely difficult; because we were told that if he was to enforce his authority to the bitter end, and complain to the Local Government Board, the *ultima ratio* would be the dissolution of the board of guardians, and the appointment of paid guardians?
Yes.

1325. And a chairman does not want to go that length, if he can help it?
It leads to great expense.

1326. It is altogether a very extreme step, and one that a chairman would not like to take if possibly he could avoid it?
Yes, and paid guardians are, of course, too extravagant; they will get in the rates.

1327. About this question of *ex-officio* guardians, you say that you have 19, and out of those there are practically only 12 to whom it is possible to attend?
Yes.

1328. There are, therefore, seven *ex-officios* who, by no possibility, could be expected to come to the board meetings?
They do not come unless there is strong pressure brought to bear, a whip.

1329. Have you ever considered that question about the impossibility of an *ex officio* guardian resigning. I suppose you know that under the present law once an *ex-officio* guardian is there he is there for life, unless he is turned out?
I did not know that he could resign.

1330. *Chairman.*] My noble friend is asking this question: Do you think it desirable that he should be able to resign?
I do, because many a man is kept on who does not want to attend, and keeps out a better local man who would attend.

1331. Viscount *Hutchinson.*] Do you believe that in the case of the Roscommon Union you would be able to fill up, from local men, these seven vacancies, and, at all events, secure a fuller attendance of *ex-officios* than you have got now?
I anticipate that there will be a much better attendance from the large accession to the magistracy. The primary qualification for an *ex-officio* guardian is residence, and there are a lot of new magistrates coming in who very soon will change the aspect of the *ex-officio* portion of the board.

1332. Quite so; but in what way will they change the aspect of it?
I take it that those having the disposal of the commission of the peace will look at the qualification in the way of ratepaying, and that those appointed will be large ratepayers, as a rule.

1333. But as I understand it, all the evidence shows that now the *ex-officio* element of the board is the element which represents property?
There is a theory that it did, but I am afraid the *ex-officio* was taken to represent loyalty.

1334. I think

12th May 1885.] Mr. SMYTH. [Continued.

1334. I think you will find the original idea was that he represented property. Are you inclined to think that the new class of men, the accession you look forward to in the magistracy, will represent property?
I think that those having the disposal of the commission of the peace will always look largely to property.

1335. Have you never considered whether there would be any other means of representing property besides *ex-officio* guardians?
I read Mr. Bagwell's proposition; I doubt its workability.

1336. Why?
I think it is a complicated plan. Landowners are a divided lot, living at far distances, and they will not all go together; and unless they gave their land agents their absolute power of proxy voting and authorised them to elect persons, not much could be done. If in the power of attorney which they give to collect rents and represent them, they included a power of attorney to look after their voting interests, something might be done.

1337. If I remember Mr. Bagwell's suggestion aright, his suggestion was that there should be a property qualification, and that the voting should be by means of voting papers?
Yes, that the landlords should vote for special candidates.

1338. A scheme of that sort would have the advantage of any scheme which involves representation by election over a scheme of selection like the one that exists now?
In the abstract it would certainly be fairer.

1339. And do not you think you would be likely to get a class of people, who, by being elected representatives, would be driven to take a greater interest in the proceedings of the boards of guardians than any selected persons would do?
Yes, I think you would. My dread is that the system is so complicated that you would not get the owners of property to take that interest in it which they ought to take.

1340. How "complicated"; if there is a system of election for occupiers for the elective guardians, would it not be just as easy to devise some system of election for property owners?
If a system could be devised, it would be a good thing; but they live so far apart in every union, and they are such a very divided number of people, and there are so many middle interests in Ireland, that the difficulties in the way would be great. In my union Lord Essex owns the whole fee of the union. Then under him there are half-a-dozen interests, large valuable estates in property under him; and then there are divisions and sub-divisions, plenty of men having considerable interests, who in England you would think were only ordinary farmers, and should never have sub-let at all.

1341. You think it would be a very difficult thing to work?
Yes. I think in dealing with sanitary matters we find great difficulties in getting at the real owners in towns in Ireland, there are so many middle interests, leases and sub leases.

1342. Viscount *Powerscourt*.] There are a great many middle interests in England too?
I have not been much in England for over 30 years.

1343. *Chairman*.] Might it not tend to embitter class animosities if there were such a system of electing representatives of property?
That is one thing.

1344. The object of every loyal man ought he to smooth those distinctions?
We have been trying to do that.

1345. Viscount *Hutchinson*.] That class difference exists now, does it not?
It does.

(0.1.) Q 4 1346. There

1346. There is a class feeling between the elective guardians and the *ex-officio* guardians, just as there would be between the elected representatives of occupiers and the elected representatives of property owners?
Yes.

1347. *Chairman.*] And this would intensify it more, you think?
Yes.

1348. There would be some difficulty also in distinguishing the case of a man who was owner as well as occupier, and deciding which class of guardian he was to vote for?
There would be, I think, some difficulty there.

1349. Lord *Saltersford.*] But would there not be a good many people holding the middle interests, whose feelings would go very much with the actual occupier; in that multiplicity of interests, taking the smaller immediate lessors, as well as the greater, their interests would be very much with the occupier, would they not?
My experience in Ireland is that once you become a landlord, you have a landlord's interests. Very strong class distinctions are widening, I am sorry to say.

1350. Lord *Shute.*] In answer to Lord Donoughmore just now, you said that in sanitary matters in Ireland there would be great difficulty in finding out the real owner; is it not the business of the inspector of nuisances to find out who the real owner is?
He tries to do so.

1351. What are the difficulties?
Take the town of Roscommon; Lord Essex made a lease 70 years ago, a building lease; a man built a house; on that the rent was 4 *l.* or 5 *l.* probably then, and that house was worth 30 *l.* or 40 *l.* or 50 *l.*; it at one time went up to be worth 70 *l.*, and that man set, or sold, or became bankrupt or died, and then left it to somebody who married somebody else, and it went into settlement with the lawyers, and Heaven knows how many interests have been created for children and the different parties voting out of the one title.

1352. Lord *Saltersford.*] Would not the immediate lessor in the rate book be the person to apply to for the abatement of the sanitary nuisance?
Yes, and there are special provisions in the Sanitary Acts to get over those difficulties as well as we can; but that is one of the things that causes trouble in working the Acts, the multiplicity of titles.

1353. *Chairman.*] Did I rightly understand you to say that there is at the present moment a large increase proposed in the magistrates of your district?
There has been a considerable increase in the county.

1354. Is there any particular reason for that?
The idea is that the present Government wish to widen the magistracy, and to appoint every eligible Roman Catholic; that is the popular idea.

1355. If you had an increased number of magistrates, you might have a number from whom to select the *ex-officios*, supposing that the elective principle was introduced in their selection as has been suggested by some witnesses. At present, as we know, the highest rated magistrates are the *ex-officios*, no matter whether they are resident or not, or whether they attend or not?
Yes.

1356. It has been suggested that the magistrates should elect out of their own number certain persons to form the *ex-officios*?
Yes.

1357. And the theory is that men who are elected for a purpose are more likely to attend to the business for which they have been elected than those who are simply there by accident or birth; supposing the number of magistrates, qualified or unqualified, at present in your district to be increased, do you think it desirable that that elective principle should be introduced in the selection of the *ex-officios*?

I think

12th May 1885.] Mr. SMYTH. [Continued.

I think that is a very good idea, but I do not know that it would commend itself to what is called the popular party at all.

1358. Lord *Saltersford*.] Is it not so at present, when the number of magistrates resident in the union exceeds the number entitled to attend at the board?
That is quite so. Residence gets the first; and in Tipperary there are a very large number of magistrates, and probably there are quite enough of resident *ex-officios*.

1359. *Chairman*.] But the suggestion that my Noble friend has made is, that when there are more qualified magistrates than there are places for on the board, the magistrates then select those who should fill the position; can you tell us how that is?
I can hardly contemplate any union where there would be more resident magistrates than there would be room for, except in Dublin, where a great lot of gentlemen are appointed to the commission of the peace merely for political purposes.

1360. Honorary purposes?
Yes, honorary purposes.

1361. Lord *Monk-Bretton*.] Is it not the law that in any union in which there is a greater number of qualified resident magistrates than the number who may sit as *ex-officios*, then the highest rated are taken?
I should say it is. Of my own knowledge, I could not tell you that there is such a clause in the Act, but I should imagine it is so; that the clerk goes through them and takes the highest rated; he takes the farmers according to the rating.

1362. *Chairman*.] Where there are not a sufficient number in residence he then selects the highest rates on the list?
Yes.

1363. That we know; but in the case where there are too many to fill the number of places, does he select from the number of those who are highest rated?
I could not say from my own knowledge.

1364. As a matter of fact, it is the clerk who selects them and not the magistrates?
Yes, the clerk is the returning officer.

1365. Viscount *Hutchinson*.] With regard to your own union, I want to ask you a question arising out of Lord Monk-Bretton's question; you say that there is a large increase in the magistracy in Roscommon; now, supposing that the power of resignation were to be exercised, do you believe that among the new magistrates fit and proper persons could be found, who would be more likely to attend the board of guardians than the present *ex-officios*?
I think that if there was a power of selection of resident men, it would be for good.

1366. Not "power of selection," but power to create vacancies or possibility to create vacancies, is what my question points to?
It would come to the same thing. I think the power of resignation would be a very good one, because, I think, any man who never attends at all had better resign, and make room for one who would attend.

1367. What would be the effect of it, in your opinion?
I ought first to explain that I did not mean that in the Roscommon Union, but in the county of Roscommon, there had been a large increase of the magistracy.

1368. *Chairman*.] Your union extends over some adjacent counties?
Yes, it is only a portion of Roscommon; we take in a part of Galway, a little part; but we are chiefly in Roscommon.

The Witness is directed to withdraw.

(O.1.) R

12th May 1885.

Mr. JOHN B. HEWSON, having been called in ; is Examined, as follows:

1369. *Chairman.*] I THINK you are a magistrate of County Limerick ?
Yes.

1370. And you have had some experience of the poor law system ?
I have been 32 years a guardian.

1371. Of what union ?
Rathkeale.

1372. During a part of that time as an elective guardian, I believe ?
Ten years as an elective guardian.

1373. And during the remainder as *ex-officio* ?
Yes.

1374. And, I believe, for the last 15 years you have been vice chairman of the board ?
Yes, and previous to that I was deputy vice-chairman.

1375. Looking at the Bill now before the House, I believe you approve of the proposal that elections for the future should be conducted by means of the ballot ?
Yes.

1376. What do you say as to the question of a separate voting paper being given for each vote ?
I think the best way would be to give a separate voting paper for each vote a man is entitled to. What I would propose to do would be to have a book with blocks, and the numbers corresponding in the blocks with the voting papers, and when a person came into the booth to apply for his vote that the assessor should look to see how many votes he had, and give him the number of voting papers corresponding with the number he was entitled to, and he should sign these and put them in the ballot box.

1377. Do you think it is desirable that provision should be made for that by the Act, and that it should not be left for the Local Government Board to frame the conditions by Order ?
Yes, I think it would be better to have it in the Act.

1378. Have you any other suggestion to make with regard to the ballot ?
I would have the dispensary districts the places for taking the ballot. There would be half-a-dozen electoral divisions perhaps in each dispensary district, and the electoral divisions are generally grouped round the dispensary ; and there is generally a court house in the place where the dispensary is.

1379. Are the dispensary districts and the electoral divisions always coterminous ?
Yes.

1380. But one dispensary district would contain a large number of electoral divisions ?
Yes, but the electoral divisions are always in a ring close round it ; and I think it would be no hardship to the people who wanted to vote to have to come to the court-house where the dispensary is, or the dispensary house, and vote there.

1381. Some of the dispensary districts extend over a vast number of miles, do they not ?
Not in the south of Ireland ; they may in some of the out of the way places in the west of Ireland.

1382. For instance, my own dispensary district of Blessington and Ballimore Eustace, is 12 miles round ?
They could increase the number of dispensary districts if they wished.

1383. But

12th May 1885.] Mr. HEWSON. [Continued.

1383. But taken as a rule, in the southern districts of Ireland, the dispensary districts are not large?
No; it would not be right that they should be, because the people have to go to the dispensary in order to get medical relief.

1384. And that plan would get rid of the cost of hiring a room for the purpose?
Yes.

1385. But supposing any expenses to be incurred, do you think it right that they should be put upon the rates, or that the candidates themselves should bear them?
I think they should be put upon the rates; it is a public matter.

1386. What do you say to the proposal to abolish proxy voting?
I think it would disfranchise the greater part of the landowners in Ireland. I think the larger part of the property in Ireland is held by people who do not reside, and they would lose their power of voting entirely.

1387. I believe you rather want to extend it than abolish it?
I would rather extend it in a modified degree.

1388. In what way?
I think it is hard on very large proprietors now that their maximum number of votes stops at 200 *l*.

1389. But that observation applies not only to the proxy vote but to the occupancy votes?
It does. I would extend the occupancy votes too.

1390. Do you think, also, that the power of giving a proxy vote should be extended?
Yes; I think the power of giving a proxy vote should be extended to land in the owner's occupation. At present, the owners have the right of voting as occupiers and also as owners of the land they occupy; and there are many owners that occupy but do not reside, and these owners lose their power of voting for the land they occupy by not having the right of appointing a proxy.

1391. Take an instance of a farm of 200 *l*. held in fee; the owner there would have 12 votes, six as occupier and six as owner?
Yes.

1392. If he did not reside, as I understand your proposal, it would enable him to give six of his 12 votes by proxy?
Yes, and now he loses both. He cannot vote as occupier, because he does not reside; and he cannot vote as owner, because he cannot appoint a proxy for land in his own occupation.

1393. What do you say as to compelling an owner to re-register his right to vote?
I think it is very hard lines. I think that once a man establishes his claim to vote, unless it comes under the cognizance of the clerk of the union that he has lost the qualification, he ought to be entitled to hold it for life. An occupier, once his claim is established, remains on the rate book, and is never taken off; but the owner, unless he renews his claim every five years, now loses his right to vote.

1394. Can you see any reason why that should be so?
I see none. It is a great deal more difficult for the owner to establish his claim in the first instance than for the occupier; in fact, the occupier has to do nothing except have his name entered in the rate book, while the owner has to go through a very troublesome form.

1395. What do you say about the provisions for election petitions in the Bill?
I think, so far as I could see, the Bill is very fair about that; I think there is no amendment I could suggest in it; I think the county court judge is the proper person to hear the petition.

(0.1.) R 2 1396. A suggestion

1396. A suggestion has been made that in order to prevent frivolous petitions, the petitioner should be obliged to lodge security for costs?
I approve of that.

1397. You think it a wise suggestion?
That is a proper safeguard.

1398. What do you say as to the provisions for preventing a minor from voting?
I would allow the minor to vote through his guardian.

1399. Through his guardian or trustee?
Yes. At present I think neither lunatics nor minors can vote.

1400. What do you say to the proposal to reduce the qualification for an elective guardian, and fix it at 12*l*.?
I would abolish the qualification entirely. I would have no qualification. I think that where a man represents others he need have no personal qualification of his own; that is to say, no property qualification.

1401. Then you think the same rule ought to apply to the guardians as to Members of Parliament, who we all know may be men of no property whatever?
Yes, and I will tell my reason. There is very often a difficulty in getting proper people with the required qualification. In the union where I live I took a great deal of trouble to make property votes in a place where there was an ex-suspect as guardian; I wanted to get the division contested; and there were only about half-a-dozen people that were qualified, and the result was that I could not get any of them to contest the place; and if the qualification had been greatly extended I could have got plenty of men.

1402. Then your motion, as I understand it, is that if anything is done about the qualification, it ought to be to abolish it altogether?
I would abolish the property qualification altogether.

1403. What do you say to the proposed reduction of the number of *ex-officio* guardians?
I think it would be very unfair; I think that either the *ex-officio* guardians or the people representing property, should be equal in number to the elective guardians.

1404. What do you think would be the result if the proposed reduction were carried out?
The result would be that it would throw the whole management of the unions into the hands of the men that represent the farmers now, and that while the owners were paying the larger amount of the rates they would practically have no voice in the management of the unions.

1405. What do you think would be the result of that?
The result would be what it generally is where people are dealing with other men's money; they are generally very lavish in their expenditure.

1406. And you see no reason to think that there would be any departure from the ordinary rule in this case?
No; in fact, my experience shows that in unions where they have the management they are most extravagant, even with the present safeguards.

1407. Can you give any instances of that?
Yes; in the Rathkeale Union, up to the year 1862, the management of the union was entirely in the hands of the *ex-officio* guardians. At that time there was a great deal of sectarian feeling in the union, and a great change was made in the board, and it came entirely under the hands of the farmer guardians, and the result is an enormous increase in the rate. In the year 1859 (which was the only year when I could get at the return; the reason I selected it was because I could not get the returns for 1863 or 1862, because you cannot put your hand upon the old papers) the rate in our union was only 2,592 *l.* as the whole rate for the year. That was an average poundage of 11½ *d.* The numbers allowed

out-door

12th May 1885.] Mr. Hewson. [Continued.

out-door relief that year were only four. In the year 1884 the rates were 7,917 *l*., and the average rate was 2 *s*. 10 *d*., and the numbers on out-door relief were 810, and the numbers in the workhouse were only 160.

1408. Viscount *Hutchinson*.] Have you a large town in your union?
There are two or three towns. Rathkeale is the second town in the county, and Askeaton is a populous village, and also there is another village, Pallaskenry.

1409. *Chairman*.] Has the population increased?
No, the labouring population has diminished one-half.

1410. With half the population the rate has increased in this enormous manner, you say?
Yes.

1411. And the out-door relief also?
Yes.

1412. Lord *Ker*.] What was the average out-door relief in 1859?
I could not tell you; some very small fraction.

1413. Would 10 *s*. cover it?
I suppose 4 *l*. would cover it.

1414. *Chairman*.] To what do you attribute this increase in the rates?
To the management of the board having got into the hands of the elective guardians, the representatives of the farmers. I am afraid that the out-door relief is used now in supplementing the wages of workmen and herdsmen; that is to say, a berdsman will be herding a farm, and he will get no regular wages from the farmer. He will have his house, and he will have a little plot of ground, or perhaps grass for some goats and a cow, or something of that kind; and he will have an old mother living with him, and the old mother will be put upon out-door relief. That helps the family to herd the land.

1415. Under these circumstances, would the herd be a herd to one of the poor law guardians?
He may be, or to some friend of a poor law guardian, or to some person who takes an active part in returning that poor law guardian.

1416. Have you known out-door relief given in any other irregular manner?
Yes, I have known one case where out-door relief was given to a tailor to buy a sewing machine; I think 6 *l*. was given. I was not at the board the day it was given, but I heard it afterwards. And I knew another case where money was given to a smith to roof a forge. It did not appear in that way on the books. The appearance on the books is, so much a week given; but the relieving officer was authorised to give so many weeks *in globo*. It appeared all right in the book.

1417. Lord *Monk-Bretton*.] How was it put down?
The man was put down under the medical head as not being very well.

1418. The sewing machine was charged as medical relief?
I will not say exactly as medical relief, but there is a column in the relieving officer's book where he must put down the qualification for a man to get relief; and in this case he was put down as suffering from debility or something of that kind; some expression that had a very wide meaning.

1419. Viscount *Hutchinson*.] The Chairman asked you the question whether it was not possible for the herd, whose family or mother was being relieved, to be the herd of a poor law guardian?
He might be herd for a poor law guardian.

1420. Do you find it at all common, when a guardian of a certain electoral division is anxious to get anything of that sort done, that he finds a good deal of support from guardians of other electoral divisions in hopes of favours to come?
Yes, according to the old saying "Scratch me and I will scratch you." I have often known very large amounts of out-door relief to be given to evicted tenants.

tenants. I knew one case in which an evicted tenant got 1 l. a week. I was chairman the day it was given to him. I was told that the Local Government Board had sanctioned the giving of a large amount of relief to evicted tenants, but I did not know at the time what I heard afterwards, that the man had cattle and other means of living. The usual relief to a family would not have exceeded 5 s. or 6 s., but because he was an evicted tenant he got that large amount.

1421. *Chairman.*] You were in the chair you say on that occasion?
Yes.

1422. Did you sanction that?
I sanctioned it. I was told that the Local Government Board permitted four weeks' relief to be given to an evicted tenant, allowing the guardians to give what they thought proper whether the men were able-bodied or not.

1423. You mean by that, I suppose, four weeks to be given at once?
No, but to get the relief for four weeks in weekly payments.

1424. Lord *Ker.*] Did he get it in money?
He got it in money.

1425. *Chairman.*] Then does the 1 l. mean four weeks at 5 s. a week?
No, it was each week 1 l. a week.

1426. Viscount *Powerscourt.*] You said that dispensary districts might be increased in number to meet the convenience of electors?
Yes.

1427. How do you propose that should be done?
The Local Government Board have the power of making any number of dispensary districts they wish in a union.

1428. Lord *Saltersford.*] It is in the power of the guardians, is it not?
No, I think the Local Government Board have the power.

1429. Viscount *Powerscourt.*] Would not that very much increase the expenses of the union?
They might divide the present medical district, with one medical officer doing in two divisions the work he is now doing in one division. The present districts are attended to by medical officers, and they would take two districts in place of one. I have known two districts amalgamated into one, and I do not see any reason why one should not be divided into two. I may observe that I think it would be very well to avoid bringing electors into one locality at the time of an election. If they were required all to attend at the poor house to vote, the mob influence would have more power than it has at present. It has been found in the county elections that where the number of polling places was increased the power of the mob was decreased very much by scattering the voting about in different places; and I think the same would happen in regard to the voting for guardians.

1430. *Chairman.*] We were speaking of what was likely to be the result, supposing the elective guardians or those elected under the present state of feeling were to get matters altogether into their own hands; I think you have some instances to give us of the kind of animus that they display towards the landlords, for instance, with regard to labourers' cottages?
Yes. In our union they have selected boycotted farms and places of that kind, in many instances, to put these labourers' cottages on; the object, I believe, is to put the evicted tenant in as occupier of one of the houses to annoy the landlord, or any other person taking the evicted farm.

1431. With regard to excessive out-door relief to evicted tenants, have you known instances of that?
Yes; I knew one instance which I particularly remember, where a man got a pound a week.

1432. An evicted tenant?
An evicted tenant.

1433. What

12th May 1885.]   Mr. Hewson.   [Continued.

1433. What is the usual amount?
The amount, I think, generally does not exceed 5 s. or 6 s. a week, unless in case of sickness; we sometimes give more than that if a family are all ill, but that is about the maximum.

1434. Now with regard to the striking of dispensary committees, that is done once a year after the formation of the new board?
Yes, after the formation of the new board.

1435. Have you known any political feeling introduced into that matter?
Yes, that is a very common thing to do whenever there is going to be an election, or whenever it is anticipated that there will be shortly an election of doctor for a dispensary district; for instance, if the doctor is very ill, and it is probable that he will either die or resign, there is immediately an attempt to manipulate the committee for the coming election. There are a certain number of men who are neither elective guardians nor *ex-officios*, who are members of the committee, and these are elected by the boards of guardians, and the great object is then to put on the committee as many of these people as it is thought will be safe to vote for a certain candidate.

1436. Have you known them strike off desirable members of the committee on political grounds?
I have known men that were for years members of the committee struck off just on that particular occasion, in order that they might not have a vote for the election of doctor; and some of these men would be perhaps put on again after the election was over, the next time. Talking of the election of the dispensary committees, I would suggest that whoever represented the landlords, whether *ex-officios* or whoever they may be, they should be appointed at the same time that the other guardians are appointed, because difficulties occur now upon the dispensary committees. The *ex-officio* guardians are appointed now after the 29th of September every year; the elective guardians are appointed after the 25th of March; the dispensary committees are appointed after the 25th of March; and the *ex-officios* are all members of the dispensary committees where they own property; and the result is this: that sometimes a committee will be appointed on the 25th of March, and an *ex-officio* guardian will come on on the 29th of September, and some member of the dispensary committee must go off then to admit the *ex-officio* guardian; and there is always a great piece of work then as to who is to come off, and that leads to a great deal of ill-feeling; but if the dispensary committees were formed at the same time, that is, if the *ex-officios* were all appointed at the same time as the elective guardians are, nothing of this kind would happen. The dispensary committees are formed on the 25th of March; the *ex-officio* guardians are re-appointed every 29th of September as guardians. There is continually a change in the *ex-officios*; and when men leave the union, the magistrates who reside in the union have a precedence over the magistrates who do not reside; but as soon as a man leaves the union some other person comes in in his place; his appointment takes place the 29th of September; the committees are already formed at that time, and as soon as he is made an *ex-officio* guardian he must be made a member of the dispensary committee, and the committee have to be re-constituted again in order to admit him, and that obliges sometimes two elections in the year instead of one; whereas if the *ex-officio* guardians and elective guardians were appointed at the same time the committees could only be appointed at one time in the year.

1437. Viscount *Hutchinson*.] The only possible way we have been told by which an *ex-officio* guardian can vacate his office is by giving up his qualification?
The Poor Law makes no provision for the resignation of an *ex-officio* guardian. If a magistrate resides in a union he becomes an *ex-officio* guardian without any assent on his part; and it is doubtful whether his name could be removed off the list upon his own application. If the number of resident magistrates is insufficient to balance the number of elected guardians, the clerk of the union has to look out that magistrate who though non-resident is highest rated, and if he assents to his appointment he is put on the list; if he does not assent, then

12th May 1885.]   Mr. HEWSON.   [Continued.

then the next highest is asked will he accept, and so on till the required number is obtained. The law appears to be unsettled as to their power of resigning when once appointed.

1438-39. With regard to the unbusinesslike manner of proceeding in the unions where the League have it their own way, are you aware of any instances of that kind?
Yes, I know that all kinds of foolish propositions come from other boards of guardians.

1440. Do you know anything about rate collectors making default?
Yes. There is a union adjoining ours, the Croom Union; I knew two collectors to go off there owing a whole lot of money; and in one instance, at all events, it was found that the securities were no guarantee for the money, and the money was all lost. It is the business of the guardians to see that there are proper securities, but the board had been for years in the hands of the Land Leaguers, and they did not look after the securities, and the rates had all to be collected from the people again.

1441. Before we leave the subject of the dispensary committee, there was a suggestion which, I believe, you wished to make with regard to the powers of the members of the committee who are not guardians?
I would abolish them altogether.

1442. Viscount *Powerscourt*.] Abolish what?
Abolish the men who are not members of the board of guardians now; I do not see what they are wanted for.

1443. Lord *Saltersford*.] But is it not a great inconvenience to persons in need of medical relief not to be able to get dispensary tickets?
Yes, but you can appoint wardens; the wardens have no power of doing anything except just issuing tickets.

1444. *Chairman*.] I think your suggestion comes to this: that those members of the dispensary committee, who are not guardians, should be only permitted to issue tickets for medical relief, and should not possess any other powers?
Yes.

1445. Then with regard to these extraordinary resolutions which are sometimes passed by boards of guardians, I believe you have something to say upon that subject?
One resolution came before us a short time ago from the Kildysert Union, in the county of Clare, calling on the Government to order the Land Commissioners to reduce the present judicial rents 50 per cent., and this was immediately proposed to the board and carried.

1446. Who was in the chair then?
I do not know exactly who was in the chair; I was not; it was hearing the minutes read of the former day's proceedings that gave me the first intimation about it.

1447. And supposing the chairman wished to put a stop to such an irregular proceeding as that, what course could he adopt?
The only course he could adopt would be to refuse to put the question. It would be rather arbitrary, but he might say, "It is a political question, and I will not allow it to be discussed."

1448. A strong chairman, who takes a proper view of his functions, would, under those circumstances, be of enormous importance?
Yes.

1449. Viscount *Hutchinson*.] Have not cases often happened in which the chairman has acted in that manner, and has refused to put resolutions to the board, and has vacated the chair, and then the moment he has gone out of the room the guardians have called somebody else to the chair and passed them?
If the clerk knows his business he should refuse to go on. The clerk should get up, take the books with him, and walk out of the room.

1450. Lord

12th May 1885.]　　　　　Mr. Hawson.　　　　　[Continued.

1450. Lord *Saltersford*.] But if the chairman persists in refusing to put the question to the board, what can the board do but proceed to other business?

They may go on talking and making such a noise that he cannot go on with the business that ought to be done. They get up and leave their seats, and talk to their neighbours, and you have a regular bear garden.

1451. Lord *Shute*.] But if the chairman persists in that way they cannot proceed to any legal action?
No.

1452. *Chairman*.] I suppose you think it would be very desirable that some regulation should be framed which should exclude this extraneous business from the boards?
Yes, if I saw the practicability of it.

1453. The possibility of it, you mean?
But I mean how it could be practically carried out. The chairman should be the person to judge whether it was right or wrong.

1454. Viscount *Powerscourt*.] You have given the Committee a new idea; you said that you would abolish the property qualification for guardians altogether?
Yes.

1455. How do you imagine that would work?
My idea is that when any person represents others, he would go there as the representative of others, and not as representing himself in any kind of way; and I do not see what a qualification of his own would have to do with it. The people who appoint him could turn him out if he did not carry out their views. And I think to abolish the qualification would enlarge the sphere of people from whom you could choose. I am also in favour of abolishing the qualification for men representing the landowners. I would let the landowners elect their own representatives without any qualification being required from them.

1456. *Chairman*.] Have you any other general observations you wish to make about the Bill. I believe you have a Table showing the result of contested elections, have you not, in two electoral divisions?
Yes.

1457. And the value of the property votes in each?
Yes, I have taken two electoral divisions where contested elections were held this year. These Tables show what influence the property vote has in a contested election. One was the Castletown Electoral Division. The valuation of the electoral division is 2,636 *l.*; in the owners' occupation there is 1,267 *l.* The Loyalist candidate had 40 occupier votes, which represented a valuation of 1,699 *l.*; he had also 37 property votes. The Nationalist candidate had 44 votes, which represented a valuation of 628 *l.*; they would have carried the election against the occupier votes, representing 1,699 *l.*, but all the property votes he had were 5, and they represented a valuation of 6 *l.* These were labourers' houses that some of the tenant farmers were immediate lessors for, and had property votes out of them on that account. Anybody that has a house on their land can make a property vote out of it, supposing the house is only valued at 5 *s.*

1458. That is in consequence of the recent decision in Lord Fitzwilliam's case, is it not?
No; I think that has always been the law. You are liable for the rate, because there is a tenement under 4 *l.*, and you can make a property vote out of that. You are proprietor of that; you are occupier of your own farm, and vote for it, but you are proprietor of this house, and the person living in it is your tenant, and for that you can make a property vote, supposing it were only valued at 5 *s.* The influence of the whole property vote in that electoral division was 37; that was the whole property vote, and the landlords in that division occupied more than half the land themselves, and their votes, both taking them as occupiers and as landlords, only counted 37; while the tenants' votes counted

(O.1.)　　　　　　　　　　S

counted 84. In that case the landlords paid two-thirds of the whole rate, and the votes only counted 37, while the tenant votes counted 84.

1459. Lord *Monk-Bretton*.] You say there were 37 property votes, and 84 occupier votes?
Yes.

1460. Can you say how many owners gave the 37 property votes?
I think about six; but they were occupier votes, some of them, as well as property votes. I can tell you how many of the 37 were occupier votes; I suppose about half of them were occupier votes.

1461. But six persons gave those 37 votes?
Yes, as occupiers and owners.

1462. Then how many persons gave the 84 occupier votes?
I could not exactly tell you, but it must have been a considerably less number than the 84, because some of these people have two or three votes.

1463. Could you tell approximately?
I could not. I have the figures in town, but I did not bring them here; I did not think the question would be asked.

1464. Would it be 40?
Very likely; or I will say 30. The other is the Pallaskenry Electoral Division. The valuation of this electoral division is 2,510 *l*.; the land in the occupation of the owners in that electoral division is only 42 *l*.; the owners do not reside. The Loyalist candidate there got 38 occupying votes, representing a valuation of 700 *l*.; he got of property votes 21, representing a valuation of 2,510 *l*, and they altogether counted 59. The Nationalist candidate got 58 votes, representing in occupation value 1,227 *l*., and he got no property vote. The Loyalist was returned by a majority of only one; that is, the whole property vote of the division was only able to turn the scale by one.

1465. *Chairman*.] Were proxies used?
Yes, they were all proxies. I hold some of the proxies myself in that division; the proxy of a gentleman who lives in another county.

1466. Notwithstanding that enormous preponderance of the valuation of those who gave votes for the Loyalist over that of those who gave votes for the League candidate, the League candidate would have won the day had it not been for the proxy vote?
Yes.

1467. And that only enabled the other to win by one?
Yes, by one vote; and all the proxy votes that could be made are made in that division.

1468. Lord *Monk-Bretton*.] Now, in that case, can you tell how many persons voted for the Loyalist candidate, and how many for the League candidate?
I think the number of persons that voted were pretty equal, because I have the figures at home, as I say, and my recollection is that the smaller men generally voted for the Loyalist candidate; it was the larger farmers that voted for the Nationalist, and the numbers were 58 and 38; but I think the voters were very nearly equal in number.

1469. The Loyalist had the votes of the owners and the smaller occupiers, I understand you?
Yes.

1470. And the larger occupiers voted for the Nationalist?
Yes, the larger occupiers, not owners.

1471. So that the number of persons voting was about equal?
The number of persons voting was about equal. I have another table here showing the relative amount of rates that are paid by the landlords and by the occupiers in the Rathkeale Union. The valuation of the union is 56,240 *l*. The total amount of poor rate in 1884 was 7,917 *l*.; the valuation of the land
in

12th May 1885.] Mr HEWSON. [Continued.

in the owners' possession is 9,669 *l*.; the amount of the present rate payable by them on this valuation is 1,302 *l*.; the approximate valuation of tenements under 4 *l*., for which they are liable for the rate, is 600 *l*., and the rate they would pay upon that would be 75 *l*. They also pay half the rate upon a valuation of 45,971 *l*.; that would be 3,275 *l*; making the total rate paid by the landlords in the union 4,562 *l*.; while the occupiers would only pay half the rate upon 45,971 *l*., which would be 3,275 *l*.; that is, the landlords' rate would be 4,652 *l*., while the occupiers' rate would be only 3,275 *l*., something like 7 to 5. I have another table showing the voting power of owners and tenants in eight electoral divisions. The reason I took eight electoral divisions, and not the whole union, was that it is very troublesome making out these figures, and I have not time to make the whole of them out, but I will undertake that they represent the union properly, that it is a proper representation of the whole union. I am taking the total powers of the landlords now. Supposing that every vote they could make was made (they are not half or one-third of them made), I find that the whole voting power of the landlords in these eight electoral divisions would amount to 453 votes, and the tenant votes would amount to 1,066; and in these votes for the landlords I take their occupation votes as well as the property votes, and they occupy something between one-fifth and one-sixth of the whole union.

1472. Now in that case can you tell the number of persons who give those 453 votes?
I could not; I could tell you if I had the papers I took these from; these are only epitomes.

1473. But you do not know what number of persons the 452 votes and the 1,066 respectively would represent?
No, I could not tell off-hand.

1474. *Chairman*.] Have you given the proportion of rates which they pay?
I gave it in the union; I did not give it in these eight electoral divisions, but in the whole union. They bear the same proportion that the eight electoral divisions would bear to the 18.

1475. Lord *Monk-Bretton*.] These eight are so perfectly typical of the 18?
Perfectly typical. These are the electoral divisions that are around where I live myself, and they are the places which I know the best.

1476. Are all the electoral divisions in this union rural divisions, or are there some urban?
There are some urban.

1477. And in the eight which you have given us, are there some urban?
There are two urban; and there are some of the electoral divisions. I took where the largest proportion of the land is held by the landowner; that would diminish the number of the occupier votes; and in some of the divisions that I did not take, the landlords do not occupy at all, so that it was perfectly fair in the way I took it.

1478. You told us that you are in favour of having a great number of polling places to avoid mobbing?
Yes.

1479. In what buildings would the poll be taken?
In the petty sessions courts.

1480. But would they afford a sufficient number of places?
Yes; it is in the petty sessions courts that the present election of members of Parliament takes place.

1481. And would they be conveniently situated?
Very conveniently situated. There are plenty of petty sessions polling places.

1482. If they were used for the purpose, that would answer your object of having a multiplicity of polling places and avoiding crowds?
Yes.

12th *May* 1885.] Mr. HEWSON. [*Continued*

Yes. The only thing I see about it is that the elections might not all be able to be held the same day; you might require two or three days to hold the elections.

1483. In different electoral divisions?
Yes. The clerk would hold the election in one dispensary district to-day and another to-morrow, and so on; it would take two or three days perhaps.

1484. When you said that 1 *l.* a-week was paid to evicted tenants, was that paid in money or in kind?
It was one evicted tenant I mentioned. It was paid in money. We do not give relief in kind at all in our union; the relieving officers say they could not carry it out.

1485. You said that a change came over the character of your board some years ago, when the power passed into the hands of the elective guardians; what was the immediate cause of that?
I think at that time there was some sectarianism in the country, which, I am happy to say, does not exist in the union at all now; we are very free from it. But at that time there was a cry that the Protestant guardians had too much influence, and that was, I think, the cause of it; and then there was a change when the *ex-officio* guardians ceased to attend almost entirely.

1486. For how long a period did that sectarian spirit prevail?
I could not exactly say how long, but it died away entirely; and, I am happy to say, there is nothing of the kind now.

1487. It lasted some years?
Several years.

1488. You are in favour of increasing the number of votes in some proportion to property in the case of both owners and occupiers?
Yes.

1489. Up to what number of votes would you give an owner voting power?
It would limit itself in this way: that the electoral divisions are small, and that there are very few cases indeed where one man owns the whole electoral division. That would limit itself; but what I propose is, let the votes go on up to 200 *l.*, as they are, and after that I would give an additional vote for every 100 *l.*

1490. Without any limitation?
Yes; but I say it would limit itself, because the electoral divisions are generally small; from 2,000 *l.* to 3,000 *l* is generally the valuation, and it is very rarely indeed that one proprietor owns the whole electoral division. Even in the cases of very large proprietors you generally find the property scattered over several electoral divisions, and other owners will come in in each division, and they would only have these votes in each division according to the value of the property they owned; their votes would not reckon *in globo* in the whole union.

1491. And you would give an occupier votes in the same way?
I would give an occupier votes in the same way.

1492. We have been told that under a recent decision one man can now have as many as thirty votes?
Yes, I was aware of that before the decision.

1493. And under your system can one man have a considerable number of votes still?
A man may have thirty votes, but I never knew a case in which he had, because he would require to be an owner of tithe rentcharge, as well as an owner of property, to have 30 votes, and there are very few such people; it is only a possible case.

1494. How many votes have you known one man have?
Six as occupier, six for the land he occupies, and six for tenements over 4 *l.*; I never knew a man to have six votes for tenements under 4 *l.*, and I do not think there is such a thing in any one electoral division in Ireland, as a man
having

12th May 1885.]   Mr. HEWSON.   [*Continued*.

having the maximum number of votes. I have a large number of tenements under 4*l.* myself, and I do not think they are valued at as much as 60*l.*

1495. Have you ever known a man have as many as 24 votes?
No. Eighteen, I think, is about the maximum I have known, and I do not think my proposition would increase the votes of the owners very much either.

1496. But there must be many instances in which an owner has more than 200*l.* in one electoral division?
Yes, but he should have 200*l.* in tenements under 4*l.* in order to get the full number of votes, and I do not think that such a thing exists. All these cabins are only rated at 10*s.* or 5*s.*: you would want a thousand of these to make it up. But I would like to see the owners represented by men elected by themselves. I would abolish the *ex-officio* guardians entirely.

1497. You would be in favour of having a constituency of owners, and a constituency of occupiers?
Yes, and I do not think it would create class interests a bit more than now. I think one of the causes of the unpopularity of *ex-officio* guardians is that they are supposed to represent the Government in a great degree. They only represent the Government and themselves; they are not elected by anybody.

1498. *Chairman.*] I suppose there is nothing so unpopular in Ireland as the Government?
Nothing so unpopular as the Government.

1499. Viscount *Powerscourt.*] Whatever Government?
Whatever Government there is; I do not mean any particular Government.

1500. Viscount *Hutchinson.*] I daresay you have heard what the last witness said: he saw great difficulties in forming a constituency representing property?
I do not see those difficulties at all. I was listening to the evidence; I think he is quite mistaken; I think the rate books will supply all the necessary information. Supposing one large owner owns, say, 30,000 acres of land in one county, and supposing that he has let on fee farm grants to six other people, and supposing these people have this sublet to, say, 600, they would each vote out of the amount of property they had; they would not interfere with one another. This large proprietor would have his votes to 200*l.*; the six other voters might have their votes up to 200*l.* each, or they might not; each of the occupiers would have their votes, and it would go down entirely to the labouring men, or to the tenements under 4*l.*, perhaps the labouring man's house. So I do not see the slightest difficulty in carrying it out. Then again, the proxies could be given for the votes just in the way they are given now; and there would be this great advantage, that there are men now who cannot be on the boards at all, who might represent the landlords. For instance, I know tenant farmers that would sometimes represent the landowners.

1501. That would bring in an entirely different class of persons. Are there a number of tradesmen and other people in the towns who would come forward?
Yes; it would not be exclusively what are commonly called landlords. They would be men who had property, but a different kind of property; they would represent the property class, but not merely the landlords. Then again, one would see agents representing property; one would see sons of gentlemen who are not rated at present; they might represent the proprietors. And at present the *ex-officio* guardians do not give any undertaking, either complied or actual, that they will attend, and they are under no obligation to attend; and they do not represent any class at all; they represent themselves and the Government, and nobody else; and the way they are talked about at the board is generally this: "You are an *ex-officio* guardian, but the elective guardian represents the ratepayers." "So he does." The other man may have more property than all the elective guardians put together, but he only represents himself and not any class. I may say that there was a meeting of landowners in the county of Limerick and this question was discussed, and I proposed that we should adopt this plan, and it was at first opposed, but I brought the whole meeting round to my views, and it was endorsed by them as their opinion.

1502. By

12th *May* 1885.] Mr. HEWSON. [*Continued.*

1502. By "this plan" you mean Mr. Bagwell's scheme?
I have not seen Mr. Bagwell's plan; it was my own idea.

1503. Viscount *Powerscourt*.] It is that the whole board should be elected; that is what you mean?
That the whole board should be elected.

1504. By two different classes?
Yes. I would give the landlords that occupied their occupation votes as tenants, and I would give them their property votes to vote for the representatives of property.

1505. Lord *Shute*.] I want to hear a little more, if you please, about the relief given to these evicted tenants. We have heard it said that the ordinary relief is about 3 s. a week, but as a general thing it is 1 l. a week that is given to evicted tenants?
Yes.

1506. Upon what do you base that relief; do you base it upon the estimated income of the evicted tenant before he was evicted, or what?
I do not think it was based on any particular thing. I am sorry to say that a great many of our boards now are under the influence rather of the Land League in Dublin, and whatever they are told to do they do. I think it is something of the same amount as the Land League were giving themselves when the funds came from America.

1507. The Land League were giving out of their own pockets, but the board of guardians out of the pockets of the ratepayers, that money being public property?
Exactly so.

1508. *Chairman*.] Although the *ex-officios* are nominated by the Government, do you think that it would be altogether untrue or an exaggeration to say that the elective guardians are now to a great extent nominated by the Land League?
There is no doubt of that. The question was entirely, Are you a Land Leaguer, or not?

1509. And they act upon the orders they receive from the Central League in Dublin?
Yes; the whole thing is moved by one machine; it is a part of the whole system; the one object is to throw all the power, taxing power and everything into the hands of the Land League.

1510. Have you heard of a difficult question coming before the board of guardians, and being referred back to the head office of the National League in Dublin?
No, I have not; it did not occur when I was there.

1511. However, such a thing would not surprise you?
No, such a thing would not surprise me; nothing would surprise me; they get regular legal advice on every subject.

1512. Lord *Ker*.] As to the *ex-officio* guardians being unpopular, are they unpopular with the smaller ratepayers, do you think?
I think they are more unpopular with the larger ratepayers. I think this agitation is more carried on by the large farmers than by the small ones. It is the larger farmers that expect to shove the gentry out and take their place.

1513. You said that the rates have gone up very much since the *ex-officios* have not attended; do you think that the smaller ratepayers recognise that fact?
No doubt of it.

1514. Therefore they would be sorry to see the *ex-officio* guardians abolished?
They would be sorry to see the representatives of the landlords abolished; they do not know anything about *ex-officios;* they only know them as landlords.

1515. I think

12th May 1885.] Mr. HEWSON. [Continued.

1515. I think you just now rather endorsed the expression of opinion that the *ex-officio* guardians only represented themselves?
I think they do; I mean by that that they actually only represent themselves.

1516. But, on the other hand, you say the small ratepayers look up to them as protectors?
I am talking of the men that reside in the neighbourhood now; of course they know nothing about the men they never see; but the men in their own neighbourhood exercise a certain amount of influence over them, and they look up to them in a certain degree; but I do not think that as *ex-officios* they represent anybody. Then again another thing must be remembered; the late appointments of *ex-officio* guardians are not connected with property at all; they are merely political appointments, and according as these appointments are made the *ex-officio* guardians will less and less represent property. I think it would be a very wise move to change that.

The Witness is directed to withdraw.

MR. HENRY RINGWOOD, having been called in; is Examined, as follows:

1517. *Chairman.*] I BELIEVE you are an elective poor law guardian?
Yes.

1518. In the union of Gorey?
Yes.

1519. And deputy vice-chairman?
Yes.

1520. Have you considered the Bill now before the House?
Yes.

1521. With regard to the provision for triennial elections, do you approve of that?
I quite approve of it.

1522. And voting by ballot?
I do not approve of voting by ballot.

1523. On what ground?
I do not approve of it except as applied to the residents of the union in question; I think it would be unfair to non-residents.

1524. On what ground?
A non-resident might have property in several different unions in Ireland, north and south, east and west, and the elections might all fall upon the same day, and he could not possibly vote in person at each election, and therefore, would lose his vote; that is one reason.

1525. Of course he would still retain, unless this Bill is passed in its entirety, his proxy vote?
Yes.

1526. You mean that his occupation vote would be lost; is that so; I do not quite follow you; are you anticipating the loss of the proxy vote when you make that answer?
I am.

1527. Please do not do that; supposing the proxy vote to be retained as it now exists, what objection do you see to the general use of the ballot?
A man may have two or three residences in Ireland, and the elections might come on on the same day in each, and he could not possibly attend all; he might be the owner of a very large property, or he might be ill, so that he could

could not attend; and, I think, it would be an injustice to have him lose his vote on that account.

1528. You mean that you can conceive cases where the occupier would be totally unable from physical reasons to vote under the ballot?
Yes.

1529. And, of course, as an occupier he would have no proxy vote, as you know?
Yes.

1530. In case of an infirm person it might be a disadvantage, or in case of a woman?
I think it would.

1531. What do you say to the proposed abolition of the proxy vote?
I think it would have a very prejudicial effect on the unions in Ireland; at least in three of the provinces in Ireland.

1532. On what ground have you come to that conclusion?
I have come to this conclusion on that matter; I think that the best guardians are those that are helped into their election by the aid of the proxy votes; they are the best men.

1533. That is your experience?
That is my experience.

1534. Does the proxy vote often turn an election in your district?
We very seldom have a contest in the union in which I reside; but I have known contests to take place in the other unions in the county in which I reside, and the proxy vote is not able to carry the day. In fact, in those unions just now it has not been worked up, and even if it was worked up, I do not think it would be able to elect the candidates that the property owners would wish to have in. It depends a great deal upon the size of the farms in each union.

1535. Are you tolerably well acquainted with the opinions of the people at large in your union in this matter?
I am.

1536. Have you heard them express any feelings against the proxy vote?
I have.

1537. The people at large?
Yes; the people at large.

1538. What do they say about it?
They say that it is unfair to thrust in a guardian in such a manner; that he should be elected by the ratepayers.

1539. But so he is by the proxy vote?
Yes, but that he should be elected by those who are not owners of property.

1540. What class of persons have you heard express that opinion?
Small farmers.

1541. Are those persons who have expressed that opinion men who hold strong political opinions?
They are.

1542. Members of the Local Land League, I presume?
Yes.

1543. And do they look upon this election as a political one or as one to secure a good result in the carrying out of the poor law?
They look on it in my opinion as a political matter.

1544. And they feel it a great hardship that they are prevented by the proxy vote from electing candidates who hold their own political views; is that what you mean?
That is what I mean, exactly.

1545. Supposing

1545. Supposing the proxy vote to be abolished, can you see any mode by which owners of property non-resident would not be disfranchised; do you see any other mode by which they could exercise their power to vote in respect of the rates they pay?
I cannot see how they could do so, if the Bill is passed in its present form.

1546. Do you think that the abolition of the proxy vote would disfranchise owners of property who are non-resident?
I think it would.

1547. What do you say to the proposed reduction of the *ex-officio* guardians?
I think it would have a very prejudicial effect upon the working of the unions with regard to the expenditure of the public money; the rates would be surely increased if the *ex-officios* were reduced.

1548. Why do you think so?
I have seen this in other unions in the county, that where officers are required for any particular purpose it is not according to their qualifications for that purpose that they are elected, but simply because they belong to the popular party.

1549. You mean in other unions where the *ex-officios* are in a minority?
Exactly so; where the proceedings of the board are worked by the representatives of the popular party. I have evidence here in black and white, the report in the paper of proceedings that took place in a union in the county where there were officers required as inspectors, to see after the building of the labourers' cottages that were going to be erected in the county; clerks of works, in fact, I may call them; and there were several candidates. Some of them were experienced builders, I believe, themselves; some of them were clerks or foremen belonging to builders; and others of them were representatives or the nominees of the popular party, that knew nothing whatever about building, and they were brought forward as such. I shall read you, in fact, the way one of them was proposed as clerk of works. "Mr. N. Codd proposed Mr. Ryan as clerk of works. He was a fit and practical man, who understood every kind of business; another thing, ever since the agitation started he was a foremost man whenever he was wanted. Mr. Cassin: That might be left overboard; you should not bring in such things as that here; keep that in your own bosom. Mr. N. Codd: You should not get up to reprimand me, sir." Then it went on in that style; but this man that Mr. Codd proposed, although there were four or five candidates, was elected by a large majority. His proposer was asked if he knew anything about building. "Mr. Cassin: I wish to ask you a question. Have you any experience of that man 'doing' a building, as you spoke so highly of him? (After a pause), Silence gives consent. Mr. N. Codd: Whatever he took in hand he performed. Mr. Cassin: I am not speaking to you; if you wanted a ploughman would you go in for a tailor? I have no objection to Mr. Ryan; but I think he got his share, and the situation ought to be given to a man that served his time and had experience. I'll propose that Dennis Dempsey be accepted. If he came forward to value land I would throw him overboard." But it resulted in this man, who knew nothing whatever about building, being elected as clerk of works.

1550. What union was that in?
That was in Wexford Union.

1551. That is a union where the *ex-officio* element is not very strong, I believe?
Not very strong. Then I have another union here, the Athy Union, where they wanted to elect a relieving officer, and there were four candidates. "Thomas Clearcy was recommended by the committee of the National League, Monasterevan. Mr. Kilbride hoped that every member of the National League at the board would support him;" and Mr. Thomas Clearcy was elected by a large majority.

(O.I.)   T   1552. I believe

1552. I believe the *ex-officio* guardians have practically given up attending Athy Union?
No; a few of them attend, but they have very little control over the proceedings of the board there.

1553. Viscount *Powerscourt*.] Does Lord Drogheda attend?
I do not think he does; I do not see his name, generally speaking, as at the meetings.

1554. Lord *Monk-Bretton*.] How many does the board consist of?
I am not intimately acquainted with the Athy Board, excepting from seeing the reports in the papers.

1555. Lord *Saltersford*.] Do you know anything of contracts being given for political reasons by the Enniscorthy Board?
I have heard of a contract for tea being given at a farthing a pound more than what the tea was offered for by another party to the board, and it was given to the contractor, it was declared, on account of his nationality.

1556. Lord *Monk-Bretton*.] That is what you have heard; not within your own knowledge?
I cannot speak of it as within my own knowledge, but I have heard it from what I should consider the best authority.

1557. It is not in your own union?
It is not in my own union: Gorey is my union.

1558. *Chairman*.] And in Gorey the League element does not prevail?
The League element is not so strong there as in other unions, but we have plenty of the League spirit in the Gorey Union among those that attend the board there.

1559. Have you a good attendance of *ex-officio* guardians?
Tolerably good.

1560. How many *ex-officio* guardians are there on your board?
I cannot state the exact number. I may say that I am not as well prepared for this examination as I otherwise would be. It was only last Wednesday that I definitely decided upon coming here, and that I understood that it was definitely decided that I was to come. I thought that my name was to be submitted amongst other names, and that your Lordships would choose five or six, and that my name might not be one of them.

1561. Viscount *Hutchinson*.] Can you tell me how many elective guardians there are?
I cannot; I think somewhere about 20.

1562. Lord *Saltersford*.] I think I should not be very far astray in saying 19, should I?
I made a very good shot at it in saying 20.

1563. Do you happen to know whether the full number of *ex-officio* guardians are on the board, whether there are 19 *ex-officio* guardians on the board?
I think there are an equal number.

1564. Are there not some that reside at such a distance that it is impossible for them to attend except on very rare occasions?
Yes, there are. They could not possibly attend the board every day. I think those *ex-officio* guardians that reside in the locality give a very fair attendance.

1565. Did you ever see Lord Powerscourt at the board; he is, I believe, an *ex-officio* guardian?
No, I do not remember seeing Lord Powerscourt there. I may mention that no matter whether they reside in the locality or not, whenever there is any important business to be transacted at the Gorey board of guardians, the *ex-officio*

ex-officio guardians attend very largely; and I think they cannot be blamed so much for their absence on other occasions, because a great many of them have their magisterial duties to attend to, and they have a great many private duties to attend to, and they could not possibly be at the board as often as some of the elective guardians are; but they consider (and I quite agree with them) that the next best thing they can do when they cannot attend regularly, is to attend on such days as when officers are to be appointed, or contracts to be given, chairmen to be appointed, or such matters to be considered; and that they can feel their minds more at rest if they attend and secure the election of good men to fill such positions; just the same as if they were in a mercantile way, and had branches of their business in different towns or counties, and could not give their personal attendance in each of those towns or counties, they consider that the next best thing they could do then was to get a proper conductor or manager in whom they could place confidence.

1566. *Chairman.*] Then I gather that you, as an elective guardian, would not like to see any diminution of the *ex-officio* element on your board?
I would not object to see the *ex-officios* reduced if they were not ratepayers.

1567. Viscount *Powerscourt.*] Will you explain that?
If the *ex-officio* was not a ratepayer, I mean.

1568. Viscount *Hutchinson.*] You would not like to see people who were not ratepayers appointed *ex-officio*; that is what you mean?
Yes.

1569. *Chairman.*] But you do not wish to see the number of *ex-officios* diminished?
No, I do not.

1570. Lord *Monk-Bretton*] Do I understand you rightly, that you would rather have the number diminished than have men as *ex-officios* who are not ratepayers, and are not interested in the district?
I would not object to have the number diminished if there were any on the list who were not ratepayers.

1571. Viscount *Hutchinson.*] But then you consider, do you not, that it is perfectly right and fair that as the owners of property bear more than one-half the rate, they should have at least one-half of the representation on the board?
Yes, I think it would be a great injustice to deny them that.

1572. Your remark comes to this, that you would like to see people struck off the roll of *ex-officio* guardians who were not ratepayers?
Yes.

1573. But you would not object to seeing them replaced by people who were ratepayers?
Certainly not.

1574. Lord *Saltersford.*] Can you give the Committee a comparison between the amount of rates paid in the Gorey Union, where the *ex-officio* element has considerable influence, and the amount of rates paid in other unions, where the *ex-officio* exercise a smaller influence?
I can. In the Wexford Union, in the year 1882, the average poor rate was 1 s. 5¼ d. in the £., in Enniscorthy it was 1 s. 1/1 d., in New Ross it was 1 s. 8 7/8 d., in Gorey it was 10 d.

1575. You have not told the Committee yet anything as regards the *ex-officio* element in those four unions?
The *ex-officio* element in Gorey is far stronger than what it is in the other three unions, and the rates are entirely lower in Gorey. Then in the year 1883, in Wexford Union the rate was 1 s. 7¼ d., in Enniscorthy Union it was 1 s. 6¼ d., in New Ross it was 2 s. 6¼ d., in Gorey Union in the same year it was 1 s. In 1884, in Wexford Union it was 1 s. 6½ d., in Enniscorthy it was 1 s. 8¼ d., in New Ross it was 1 s. 10½ d., and in Gorey Union it was 1 s. 1½ d.; and I attribute the low rate in the Gorey Union to the attendance of the *ex-officio*

12th *May* 1885.   Mr. RINGWOOD.   [*Continued.*

officio guardians, and the guardians that are helped to be elected through the proxy vote, and I consider they are the best business men.

1576. *Chairman.*] There is no circumstance in the population or valuation of the three unions you have mentioned that would account for that difference, I suppose?
The population in Gorey Union is smaller I know, but the valuation is smaller too in proportion.

1577. Then there is no circumstance with reference to the population and valuation which would account for that?
I think not.

1578. Lord *Monk-Bretton.*] Are they all rural unions or urban; is the character of the population the same in these different unions?
Yes, I should say it is.

1579. Are they agricultural?
Yes, all four unions are agricultural unions.

1580. Lord *Saltersford.*] I think the presence of the towns of Wexford and New Ross would probably make a difference, would it not; would there not be more poverty in the towns of Wexford and New Ross than in Enniscorthy and Gorey?
The rates in Enniscorthy are far above the rates in Gorey; there is very little difference between the rates in Enniscorthy and the other two unions that are seaport towns. The great increase in the rates in the other three unions, in my opinion, is in some degree owing to the liberality with which they give out-door relief; and, as a rule, the guardians that are elected by the popular voice are to a man all in favour of out-door relief, and they even propose to give as much relief as would be necessary for the whole support of a family. They frequently object to a small amount being given, saying that so much would not support a family; whereas out-door relief, in my opinion, was never intended except as an auxiliary to the support of a family, or at all events, not intended by the Poor Law Act. They appear to ignore the fact that if there was no one at all in the house we should have to keep up our staff of officers still, at great expense; and the sure test of destitution is the offer of the house to an applicant. We would find 50 who would call themselves destitute and accept the out-door relief, to one that would accept the house.

1581. Lord *Monk-Bretton.*] In your union do you insist on the house test?
We do not go into it strictly, but we go into it far more strictly than what the other three unions do.

1582. In your opinion, does the Gorey Union enforce the house test strictly enough?
I think they enforce it strictly enough, but they do not enforce it with severity. They are very liberal; if the breadearner of a family gets disabled through wounds or sickness, they are very liberal in giving out-door relief to that man; or if there is a poor widow that is making some exertions to support herself, they will give out-door relief to her if she has a couple of children; but they object to giving out-door relief to parties who go about begging, and simply calculate upon this out-door relief as a means for their subsistence in addition to what they can get by begging; and then their children are neglected. They idle about the streets in the different villages, they are not sent to school, and they also make a trade of begging. And I think it was to prevent such consequences that the workhouses were established.

1583. Viscount *Hutchinson.*] And it is that class of men that you find refuse the house test more often than anybody else; it is that class of persons that are always applying for out door relief, is it not?
Yes, principally.

1584. And that class of persons, if you offer the house to them, generally refuse it?
Decidedly,

Decidedly, they would refuse it; they would rather stay out. But I very seldom see the guardians that I spoke of elected by the popular vote refuse outdoor relief to any applicant except in very extreme cases. They go on to calculate that if they come into the house, they would cost so much per week, and that if you give them half the amount outside they will be satisfied with it; and so they say it would be better not to bring them into the house.

1585. Lord *Monk-Bretton*.] Do you find in your own union that the elective guardians are weakly inclined to give out-door relief; that they have a weakness in that direction?
I consider that they have.

1586. *Chairman*.] I suppose considerable pressure is sometimes put upon them to give it?
I daresay it may be.

1587. More pressure put upon them than is likely to be put upon the *ex officios* by their neighbours, I mean to say, and so forth?
Yes, I daresay there may be; in fact, I feel nearly sure there is.

1588. Lord *Saltersford*.] I daresay you may have heard the evidence of former witnesses with regard to the difficulty the chairman of a board of guardians is put in preventing political matters being brought forward; do you find from your experience that if the chairman is firm in the matter, he can prevent political matter from being brought forward?
I find that that is my experience in Gorey Union.

1589. That political matters are not pressed if they are brought forward?
They are not pressed latterly, because it has been tried over and over again, and the parties trying to force them forward have failed.

1590. Lord *Shute*.] Are reporters always present at the meetings of your union?
A reporter is. We have a second reporter, but he is not able to write shorthand, and that alters the matter considerably.

1591. There is always a reporter, I understand you to say?
Yes, there is always a reporter.

1592. Lord *Monk-Bretton*.] You told us that you are an elective guardian?
Yes.

1593. Are you a landowner?
I cannot say that I am; it is only to a very small extent. I will not call myself a landlord, but I have an interest derived out of land.

1594. Lord *Saltersford*.] Not in the Gorey Union, I think?
Not in the Gorey Union.

1595. I think you do not come here as the representative of the Gorey Board?
I come here as the representative of my own ideas.

1596. Exactly; but would you have any hesitation in saying that there are a considerable number of elective guardians on the Gorey Board who share your opinion; I do not say a majority, but a considerable number of elective guardians who share your opinion?
I think there are, but I feel sure that if the Bill before the House in its present state becomes law, that number will be considerably reduced in future.

The Witness is directed to withdraw.

Ordered, That this Committee be adjourned to Friday next, at Twelve o'clock.

Die Veneris, 15° Maii, 1885.

LORDS PRESENT:

Lord President.
Earl of Milltown.
Viscount Powerscourt.
Viscount Hutchinson.
Lord Saltersford.

Lord Ker.
Lord Shute.
Lord Monk-Bretton.
Lord Sudley.

The EARL OF MILLTOWN, in the Chair.

Mr. EBENEZER MOLLOY, having been called in; is Examined, as follows:

1597. *Chairman.*] I BELIEVE you are Clerk to the Naas Poor Law Union?
Yes.

1598. How long have you held that appointment?
Thirty-four years.

1599. You are also, I believe, President of the Union Officers' Association?
I am.

1600. And they have deputed you to give evidence before the Committee with regard to the Bill?
Yes.

1601. Perhaps you will tell the Committee what the Union Officers' Association is?
It is composed of the clerks, and masters, and all the officers of the unions in Ireland, and it has been formed for the purpose of looking after their interests generally.

1602. Have you given your attention to the Bill now before this House?
Yes, I have looked over it carefully.

1603. What do you say to the proposal that elections should be triennial, instead of annual as now?
I would approve of it.

1604. You think it would be an improvement?
I think it would be.

1605. With regard to the proposal that vote by ballot should be the mode of election for guardians, what do you say to that?
I would also approve of the vote by ballot, on the ground that the present mode of voting is open to abuse by candidates and others being allowed to take lists of all persons recording their votes. Were it not for that, I think the present system is just as good.

1606. You mean that the present system would ensure jealousy?
Certainly, if it were confined to the constabulary and the returning officer.

(O.I.)   T 4   1607. But

15th May 1885.] Mr. MOLLOY. [Continued.

1607. But what guarantee would the ratepayers then have that the votes were truly recorded?
It could be ascertained by a sworn inquiry.

1608. Would not that be rather a cumbersome mode of conducting an election?
I do not think it would. At present the returning officer has the power of excluding the general public from the scrutiny of votes, and, if he can show good reason, the candidates also, under the existing regulations.

1609. He has that power, you say, at present?
He has that power under the existing regulations.

1610. We have had evidence that it is sometimes done, but I did not know that it was legally done?
Yes, it is so.

1611. Who ascertains whether at the scrutiny, the voting is correctly inquired into?
If it is objected to afterwards, application is made to the board of guardians; that is to say, the person aggrieved applies to the board of guardians, and the Local Government Board are communicated with, and, if they think it desirable, they order a sworn inquiry.

1612. At any rate, as the elections are at present conducted, I suppose there is not much secrecy?
There is not.

1613. Is there much intimidation as far as you know?
Not in my union; I do not know of any.

1614. Do you see any objection to the ballot?
In this way: I think that there are a great many women who at present have the right of voting, and exercise that right, and I doubt very much whether they would go to the polling booth to record a vote; and if they did not they would be disfranchised by the ballot. And then I apprehend the expense would be very great; whereas the expense of the present mode of electing guardians is very trifling indeed. Unless the police were appointed as assistants to the returning officer at the polling booth the expense would be very great.

1615. That suggestion has already been made, as also that one of the petty sessions courts should be used for the purpose of polling booths, to save expense; do you approve of that suggestion?
I do.

1616. And that the dispensary district should be made the electoral district?
I think the dispensary district would be too large. People would have to travel perhaps 14 or 15 miles to record their votes.

1617. That struck me as an objection when the suggestion was made, knowing as I do the large size of some of the districts?
For instance, in the county of Wicklow, men would have to travel from Lacken to come to Blessington.

1618. But that is rather an exceptional case, is it not, that being a mountainous country and thinly populated. As a rule, I suppose, where sick people are able to attend at dispensaries, voters might go to them?
I think that is the only district, perhaps, that the objection would apply to. There are districts, and several of them, where they are certainly seven or eight or 10 miles across.

1619. But that is supposing an extreme case, that a man would have to go from one end of the district to the other. The radius would be not so considerable?
No.

1620. Then with regard to infirm persons, do you think that they might have
some

some difficulty in giving their vote by ballot. You have said that women would have some difficulty; might infirm persons also?
Of course the same thing would apply to infirm persons.

1621. Have you any suggestions to make to the Committee which might obviate that difficulty; do you think, for instance, it would be possible to give them a proxy vote?
No, it would not.

1622. You could not entertain the idea of giving that to the occupier?
No.

1623. Why not?
I am afraid it would be too largely availed of. Everyone would take advantage of it.

1624. I only suggested it in the case of women or infirm persons?
Unless they were qualified as the owners of property to appoint proxies, I do not see how they could have a proxy.

1625. Not under the exisiting law, that is to say, but I am now suggesting to you an alteration of the law; it has been suggested by some of the witnesses that it might be desirable, instead of abolishing, to extend the proxy vote, and to give it to those who do not at present possess it; occupiers, for instance, who could not attend well; you do not seem to approve of that suggestion?
I do not approve of it.

1626. Is there anything else you would like to say on the question of the ballot?
I think not.

1627. Then, turning to the proposal in the Bill, in Clause 9, to abolish the proxy vote, what do you say to that?
I am decidedly of opinion that the proxy vote should not be abolished.

1628. On what ground?
It would deprive owners of property in different unions and different electoral divisions of all power of voting; for instance, in my own union, I know several owners of property in several counties, and if the elections were all to take place at the same time throughout Ireland it would be utterly impossible that they could record their vote.

1629. If they had to attend personally, you mean?
If they had to attend personally.

1630. So that you think it would amount to their disfranchisement?
I think so.

1631. And it would be an example of taxation without representation?
Quite so.

1632. Does the proxy vote of ten turn an election, in your experience?
Indeed it does.

1633. The contests then, I suppose, are rather close?
Where there are proxy votes they are. I will give you an instance of it, if your Lordships wish.

1634. If you please?
I will mention two cases. In the Carnalway electoral division the Loyalist candidate got, occupation votes, 136, and proxies, 44; the Nationalist got 153 occupation votes, and no proxies.

1635. In that case the Loyalist candidate was returned by a small majority?
By a small majority; excludingth e proxies, the Loyalist had only 136 votes, against 153.

1636. What was the relative amount that those parties contributed to the rates?
I should

(0.1.). U

15th May 1885.] Mr. MOLLOY. [Continued.

I should say that in Carnalway the Loyalist party contribute three-fourths, or very close on three-fourths. It is an electoral division in which a great many owners of property reside.

1637. And yet, though they pay three-fourths of the rates, they could not return a guardian without the aid of the proxy vote?
They could not.

1638. Have you any other instance?
Yes, that of Gilltown. The Loyalist got, occupation votes, 70; and proxies, 80; the Nationalist got, occupation votes, 143; double the amount of the Loyalist.

1639. And in that instance again the Loyalist was returned by a very small majority?
A very small majority.

1640. What proportion did the votes there bear to the payment of the rates?
Very close on the same proportion as in Carnalway.

1641. What is the total valuation of Naas Union?
£. 153,106.

1642. How do you divide that; what is the valuation of land in the owners' occupation?
£. 19,300 is the valuation of the land in the owners' occupation. If I am allowed to include in that railway and canal (who are the owners in fee), it is 36,049 *l.* Then taking the holdings rated at and under 4 *l.*, the limits under which the landlords are liable, their valuation is 2,854 *l.* Then the landlords pay in the aggregate, 96,005 *l.*, and the tenants, 57,101 *l.*; that is, the owners of property pay five-eighths of the entire rate.

1643. And in how many electoral districts are they able to return a representative; are you able to state that?
Which party does your Lordship refer to?

1644. I mean to say, in how many districts are those who vote for the Loyalist candidate (without speaking of any parties) able to return him?
There are only three (if I may use the expression) Loyalists out of the 33.

1645. The others are Non-Loyalists, we mean by that; all through this inquiry (not wanting to use a term that is disagreeable to anybody), the League candidates?
Quite so.

1646. Is there anything else you would like to say on the proxies?
I think if the proxy votes were abolished, property would not be represented.

1647. Now, passing to Clause 11, which provides that a day shall be fixed to hear claims of persons entitled to vote, what have you to say about that?
In the first place, I think that the time specified for the returning officer to sit appears unreasonable. From 10 to 5, as at present, I think would answer all the purposes, in place of from 9 to 6; and I think that the nomination of candidates should be made 21 days before the day of polling, and that only lists of the persons entitled to vote in contested electoral divisions should be printed, thereby saving a great deal of unnecessary expense.

1648. You mean that, by having 21 days' notice of a contest, you would be able to decide in what cases it would be necessary to print the lists?
Yes, and I would get time enough to get the lists printed, and to give the prescribed notice that they were open for inspection within that time; and then there might be only five or six contests out of 29 districts.

1649. How many do you usually have?
Last year we had 11. In years gone by, for very many years, I suppose for 25 years, we seldom had more than two or three, but of latter years they have increased.

1650. Is

15th May 1885.] Mr. MOLLOY. [Continued.

1650. Is there any other object, except that which would be gained by sending in the names 21 days before ; or is that your only object ?
Nothing more, I think, than the avoiding of the unnecessary expense of printing the lists where there is no contest. The returning officer could not possibly find time to write the lists.

1651. You suggest that they should be printed ?
Certainly.

1652. They are not now printed ?
They are not.

1653. Lord *Saltersford*.] A list of voters you mean ?
Yes. And I think that no right of appeal should be given unless the objection was made before the returning officer, and before the register was signed. Those lists being published, and the public having an opportunity to see them for seven days, people could then make their objection ; and if the returning officer ruled against that objection, then they might have a right of appeal ; but I do not think it would be fair or reasonable that after the register was signed, there should be an appeal.

1654. *Chairman*.] You are going to pass now to the question of appeals ?
Yes.

1655. Will you explain that a little more fully ?
I think there should be no right of appeal, unless the objection was made before the returning officer, and before the register was signed. I take it that the lists would be printed and published, and that then all parties concerned would have ample opportunity of finding out if there was anything wrong in connection with it, and that they should then and there make the objection. If the returning officer ruled against that objection, then of course they should have the right of appeal to the county court judge.

1656. Then, under those circumstances, do not you think that all the lists ought to be printed and published ?
But you know it would be only in the case of a contest that any objections would arise.

1657. How can you tell when there will be a contest. If we adopt the proposal to have triennial elections, then if there is an accidental vacancy during the three years, a contested election may come on, and on a wrong register, may it not ?
I was not aware that it was contemplated that the register should last for a year. Is that contemplated, may I ask ?

1658. I understood that the proposal was for three years ?
I say it could not last without correction for longer than six months, because the rates are generally made in the month of September, and the register only lasts from March to September, and would be subject to revision after that, as the books would be revised.

1659. But the additional expense of publishing all the lists would be very small surely ?
There are 29 districts, it must be remembered.

1660. There is no other objection, I suppose, except the ground of expense ?
I think not.

1661. Can you give us any idea of what the expense would be ?
I could not, because it is quite a new thing. We always wrote them before. The jurors' lists at present, on which there are about 600 names, cost something like 9 *l*. for printing.

1662. What do you say about a proposal which has been made, that petitioners should lodge security for costs ?
I think that it would not be fair to subject the returning officer to be mulcted in costs, unless it could be proved that he was guilty of gross negligence, or of wilful or improper conduct.

1663. We

15th May 1885.] Mr. MOLLOY. [Continued.

1663. We will come to that presently. In order to prevent frivolous petitions, would you say that, as in the case of an appeal in the county court, the petitioner should give security for costs?
I decidedly think that the party making the appeal should give security for costs.

1664. Now, coming to the other point to which you were just advancing, the question of on whom the costs should fall, what do you say about that?
I think they should fall on the defeated party and not on the poor rates; I think it would be very unreasonable to have any of the expense coming out of the poor rates.

1665. But supposing the mistake had arisen through the carelessness of the returning officer?
I think he ought to be made to pay the costs himself if it could be proved to have arisen through utter carelessness on his part.

1666. Supposing it did not go so far as that; supposing that the mistake had arisen not through utter carelessness, but through an excusable lapse of some kind or another, it would be rather hard to call upon him to pay, and yet it would be very hard, would it not, to call upon either of the parties to pay?
It would; in that case I suppose it should come out of the poor rate.

1667. But you think, except in that case, it ought not to come out of the poor rate?
I do.

1668. Turning to Part III. of the Bill, what do you say to the first sub-section: "No person under the age of Twenty-one years shall be permitted to vote at any poor law election"?
I think that every person rated ought to have a right of voting.

1669. No matter what his age?
No matter what the age was, either to vote himself or through his guardian or trustee.

1670. What do you say to Sub-section (3), which provides that, "No justice of the peace shall be qualified to be an *ex-officio* guardian of any poor law union unless he is a ratepayer of such union"?
I quite agree with that; I think he should be a ratepayer; I think the qualification of being only a justice of the peace should be done away with.

1671. What do you say to the proposal to reduce the qualification for elective guardians, and fix it at the hard-and-fast line of 12 *l.*?
It is too low entirely. At present it varies. I believe it is as low as that, or perhaps lower in some unions in Ireland; I am not prepared to say positively, but I think it is so; but it would be absurd in the part of Ireland in which I live to reduce it to 12 *l.*

1672. What is your limit?
£.25 is the qualification in Naas; and taking into account the large number of very largely rated occupiers, I consider that too low.

1673. We have already heard that the Local Government Board can fix it at any sum they like?
Quite so.

1674. And that in fact in districts where it is difficult to find highly rated occupiers, they do fix it much lower?
They do; and I may observe that to be a member of the dispensary committee of management, if elected by the board, requires a qualification of 30 *l.*

1675. Can you tell us how that qualification is fixed for the dispensary committee; is that fixed by statute?
Yes; 14 & 15 Vict. c. 68, s. 7.

1676. I have

15th May 1885.]   Mr. MOLLOY.   [Continued.

1676. I have asked the question of several witnesses, and I have not been able to ascertain how that is?
Perhaps I may be wrong, but my impression is that it is fixed by Statute.

1677. It seems rather absurd, does it not, that the qualification for the committee of a body should be higher than that for the body itself?
That is what struck me.

1678. It was suggested by a witness on our last day of meeting, that the qualification should be abolished altogether for the office of elective guardians; what do you say to that?
I do not agree with that at all. There is a greater amount of intelligence in towns than in rural districts. A man rated at 12 *l.* in a town would make a better poor law guardian than a man rated at 60 *l.* in the country.

1679. That seems to be an argument for lowering the qualification, does it not?
So far as towns are concerned.

1680. But you must make it uniform, I suppose?
The majority of the guardians are rural guardians.

1681. Viscount *Hutchinson.*] I fancy the idea of the suggestion that was made, that there should be no qualification required for elective guardians, was this, giving a larger field of selection. The idea was that people who perhaps were not in any way connected with the union, should come in and act as guardians for the union if the ratepayers chose to repose confidence in them; in the same way as Members of Parliament often have practically no connection with the locality which they represent. Do you think that it is likely that under such a system of no qualification persons would come from outside and take office of poor law guardian?
I am certain they would not, unless they were paid for it.

1682. Lord *Salterford.*] Do you know any case where the question of qualification has been raised, in a contested election, for instance?
No; it was never raised in my union.

1683. Do you think it might have been raised in any case?
I never remember its being raised.

1684. *Chairman.*] But do you think that the rule is evaded or broken through?
I do not.

1685. Do you think that most of your guardians really have the qualification necessary by law?
I must ascertain that myself as I am responsible for it; I must find that the candidate has the rating qualifications, 25 *l.*

1686. Viscount *Hutchinson.*] What course would you have to take supposing there was a candidate proposed for the office of poor law guardian in a certain electoral division of our union, and you found that he was not duly qualified?
The nomination would be invalid.

1687. You would declare the nomination invalid?
Quite so.

1688. *Chairman.*] Is there any complaint amongst the people of the union that the qualification is too high at present?
I never heard it mentioned.

1689. Has it never been brought forward at the board?
Never; I never heard a question on the subject, I never heard the matter mentioned before in my life till I saw it in the Bill.

1690. Viscount *Hutchinson.*] What would be the effect of lowering the qualification in the Naas Union?
Getting very stupid guardians, I suppose.

1691. And

1691. And you would have a great increase of contested elections?
There would be a great increase of contested elections, and certainly would not improve the status of the board.

1692. *Lord Shute.*] Do you find that in Ireland people are not so very anxious to be elected guardians of unions?
Indeed they are not.

1693. *Chairman.*] Would you like to say any more on the question of the reduction of the qualification?
No; I would not be an advocate for reducing the qualification at all; and certainly to elect people without any rating qualification, I think would not answer.

1694. But if the law were that, if the constituency chose, in their wisdom, to elect a man who had not such a qualification, they might do so; how do you think that would work?
Then the chances are you would turn the board of guardians into a political arena more than it is at present; the poor would be left to take care of themselves.

1695. Then, coming to the proposal to reduce the number of *ex-officios*, what do you say to that?
I say decidedly not. The owners paying five-eighths of the rates, I consider that the *ex-officios* should, in fact, rather be increased than diminished. The elected guardians do not represent the owners of property, and they acknowledge that they do not, because they are not inclined to do it.

1696. They say that they represent the occupiers; is that so?
They say that they represent the occupiers, and that the owners of property have no right to be there at all, although they pay five-eighths of the rates. I certainly, on the face of it, think that instead of reducing the *ex officio* element it should be the other way. If the number is reduced to one-third, though I would not, as an official, like to express an opinion, I have very grave doubts, judging what they do in other unions where there is a paucity of justices, whether it would not be very disastrous; more than that I would not like to say.

1697. *Lord Shute.*] I suppose that opinion, to which you alluded just now, is not the general opinion, that owners of property have no right to be guardians?
I think the owners of property are not considered to be Irishmen; it is only the people that are to be looked after now-a-days.

1698. Then it is the general opinion?
I think so.

1699. *Chairman.*] Not the general opinion, is it?
I will not say the general opinion.

1700. But the opinion of some of your guardians?
Yes. Now, I will give, if the Committee will allow me, an instance of one union where there are very few resident justices, that is the Athy Union. The clerk of the union applied to that board to have the rate collectors appointed him as assistant overseers, under the Representation of the People Act, and the board, instead of acceding to his request, appointed the secretaries of the different Land Leagues as his assistants. The Local Government Board remonstrated with the board, and still they refused to accede to the wishes of the Local Government Board, and let the collectors discharge the duty.

1701. And in what position does the matter stand now?
The matter stands now, that the secretaries of the Land League are the assistants to the clerk of the union, and are serving the notices which are required under the Act.

1702. And

15th May 1885.]   Mr. MOLLOY.   [Continued.

1702. And can a board of guardians set the Local Government Board at defiance in that way?

It appears that they did in that case. I do not know what action the Local Government Board will take in the matter now. Of course, if they are very obstinate, the Local Government Board have the power of dissolving them altogether. If you wish it, I will read the correspondence between the Local Government Board and the board of guardians.

1703. If you please?

"The Local Government Board for Ireland have had before them the minute of the board of guardians of the Athy Union, on the 21st instance, relating to duties to be discharged under the Representation of the People Act, 1884, from which it appears that the board have directed that the books of two of the poor rate collectors should be handed to persons who had been named at a previous meeting of the board, to assist the clerk of the union in the discharge of the duties under the Act referred to. The board have also had before them the minute of the board of guardians of the 7th instant, when the guardians named certain persons, three of whom are collectors of poor rate in the union, and four of whom are not, to assist the clerk, the attention of the board having been drawn to the subject. In reference thereto, the Local Government Board desire to point out that it is obligatory on the clerk of the union to take the necessary steps under the Act, and that the responsibility rests with him. The several poor rate collectors are also bound to perform all duties imposed upon them by the Acts in force relating to the representation of the people, and that the six collectors of rates employed in Athy Union should be called on and required to aid the clerk. The collectors cannot be absolved from the discharge of this duty, and the appointment or nomination of the persons made by the guardians on the 7th instant were irregular and *ultra vires*. The books of the poor rate collectors should on no account be entrusted to other persons. The guardians will at once recognise the paramount importance of the collectors retaining their books in their own custody. It is competent to the board of guardians, with the approval of the Local Government Board, to remunerate the clerk of the union, in pursuance of Section 73 of the Act of 13 & 14 Vict. c. 69, to such extent as will enable him to employ and pay such assistants as may be necessary for carrying out the provisions of the Act referred to; and as above pointed out, the collectors of rates are the proper persons to be employed. The Local Government Board request the immediate attention of the board of guardians to these important matters." Then at a meeting of the guardians, Mr. Kavanagh said, "I would suggest that the following reply be sent to the Local Government Board: 'That, inasmuch as the several parties appointed have been working at duties of overseers under the Act, the guardians do not see the advisability or necessity of making any further change, as we consider those appointed fully competent, and more especially as the time is now very limited to fulfil the duties required under the Act.'" Mr. Orford seconded Mr. Kavanagh's proposition, which, on being put to the meeting, was unanimously adopted, and the discussion on the subject dropped."

1704. Now, in your union, do the *ex-officios* attend tolerably well?
They do.

1705. And do you consider that advantageous or disadvantageous to the proper administration of the poor law?

I consider it most advantageous. There are several *ex-officios* of my board who take a very lively interest in the taking of contracts, and I attribute a great deal of the good feeling, if I may say so, that exists in the Naas Union, to the committees being mixed committees for entering into contracts and taking stock, and all those sort of things.

1706. Viscount *Hutchinson*.] What is your average attendance of *ex-officios*; how many come out of the 33?

I believe the attendance in the different unions is published, but I did not bring it with me.

1707. *Chairman*.]

15th May 1885.] Mr. MOLLOY. [Continued.

1707. *Chairman.*] A suggestion has been made here, that the *ex-officio* guardians should have the power to resign their position; will you tell us what is the law on that point, because that has been variously stated here?
The law, as I understand it, is that if in a union where there are, for instance, 33 *ex-officios* required, if there are exactly that number of justices qualified within the union, they are everyone of them bound to act, and they cannot refuse to act; they cannot resign.

1708. The only question I want to ask is, has an *ex-officio* now, by law, the power to resign?
I think not.

1709. Do you think it desirable that he should have such a power?
I think so.

1710. In the case of a man who is unable to attend, for example?
In the case of a man who is unable from old age or any other circumstances to attend, I think it would be reasonable that he should have the power of resigning.

1711. How would you suggest that his place should be filled up?
I think some one should be elected by the magistrates amongst themselves, irrespective of qualification.

1712. Viscount *Powerscourt.*] Irrespective of any property qualification, you mean?
Yes.

1713. *Chairman.*] But you have just assented to the proposition that every *ex-officio* should be a ratepayer?
Quite so; but what I mean to say is that a justice rated at 100 *l.* should not take precedence of a justice rated at 50 *l.*; but supposing that there are 50 justices resident and non-resident connected with the union, I say that those should meet, and from their body elect 33, or whatever is the number required, choosing them from their own body.

1714. Viscount *Powerscourt.*] That is, in fact, that the whole board should be elected?
I think so.

1715. Part by the ratepayers and part by the magistrates?
That the whole of the *ex-officio* guardians should be elected from the whole body of owners of property.

1716. Lord *Monk-Bretton.*] Instead of putting on those who are most highly rated?
Yes, for this reason, that the highest rated may be a very old man, or he may live at a very inconvenient distance, or for a great many other reasons may be unsuitable.

1717. Viscount *Hutchinson.*] Now we will suppose (rightly or wrongly) that the *ex-officio* guardian has a power of resignation; I dare say there are a great many of *ex-officio* guardians in your union, who, by no possibility, are able to attend, because they live at too great a distance, or something of that sort?
Yes.

1718. Supposing there were a power of resignation on their part, would you be able to find proper men to fill their places?
If you mean local magistrates, no, I would not, but if there are not enough resident justices, I would get the non-residents.

1719. But in that case would you be able to find people who would be more likely to attend than some who are on the board now?
I could not say that.

1720. But you suggest, I understand, that there should be a form of election for *ex-officios*, and a form of election for owners of property?
Yes.

1721. *Chairman.*]

1721. *Chairman.*] Do you mean that the magistrates should elect out of their own body?
Yes.

1722. Not that all owners of property should join in the election?
The owners of property, you know, in nine cases out of ten, are magistrates.

1723. Viscount *Hutchinson.*] But I will tell you why I ask you the question, because we have had the matter before us; Mr. Bagwell, and other witnesses, on the last occasion, suggested schemes by which property should be represented?
I think it would be very difficult to get the owners of property to elect. I think it would be sufficient to have them elected by the magistrates from their own body.

1724. There are a great many owners of property who are not magistrates; taking it all over Ireland, the majority of owners of property are not magistrates, I suppose?
In the union I represent, I hardly know an owner of property who is not a magistrate, unless in the case of people living away from Ireland altogether.

1725. If a scheme of the sort were entertained, by which, instead of *ex-officio* guardians as they exist now, we should have a separate class of guardians who should represent property, as against the guardians who represent the occupiers, you would not see any difficulty, would you, in organising a scheme by which a constituency could be formed, and could proceed to the election of such guardians?
There could be no difficulty, of course, that I know of, in the owners of property electing amongst themselves people to represent them outside their own body.

1726. Do you see any advantage in that?
I do not see any advantage that would be gained.

1727. You do not think that it would have this advantage, that it would be in the power of owners of property to choose a certain class of local men who are never on boards of guardians now: I mean men who are representatives of property in a certain way, though perhaps not of property in land?
I do not think it would be any advantage whatever electing them. I think the *ex-officio* guardians would be just as likely to attend as any class that they would elect.

1728. Lord *Saltersford.*] But do not you think that a person who was specially elected for the purpose of attending would be more likely to give a regular attendance at the board than one who simply comes into it as an *ex-officio*?
But my experience is that the *ex-officio* guardians, a good many of them, take just as large an interest in the business of the union as the elected guardians, and are as great economists.

1729. Viscount *Hutchinson.*] Do you look upon it as absolutely and entirely necessary that the representative of property should be a magistrate?
Well, I do not say it is absolutely necessary that he should be a magistrate; but I think the magistrates are as good a class as the owners of property could be represented by.

1730. But there are a great many other people who would do just as well as magistrates, are there not, to represent property?
I would be very sorry to say that there are not. I do not mean to say that the whole intelligence of the country is concentrated in the magistrates.

1731. Viscount *Powerscourt.*] To put it shortly, would it not be possible to find men to represent property who were not magistrates?
I have no doubt it would; there can be no question about that; but whether you would secure a better attendance by it or not is another thing.

(O.I.)   X   1732. *Chairman.*]

1732. *Chairman.*] Your idea is that the *ex-officios* should be preserved pretty much as they are, but that they should be selected by the magistrates from amongst their own body?
Yes.

1733. You have not adopted Mr. Bagwell's proposition?
No. I am an advocate for the existing magistracy electing from their own body the number required to represent each union.

1734. And I think this Bill, in fact, provides that they shall elect from their own number; do you wish to say anything more on that point?
No.

1735. Lord *Monk-Bretton.*] Is the effect of the Bill, as it stands, that the magistrates are to elect out of their own body?
Yes.

1736. Is that the effect of the Bill as now worded?
Yes, I think so.

1737. *Chairman.*] I find that the words in Sub-section 5 of Clause 26 are: "In every case in which the number of justices qualified to be *ex-officio* guardians shall exceed one-half the number of the elective guardians, the justices to serve as *ex-officio* guardians shall be selected from among the qualified justices at the prescribed time after the passing of this Act, in the manner provided by the Sixteenth Section of the Act of the Session of the Tenth year of the reign of Her present Majesty, chapter Thirty-one." What clause does that refer to?
The one which says that the highest rated should be taken, if the number of justices in a union exceeds the number that are to be on the board; they have to be written to to know if they are willing to act, and then, having ascertained that, they are selected according to their rating.

1738. Lord *Monk-Bretton.*] Therefore, the Bill in that respect retains the existing law?
Yes.

1739. Lord *Shute.*] I believe that a great many agents of owners of property are magistrates in Ireland?
They are.

1740. I suppose you would hardly think they were proper persons to fill the office of *ex-officios*, as they are not necessarily ratepayers?
I would not have them on unless they are ratepayers. I would not have any magistrate on a board of guardians in virtue of his being a magistrate unless he was a ratepayer.

1741. Even though the agents represent the property of their employers, you would not have them on the board unless they were ratepayers?
I would not. I would require a property qualification from the *ex-officio* guardians.

1742. *Chairman.*] I suppose there is a certain amount of jealousy felt amongst the guardians at persons who are not ratepayers interfering in the affairs of the union?
I think so, naturally.

1743. Now with regard to Sub-section (6), which provides: "No ratepayers shall be entitled at any poor law election to more than 18 votes": what do you say to that?
I think that is a very good arrangement too; I would be very much inclined to go back, and let things be as they were before the decision in the Fitzwilliam Case. According to the law as it stands now it would be possible for the owner of property to have 30 votes; that is, 12 as owner and occupier, 12 as the owner of property, rated at and under 4 *l.*, and six as the owner of property over 4 *l.*; that would give him 30 votes; I think 18 is quite enough; I would be inclined to let the holdings valued at and under 4 *l.* be, as heretofore, added in to the first claim to vote.

1744. Be aggregated, you mean?
Be aggregated.

1745. And the effect of that decision to which you have referred has been to alter that rule of aggregation?
It has, and I do not think there are very many, perhaps not more than one or two landlords in Ireland that could by any possibility have as many as 30 votes; I doubt if there are very many that have tenants under 4 *l.*, valued at 200 *l.* and upwards.

1746. They have not a sufficient number of tenants at 4 *l.* and under to make up the 200, you mean?
Just so.

1747. Are there any other observations you would like to make with respect to this Bill?
I think not.

1748. Lord *Monk-Bretton.*] How many electoral divisions are there in your union?
Thirty-seven. There is a difference between electoral divisions and electoral districts.

1749. How many electoral districts are there?
Twenty-nine.

1750. And how many elective guardians?
Thirty-three.

1751. How many of those are owners?
Not one.

1752. How many *ex-officios* are there?
Thirty-three, the same number as the elective guardians; all resident, and all rated, either owners or occupiers of property.

1753. And what is the number of voters in the union?
In the entire union, do you mean; I could not answer that question. The entire union was never contested; every electoral division was never contested at any time.

1754. Then you do not know the number of electors who could record votes in case the whole union were contested?
I should suppose close on 4,000.

1755. Out of those 4,000, how many would be owners?
I could not answer that question.

1756. A fourth?
No, not so much as a fourth.

1757. An eighth?
I would not like to say.

1758. You could not tell approximately?
I could not; the question has never cropped up; I never thought on the matter.

1759. Is any complaint ever made of the power of voting by proxy which is now enjoyed?
Well, yes; people grumble at it.

1760. To any great extent?
No.

1761. *Chairman.*] What sort of people grumble at it?
The candidates themselves.

1762. Do the people at large?
No.

1763. Lord

1763. Lord *Monk-Bretton.*] You mean the candidates who think the proxy votes will go against them, I presume?
Quite so.

1764. You mentioned the Fitzwilliam case just now; what is the name of that case?
Earl Fitzwilliam v. The Shillelagh Union, I believe. It is familiarly called the Fitzwilliam case.

1765. Can you tell me where it is reported?
I cannot.

1766. I think you said that you considered that the absence of owners as *ex-officio* guardians from the boards would be disastrous; you used that expression?
I think so, if that element was left out altogether.

1767. Why would it be disastrous?
I mean that the boards would become political bodies pure and simple, to discuss political matters, perhaps to the detriment of the legitimate duties which they have to discharge. The tendency is that way at the present time.

1768. Do you think that the Poor Law would be less strictly administered?
I do, decidedly.

1769. There would be a tendency to give out-door relief more freely; is that so?
I do not go that length. The out-door relief, as far as I know, has enormously increased of latter years, but I do not think it is on the increase at present, and likely to go beyond the point it has reached.

1770. Is the house test less severely applied now in the unions than it was some years ago?
No, I think not. I do not think boards of guardians are disposed to give out-door relief unless in extreme cases, and to those legally entitled.

1771. You do not think that the strict administration of the Poor Law has been unduly relaxed of late years?
I do not. There are three classes of persons entitled to out-door relief; the permanently disabled by reason of old age; the temporarily disabled by reason of sickness or accident or otherwise, and widows with two or more children. With regard to the third class, widows with two or more children, I think it very desirable that they should get out door relief, because the mother may be able by her industry to supplement the relief, and rear her family out of the house, which I think is very desirable, for I am afraid that children brought up in a workhouse do not turn out very well as a rule.

1772. Lord *Saltersford.*] Have there been any cases of guardians surcharged for giving illegal out-door relief in the Naas Union in your recollection?
I do not think there was ever a surcharge in the Naas Union that I recollect.

1773. Lord *Monk-Bretton.*] Upon Clause 11 of the Bill, do you think that the returning officer should hear objections to persons who have been put on the list, at the same time that he hears claims from persons who have been omitted from the list?
I think so.

1774. You would amend the clause in that way?
I would; and as I stated before, unless objections are made before the register is signed, they should not be made afterwards, the public having had ample opportunity of making the objections before.

1775. You would not allow an appeal, unless the point had been raised before the returning officer?
Quite so. I think that would be but reasonable, for I am afraid the returning officer might get a great deal of annoyance otherwise. A trivial mistake that

that might have been pointed out and rectified before the register was signed, might be brought against him afterwards.

1776. *Chairman.*] You have always had a good attendance of *ex-officios* at your board, I gather from you?
Very fair.

1777. Throughout the whole of this agitation it has not made any material difference?
There has been a very fair attendance. I suppose the average attendance of *ex-officio* and elected guardians would be about 10 or 11. Then there would be always a good third of them, I should say, *ex-officio*.

1778. In fact, the Naas Board has never been, what some of the other witnesses have called, "altogether in the hands of the League"?
It has not.

1779. Lord *Shute.*] Are the *ex-officios* well treated by the other guardians in your union?
I cannot say that they are treated with a great deal of politeness; it does not seem to be the order of the day now. A gentleman appears to be nowhere; there is no doubt about that.

1780. They never agree with them?
Very seldom; there are very few subjects that they agree on.

1781. Is there any very strong language used?
No, we do not go so far as that.

1782. Order is well kept?
Order is well kept.

The Witness is directed to withdraw.

MR. HARRY M'CANN, having been called in; is Examined, as follows:

1783. *Chairman.*] ARE you a Magistrate?
No.

1784. An elective guardian?
I am an elective guardian. I was a magistrate at one time, and I was an *ex-officio* guardian for four years, in virtue of my position as magistrate, and I have been an elective guardian for the last eight years.

1785. In the Longford Union?
In the Longford Union.

1786. I believe you are vice-chairman of the board of guardians?
Deputy vice-chairman.

1787. Have you considered the Bill now before the House?
I have looked into it.

1788. We should be very glad to hear what you think about it; what clause would you first wish to call our attention to?
I would be satisfied with a triennial election for the guardians; I think that is the first matter.

1789. That is Clause 4?
Yes; the others before that are merely defining clauses.

1790. Viscount *Hutchinson.*] We have had it suggested to us by another witness that one-third of the board should retire every year, so that there should always be on the board two-thirds of the old members; that, in fact, the re-election of the board should take place by thirds; what do you say to that?
Theoretically, it would be the case that it might be better to have some of the

the old members on in that way; but, practically, the majority probably of the old members would still remain on without that.

1791. You do not see any great advantage in a third retiring every year?
No; I do not see any great advantage in their retiring in the case of boards of guardians, as they do in many other public bodies.

1792. I ask the question, because it was suggested to us that by that means you would have men of experience always on the board?
That is the reason why I wish you to have triennial elections; because otherwise one man goes out one year, and another comes in for the next who does not know anything of his business; in theory it might be better to have a third retiring annually, but I think practically a sufficient number of the old guardians would be re-elected without that.

1793. *Chairman.*] What do you say to the proposal of the Bill to adopt the ballot for these elections?
In the present degenerate state of feelings on the subject, I am greatly afraid it is necessary for the protection of some of the people from every sort of influence. I prefer to vote publicly myself.

1794. What kind of influence is now exercised?
A great deal of influence is used on every side; I do not distinguish; I think there is popular influence and landlord influence; I dislike using the words, but the Committee will understand what I mean.

1795. How can a landlord use undue influence under the present state of the law?
I hardly like to go to particulars, but we have had in our county, very recently, some very serious cases of undue influence on the part of landlords. We had an election for Poor Law guardians not very long ago, in which every tenant of a certain landlord (I hope you will not ask me to mention the name: I will mention the name privately to you) who voted for a particular guardian was deprived of his turbary.

1796. Had he a legal right to it?
No, he had a permissive right; and those who voted in a particular way were deprived of it. There is no system of voting more liable to intimidation than this voting paper system. There is much less intimidation possible where a man comes up and publicly votes, than where he gets a voting paper, because in the latter case he may be tampered with in every way.

1797. You are opposed, therefore, to the present system?
I am opposed to the present system. As we have the ballot for Parliamentary elections, I suppose we require it for these elections; I know that the other system is most unsatisfactory. One party goes in and gets the voter's voting-paper filled up, and immediately afterwards the opposing party comes in and gets the voting paper spoiled.

1798. On the whole, then, you think that it is desirable to have the ballot, to prevent undue influence from any side?
I think it is necessary.

1799. Is there any suggestion you would like to make for carrying out the machinery of the ballot?
No, I think it can be carried out just as at the election of town commissioners. At present town commissioners are elected by the ballot; I see no difficulty in it.

1800. Do you not think that women and infirm persons might have some difficulty in exercising their vote by ballot in these Poor Law elections?
The women vote for the town commissioners, and they seem to exercise their vote in Longford as vigorously as the men.

1801. They are not too timid?
No, not there; they may be in other parts of Ireland, but with us they are just as anxious to record their votes as any man.

1802. Is

1802. Is there anything else you see in the Bill to remark upon before you come to Clause 9?
No, not till we come to the proxy voting.

1803. That is Clause 9; what do you say to that?
I am opposed to voting by proxy.

1804. On what grounds?
On the ground that it is an invidious distinction. It is given to a certain class, and not to another.

1805. But it is only given to a certain class, we have been told, because they could not vote in any other way?
Why not; could not anyone come personally there and vote, if it is worth his while?

1806. How could he be in two places at once; that has been a suggestion that it would be impossible, as the Poor Law elections are conducted all on one day, for a man who had property in various unions to vote in all of them in person?
But that affects also the ratepayers in various unions. If the proxy vote were continued, I should say it should be given to ratepayers as well. I do not see why vote by proxy should be proper in the Poor Law election, unless it is in the Parliamentary election too.

1807. Do not you see any distinction between the two cases?
I see the distinction that your Lordship suggests, still I do not think it is a difficulty that should override the objection generally felt to voting by proxy as an invidious distinction.

1808. But an invidious distinction, because it is an unnecessary distinction, in your opinion?
If you would extend it to all, I would have less objection to it.

1809. There has been a suggestion made by a witness that it should be extended, in certain circumstances, to occupiers?
I would have less objection to it then. I have not studied the question in reference to that; it never struck me.

1810. The objection to proxy voting is a sort of sentimental objection on your part?
To a certain extent it is, but certainly my objection would be considerably lessened if the distinction were removed.

1811. *Lord Shute.*] But an occupier is not likely to occupy one farm a very great distance from another, is he?
I occupy land myself in more than one union.

1812. Fifty or 100 miles apart?
No so far, but some 40 or 50.

1813. Supposing an owner of property had got property 50 or 100 miles off?
I am in that position myself; I am an owner of property as well as a ratepayer; I can vote by proxy, I think, in three unions, but I have never used the power.

1814. *Chairman.*] You wish to be prevented from voting by proxy?
I have never used it, so it is immaterial to me if I am prevented.

1815. *Lord Saltersford.*] But you think it would be fair that there should be a proxy for a simple occupier's vote?
Yes, if there be a proxy vote at all.

1816. In point of fact, that would be extending the proxy vote, would it not?
Yes; as his Lordship says, it is probably rather a sentimental objection on my part; I am opposed to a distinction in the nature of the voting between different parties.

15th May 1885.]   Mr. M'CANN.   [Continued.

1817. *Chairman.*] But you do feel that it would be somewhat of a hardship that those who pay a large proportion of the rates should have no voice in the election of the Poor Law Board?
Those who have property in different unions would be incapacitated from voting, probably, if the proxy vote were taken away.

1818. So that it would amount to taxation without representation?
It is the case, you know, in the Parliamentary elections.

1819. Lord *Ker.*] If the proxy vote were not exercised, would it not practically throw, or very much throw, the whole election into the hands of one class?
It would, perhaps, to a considerable extent; but practically the other class (though I do not like to talk of classes) are protected by the *ex-officio* guardians.

1820. That brings us to another question?
You must take them together; at least, in my mind, I feel that I must. At present the *ex-officio* guardians are a sufficient protection for the property vote, because they have an equal number of guardians.

1821. Lord *Shute.*] You are aware that in England we have the *ex-officio* guardians, and it has answered well?
And so in my part of Ireland we have got on well; we have no complaint, except that the *ex-officios* never attend.

1822. *Chairman.*] Let me put to you this frank question: until the political element was brought into these questions, was there ever an objection raised to the proxy vote?
Yes, I have always had that objection, and I am not a politician; I have never taken part in politics. The thing I principally want altered is this; I think it is a mistake to have the returning officer also the revising officer.

1823. What clause is it in the Bill which deals with that?
Clause 11. It comes to that; I think a great deal of the disturbances and annoyances at elections arise from that fact.

1824. And what alteration would you suggest?
I think it would be very simple to have the list of poor rate electors revised by the county court judge, as the Parliamentary list is, and made some considerable time before; and all objections made before him; and once that register is signed by the county court judge, let that register be final. I think that is really the most important thing that could be done with regard to the administration of that part of the Poor Law in Ireland, and it would save expense also.

1825. Lord *Dudley.*] How often would you have that revision?
Every 12 months. I do not see why it could not be made at the same time as the Parliamentary revision; and I think that that is really of more importance than the question of *ex-officios*, or the ballot, or anything else.

1826. Lord *Saltersford.*] How would that save expense?
Because it would stop a number of contests; contests are now started on the possibility of finding fault immediately after the election with the revising officer's conduct. The contest is often owing to some complaint against the action of the revising officer just before or at the revision of the list; and if it were carried out before the county court judge, all this would cease, and these contests are very expensive.

1827. *Chairman.*] What should you say is the expense of these contests?
In a large division it would be 10 *l.* or 15 *l.* out of the rates.

1828. But that expense would be increased, I am afraid, by the introduction of the ballot?
Of course it would; but contests would be fewer.

1829. And are the costs paid out of the rates now?
They are paid out of the rates.

1830. Do you approve of that?
I think

I think so; it is a difficult question; I have often thought of making the defeated candidate pay the costs; but still it would be a difficult question. I think all these objections to returns are merely founded upon errors supposed to have been made by the returning officer.

1831. What do you say to having the lists of voters printed?
That is my idea. I think they should be printed in about the month of July; the taxes paid before the 1st of July, and the lists prepared by the collectors, and printed in the month of July; and any objections made then before the sitting of the county court judge in August.

1832. And do you think that all the lists ought to be printed and published, and not alone those where there is a contest?
In my view they should be printed; long before there is an idea of a contest.

1833. Do you think that that would add much to the expense?
It would decrease the expense considerably, because often there would be no contests if that were done.

1834. Viscount *Hutchinson.*] It would increase the expense at first, and decrease it eventually, you think?
Yes.

1835. *Chairman.*] What do you say as to the petition to the county court judge?
That would be very much simplified again by my proposition if carried out, because the greater number of the grounds of petition would be removed. Unless for improper conduct on the part of the returning officer, there could be no petition.

1836. And do you approve of the suggestion that the petitioner should give security for costs?
Yes.

1837. To prevent frivolous petitions?
Yes, and it also would decrease the number of petitions.

1838. And with regard to the costs on petitions, is there anything you would like to say about that?
No, I think they would be very trifling.

1839. Do you think they ought to fall on the rates?
No; I think not.

1840. Under no circumstances?
Under no circumstances.

1841. Take the case I have put to one of the witnesses, of the fault being that of the returning officer, although not such a grievous fault as to make him liable in damages; still, it would be very hard on the parties then to have to pay the costs?
I think that might be left, as it is in many cases, to the discretion of the county court judge. If the county court judge considered that the returning officer was in fault so seriously that he should pay the costs, it would be in his power to put the costs on him.

1842. And if not?
If not, that they should be paid out of the rates, if it was a sort of excusable informality or oversight. I would leave that to the discretion of the county court judge; but I anticipate that there would be very few petitions were the revising officer not the returning officer also.

1843. Lord *Ker.*] The list would hold good for the whole year, I suppose, from one July to the next July?
That would be my suggestion.

1844. *Chairman.*] What do you say to the proposal of excluding a minor from

15th *May* 1885.] Mr. M'CANN. [*Continued.*

from voting; it has been suggested that he might be enabled to vote through his trustee or guardian; do you approve of that?
I certainly think it looks very odd to have a minor voting; I would object to a minor having a vote.

1845. But do you object to his being allowed to vote through his guardian, or next friend?
No. I think some provision might be made to enable, not him personally, but some person to vote for him.

1846. And I suppose you approve of the proposal that a justice of the peace should not be qualified to be an *ex-officio* guardian unless he is a ratepayer?
In some sense, although it is not so with us. I know unions where it would be a great pity that, in order to serve as a guardian, a justice of the peace should be necessarily a ratepayer; it is not so in our union, because we have no justice of the peace that is not a ratepayer.

1847. Lord *Skute.*] If you do not object to somebody voting for a minor, you do not entirely object to proxy voting?
No, I do not.

1848. Lord *Sudley.*] If the power of proxy voting was extended to occupiers who hold land in different unions, would that do away with your objection to proxy voting?
It would, to a considerable extent.

1849. *Chairman.*] You are in favour of retaining the law as it is, with reference to the question of a justice of the peace being a ratepayer?
Yes.

1850. Is there not a certain amount of jealousy, which one could perfectly well understand on the part of the elected guardians, against a person who is not a ratepayer being a guardian, and dealing with the rates in poor law affairs?
Not in my judgment. There is a certain amount of jealousy in regard to the agent of a landlord, even though he be a ratepayer, being an *ex officio* guardian, but it does not extend to a man because he is a magistrate being *ex officio*. A landlord himself, for instance, represents his own property, and his agent is an *ex-officio* guardian because he is a justice of the peace; but he may be a ratepayer; a resident agent is always a ratepayer; but I do not think there would be a jealousy against a man individually because he happened not to be a ratepayer; the jealousy would be with regard to the double representation of the same property.

1851. Viscount *Hutchinson.*] But it may happen, may it not, that a man who is not a ratepayer, but is a guardian, represents nobody?
We had one, years ago, and we used to call him guardian for the union at large.

1852. *Chairman.*] What do you say, coming to the next proposal of importance, with regard to the proposal to reduce the number of *ex officio* guardians?
The matter does not affect us very much, because we have only two *ex officios* that ever attend. They have such confidence, I suppose, in the elective guardians that they leave us to ourselves. Lord Granard, an *ex officio* guardian, is our chairman, and Mr. James Bond, another *ex officio* guardian, is our deputy chairman, and they are very regular attendants; and I do not think any other *ex officio* attends three times in a year.

1853. Viscount *Hutchinson.*] How many are you now on the board?
We have 19 electoral divisions, 21 elective guardians, and 21 *ex officio* guardians.

1854. Do you suppose some of them do not attend because it is impossible, from the fact that they live too far off, or are too old?
Those who live nearest attend worst. We have some who live within a mile or half a mile of the workhouse, and never come in to the board meetings.

1855. *Chairman.*]

15th May 1885.] Mr. M'CANN. [Continued.

1855. *Chairman.*] But do they give any reason for not attending?
No; they pay Lord Granard the compliment of coming in to attend at his election; they come in then.

1856. Viscount *Hutchinson.*] You have had no contest for the election of chairman for the last few years, have you?
For the eight years that I have been there, I do not remember any contest for the post of chairman.

1857. *Chairman.*] As far as you know, when the *ex-officio* guardians attend, are they subjected to any insult or annoyance of any kind?
Certainly not in our union; on the contrary, we are always most anxious to have the *ex-officios* there; we like to have them in.

1858. Then I presume from that answer that you are altogether against reducing their number?
No, I am not. I consider that the *ex-officio* principle is a bad one. I think they should be elected. I would suggest that the owners of property should elect 21 of the guardians, and the ratepayers elect the other 21.

1859. Viscount *Hutchinson.*] In fact, on grounds of strict justice, you prefer that to the system proposed in the Bill that the *ex-officio* guardians should be reduced?
I would suggest then that there should be independent representatives upon the board, for the owners of property, and for the ratepayers. I never heard it suggested before, but it was in my own mind for years, and I had formed that idea.

1860. You did not see Mr. Bagwell's scheme?
I did not read it; and that plan would obviate the evil of the non-attendance of the representatives of property.

1861. Your practical objection to the *ex-officio* is that he does not attend?
That he is no use; and that is the case in the surrounding unions as well as in our own.

1862. I suppose it is, perhaps, because he is selected, and not elected, that he does not attend?
It would not be necessary to have that gentleman a magistrate. In my mind he might be a representative of property, without being a magistrate in any sense of the word.

1863. It has also been suggested to us here, that if you had that mode of election you would get a much larger class of people to select from as representatives of property, not only people who own land, but there are plenty of people in towns engaged in business and trade, whose interest are mixed up with landed property to a great extent, and you would have the advantage of that class to choose the representatives of property from?
We would have property represented, not a class of property.

1864. Practically, your only objection to the *ex-officio* guardian is that he is no use?
Yes.

1865. And you think he may just as well be reduced as not?
That is the result of my long experience.

1866. Of course you are not at all looking at it from the point of view from which some people look at it, that the *ex officio* is the only representative that property gets?
Why should I object to property being properly represented? The mistake on most poor law boards at present is that property is not properly represented; whether it is from the evil of their being *ex-officios de jure* and not selected for the purpose, or for whatever reason, they do not attend. In all probability the owners of property, if they elected them, would encourage them to attend; they would not elect a man that would not attend; the very election would encourage him to attend.

(0.1.) Y 2 1867. You

1867. You have heard what has been said by other witnesses as to the proportion of rates paid by the different classes of owners and occupiers; do you know, from your experience, what it is?
I have calculated that it is about 3-8ths in our union; the owners pay about 5-8ths.

1868. He is fairly entitled, under those circumstances, to a half of the representation?
To 5-8ths of the representatives. He has that practically, in the division that I represent; the owners of property there could elect the guardian. I represent the division of Corboy, in the county of Longford, and the owners of property could elect the elective guardian there; that is to say, their voting power is greater than that of the occupier voting power in that division.

1869. *Chairman.*] That must be exceptional?
I presume it is. Should the present law remain as it is, with the 36 votes carried out in Longford, the power would be in the hands of the owners.

1870. Thirty votes is the maximum, is it not?
I think I could show that a man can possibly have 36 votes; I do not suppose, practically, he has; but if he had, in the Longford division itself, the property vote would outvote the occupiers. I am not certain that Lord Longford has not 36 votes in Longford if he chooses to exercise his right.

1871. That must be a very exceptional case?
Even with the 18, the property vote could outvote the occupier vote in Corboy.

1872. Lord *Ker.*] We have been told that it is not possible for any one individual to have more than 30 votes; but you do not agree with that?
Theoretically it is possible; a man can have 12 occupier votes, and he can have 24 votes as an owner of property.

1873. Lord *Saltersford.*] In the newspaper it was stated in a recent case, the Fitzwilliam case, that 30 was the largest number of votes possible?
I think I could prove that it is 36.

1874. *Chairman.*] Are you in favour of reducing the number to 18 as the maximum votes that any man could have in any one electoral division?
That has been the law so long acted on; it has so long been the practical law, under the direction of the Local Government Board, that I think I would be in favour of keeping that.

1875. You think that that would be right; and the proposal of this Bill is to limit the number of votes that one man can give to 18; in fact, to revert to what has been the practice hitherto?
If the *ex-officio* guardians were elected as I propose, it would make no difference what the number of votes that one man could give was.

1876. How do you make that out?
Because the property vote would not interfere in the election of elective guardians.

1877. Surely an occupier would be entitled to vote for an occupier candidate?
An occupier can only have 12 votes under any circumstances.

1878. Lord *Ker.*] You would have two separate classes of representatives?
Yes.

1879. The elective guardians elected entirely by the occupier vote?
Yes.

1880. And the owners of property elected entirely by the property vote?
Yes.

1881. An equal number?
An equal number as at present.

1882. Viscount *Hutchinson.*] One point has arisen in the course of the evidence

evidence before the Committee about the ballot; if the secrecy of the ballot is to be preserved, how are you going to do that; when there are certain people who have a certain number of votes; we will say one person has five, another 12, another six, and so on; when it comes to revising the votes, people will be able to make a pretty good guess as to who voted upon these different voting papers; would you suggest, in order to obviate that, that there should be a separate paper for each vote?
Yes; if a man has 12 votes he should have 12 papers.

1883. Lord *Shute*.] What is the out-door relief in the Longford Union?
£.1,000 a year at present, I am sorry to say.

1884. I mean in individual cases?
We have 233 cases of out-door relief.

1885. What do they individually get?
I daresay it will average about 2*s*. 6*d*. a week; some get a great deal more; some have five or six children, and they may get as much as 6*s*. a week.

1886. Do any of them get as much as a pound?
No.

1887. You do not give evicted tenants, or persons of that sort in your union, a pound a week?
We may have given relief to evicted tenants, but not because they were evicted tenants.

1888. You never gave them as much as a pound a week?
No.

1889. Lord *Ker*.] Do you know what maximum has been given?
I do not think we ever exceeded 6*s*.; in no case has it been given to an evicted tenant as such, but an evicted tenant may be an object for out-door relief. We would not exclude a man from out-door relief, if he was otherwise entitled to it, because he happened to be an evicted tenant.

1890. *Chairman*.] Is there anything you would like to say generally to the Committee, on the subject of the Bill before us?
Nothing more, except that I may add that we have a most exemplary revising officer ourselves, and he is found no fault with; but in reading the papers I find that all those discussions which have occurred on this subject in the House of Commons, arose out of some questions between the candidates and the returning officer; and if he were not the revising officer as well, those contests could not arise.

The Witness is directed to withdraw.

Mr. RICHARD EDWARD FOX, having been called in; is Examined, as follows:

1891. *Chairman* You are a magistrate; for what county?
The county of Longford.

1892. And an *ex officio* guardian of the Ballymahon Union?
Yes.

1893. You have been so, I believe, for the last 15 years; and since March last you have been appointed deputy vice-chairman of the Board?
Yes.

1894. What do you say to the proposal in this Bill for triennial elections?
I am not in favour of it.

1895. Why do you object to it?
I think, under the present state of things, taking the guardians that would be put in, it would be undesirable to have them for three years without a controlling

trolling election; that is to say, I think we would get a bad class of guardians for three years, such as we have at present. I am speaking of my own union.

1896. But why should you get a worse class?
I said as had a class as we have now.

1897. Then it would make no difference, would it, if the elections were triennial?
But we should have them for three years.

1898. But if you keep on having them for one year, it cannot make much difference?
If this had been proposed four years ago, I should not have objected to it at all, and it is possible that I should not object to it three or four years hence, but I am speaking of the actual men we are likely to get.

1899. Viscount *Hutchinson*.] What is the actual qualification in your union?
£. 20.

1900. *Chairman*.] You think, as I understand you, that it would he bad to stereotype the guardians who are elected under the present period of agitation?
Yes, and I hope we shall have a better class.

1901. What do you say of the ballot?
I would approve of it.

1902. I believe you would prefer that the election should be held in August instead of March?
Yes.

1903. On what ground?
I think it is an anomaly that an elective guardian coming in in March should strike the rate in September, and that if he was put out, his successor should he liable for the administration of one-half of the rate that his predecessor struck. I think the election ought to be in August, and the rate struck in or about September.

1904. Viscount *Hutchinson*.] At present I understand that the elections for the elective guardians take place in March?
In March.

1905. And that the *ex officios*, if any, are nominated in September?
The *ex officios* are practically nominated in September.

1906. And that is more or less anomalous in itself, is it not?
It is curious.

1907. Looking upon the *ex officios* as, I suppose, they ought to be looked upon, as representing the property-owning class?
Yes; but it strikes me that the guardian who strikes the rate should administer that rate.

1908. Should be responsible for the administration of the whole of it, you mean?
Yes.

1909. *Chairman*.] What do you say about the proposed abolition of proxy voting?
That I am entirely opposed to.

1910. Why?
It would disfranchise, in fact, the representatives of property, of ownership, to a great extent.

1911. Do you mean to say that owners of property could not exercise their vote without that power?
They could only partially exercise it.

1912. Do you see any evil in the system of proxy voting as it exists at present?
No.

1913. How

1913. How many owners of property are there in your electoral division?
Eight.

1914. How many of them are resident?
There are two actually in the electoral division, one about a mile outside it, whom I practically count as resident.

1915. Then there are three, you may say, resident and five non-resident?
Five non-resident.

1916. Would the effect of the abolition of the proxy vote be to disfranchise the five out of the eight?
Yes.

1917. What proportion of the rates do the owners pay to the occupiers in your electoral division?
The owners pay 92 *l*. 9 *s*. 5 *d*., and the occupiers pay 55 *l*. 19 *s*. 3 *d*.

1918. I believe you can produce some table to show what occurred at the last election in your union?
Yes.

1919. And what does that table show as regards the numbers voting for the Loyalist candidate, and those who voted for the League candidate?
For the Loyalist candidate there was 51.

1920. Fifty-one votes were given, you mean?
Fifty-one votes.

1921-2. And for the other?
Eighty-two.

1923. What proportion of rates were paid by those who voted for the Loyalist?
£. 98. 16 *s*. 10 *d*.

1924. And for the other?
£. 39. 10 *s*. 1½ *d*.

1925. Less than half.
Less than half.

1926. And yet they carried the election by a majority of 30?
Yes.

1927. What is the amount of the rate in your electoral division.
£. 148. 8 *s*. 8 *d*.

1928. Have you got a table showing how that is made up?
Yes; exactly.

1929. Will you shortly tell us that?
Landlords and Loyalist tenants who voted contribute 18 *l*. 9 *s*. 6½ *d*.; landlords for occupations and for holdings valued at 4 *l*. and under, contribute 33 *l*. 6 *s*. 9½ *d*.; landlords for 14 tenants, votes spoilt or otherwise useless, contribute 7 *l*. 10 *s*. 4½ *d*.; landlords on account of Nationalist votes contribute 39 *l*. 10 *s*. 1½ *d*.

1930. You have got also, have you not, an analysis of the rates contributed by owners and occupiers?
£. 92. 9 *s*. 5 *d*. contributed by owners.

1931. And what is the number of votes which that gives the owners?
Thirty.

1932. And how many of the 30 are proxies?
Twenty-four may be proxies, or are proxies.

1933. And of the occupiers, what is the number of votes?
One hundred and twenty votes.

1934. And

15th May 1885.]   Mr. Fox.   [Continued.

1934. And how much do they pay?
£.55. 19 s. 3 d.

1935. So that, according to that, were it not for the proxies, the owners' votes, though they contribute 92 l. 9 s. 5 d., might be only six, while that of the occupiers, who contribute only 55 l. 19 s. 3 d., will be 120?
Yes.

1936. I believe you also have an analysis of the votes given in the electoral division of Forgney?
Yes, I have.

1937. Will you shortly state the result of it?
The amount of rate paid by owners, 174 l. 18 s. 8 d.; the owners' votes, 87.

1938. And how many of those might be proxies?
In my table I have 61, but on copying it out this morning it struck me that there was a mistake; it should be 49, I think.

1939. The amount of rate paid by occupiers?
£.100. 9 s.

1940. And their votes?
Two hundred and fifty-three.

1941. So that although they only pay 100 l. 9 s., they would have 253 votes, while the owners who pay 174 l. 18 s. 8 d. would, without proxy votes, have only 38?
Yes.

1942. Lord *Monk-Bretton*.] When you say that without proxies the owners would only have so many votes, you mean assuming that each owner has one vote only?
No.

1943. How do you arrive at that conclusion?
In the electoral division of Forgney, which I am answering about now, there were actually given 49 proxy votes by a certain number of owners.

1944. Then I understood you to say, that if proxy voting were abolished there would have been only so many owners' votes?
It would have taken away that 49; if proxy voting were abolished the owners would then have 38 instead of 87.

1945. Why would those 49 votes be lost?
The 49 are given, I may say, almost entirely by people who reside out of the union; most of them are in professions in the army and otherwise.

1946. Then you arrive at the conclusion that those 49 votes would be lost if proxy voting were abolished, on the assumption that none of those people who possess those votes would be able to come up and vote in person?
They would be absolutely lost if proxy voting was abolished, unless they were allowed to vote in a way in which they are not allowed to vote now. These proxy votes, as I understand the matter, could not now be brought in, even if the owners were upon the spot. I may be wrong, but I have always seen that when the owner is on the spot he exercises his vote and his claim, his proxy.

1947. Viscount *Hutchinson*.] Can he vote twice over; in person, and by proxy as well?
So I have always understood.

1948. Lord *Saltersford*.] Not on the same qualification?
No.

1949. Out of the same qualification, why should he not vote in person?
I see no reason why he should not; but it is not done in my experience.

1950. Lord *Monk-Bretton*.] Then I will put my question again: you arrive at the conclusion that if proxy voting were abolished these 49 votes would be
                                                                          lost,

15th May 1885.] Mr. Fox. [Continued.

lost, on the assumption that the people who possessed these votes would not come up and vote in person?
That is so.

1951. *Chairman.* And do you think it would be very difficult for them to do so?
In the majority of these cases it would be absolutely impossible, that is, to do so continuously. For instance, at this election I knew a gentleman who was an officer in India at the time the election took place, and he happened, after it was just over, to be back in Ireland.

1952. I believe you also produce a Table showing the amount of rateable property in your union and its division, according to the Poor Law Act, between owners or immediate lessors and tenants?
Yes.

1953. What does that Table show?
The amount of rateable property in the union is 62,004 *l*. 1 *s*.; the valuation of rateable property in the occupation of owners, or immediate lessors, is 9,723 *l*. 17 *s*.; the valuation of holdings rated at 4 *l*. and under is 2,036 *l*. 17 *s*; the valuation of holdings rated at over 4 *l*. is 50,243 *l*. 7 *s*.

1954. How much of that is contributed by each class?
The amount of the gross rate is 3,780 *l*. 5 *s*. 6 *d*.; the amount of rate contributed by owners or immediate lessors for property in their occupation is 627 *l*. 2 *s*. 8¼ *d*.; the amount of rate contributed by owners for holdings rated at 4 *l*. and under is 137 *l*. 16 *s*. 10½ *d*.; the amount of rate contributed by owners for holdings rated at over 4 *l*. is 1,487 *l*. 2 *s*. 11¾ *d*.; the total amount paid by owners or immediate lessors is 2,252 *l*. 2 *s*. 6¼ *d*.

1955. And the total amount paid by tenants for holdings rated at above 4 *l*?
Tenants for holdings rated at over 4 *l*, 1,487 *l*. 2 *s*. 11¾ *d*.

1956. Against 2,252 *l*. 2 *s*. 6¼ *d*.?
Yes.

1957. Can you tell us what that proportion is?
It is approximately two-thirds.

1958. Now, without the proxy vote, how would it be in the electoral division of Forgney?
Without the proxy vote in the last election the numbers would have been 253 tenants' votes to 38.

1959. The voting power of the tenant would have been represented by 253, and that of the owners of property by 38?
Yes, if the proxy were abolished.

1960. Although the proportion of the rates was what you have just told us?
Yes.

1961. Do you think that the proxy ought to be given for each election, or for how long a period?
If the triennial elections were to come into force, I think the proxy should be given for the three years. I should make the proxy and the period of the duration of the man's occupancy of his place coterminous.

1962. That is to say, the proxy to be used for the general election, and for any bye-election that may take place during the board is to last?
Yes.

1963. I believe you approve of the suggestion of security for costs being on election petitions?
Yes.

1964. Do you approve of the suggestion made by the last witness, Mr. M'Cann, that the lists should be revised by the county court judge?
I do not think it wise, and I think it scarcely practicable.

1965. Why?

1965. Why?
I think, if the appeal is to go to the county court judge, he should not be the man who prepared his own lists.

1966. How is it in the case of the Parliamentary List?
The appeal against an election in Parliament does not lie with the revising barrister.

1967. It lies from the barrister to the judge of assizes?
The appeal goes before the election judges in Parliamentary matters; but if you appeal from a Poor Law election, under the proposed Act it will go before the county court judge, whom Mr. M'Cann proposes to make the revising officer.

1968. Have you anything to say with regard to that part of the Bill?
No, on the election portion, I do not think that I have.

1969. Lord *Saltersford*.] If I am not mistaken, the Bill here proposes that there should be a list of ratepayers drawn out immediately before each election. Do you think it desirable that there should be a list that should be drawn out immediately with a view of the contested election?
Not immediately.

1970. Unless I am mistaken, the Bill appears to provide for that. Do you happen to recollect when the clerks in unions prepare the list of Parliamentary voters and jurors?
No, I cannot tell you the exact period.

1971. However, whatever the time may be, do you see any difficulty in arranging that the clerk, at the same time that he is making out the list of the Parliamentary voters and jurors, should also make out the list of those qualified to vote at Poor Law elections?
I do not see any difficulty beyond the time it would take.

1972. They would be the same names, I suppose, except that there would be a small addition: it seems to me that if he has to make out the list of Parliamentary voters and jurors, he should at the same time make out a list of those qualified to vote at Poor Law elections; does it strike you in the same way?
There would be a great many additional names of persons entitled to vote at the Poor Law election below the qualification of a Parliamentary elector.

1973. But there would be a great many the same?
A great many; it would be a simple addition to the other one, I think; but he would also have to specify the number of votes belonging to each individual.

1974. Lord *Monk-Bretton*.] The constituency for Parliamentary elections, and the constituency for Poor Law Board elections, are not the same?
No; the constituency for the Poor Law elections is wider, and also its members are entitled to various numbers of votes, according to their qualification.

1975. Women vote also at the Poor Law election?
Women vote also.

1976. *Chairman*.] What do you say to the proposal in the Bill of reducing the qualification of guardians?
I do not like that at all.

1977. On what ground do you object to it?
I think that by reducing it to 12 *l*., as suggested in the Bill, you would be bringing in, in these unions where they are now qualified at a higher sum than that, a class of men that are not quite fit to do the work.

1978. What do you say to the proposed reduction of the number of *ex-officio* guardians?
That I am quite against; I cannot see any reason for that at all.

1979. On what ground do you oppose that, chiefly?
Because I think, even as it is, owners of property are not sufficiently represented; they are not fairly represented if you think of the amount of rates they pay;

pay; at the same time I do not propose that their representation should be larger.

1980. Lord *Saltersford*.] You think they are already not sufficiently represented?
I think they are not, if you go by the exact figures?

1981. Under the present system, you mean?
Under the present system, I scarcely think they are.

1982. Viscount *Hutchinson*.] Do you mean, taking all the circumstances of the non-attendance of the *ex officios*, and so on, into consideration, or the actual number of representatives of property?
If you compare the number of representatives as *ex-officio* guardians, and the amount of rates paid by the owners, I do not think that they are represented really in that way, if you go by the strict letter. May I make a remark of my own?

1983. *Chairman*.] Certainly.
I cannot see that the fact of *ex-officio* guardians not attending can do anything but go towards strengthening the propriety of increasing the representation of ownership upon the board, or extending the *ex-officio* guardianship, and not reducing it.

1984. Viscount *Hutchinson*.] You think it is an argument in favour of extending it?
If it is to be used as an argument at all.

1985. *Chairman*.] What do you think would be the result if the *ex-officio* element were diminished?
The increase of the rates; and, judging from present things, the probable bankruptcy of most of the unions in Ireland.

1986. On what do you found that supposition?
First of all, as to the increase of the rates, I find that the poor rates have gone up, I believe generally, at all events considerably in my union, simply by the influence of the National League guardians, their regular attendance being larger than that of the *ex-officio* guardians.

1987. What do they do to increase the rates?
Simply outvote the *ex-officio* guardians.

1988. On what subjects?
I am speaking particularly of out-door relief.

1989. You think that the League guardians are in favour of increasing out-door relief?
I am certain of it.

1990. Has it increased considerably in your union of late years?
It has increased in ten years from 300 *l*. 7 *s*. to 730 *l*. 1 *s*.; that is up to the 25th March last.

1991. Lord *Shute*.] Do they give increased relief to evicted tenants in your union?
Not increased relief; nothing exorbitant. Relief has been given, but not to such exorbitant sums as I have seen reported from other unions.

1992. You do not know of a pound a week being given?
No, we have had no such case.

1993. Is it a common occurrence, or uncommon, to give high relief to evicted tenants?
If I can speak from reports I see in the newspapers, I should say it was done frequently; I have not seen it in my union.

1994. You believe it is done in many unions?
Yes.

(0.1.) z 2 1995. *Chairman*.]

1995. *Chairman.*] Are you acquainted with the facts with reference to the union of Longford?
I know the amount of out-door relief for the last five years.

1996. Can you give it to us?
I can state it from 1879 to 1884. In 1879 it was 763 *l.* 12 *s.* 9½ *d.*

1997. In 1880, what was it?
In 1880 it was 905 *l.* 11 *s.* 6 *d.*

1998. In 1881, what was it?
£. 1,097. 0 *s.* 11 *d.*

1999. In 1882, what was it?
£. 1,275. 12 *s.* 10 *d.*

2000. In 1883, what was it?
£. 1,349. 6. 9.

2001. And in 1884, what was it?
£. 1,286. 7. 3.

2002. Was there any increase in the population or destitution of the union to account for that?
In the destitution of the union certainly. Though I am not a member of the union, I see a great deal of it.

2003. Then you think that that would account for it?
That would account for the increase up to a certain date; I do not know that it would account for its maintenance. One portion of the union of Longford is poor.

2004. Is the Longford Union one which is in the hands entirely of the League, or one where the *ex officios* attend in large numbers?
I believe the *ex officios* attend, as Mr. McCann has stated, very rarely.

2005. Lord *Shute.*] Do you give relief now in your union, out-door relief, I mean, simply for destitution?
No, the strict working of the Act has been considerably relaxed in our union.

2006. Viscount *Hutchinson.*] According to the strict working of the Act, there are only three cases which are supposed to be proper cases for relief in that way?
Yes.

2007. Lord *Shute.*] And I suppose that offering the house is no use at all?
It is very seldom done.

2008. You do not find on offering the house that the people can do without the relief?
The test is very seldom put; the rate is voted without it.

2009. Viscount *Hutchinson.*] Has that been your experience in the union of Ballymahon?
Yes, that has been my experience in the union of Ballymahon.

2010. That the guardians are unwilling to put the house test in force?
Yes, that is the League guardians.

2011. Do you know the reason?
No. I really could not say any reason.

2012. We have had a financial reason given us, namely this, that the guardian thinks it better to give a person 2 *s.* 6 *d.* out of the house rather than to have him in the house at a greater cost; that has something to do with it?
I have often heard that put forward.

2013. *Chairman.*] I understand that in your judgment the elective guardians are not so economical in regard to the rates as the *ex officios*?
Certainly not.

2014. Have

2014. Have you any instances to prove that assertion?
I have given you the out-door relief, as far as that is concerned, for one thing. The contracts, in my opinion, are not properly taken, even in my own union?

2015. How do you mean "not properly taken"?
I mean to say that there is not a due consideration of what would be the proper price for an article.

2016. Then on what consideration are the contracts granted, as a rule?
To speak my own opinion, I am quite convinced that the majority of the elective guardians when they come into the room recognise the samples; they know from which shop such and such an article comes. May I explain? The samples are all put upon the table, and though we always appoint a committee as it were, to take off any distinguishing mark, yet in spite of that, I am convinced that the elective guardians do recognise them, and the contractors that are appointed are nearly invariably the same.

2017. Do you mean to say that they give the contract not to the best sample, but to that which comes from their own friends?
That is what I say.

2018. Is there any other instance you can suggest, showing that they are improvident in the management of the rates; you have not hitherto given any other distinct reason for that suggestion?
No, I do not think that I can.

2019. Viscount *Hutchinson*.] You have told us that in your own union you have had a very large increase in your outdoor relief?
Fifty per cent.

2020. That is in the last 10 years?
Yes; but I could make that stronger, if we were to take a shorter period.

2021. But I want to know, can you give us any idea whether the attendance of *ex-officio* guardians has increased or fallen off in those 10 years?
I should say that it had fallen off. I believe that our average attendance in Ballymahon is eight; I cannot speak with certainty as to that; but our general attendance for working days is four.

2022. That has been lately?
Lately; I believe our average is eight altogether, but I cannot be certain.

2023. *Chairman*.] Do you think that the fact that the landlords have to pay more than half the rates has any effect upon the elective guardians when they are voting away the poor rate money?
I am quite sure of it.

2024. Have you ever heard that said?
I have heard it said in the board room.

2025. What have you heard said?
I have heard a charge consented to when it was supposed to come off the rate and dissented from when it was pointed out that it would come off the county cess; and the reason given was because the landlord would not have to pay one-half of it. I heard that on the 1st of January this year.

2026. Lord *Saltersford*.] That is to say, if put on the county cess the tenant would have to pay the whole; if put on the rates it would be divided between the landlord and the tenant?
That is exactly what was said.

2027. *Chairman*.] How many of your elective guardians are Leaguers?
Seventeen.

2028. Out of a total of 20?
Out of a total of 20.

2029. So

15th May 1885.]　　　　　Mr. Fox.　　　　　[Continued.

2029. So that, notwithstanding the enormous proportion of the rates paid by the owners and Loyalist occupiers, they are only able to return three out of 20 guardians?
That is all.

2030. Lord *Sudley*.] Is it your opinion that any one owner can have as many as 36 votes?
Thirty, in my opinion, is the maximum.

2031. The last witness said he thought he could prove 36?
I do not agree with him.

2032. Viscount *Hutchinson*.] I asked a witness the other day whether he did not think it possible that a guardian who wished to do something good-natured in his own electoral division in the way of out-door relief might secure the votes of other guardians in other electoral divisions in view of favours to come; does that happen, do you think, sometimes?
Certainly; I have been canvassed myself.

2033. Do you suppose that if a guardian for an electoral division had a direct interest in keeping down the rates in the whole union, instead of merely keeping them down in his own electoral division which he represents, and beyond the four corners of which he has no interest in keeping them down, it would make any difference; do you think it would be possible then for a man who represents an electoral division in one part of a union, to go to a friend on the other side, and say, "Help me to put something on my rates, and when you want it done I will do the same for you"?
If his friend, the other man, had the interests of the whole union at heart, he could not do it, or would not, if he knew it.

2034. *Chairman*.] Have you anything that you wish to say generally on the Bill?
No; I do not know that I could add to my evidence, except to say that it has struck me that it is the most unseasonable time to introduce a Bill of this sort at all.

The Witness is directed to withdraw.

MR. PETER WALSH, having been called in, is Examined, as follows:

2035. *Chairman*.] You are a magistrate, I believe?
Yes.

2036. For what county?
For the three counties of Kilkenny, Tipperary, and Waterford.

2037. And you are an *ex-officio* guardian for Carrick-on-Suir Union?
Yes.

2038. And have been so how many years?
Over nine years; nine years last January.

2038*. Viscount *Hutchinson*.] Carrick-on-Suir Union is in these three counties?
Yes.

2039. *Chairman*.] Are you a good attendant at the Board?
Pretty fair; I attended 21 times last year.

2040. With regard to this Bill before the House, have you given it your consideration?
Yes, I have.

2041. Do you approve of the provision for holding the elections every three years instead of every year?
I do.

2042. And

2042. And of substituting the ballot for the present mode?
Decidedly.

2043. What do you say about proxy voting?
I say that it is absolutely necessary if landed property is to be represented at all; I do not see any other way of representing it, except by a cumbersome method; if you want property to be represented on the Board, I think proxies should be retained.

2044. Do you see any hardship in the proxy vote to any class of the community?
I do not.

2045. Is there any complaint amongst the people at large about the proxy vote?
No, not amongst the people at large; but of course the Leaguers complain of it.

2046. Does it bear a large proportion to the occupation vote in your district?
Not very large.

2047. How many proxies were used at contested elections from 1877 to 1885?
I have a table which shows that. In the electoral division of Ballydurn there was an election in 1884, and there were occupier votes 55, and proxy six. Then in Boolyglass there were 50 occupiers' votes recorded, and proxy votes eight.

2048. Perhaps the shortest way would be to give us the total, without going through all the names?
The total number of votes recorded was 3,544 occupation, and 781 proxy votes.

2049. Has the proxy vote any effect now?
It has. Without the proxy vote the League would carry the whole union.

2050. What is the result at present?
At an election for chairman, &c., that was held in 1882, there were present 23 *ex-officio's* guardians and 23 elected guardians; 26 each was the full Board. Mr. Malcomson, an elected guardian, voted with the *ex-officios*; the result was that the *ex-officios* carried the election by 24 to 22. At subsequent meetings an extraordinary state of affairs ensued, so much so that no business could be transacted.

2051. How many Loyalist guardians are elected now?
Now, seven.

2052. In case the proxy vote was abolished, should you be able to elect those seven?
Not one.

2053. And in those seven electoral divisions, what proportion of the rates are paid by the owners to those paid by the occupiers?
In the whole union, five-eighths, within a very small fraction.

2054. Even in those seven electoral divisions the owners could not return Loyalist representatives without the aid of the proxy votes?
No; and they would be afraid to stir without these at their back.

2055. I believe you, yourself, are a tenant farmer as well as a proprietor?
I hold two farms on my own hands, for which I pay rent. I have property in three unions.

2056. Could you exercise your vote without a proxy?
I could not exercise my voting powers without the proxy, when the elections are all on one day.

2057. Viscount *Hutchinson*.] And that they generally are?
Yes.

2058. *Chairman*.] What do you say to the proposal to reduce the qualification for guardians?

I am decidedly opposed to any such proposal; I certainly would prefer to increase rather than reduce it.

2059. Viscount *Hutchinson*.] You were saying that ever since a certain time everything got into the hands of those elected guardians, and the consequence was that things went from bad to worse?

Mr. Malcolmson was elected chairman, and I was elected vice chairman; and then the Land Leaguers brought forward different resolutions, and of course we would not have them.

2060. You would not put them to the vote, you mean?

We would not. At one meeting at which I was chairman, the Leaguers proposed a political resolution, which I declined to put. They said they would leave the board room. I replied, "Very well, gentlemen, there are plenty here to do the work." They left, but returned. At a subsequent meeting, Mr. Malcomson, in the chair, adjourned the board on their motion, in consequence of his refusal to put political resolutions from the chair. On the next day of meeting he commenced the business where he had left off, and they would not allow anything to be done; several meetings were then adjourned. At one of the last meetings they would not even allow a letter from the Local Government to be read, though requested to do so by the Poor Law Inspector; nothing was done, consequently the Local Government Board dissolved the board of guardians.

2061. Lord *Monk-Bretton*.] What were the matters they wanted to bring in; political questions?

Yes, Land League resolutions from other unions; and we refused to discuss them.

2062. Viscount *Hutchinson*.] Resolutions which had nothing whatever to do with the administration of the Poor Law?

Nothing.

2063. Lord *Saltersford*.] Was it the case that out-door relief could not be given in consequence?

Yes, it was; the clerk had to give his own cheque for three consecutive weeks for that purpose.

2064. In fact, the relief was stopped?

Everything was stopped. No rate was struck, consequently some persons were defranchised for the year. The next board was somewhat modified by the help of proxy votes, and since then there has not been much difficulty in carrying on the business.

2065. *Chairman*.] You have a majority with the aid of the *ex officios*?

Yes; we had only nine the first year; but we have seven Loyalist elected guardians now.

2066. What do you say to the proposal to lower the qualification for elective guardians?

It would not be desirable. I think it would admit men of insufficient independence, and too much subject to outside influence, and the lower the qualifications of guardians, the less interest they would have in the proper management of the rates. I never heard any complaint against the present qualifications of guardians.

2067. What do you say to the provision in the Bill for diminishing the number of *ex-officio* guardians?

I think it would be most injurious; I would have the number equal, as they always have been. Their being equal has never done any injury to the administration of the poor law within the union, and I am convinced the people think so, and have no objection to the *ex-officios* being equal in number to the elected guardians.

2068. You think that the mass of the ratepayers do not look with any hostile eye upon the *ex-officio* element on the board?

Certainly not.

2069. Would

2069. Would they, to a certain extent, protect them?
I think they would have more confidence in them than in some of the men they elect themselves.

2070. And do you think that the poor look upon the *ex-officios* as their protectors to any extent?
I think they do; but there is such a terror exercised over the people now that they would actually do what they know is wrong.

2071. What do you think would be the practical result of diminishing the number of *ex-officios*?
It will have this effect, that if the number were diminished, property paying the larger portion of the rates could not be sufficiently represented. It is hard enough to get candidates to come forward for election, and we could not possibly get them, because they would be in the minority, not having *ex-officios* to support them in the board-room.

2072. The few that now attend you think would be prevented from attending?
If you diminish the number, certainly I think so, and I believe it would have the effect of considerably increasing the rates.

2073. Viscount *Hutchinson*.] Can you give me any idea what the average attendance of the *ex-officio* guardians is, now you are 20 to 26 you have told us?
My attendance was 21 last year.

2074. You attended 21 board meetings?
Yes.

2075. You have fortnightly board meetings, have you?
No, weekly. Lord Bessborough attends very frequently, and some others.

2076. When you do go to a board meeting, an ordinary board meeting, how many are there generally there?
We have them nearly equal. There may be six or eight elected guardians, and there would not be so many *ex-officios*, perhaps five or six.

2077. Your ordinary meetings average about 12?
Twelve or 14.

2078. And you do not have much difficulty now, I suppose?
Not much; the business is very fairly done by the elected guardians, so long as political or party matters are excluded.

2079. Lord *Shute*.] Are the *ex-officios* well treated by the other guardians, the elective guardians?
Quite so, except when the elected guardians introduce party or political matters.

2080. Lord *Saltersford*.] Are you an *ex-officio* of any union besides Carrick?
No, I am not; in fact, I did not register any claim in any other union.

2081. You might have been put on by the clerk without claiming it?
I was within one of being in for Clonmel.

2082. *Chairman*.] As I understand you, in 1882 the board rather got into the hands of the Leaguers; was not that what you were just now saying to my noble friend, that in 1882 the Leaguers got a majority on the board?
They had a majority of the elective guardians.

2083. You told us that disastrous things resulted?
Yes.

2084. Were there any instances then of excessive out-door relief?
Yes, there were two cases; there was one case where they ran it up to 30 *s.* a week, the case of Pierce Power.

2085. Viscount *Hutchinson*.] What was he?
An evicted tenant; and another case was that of a man of the name of Whelan;

Whelan; he was getting 12s. 6d. a week at one time, and then they wanted to give him 1l. a week, and I was in the chair that day, and I made the man acknowledge that he had 40l. which he could not account for, and then I refused to give it to him at all. They all went against me, and then one young fellow, an elective guardian, said to me afterwards, it was the best thing that had been done for a long time, my preventing that man having it; and I said, "Why did you go against me?" He said, "Because otherwise I could not stay in the country." Then another time there were two evicted tenants, and they applied for out-door relief, and the man whose case came on first was a man that had means, and we knew it, and we all refused to give it to him, and the chairman would not put it; and then there is another man that we all knew that wanted out-door relief, and we all wanted to give it him, but the Land Leaguers voted against giving it to the man that was poor, because we would not give it to the man who was not in want of relief.

2086. *Chairman.*] I understood you to say just now that it was in consequence of political resolutions having been brought forward, which the chairman refused to put, that the business of the board was brought to an end, and that the ordinary business could not be transacted?
The chairman took up the business where it had been left off. At the previous meeting they immediately renewed their opposition at the old point. They would not allow anything to be done, unless we passed the political resolutions which the chairman had previously declined to put to the board.

2087. Is it not the rule at poor law unions that these resolutions cannot be put till the ordinary business is over?
Yes; but when the board is adjourned, then, I suppose, they consider it right to begin where the business was stopped.

2088. I cannot understand how the refusing to put the resolution put a stop to the ordinary business, when the rule is that these resolutions are not to be put till the ordinary business is over?
That is how it was transacted. It was held that when the board was an adjourned board, you could take it up where you left off.

2089. Lord *Saltersford.*] I am under the impression that each board has power to regulate the order of its own business; that is so, is it not?
No, there are new rules brought in since then, and there is a regular order of procedure that we must all obey.

2090. Lord *Sudley.*] From the Local Government Board?
Yes.

2091. *Chairman.*] Such an occurrence would now be impossible, would it?
I should think so, except that business being adjourned at a certain point they would take it up at that point when they commenced again; and it was taken up at the very same point.

2092. But can you do that under the new rules?
I should think not.

2093. What do you say to the proposal for electing magistrates?
I think it would be a better way; then you would have men that would attend.

2094. You think that the magistrates should elect their representatives out of their own number?
Yes; but the poor law gentleman that gave the evidence on that subject has, I think, made a mistake. The way it is is this, that every magistrate resident in the union is an *ex-officio* guardian, and every magistrate that is a non-resident goes in according to his qualifications; but then a subsequent Act says that he must have a 50l. qualification in order to entitle him to be a non-resident guardian; but then there is another thing that keeps off a great many justices. The Local Government Board hold (and they refused it to me) that if you are not rated directly, either for occupation or small holdings, no matter if you have 1,000l. a year, you are not to be put on.

2095. Viscount

15th May 1885.] Mr. WALSH. [Continued.

2095. Viscount *Hutchinson*.] If you were going to have an election of magistrates by magistrates would you not find yourself in the same position as you are in now, that you would not get men to serve. After all, it is a pretty general complaint that the difficulty is to find people who can attend?
We should try to choose magistrates who would probably attend, their residences being sufficiently near.

2096. I mean apart from the Land League altogether, it is almost impossible, is it not, in any area like the Poor Law union, to find a sufficient number of magistrates who will give a regular attendance at the board of guardians?
It is very difficult to find them.

2097. An idea which has been suggested is that there should be an entirely new constituency of the owners of property, and that would give you a much larger class of people to choose from?
I would not like that at all.

2098. Why not?
You hand over the elective guardians entirely to political organisations. That is my view of it, and I am convinced that would be the consequence of any such arrangement.

2099. *Chairman*.] Do you think that there might be a possibility of filling up vacancies amongst the *ex-officio* guardians, which might arise from resignations of persons unable to attend the union, by justices who are in adjoining districts, but who are near enough to attend the union?
Yes, if they be ratepayers; but I would not allow any justice to be an *ex-officio* guardian except he were a ratepayer, except in this case: that where it is impossible for a landlord to attend, I certainly say that the landlord's property should be represented by his agent; but not by the landlord and agent both together, except the agent is a ratepayer.

2100. Viscount *Hutchinson*.] It does often happen that a landlord is represented by an agent?
Yes; it may be if he be a rated justice.

2101. And I have known cases where the Local Government Board have nominated an agent on the understanding that he and his landlord do not attend the board at the same time; perhaps you have known such?
There is nothing to prevent their both attending, if qualified.

2102. *Chairman*.] Are there any instances in your union of magistrates who reside in adjoining counties, and who pay a good deal of the rates in your union, but cannot be *ex-officio* guardians because they are non-resident?
Not for being non-resident, but for not being directly rated; as, for instance, Mr. Power, of Bellevue.

2103. Does he live within an easy distance?
He owns a townland, valued at about 1,400*l*. a year, close to my residence, but not being directly rated he is not an *ex-officio*, as the number of resident and non-resident qualified justices exceeds the number of elective guardians.

2104. Will you explain what you mean by "directly rated"?
He is not rated for land in his occupation, or for holdings under 4*l*.

2105. And therefore he is passed over?
He is passed over.

2106. And, perhaps, men with much less interest are *ex-officio* guardians?
Yes; the proper way would be that every person who has to pay rates, directly or indirectly, should be considered as rated.

2107. What do you think of the proposal to reduce the number of votes which should now be given, from 30 to 18?
Instead of that, I would increase it. As I said before, here is a landlord with an income of 1,000*l*. a year, and paying half the rates on 1,000*l*. a year in one electoral division, and he has only six votes, whilst his tenants, paying the other half,

(0.1.) A A 2

15th May 1885.] Mr. WALSH. [Continued.

half, have 60; and in another case, two landlords have six each, and their tenants 100. I would give them all votes in proportion to their rating qualification. It is so up to 200*l.* qualification rating, and for every additional 50*l.* of rating there ought to be an additional vote given to both landlord and tenant, because I think the rates ought to be fully represented.

2108. With regard to the aggregation of the valuation, what do you say?
If it were to be reduced, I would fall back on the original way; that is to say, aggregate the small holdings with occupation, and then give six votes for proxies and 12 for the occupation of the small holdings; that is the way it was originally.

2109. Have you any other observations you would like to make on this Bill?
Yes, as to the lists; I would certainly have the lists last for the three years. If you had a triennial election, then I would have the lists made out for every bye election, and for the general election, and let them be completed, say, at the January Sessions; the other is the October Sessions; but then you could not have the rates paid, for we strike our rates in July, and they are never paid up until Christmas, and then you would disfranchise a lot of people. I would have the list revised up to the 31st of December; and then every man that has rates paid one month previous to that, or two months, let him go on the register, and then let it stand till that time three years, provided he kept his rates paid each year.

2110. What do you say to Mr. Fox's proposal, that the election should be in August instead of March, the object of that being that the guardians that struck the rates should be liable for the spending of them?
I think it would not have any effect on the rates. I wish to add, we strike our rates in June or July, as it is more convenient to the farmers to pay from that time to the end of the year than any other. We have, after providing for the requirements of the union for the past year, a sum of 1,842 *l.* remaining to our credit, and the estimate for the current year, including a sum of 475 *l.* to meet the requirements of pending legislation on education, is very low; from 8*d.* to 2*s.* in the £. on the various electoral divisions. I wish to add that I got returns of our out door relief. In 1875, it was 10*l.* 16*s.* a week; in 1876, 11*l.* 16*s.*; in 1877, 11*l.* 8*s.* 6*d.*; in 1878, 10*l.* 3*s.*; in 1879, 9*l.* 3*s.*; in 1880, 12*l.* 2*s.*; in 1881, 13*l.* 10*s.*; in 1882, 11*l.* 1*s.*; in 1883, 10*l.* 13*s.*; in 1884, 10*l.* 16*s.* That is our out-door relief.

2111. Viscount *Hutchinson.*] When was the board dissolved?
In 1882.

2112. And how long did it remain dissolved?
Only during the summer. There was a fresh election in March again.

2113. *Chairman.*] Do you think it might be desirable that the register of voters should not be questioned after an election?
No, I do not; I would let it be questioned at any time. At one time I was for the revising barrister doing it; but it would throw a great deal of work on him. I never heard of any complaint against the present returning officer doing it.

2114. Viscount *Hutchinson.*] There are a great many petitions in contested elections, on the chance of finding out something wrong in the register, are there not?
Perhaps it would be as well to have the register, if it were done by the revising barrister, final.

The Witness is directed to withdraw.

Ordered, That the Committee be adjourned to Tuesday, the 9th of June, at Twelve o'clock.

Die Martis, 9° Junii, 1885.

LORDS PRESENT:

Earl of MILLTOWN.
Viscount POWERSCOURT.
Lord SALTERSFORD.
Lord INCHIQUIN.

Lord SILCHESTER.
Lord SHUTE.
Lord MONK-BRETTON.
Lord DE VESCI.

THE EARL OF MILLTOWN, IN THE CHAIR.

MR. PATRICK A. MEEHAN, having been called in; is Examined, as follows:

2115. *Chairman.*] You are, I think, an elected Guardian of the Mountmellick Union, and also the Chairman of the Union?
Yes.

2116. What is your professional business?
I am a grocer and a wholesale butter merchant.

2117. "Grocer" includes, I suppose, as it usually does in Ireland, wine and spirit merchant?
Yes.

2118. You have told us that you are the chairman of the union; how long have you been chairman?
Since last April.

2119. What counties is your union in?
Principally in Queen's County; a small portion in King's County.

2120. Since this last election you have been the chairman?
Yes.

2121. Have you considered this Bill now before their Lordships?
I have read it over.

2122. What is the first point in it to which you would like to call attention?
The first point is the election of the guardians for a period of three years.

2123. What is your opinion on that provision?
My opinion with regard to the present system is that it is objectionable in many ways; principally because it involves a needless waste of the rates in yearly contests. There were 14 out of the 42 electoral divisions in the Mountmellick Union contested last year, at a cost of probably about 40*l.*

2124. Does that fall upon the rates?
It does. The yearly contest imposes an untold amount of trouble on the clerk of the union; it is a cause of turmoil, worry, and great loss of time to the guardians seeking election who have to do the arduous work of the union gratuitously, and who, if the dread of this yearly turmoil were removed, would set themselves resolutely to learn their duties accurately, and perform them with justice and benefit alike to the ratepayer and the poor.

2125. Then

9th June 1885.]   Mr. MEEHAN.   [Continued.

2125. Then you are in favour, I understand, of triennial elections?
Decidedly. I may add that the triennial elections will effect a saving in the rates, and will give ample time to the officers to have their lists of voters correctly made out.

2126. The next point of importance is the provision for the ballot being the mode of election in future; what do you say to that?
That is the next point that I would deal with in my evidence, with your permission. I approve of, and most strongly recommend, the ballot to be adopted in poor law elections; because, under it, intimidation and other interference with the liberty of the voter will be impossible. As showing where intimidation was practised under the present system, I instance the election for Borris electoral division, where, in the year 1882, a certain gentleman, not only unduly solicited, but threatened that, unless the ratepayers voted in accordance with his wishes, he would remember it to them, plainly intimating, that if they did not vote for the nominee of certain gentlemen, they would afterwards persecute them in any way it was in their power to do. In addition, while of course it would be a safeguard against undue pressure by the landlord, it would also be a safeguard against intimidation by any other party whatsoever.

2127. You are in favour then of substituting the ballot?
I am most decidedly in favour of substituting the ballot for the present system. I could give other instances where, to my knowledge, acts of grievous hardship were inflicted upon ratepayers who had voted against the expressed wish of some of the landholders of the district.

2128. I daresay you may also be acquainted with cases in which hardships have been inflicted on voters who have voted against the wish of some of the occupiers of the division?
I cannot remember any instance of such a kind.

2129. It has been so stated here; that is the reason I ask you the question?
To show that such has not been the case, I may state that in the same electoral division which I mentioned to you a little while ago, that of Borris, I think it was in the year 1880, there was a contested election, and there was a bog-ranger in the employment of the landholder of the district, who came to the Liberal party and stated that his employer, a landlord, had told him that he should vote for his nominee, and that in case he did not he would expel him from his employment. We immediately told him that sooner than lose his support for his wife and family he should vote as he was directed to do. In the Maryborough electoral division, which I contested several years, one year in particular, the year before last, two men who had of their own free will promised me to vote for me were intimidated and prevented from voting for me by their landlord, who told them that in case they voted for me he would evict them.

2130. Are you speaking of what you know of your own personal knowledge?
I am.

2131. Then you are strongly in favour of the adoption of the ballot?
I am; and with your permission I would wish to add that under the present system of distributing voting papers a great deal of trouble is imposed on the ratepayer, and the way opened for fraud and trickery, both before the vote is signed and afterwards. Inexperienced policemen, strangers to the locality, or but imperfectly acquainted with it, are sent to distribute the papers, with the inevitable result of mistakes and trouble to the ratepayer. If through mistake, negligence, or premeditation, voting papers are not served, the voter has to drive from eight to 10 miles to the workhouse to the clerk of the union for one. In Maryborough division, which I contested several times, I always had to take voters over to the workhouse. One year in particular there were 12 voters with whom no voting papers were left; one of them, an old woman who had not been out for eight months previous, another an old man over 80 years of age. And frequently the voting papers are mixed up and given to the wrong people. In the last Maryborough election there

there were some 20 cases where the voting papers for certain individuals were given to others. That, as your Lordships' Committee will perceive, causes an endless amount of trouble to the ratepayers, who have, in nearly every case, to go to the clerk of the union or police constable, and lose a great deal of time in inquiring for their voting papers in order to secure them. In the case of one voter, who was entitled to four votes, her papers were given to a totally different person, and her votes were lost on the contest altogether.

2132. Clause 9 of the Bill is, I think, the next clause you would like to refer to?
Would you permit me first to offer a suggestion with reference to the remedy I would propose for that evil which I have just described?

2133. The ballot is the remedy suggested, as I understand?
I would, to remedy this state of things, suggest the ballot, under which the guardians might be empowered to appoint assistant returning officers in each contested division, the election to be held in court-house, dispensary-house, or school-house, where available, otherwise a room in a farmer's house in a central position in the division to be hired for the day; the clerk of the union, as chief returning officer, to prepare list of voters. The cost of this scheme yearly would be more than the present system, but if triennial elections are adopted it will be considerably less.

2134. That answer has reference to the machinery for putting the ballot in operation. You approve of the suggestion that has been made by some previous witnesses that the petty sessions court-houses should be utilised for the purpose of the election of guardians?
Decidedly, where such would be available.

2135. It would save considerable expense?
It would; and it would render intimidation or fraud impossible, because the voter can come in there and vote by ballot for any person he wishes.

2136. Lord *Monk Bretton*.] And you mentioned also that schools might be used.
Yes, court-houses, school-houses, or dispensary-houses, where such exist. In the divisions where no such buildings exist, I would recommend that a room in a farmer's house be hired for the day.

2137. *Chairman*.] We have been told that in almost every district there is a petty sessions court; is that the case in your union?
I cannot say to my knowledge that it is, but I know that in some electoral divisions there is no dispensary-house or petty sessions-house; and in such cases I would recommend a room in a farmer's house to be taken for the convenience of the voters.

2138. The suggestion has been made that the petty sessions district should be the electoral division; what do you say to that?
I would approve of the present electoral divisions; I think they are properly divided at present.

2139. Lord *Saltersford*.] Do not you think that dispensary districts would be better as voting districts?
Yes, in the case of divisions where dispensaries existed.

2140. Viscount *Powerscourt*.] I suppose you mean that the distances would be too great in some cases?
The distances would be too great. The distance from the outer portion of Maryborough dispensary district is about seven miles.

2141. *Chairman*.] To where?
To the dispensary-house.

2142. It has been said that, if it is not too far for the sick poor to go, it ought not to be too far for the electors to go?
In very many cases the sick poor are taken in a car.

2143. Now,

9th June 1885.]   Mr. Meehan.   [Continued.

2143. Now, I think Clause 9 is the next clause of any great importance unless you wish to say anything on Clause 8?
No.

2144. Clause 9 is the one that proposes to abolish the proxy vote; what do you say to that?
I would say that that provision is a most just and reasonable one. Approving of the ballot, I must, as a natural consequence, and if possible a thousand times more strongly, urge that voters should vote in person. The present proxy system is a network of fraud, corruption, and trickery, not certainly so much on the part of the owners of property as on those in whom they misplace their trust. I have frequently known cases where double claims are lodged by the proxy for the one property, with a trifling alteration so as to mislead.

2145. Have you known frequent cases of double claims being lodged out of one property, of your own personal knowledge?
I have known that; and a case occurred in the election for Maryborough electoral division last year 12 months.

2146. How do you know that that was done?
The circumstances are these, in one case which I will select: there is a tenant farmer living adjacent to the town of Maryborough. he lodged a claim for a beneficial interest, showing the rating of his holding to be 60 l., and his rent 40 l.; whereas the reverse was exactly the case; his rent was 60 l. (in round numbers) and the valuation 40 l. His landlord's appointment of proxy and the proxy's claim on the granting of the landlord's appointment was changed, in order to sustain that fraudulent vote of the tenant.

2147. Changed by whom?
By the proxy.

2148. And is there no punishment for conduct of that character?
I do not know.

2149. Lord *De Vesci*.] Was the case investigated?
It was not.

2150. *Chairman*.] How do you know it is true?
The tenant acknowledged at the scrutiny of the votes that his statement was false, and that he did it at the suggestion of the party managers.

2151. Were you present when he made that acknowledgment?
I was.

2152. Lord *Monk-Bretton*.] Was the vote disallowed?
It was disallowed. Then there is another case: in 1883 there was a claim lodged out of a beneficial interest of 23 l. 17 s. 10 d.; a legal gentleman in Maryborough was the proxy; in 1885 there was a new appointment made to this legal gentleman's nephew; both of those claims were duly registered, and out of the one property each of those proxies voted; that was four votes where there should be only two.

2153. Was that the fault of the returning officer?
Well, it might be considered so; but I would consider that it was the fault of the proxy, who knew that the claim had been previously registered in favour of his uncle.

2154. Still if the returning officer had done his duty the fraud would not have been successful?
But still the fact that it was done is clear evidence that fraud can be practised under the system. In 1879, the first year I contested Maryborough electoral division, there was a proxy voting paper issued, and the proxy voted on the appointment of a woman who had been dead months before, and who was buried at the expense of the rates; we investigated the case, and ordered our solicitor to take proceedings against the representatives of the woman, and recover the amount of her burial; but still her proxy, who knew that she was dead (and, I believe,

I believe, attended her funeral), on the strength of the dead woman's appointment voted for her.

2155. I suppose false returns may be made, even to vote in person, may they not?
I hardly think so, because the rating of each person is in the rate book, and if a person makes a claim, of course he will have to make a personal application to the clerk, and the clerk will, on reference to his book, see what his rating is.

2156. You say a personal application; do you mean that he cannot apply by letter?
No.

2157. Is that your idea?
You cannot apply by letter unless you apply to have the name inserted on the rate book as a ratepayer, but at election time, if a voting paper is not issued or is mislaid, the voter has to go to the clerk of the union to get his voting paper; he must make a personal application.

2158. There is an elaborate provision in this Bill, not only for revising the list, but for appealing in the case of a wrong decision on the part of the revising officer.
With regard to investigating those claims, experience has proved to us that the Local Government Board, in whose hands the investigation rests, generally do not carry it out in the spirit that justice and equity would warrant them to do.

2159. Before we go any further, perhaps you will kindly explain what you mean by "us;" you have used the word once or twice?
I might say the National party.

2160. That is to say the National League party; is that what you mean?
No, not exactly.

2161. Let us have a term that we all understand; I consider myself a Nationalist, but I am afraid I am not a member of your party?
When I say "us," I mean the bulk of the people, as distinguished from those who lodge such claims as these.

2162. Do not you think we had better keep to the term which has been accepted by most of the previous witnesses, and say the National League party?
I am quite content.

2163. I do not want to use any term that is in the least offensive?
The term is not in the least offensive to me; I am proud of being a National Leaguer.

2164. Lord *Monk-Bretton*.] In regard to this dead woman's proxy; do I understand you that the claim for a proxy vote was made after her death, or that the proxy voted after her death under a proxy power which had been obtained in her life time?
My opinion is that the proxy claim was lodged after her death; I will not state that positively. My opinion was that the claim was a new claim, that it was made after her death; but I would not make the statement without being absolutely certain of it, I would say that the claim probably was the old claim, but still that the proxy knew, and admitted in the board room that he knew, that the woman was dead, and still he voted on her appointment.

2165. How long is a proxy in force after it has been given?
Five years; it must be renewed every five years.

2166. Viscount *Powerscourt*.] Is there any provision in case of the person who gives the proxy dying; would the proxy still be in force?
No; if the person dies it must be re-made. With your Lordships permission, I would also mention another case: In 1884, on the 20th of February, there were three proxy claims lodged; they were lodged in the names of three people, and there was only one of those people who was legally entitled to vote out of the

the property. The beneficial interest in the property amounted to 20l. 9s. 6d. There was a lady who was the original owner of the property; she got married; and there was a claim made for her husband, for herself as being a joint owner, and a claim for her in her maiden name.

2167. *Chairman.*] Have you any other objection to the proxy vote besides that it gives rise, as you say, to false claims being made?

Under that heading I might mention that there have been several cases where joint owners of property have been allowed votes out of very small amounts. For instance, in the Maryborough Electoral Division, two gentlemen have been allowed two votes out of an 8 s. rating. In Kilrohanbane Electoral Division, out of a net beneficial interest of 13l. 16s. 3d, there have been six votes allowed. Of course your Lordship will observe that an ordinary rated occupier would only have one vote out of such a holding as that.

2168. Do you mean to say that these votes have been legally allowed, or illegally allowed?

I believe, legally allowed.

2169. Then what you mean to say is, that a holding of this nature, you said one of 8 s., confers legally two votes?

Yes, under the present system.

2170. I cannot exactly see how?

The way is this: they held this place in fee, and, as such, they were entitled to one vote; and then they held it as occupiers (it was in their own occupation), and, as such, they were entitled to another vote.

2171. But then this person voted as an occupier?

Certainly.

2172. That does not apply to the question of the proxy vote at all?

He voted as an occupier and as a proxy as well; he appointed a proxy for the beneficial interest.

2173. How could he appoint a proxy for the land of which he was himself the occupier; that, you know, he could not do under the law?

It was my impression that a proxy was appointed for the holding, but now I remember the proxy appointment was for other property, but still the two votes out of 8 s. was allowed.

2174. Lord *Saltersford.*] I understand you to say that he gave the proxy vote in regard to the beneficial interest only?

Yes; and I could give your Lordships' Committee other instances as well, if you should think such necessary. In the neighbouring union, in Carlow, there has been an instance where there were 75 proxy votes out of a total rating of 600l., and 24 votes of those were registered from 2l. valuation.

2175. Have you any idea how many occupiers' votes there were of the same total?

I did not make that calculation.

2176. Very considerably more than the number of proxies, were there not?

I would not think so out of 600l.; roughly testing the list, I see only 38 occupier votes.

2177. Have you any other objection to the proxy votes?

I have this objection, that I think it is a very bad system; a gentleman living away from a union cannot be a good judge of the fitness of guardians for that union. It may be said that he delegates his authority to people who are competent judges of the fitness; but still I think that a gentleman of property living away should manifest some interest in the union, and the least that could be expected of him would be that he should come in person and look after his own interest.

2178. Do you think it would be possible for a gentleman who was possessed of property in various unions to vote personally in them all?

I think it would.

2179. I suppose

9th June 1885.] Mr. MEEHAN. [*Continued.*

2179. I suppose you are aware that the elections are usually held on the same day?
There are two days allowed; and by that means if an owner of property took an interest in the business, I think it might be an easy matter for him to attend.

2180. Viscount *Powerscourt.*] Suppose he had to go to five or six different elections in one day?
It would then be a case of hardship, certainly. It is very hard for me to offer any suggestions on the matter, because I have not considered it; but I think if your Lordships' Committee or the Legislature in the Bill under your consideration would follow it up, so that in cases where such fraud was proved in a court of law (there is little use in taking it to the Local Government Board), and ample punishment was dealt out to evil doers, if that power was given, and parties punished, it would tend to put a stop to it.

2181. *Chairman.*] Would that take away your objection to the proxy vote?
It would not. I still hold that it should be abolished altogether.

2182. Can you suggest any other means by which non-resident owners of property could exercise their vote?
I think not.

2183. You are aware, I presume, that taking Ireland as a whole, the owners of property pay (it has been so proved in evidence before us) about five-eighths of the whole of the poor rate?
Yes, that is the case; and of course I would not seek to deprive the owners of property of their just representation on the Poor Law Boards; but I still hold to the opinion that they should vote in person.

2184. But do not you think it would be somewhat of a hardship that those who pay five-eighths of the poor rate should have no adequate representation at the Poor Law Board?
I think that, according to the present scale of voting, the owners of property have ample representation at the Board; and I think that they should take enough interest in the county to exercise their right in person themselves, and to judge of the personal qualifications of the people to whom is entrusted the expenditure of the money. Then, taking it on another ground, of course it is the agricultural or industrial community that creates the money that enables the landlord to pay the rates. It is from the occupying tenantry of course that the money comes in the first instance, and of course they have as deep or a much deeper interest in the matter.

2185. Why have they a deeper interest in the matter, when at the most they only pay half the rates, and in many instances pay none at all?
There are very few instances in which they do not pay it; of course, people under 4 *l.* rating do not pay; but still, even taking the small sums that they do pay, it is a very much severer burden upon them than it is upon the owners of property.

2186. How have you arrived at that conclusion?
From the great depression that is in the country at present; and I know, of my own knowledge, that there are many of the ratepayers on whom it comes with the greatest severity; it is only by depriving themselves of many things absolutely necessary for themselves that they are able to meet those rates and pay them.

2187. Then, do I understand you to say, on the whole, that you think that the owners, although they pay five-eighths of the poor rate, are not entitled to a corresponding, or anything like a corresponding, share of representation at the Poor Law Board?
No; do not take me to say that. I distinctly stated that I would give the owners of property their just representation, according to the present scale of rating. I would leave them the entire vote that they exercise.

(0.1.) B B 2 2188. But

9th June 1885.]   Mr. MEEHAN.   [Continued.

2188. But you would do away with their power of exercising the vote?
No; I would give them unlimited power to exercise it, but it should be in person, and not open the door to fraud and trickery.

2189. But take the case suggested, where five or six elections are going on at different places on the same day, where it is admittedly impossible for them to exercise their vote in person; how do you propose that they should exercise it?
I have not considered the question in that light; but there are several days elapsing between the issuing of the voting papers and the time that they are counted, and I think a provision might be inserted in the Bill before your Lordships extending the time for owners of property, who have property in different unions, to three, four, or five days, in order to afford them an opportunity of exercising their right; even under the threat of penalties, I do believe that the present proxy system, if continued, will still be used for fraud and illegal purposes.

2190. I do not quite see why there should be more chance of false claims being made to proxy votes than to the personal vote; I have not gathered from you the reason?
In this way; the owner of property makes an appointment, and the proxy lodges a claim with the clerk of the union; that appointment of proxy or that claim is not made under any legal penalties that can be conveniently recovered, unless with great expense to any ratepayer who might wish to contest it in the courts, and the clerk of the union has no opportunity of judging whether that statement of claim is correct, or whether it is not.

2191. Has he not the same opportunity that he has with other claims to vote?
I would not think so, because where a proxy makes a statement of claim out of a certain rateable property, he may say that the beneficial interest is so much, whereas it may not be within 20 *l.* or 30 *l.* of as much. For instance, in that case I mentioned a while ago of the farmer that returned his farm at a rent of 40 *l.*, and a valuation of 60 *l.*, the clerk of the union had no means of finding out whether that claim was fraudulent or whether it was not.

2192. Do I understand you to say that you consider that property, paying, as you admit, five-eighths of the rates, is adequately represented under the existing system in your union?
I think it is more than adequately represented.

2193. Then how many elected guardians are elected now with the good will and consent of the owners of property?
I could answer you that by reference to the list of guardians, and I count 10, but in answer to your previous question, I would say, that giving the owners of property their present multiple vote, they exercise that right at present, and, as well, they are generally *ex-officio* guardians of the union I would say that *ex-officios* should not be in existence at all.

2194. We will come to that presently?
That is why I say that the owners of property have more than their right of representation at present.

2195. But do you think that they are adequately represented by the elective guardians?
I do, in this way; that the elected guardians may not represent the general opinions of the owners of property, but still they disburse the rates of the union as honestly and fairly as their predecessors.

2196. That is another matter; I may take that for granted; but they can hardly represent them if they do not represent their opinions?
They may not represent them in opinion, but I think they represent them very fairly in the treatment of the rates and the management of the union; they represent the majority of the ratepayers.

2197. Lord *Saltereford*.] You made sundry statements with regard to illegal claims

claims to the proxy vote; were these cases brought before the Inspector of the Local Government Board?
They were not.

2198. Then has there been any contested election investigated into by the officers of the Local Government Board?
There was no investigation.

2199. And were none of these cases brought before them?
There was not.

2200. Lord *Shute*.] Why not, if you considered it a grievance?
The reason is, that whenever an investigation is asked from the Local Government Board, they delay too long before granting it, and the elected guardians, having other business to attend to, and pressing business, because of necessity every one of them are working men, and cannot neglect their business more than one day in the week, or two in the week, to give their time to the union, could not continue this matter for the length of time that the Local Government Board would delay it. There was a tie at Mountmellick election last March, and, though resolutions were passed by the board of guardians asking for an investigation to be held, still no investigation was ordered by the Local Government Board; and, I believe, up to the present time they have not ordered a new election.

2201. Lord *Saltersford*.] But you are aware that investigations in contested elections do take place?
I am aware of that.

2202. Lord *Monk-Bretton*.] In the case of the proxy who voted under the authority of the woman who was dead; was the vote disallowed?
It was.

2203. In the case of this tie which you have just referred to, does the question still remain undetermined who was elected last March?
It does, unless an Order has come from the Local Government Board last week, of which I have no knowledge.

2204. Then, practically, one seat at the Board has been vacant?
It has, and that is the case frequently. There was a vacancy for Lacka Division about 18 months ago; and I think that vacancy existed three months.

2205. To what do you attribute the delay on the part of the Local Government Board in investigating these matters?
I really cannot say.

2206. Is it that they have so many investigations to hold that they have not staff enough to do it?
Either they have not staff enough to do it or they do not take sufficient interest in it.

2207. Has a correspondence been going on with them on the subject of this tie election?
There has.

2208. Has the board of guardians been urging them to get the matter settled?
It has; several times, I think three times altogether, they have passed resolutions asking the Local Government Board to hold a sworn inquiry into the matter.

2209. You have told us that you are in favour of having guardians elected for a period of three years; some witnesses who have been here have expressed the further opinion that it would be possible, instead of the whole of the Board retiring at the end of three years, that one-third of the Board should retire annually, as is the case in municipal bodies; what is your opinion on that point.
In one view it would be good, but it would leave the yearly contests in the Union still, and would not have a tendency to relieve the rates of the cost of these

9th June 1885.] Mr. MEEHAN. [Continued.

these yearly contests. I think an election once every three years would be the proper way to have it.

2210. For the election of the whole Board?
For the election of the whole Board.

2211. *Chairman.*] Is there an equal delay with regard to the investigation of false claims to vote as there is with regard to ordering a new election?
I could not give your Lordships any instance where there was any investigation claimed for any of those false votes; therefore I cannot say.

2212. Do you wish to say anything more about the proxy vote?
Nothing.

2213. What is the next point to which you wish to call attention?
To the *ex-officio* guardians; I consider it unfair and unjust to have *ex-officio* guardians at all.

2214. First, I will ask you in regard to the costs of petitions; it has been suggested that the petitioner should give security for costs to avoid frivolous petitions being lodged; what do you say to that?
I had a note made exactly in those same terms.

2215. You think that that is a good suggestion?
Yes, I entirely approve of that suggestion; and I believe that without some such provision frivolous petitions would be made.

2216. Viscount *Powerscourt.*] Costs to be paid by the party?
By the party on proof, of course, that the petition was frivolous.

2217. *Chairman.*] By the losing party, you mean?
Yes.

2218. It has been suggested that minors and lunatics should be entitled to vote either by their guardians or trustees; do you see any objection to that?
I see great objection to it; I do not think that any minors or lunatics should exercise any power of voting in those elections, no more than in Parliamentary or municipal elections.

2219. Then you think the property should be disfranchised during the period of their minority or insanity?
I think so, because a ratepayer who is a minor is disfranchised also under the same circumstances.

2220. He is now, but the suggestion is that he should not be?
I would say that he should be.

2221. What injustice do you see in allowing him to vote by his next friend?
I see this injustice, that probably his guardian would not at all represent his views.

2222. But supposing he is a child of three or four years old, do you consider it of very great importance that his views should be represented?
In the cases of Parliamentary elections and municipal elections those votes are not allowed, and they should not be allowed in poor law elections either; at age mentioned he could have no views to be represented.

2223. There is a provision here that would meet the case you have just suggested. Sub-section (2) of Clause 25 provides that, " In every case of vacancy in the office of elective guardian in any poor law union, the Local Government Board shall, within a reasonable time, which shall in no case exceed three months, order a fresh election to take place to fill such vacancy." That would meet the case you have just told us of in Mountmellick?
It would.

2224. Then the next point is this: that " no justice of the peace shall be qualified to be an *ex-officio* guardian of any poor law union unless he is a ratepayer of such union." I suppose you approve of that, supposing there to be any *ex-officios* at all?

Unquestionably;

9th June 1885.] Mr. MEEHAN. [Continued.

Unquestionably; I do not think that the accident of being a magistrate should entitle him to be an *ex-officio* guardian of the poor at all.

2225. Then the next provision is that which fixes the qualification of a guardian at 12 *l.* a year; do you approve of that?
I do; I think the present rating qualification is too high.

2226. You are aware, I suppose, that the Local Government Board can lower it when they think it necessary, and that they do lower it in fact in certain parts of Ireland in poor districts?
I have never known an instance where it was lowered, and I have known very intelligent men in Mountmellick and Abbeyleix and adjoining unions who were very competent to act as guardians, and the rating qualification prevented them.

2227. Lord *Silchester*.] What is the rating there?
In Mountmellick, 20 *l*, and in Abbeyleix, 30 *l*.

2228. *Chairman*.] Has there been any general complaint that the qualification is too high?
That is a general complaint.

2229. You have heard it mentioned?
Several times.

2230. Have you ever petitioned the Local Government Board to lower it?
No, I have not, nor do I know of any instance where there was such a petition sent.

2231. You were not aware that they have the power to lower it to any sum they think right?
I was not aware of it.

2232. I may tell you, as a matter of fact, that that is so; does that get rid of your objection to the present system?
By no means; I think it should be clearly stated by the Legislature.

2233. What is the qualification for dispensary committees in your union?
£. 30.

2234. This Bill would leave that unaltered?
There is not so much necessity for that in this way; that each guardian living in the district is a member of the dispensary committee.

2235. But each member of the dispensary committee is not necessarily a guardian?
No.

2236. And as a matter of fact many of them, I do not know whether it is the majority or not, but certainly many of them are not guardians?
Many of them are not, but I think there are only three in Maryborough dispensary committee who are elected members of the committee.

2237. The majority are not guardians?
Yes, 14 magistrates, eight elected guardians, and three elected members.

2238. Do not you think it would be rather an anomaly that the qualification for the Board should be 12 *l.*, and that for a committee appointed by the Board 30 *l.*?
I think both qualifications should be lowered.

2239. Then we come to the provision in the Bill reducing the number of *ex-officios*, what do you say to that?
I would say, that under the present system of electing guardians, each of the individual *ex-officios* has a greater voice in the selection of the guardians than any of the other ratepayers; that is, their number of votes is more than that of any other individual ratepayers, and not only have they a greater voice by their greater number of votes, but also by the very great influence which they exercise on the ratepayers as landlords and magistrates.

2240. It

9th June 1885.]   Mr. MEEHAN.   [Continued.

2240. It does not seem to be very successful in your union, judging from what you have told us of the results of the election?
Sometimes it has been very successful. I might mention other unions than Mountmellick, where it has been very successful.

2241. What success has the immense power which you say they possess, had in the way of enabling them in your own union to return candidates of their own selection?
It would be hardly fair to take this year as a standard point, because the *ex-officios* are outvoted this year; but in other years, I might say since the establishment of the Poor Law in Ireland, they have always been able by the exercise of the *ex-officio* vote, to carry their own nominees in the board, and if all attended this year they could carry their way.

2242. You are talking of what they do in the board room, and I am talking of their power to elect guardians. You say that they already possess so much influence, which they are able to exercise in the election, that they have a preponderating power; I ask you, what in your union is the result of that preponderating power in the election of guardians?
In some divisions that power has secured the election of men who represent the landlord point of view, the *ex-officio* point of view.

2243. In how many out of the whole number?
In 10.

2244. In 10 out of how many?
Out of 42.

2245. So that not a fourth of the elected guardians represent the owners of property, who, you tell us, pay five-eighths of the rates?
To look on it in that light, of course, your theory is right, but still you must remember that all those owners of property have so many more votes; for instance, one owner of property may have 18 or 20 votes.

2246. No doubt, and we know the result?
And I think that is very fair. It does not at all follow, because they are not able to secure a majority, they are not properly represented. If they exercise as many votes as their rateable property qualifies them to exercise, I believe that that is sufficient representation for them.

2247. If a candidate, holding diametrically opposite views to your own, was your representative, should you consider yourself properly represented?
I might not consider myself properly represented; but if I was in the minority, of course I should be satisfied. There are very many things which we have to put up with that we do not like.

2248. I suppose the real question in these contests is a political one?
Not always.

2249. What other questions arise?
Amongst the *ex-officio* class there always has been a tendency to grant higher pensions than have been granted before to officials in connection with the Board.

2250. Is that your experience?
I do not say that that is entirely the case; but that is sometimes the case. That is one of the grounds of complaint of the National League party.

2251. Lord *Saltersford*.] Pensions to whom?
Pensions to medical officers, and ex-clerks' superannuation.

2252. *Chairman*.] You say that the *ex-officio* guardians are more prone to give those high pensions or superannuations than the elected guardians?
Yes, they are. The first year that I was guardian there was a clerk, a most respectable man, I admit, who performed his duties in a first-class manner; his pension was proposed to be 120 *l.* a year, and the National party urged that 80 *l.* or 100 *l.* a year was sufficient superannuation. He was a hale healthy man, with a business in the town of Mountmellick, and they considered
that

9th June 1885.] Mr. Meehan. [Continued.

that 100l. or 80l. should be sufficient; but still the *ex-officios*, and the men returned by their votes, voted them down, and gave the 120l. a-year.

2253. Is not there a scale fixed for these superannuations?
There may be a scale; but still I think it should be left discretionary with the board of guardians, because they are the people who have to treat with those officials; and they know the proper superannuation to give them.

2254. But as a matter of fact, there is a scale?
I believe there is.

2255. And whatever sum is fixed has to receive the sanction of the Local Government Board?
I believe so; but I believe it is competent with the board of guardians to fix the superannuation at whatever they consider just, and then the Local Government Board sanctions it.

2256. Lord *Saltersford*.] Is it not this: that there is a maximum that the board cannot exceed?
I think it is that.

2257. And that the board can grant any sum less than a certain sum?
I think that is the case.

2258. *Chairman*.] How many years, for instance, had this clerk been your clerk?
I really could not say how many years.

2259. But that was a very important consideration, was it not, in the superannuation?
Unquestionably it was.

2260. But you did not consider it?
It was considered; but I cannot remember now the number of years that he was clerk.

2261. Lord *De Vesci*.] In this case, was he granted his full superannuation; the maximum?
He was.

2262. *Chairman*.] Is there any other reason which leads you to object to the existence of *ex-officio* guardians than that you think they grant too high superannuations?
On principle, I do not like there to be *ex-officio* members at all of any board, all boards should be thoroughly representative and elective. And then, in the present system of *ex-officios*, it is open to this: that magistrates in the district sometimes act as *ex-officio* guardians, though they have no rateable property whatever in the union.

2263. This Bill, you know, gets rid of that?
Yes, I see that; and that was a most necessary provision, because there is a magistrate at present an *ex-officio* member of the Mountmellick Board, who has not a particle of property in the union; at least he does not pay any rate. There is another case of an *ex-officio* guardian with only a rating of 45l.; he exercises his right as an *ex-officio* guardian and has, as well, his two votes. An ordinary ratepayer with a 45l. rating can only exercise his vote, whereas a magistrate with the same rating can act as a guardian and vote as well. Then there is another *ex-officio* guardian with an 85l. rating; he acts as an *ex-officio* guardian, and also he can exercise his right of voting. Then there is another with a 105l. rating; and the same thing applies to him.

2264. Do you attribute any evil to the presence of *ex-officio* guardians?
On the principle that there should be no taxation without representation, every member of such a board ought to be elected by the votes of the ratepayers. I do not think that the principle is at all good that because a gentleman occupies a certain position, or is entrusted by the Government with any position, that should entitle him to exercise a right denied to other ratepayers.

(0.1.) Cc 2265. That

2265. That is an objection to the principle of it; but I ask you, whether you consider that their presence at the board is injurious either to the interests of the ratepayers or of the poor?
It is in this way; that the elected guardians, who generally do the work of the union, do not take the amount of interest that they otherwise would, taking into consideration the fact that where *ex-officio* guardians have the majority, no matter what action the elective guardians take on any question, the *ex-officio* guardians can come in and vote them down; and I believe that it has a tendency to make the guardians negligent and careless in the performance of their duties where *ex-officios* have the majority.

2266. In what cases have you found that that occurs, that the *ex-officios* come in and vote down, as you express it, the elective guardians?
I have known it several times in Mountmellick.

2267. In what questions?
On three occasions. I think it was the election of officers for the year, and on other occasions it was the granting of some pensions, as well as I can remember; I think it was only twice that I remember that the *ex-officios* came there and voted in the majority, where it was a matter of the ordinary business of the board.

2268. And you object to their having done so on those two occasions. Do you think it was improper for them to endeavour to elect a chairman who, in their judgment, would adequately fill the post?
I would not think so, provided that they were satisfied to come there during the twelve months, and perform the work of the union.

2269. You think they ought not to come unless they have been regular attendants?
Decidedly; but gentlemen will come there and elect one of themselves to a position when they are not prepared to come to the board and perform the duties of guardians. We have had *ex-officios* at Mountmellick, as a rule, who never came except once in the twelve months to appoint the chairman, and were never seen there again till the next election.

2270. The appointment of a chairman is a very important matter, is it not?
It is important in many ways; it should not be a party question at all.

2271. I am glad to hear you say so, because I agree with you in that?
I believe it is the man who best understands the business of the board who should be elected to that post; and it was the *ex-officios* who set us a bad example by electing men who are incompetent to perform the duties, and who show it from time to time, and have misused the power given them.

2272. Have you anything more to say about the *ex-officios*?
I do not think so. I will only say in conclusion on that subject that as a compromise. Of course, if the *ex-officios* are not abolished——

2273. There is no proposal here for abolishing them?
Then if the suggestion that is made in this Bill that they shall not exceed half the number of elective guardians is adopted, of course on the principle that half a loaf is better than no bread, I would be very well satisfied with that provision.

2274. But you would rather like no bread at all?
I would give those gentlemen every facility to come there, yield them the right with the greatest possible pleasure, provided that they did come there and do their duty fairly; but any time that they did come there it was to flout the opinions and disregard the feelings of the elective guardians, who have had to perform all the work.

2275. Lord *Shute.*] Do I understand you to say that the *ex-officios* only come when there is a question of electing a chairman or an important officer?
That is my experience.

2276. The attendance at your board of *ex-officios* is not good then?

It

9th June 1885.] Mr. MEEHAN. [Continued.

It is not. I think I would be correct in stating that out of the 37 *ex-officios* in Mountmellick Union not more than three, or certainly not more than four, give anything like a constant attendance or take any part whatever in the business of the Board.

2277. Can you give any reason why there is such a small attendance of the *ex-officio* guardians?
I could not, unless it is that they disregard the business, and do not wish to come there to perform it.

2278. Do you think they may have any reason, in consequence of the elective guardians going always against them, or very much against them?
I would not think so, because when they secured the election of their own officers, they did not even then come there to do the business of the Board.

2279. Then, to a certain extent your objection falls to the ground; if there is such a small attendance of these *ex-officios* what is the harm that they do?
There is every harm, because they come there once in the 12 months and elect a chairman who does not represent the wishes of the working majority of the board.

2280. What does the average out-door relief to the paupers in your union come to?
I am sorry to say that I cannot answer the question correctly. I had all the returns made out of the number of paupers in the house and their different cases, the out-door and in-door relief lists, and I mislaid the paper coming over, and thought I had it with those I brought with me.

2281. The average out-door relief is what I asked for, not the relief in the house?
That was one of the matters I took a note of, but I left the paper behind me in coming from home.

2282. Do you give out-door relief to many evicted tenants?
No.

2283. Could you tell me whether you make any difference at your board, with reference to relief given to evicted tenants and to ordinary paupers?
We have not given relief to any extent to evicted tenants.

2284. In some cases you have done so, I suppose?
I cannot recollect a single case.

2285. Have you ever heard of a very much larger sum being given in other unions to evicted tenants than to ordinary paupers?
I saw it reported in the newspapers that such was the case.

2286. But that is all; you do not know anything personally?
Not of my own knowledge; and I believe there has not been a single case in Mountmellick Union where such relief was given.

2287. We have had it put in evidence before us that such was the case?
It may be; I have no recollection of it.

2288. Lord *De Vesci*.] As chairman of the board, you know probably the total amount of out-door relief that is given?
It is something like 43 *l.* a week.

2289. Lord *Skute*.] That is the amount in gross?
It is.

2290. Cannot you remember what the ordinary out-door relief is; is it 3 *s.*, or 2 *s.* 6 *d.*, or 5 *s.*?
The relief given to each pauper you mean? From 1 *s.*, I think, to 4 *s.*; 4 *s.* or 5 *s.* is the largest amount. There may be one or two exceptional cases. I think there is a case in Mountmellick, where there is a widow with four or five small children, and she is getting 6 *s.* a week; but the ordinary sums given in out-door relief are from 1 *s.* to 3 *s.*

2291. Lord *Inchiquin*.] You said just now that you thought the election of officers for the union should be non-political?

I say that politics should be kept as far apart as possible from the ordinary business of the board.

2292. But my question is as to the election of officers; you think that should be non-political?

Certainly.

2293. Are you aware that the party to which you belong have recently put forward gentlemen, and got them elected too, as officers in various unions, who have had no experience whatever in the management of union affairs?

I am not aware of that. I believe my election was not altogether on account of my political opinions, but it was principally because I took an interest in the business of the board and attended it as regularly as I could.

2294. Do you not know that through the south and west of Ireland generally there have been substituted for former officers gentlemen who have only recently had any experience of the Poor Law, and that gentlemen have been removed from offices who had for many years filled them?

I believe that is perfectly right, too, because I do not think any gentlemen should have a monopoly of those offices.

2295. I only wished to understand distinctly your opinion; you said that your opinion as a member of the Land League, and representing the Land League opinion here was, that the election of officers should be non-political?

Yes.

2296. What I want now to get from you is that that is not the opinion held by the body to which you belong?

To some extent I think it is. I daresay the body that I belong to are actuated by this motive, that men who take part in politics, who take any part in the questions of the day, if they show intelligence and a competency to understand these matters, are to be picked out simply because they are intelligent and are likely to carry out the business of the board properly. I do not believe it is quite because they are politicians that they are selected; it may be a part of the reason certainly that men who have a good public character are selected for those positions; but I will say also that as to any man who would be incompetent to perform the duties of chairman or vice-chairman, as the case might be, I do not believe the National League would elect him to the position simply because he had a reputation for politics outside.

2297. Are you aware that in some unions in the county of Clare (with which I am more particularly acquainted) the affairs of those unions got into great difficulty owing to the appointment of chairmen totally inexperienced in their duties?

I am not aware of that.

2298. Are you aware that there is one union in that county now in the possession of the bailiffs?

I saw it in the papers; but still from what I have read of it I think it was a very high-handed proceeding on the part of the gentleman who did make the seizure.

2299. Is that a satisfactory result; do you think that the cases to which I have alluded of ousting *ex-officios* entirely from taking any part in the affairs of the union have been attended with satisfactory results?

I believe that that would not have been the result; that that seizure would not have taken place if the majority of the board of guardians was of the same political complexion as the legal gentleman at whose suit the seizure was made.

2300. Lord *Monk-Bretton*.] Then you are not prepared to say that it is the ousting of the *ex officios* from the chairmanship that has led to these difficulties?

I would not say so, because the same difficulties might have occurred under the *ex-officios*. If we take their attendance as a standpoint, the business of the board of guardians could not have been carried on at all. In my experience they only come there on certain occasions.

2301. You

2301. You have told us that on your own board there were differences of opinion between the *ex-officio* and the elective guardians as to pensions ; is there a difference of opinion between them as to the administration of out-door relief; are the *ex-officios* inclined to be stricter than the elective guardians, or *vice versâ* ?

As far as my knowledge goes I think each party are equally anxious to act fairly both to the ratepayer and to the poor. As far as I can see there is a tendency in each party to give fair out-door relief to the paupers, but not to give anything that would be unjust or unreasonable.

2302. But is there a general disposition to apply the house test more strictly on the part of one set of guardians than on the part of the other ?

As far as I can recollect I do not think there is. There seems to be an anxiety amongst the elective guardians and the one or two *ex-officios* who do attend there to do things fairly and uprightly.

2303. There is no difference between them as to the policy in the administration of the Poor Law ?

There is just one circumstance I might mention in connection with out door relief in which the *ex-officios* who attended the board introduced a political complexion ; that was in the case of a woman whose husband had been accidentally killed.

2304. I was not asking as to any politics ; I was only asking as to the administration of the Poor Law itself?

I intend to answer the question in this way : This woman's husband was killed, and it was sought by a certain party to give a political complexion to it, though it was proved on oath afterwards that there was no such thing in existence ; but it had that political complexion, and though that woman was in receipt of 7 *s.* a week out of moneys collected in the town, still the *ex-officios* who were in a majority that year gave the woman 6 *s.* a week.

2305. *Chairman.*] What is the name of the woman ?

Mrs. Hennessy ; she was in receipt of 7 *s.* a week, I think, out of moneys collected for her, and the *ex-officio* guardians gave her, I think, either 5 *s.* or 6 *s.* I was guardian for the division, and sought to have the amount reduced ; I was defeated at first, but ultimately I succeeded in having it reduced until such time as the money that was collected should have been spent, and then to give her an increase if such was deemed necessary.

2306. There was one question I omitted to ask you. We have had some evidence with regard to contracts being improperly given ; in your union now, I presume, from what you have told us, what has been called the National League element is in the ascendant ?

That is so.

2307. Are there any instances of improper giving of contracts in your union ? I would not think so.

2308. Are they always given to the lowest tender ?

Not always, and I think that would be a very bad principle to adopt. The principle as far as I know that the guardians act upon at present is that they take the samples and select the best out of them, and even if that is dearer than the others, they take that in preference ; and I believe that the experience of the officials of the house also goes to prove that those samples so selected, though a little dearer, are much better. For instance, in the case of wearing apparel of the house, and the bed clothing, &c., the samples selected on that principle are always found to last much longer than the cheapest qualities.

2309. Then do you not consider the question of price at all ?

Unquestionably we consider the price ; but the difference of a few pence, or 6 *d.* or so per yard, in an article would not affect the consideration of the matter, if the guardians considered that the articles were so much better as to be worth it.

9th June 1885.]　　　　　　Mr. MEEHAN.　　　　　　[Continued.

2310. Now is there any way by which the guardians can tell which sample comes from one man and which from another?
There are the names of all the parties there on the samples, and the tender is laid on the table for the guardians to see it.

2311. So that the guardian, in judging the sample, would know whose sample it was?
Unquestionably.

2312. Might not that tend to influence his judgment as to its superiority or otherwise?
I hardly think it would, because any guardian that goes there should go there, and I believe does go there, conscientiously to perform his duties; and I do not know any case where any tender has been given through favouritism, or through a consideration of the man's political sentiments; and I believe I am correct in saying, with regard to the number of contracts in the Mountmellick Union, which I represent, that there are as many, at least there are very nearly as many, Conservative Protestant contractors as there are Nationalists.

2313. Do you mean to say that a Protestant cannot be a Nationalist?
I do not say that; but I mean Conservatives.

2314. Lord *De Vesci.*] Have there been any instances this year of the lowest tender not being taken, but the highest?
There have, for the reasons that I have stated.

2315. Lord *Saltersford.*] I understand your answer to be this, that it is because you think the good article is better value for the money?
Unquestionably.

2316. *Chairman.*] And that no other element enters into the consideration?
I do not believe there does; I state positively before your Lordships' Committee that such a consideration never entered into my mind, and I believe that the other guardians who have the same opinion as I have act in exactly the same spirit.

2317. Lord *Saltersford.*] With regard to some of the evidence you gave before, you spoke of the influence of *ex-officio* guardians in the election of elective guardians; could the *ex-officio* element return an elective guardian without the vote of the occupiers?
Of course it is the vote of the occupiers that must elect the guardian.

2318. But I understood you to say that in some instances the *ex-officio* guardians influenced the return of the elective guardians?
So they do; I do not mean to say that the influence is exercised by the *ex-officios* always at every election; but I say that from their position as magistrates, they exercise more or less influence, and also that they exercise their voting power in accordance with the rating.

2319. Would not that be obviated by the ballot as proposed by the Bill?
It would.

2320. Lord *Monk-Bretton.*] But I understood one objection which you took to *ex-officios* to be this; that you said a gentleman who is a magistrate sits *ex-officio* upon the board, and also votes for the election of elective guardians?
That is so.

2321. That would not be obviated by the ballot?
Of course it would not; but the question that his Lordship just now asked was directed to this; that under the ballot the influence of the *ex-officios* as magistrates could not be exercised, that the voter would be at perfect liberty to vote whichever way he wished.

2322. Lord *Saltersford.*] Any objection that you might have to influence used in that way might be obviated by the ballot?
Yes, I think so.

2323. Do you mean to say that as magistrates they influence voters, that they exercise their magisterial power for that purpose?

I do not mean to say that they act as magistrates in that respect; but I say that the consideration that they are such is made use of, and it often seems, I am sorry to say, that they make their power felt in an undue manner as magistrates, by people who make themselves obnoxious to them either by voting at such elections, or any other elections.

2324. Do you mean to say that in the administration of justice they make a difference in the case of those who have voted in a particular way?

I do.

2325. Has any representation been made to the Lord Chancellor to that effect?

I am not aware of it.

2326. Do not you think that the Lord Chancellor would remove such a magistrate from the commission of the peace if it were shown that the magistrate had given undue bias to a ratepayer on account of the vote he had given?

I have no doubt that the Lord Chancellor would do what was reasonable and just; and, indeed, it would be most necessary that those cases should be brought forward, and that magistrates who abuse their position so much should be removed from a position in which they bring discredit upon the law, and earn for themselves contempt amongst the people.

2327. Viscount *Powerscourt*.] You said that your opinion was that guardians should not be *ex officios*?

Yes.

2328. But supposing that there were no *ex-officio* guardians, how would you propose that property should be represented?

By each having his voting power; I would leave, of course, the multiple vote.

2329. *Chairman*.] You would take away the proxy, however?

I would take away the proxy, but leave the multiple vote by all means.

2330. Viscount *Powerscourt*.] I mean in the election of guardians; how would you propose that property should be represented?

The magistrates, of course, could exercise their voting power in the election of guardians; but what I object to is this, that they should act as guardians without being elected.

2331. You think that all the board should be elected?

Yes; that from the fact of men being magistrates it should not at all follow that they are *ex-officios* of the board. You will remember the case I cited of a magistrate with a 45 *l*. rating, who acted as guardian and also exercised his right of voting; and there are many other such cases; but other ordinary ratepayers cannot be guardians unless they are elected.

2332. *Chairman*.] In fact, your proposal is that the *ex-officios* should be abolished; that the proxy vote should be abolished; that owners of property should be left the multiple vote; and that that is the only influence they should be allowed to exercise at the election of guardians?

Yes.

2333. And that, notwithstanding the fact that even with the proxy vote and the multiple vote, they are not able to return more than one-fourth of the elected guardians, though they pay five-eighths of the rates. Is not that a good instance of taxation without representation?

In one way it may be; but if the *ex-officios* would attend and do the business of the board, there might not be any objection to that; but they have used their position not to carry on the business of the board, but for political purposes.

2334. Viscount *Powerscourt*.] It has been suggested before that half of the board

9th June 1885.]   Mr. MEEHAN.   [Continued.

board should be elected to represent property, and half to represent the ratepayers, all the board being elected; what would you say to that?

I have not considered the question in that respect. I think the owners of property having a multiple vote at present have sufficient representation; that is to say, if they exercise the right, just the same as the ordinary ratepayers, and if the majority of the ratepayers are against them, of course they should be bound by the majority.

2335. Lord *De Vesci*.] If the *ex-officio* vote was done away with and the proxy vote, do you consider that the multiple vote should be unlimited. You are aware that there is a maximum at this time?

I am.

2336. Do you think that that maximum should be done away with, and that the vote should be unlimited?

I think that owners of property should be allowed a multiple vote, as many as their valuation would give, allowing the votes in accordance with the present system.

2337. Do you mean that the maximum should remain as it does now; it is 30, I think, now?

My answer to that is this: that I would allow the owners of property a multiple vote, in accordance with whatever rateable property they would be owners of, calculated at the present scale. If *ex-officios* and proxies were abolished, I would be in favour of giving the owners of property whatever number of votes their rateable property would give them in accordance with the present scale of counting; but if the *ex-officios* were retained, I would certainly say that the present maximum should be left as it is.

2338. Lord *Shute*.] But you would only allow them to exercise a vote, provided they gave it in person?

Provided they gave it in person.

2339. Lord *Monk-Bretton*.] If the Legislature were prepared to abolish one of the two things, either *ex-officios* or proxy voting, which should you wish most to be abolished?

I should say the proxy vote by all means. I would much sooner retain the *ex-officios* than retain the proxies, because I do not believe that there is as great a tendency amongst the *ex-officios* to act in the bad spirit in which the proxies do at present.

2340. Have you any other other observations to make on the subject of the Bill before us?

I do not think there is anything I have to add to what I have stated before your Lordships.

The Witness is directed to withdraw.

Mr. EDWARD FENELON, having been called in; is Examined, as follows:

2341. *Chairman*.] You are, I think, Vice-Chairman of Naas Union?

Yes.

2342. And an elected guardian; and I believe you are a farmer in the neighbourhood of Kilcullin?

Yes; and I am likewise a farmer in the union of Athy.

2343. What is the first clause in this Bill to which you wish to direct the attention of the Committee?

To be brief, I will take the Bill as a whole, and say that I approve of it; but as to the first clause needing notice, Clause 4, "Guardians to hold office for

[9th June 1885.] Mr. FENELON. [Continued.

for three years," taken in connection with the rest of the Bill, I think it would be very valuable.

2344. You are in favour of that provision?
Yes, I am.

2345. Then the next clause is the one which provides for vote by ballot being substituted for the present system; what do you say to that?
I am likewise in favour of that, for this simple reason, that I am quite sure it would work well in this way: that it would keep parties who, to my own knowledge, have more or less influenced voters at a recent election, from exercising their influence on the electors or voters at Poor Law elections. I will give you a case in point. A man recently in the division adjoining where I live, seemed most anxious to prove that he intended to vote for a certain candidate; he called me to his house and showed me that he had a voting paper signed for this candidate; it was too late, as it was not signed when the policeman called for it, and the policeman subsequently refused to call for it when it was signed. This man wanted to evade voting, as he was employed occasionally by having his horse and car engaged carrying parties to trains, &c.

2346. The next clause, I believe, to which you wish to call attention is that which provides for the abolition of the proxy vote?
I am very strongly in favour of the abolition of proxy voting, and the reason why I am in favour of it is because I have had some experience for the last two years, and only two (though I have been a guardian, I think, for about 10 years) of proxy voting in consequence of taking up a scrutiny last year and this year; and I believe that proxy voting is open more or less to having votes manufactured, and on the smallest occasion, whether it was a justifiable one or not, votes have been manufactured; and except we go through the very tedious routine of calling for a Local Government Board inquiry we have no power to arrive at a conclusion as to whether those proxy votes are in reality legal, for the simple reason that returning officers will not allow an attorney or counsel to examine into them or inquire whether they are legal or otherwise. I can speak of circumstances which came to my knowledge this year in regard to an election that occurred in an adjoining division. A candidate was refused permission to inspect the proxy papers, which he had a perfect legal right to do.

2347. That appears to have been the fault of the Poor Law clerk and not of the system of proxy voting?
That is one reason why I object to it, the very fact of so much power being in the hands of the returning officer, together with this reason, that for the most trivial interests proxy voting has been manufactured. I believe I am justified in saying that in a property near to me, where there are some two or three landlords, out of some 23 *s.* there was a proxy vote registered; they calculated the mere nominal sum between the value and the rent which somebody paid for it.

2348. Are you of opinion that more false votes are endeavoured to be manufactured, as you describe it, for proxy voting than for personal voting?
I am, for the simple reason that there cannot be a wrong vote in personal voting. At present the clerk of the union has the name of every man and woman (and both men and women have a right to vote at present), he has all the names on the rate book, and the rate collector is there to compare them previously to the elections, to see whether any of those parties are ineligible, or whether any be dead whose names are on the books, and, if so, they are objected to. I have never known a case in which any vote was recorded in which the person named on the rate book was not living and qualified to vote.

2349. I suppose he has the names of those entitled to proxy votes?
The clerk of the union is supposed to have the names of those who lodge proxy claims. They are not eligible to be used as voting papers, unless they are in his possession one month previous to the election; but then, as I stated before, we have no means at present of arriving at a satisfactory conclusion as to whether proxy votes are legal in reality or not. A candidate within two

(0.1.) D D miles

9th June 1885.] Mr. FENELON. [Continued.

miles of me told me that, being at a scrutiny, he heard the name of one party read out recording some four or five votes in which the party was believed to be dead.

2350. That is rather indefinite evidence, is it not?
The candidate told me who was at the inquiry himself.

2351. That the person was believed to be dead?
That he believed it himself; that he did not believe the man to be in existence.

2352. But he was not sure?
I could not swear to that.

2353. But beyond that objection to the proxy vote, that it is liable to abuse, have you any other objection to it?
Nothing beyond the small trivial sums which justify at present proxy votes being registered; nominal sums.

2354. But that applies also in the case of occupation votes, does it not; for instance, a farmer who has a herd's house valued at a trifling sum on his holding, would have an additional vote for that herd's house?
I believe so; but it is not utilised.

2355. It can be, however?
I believe so. I am determined to try it myself. I am in a position to do it myself, but have never done it yet.

2356. Viscount *Powerscourt*.] And other people might do it?
Certainly; but in my union of Naas I have never heard of an instance of it.

2357. *Chairman*.] Still it is the law?
I believe so. As to a herd's house, I am not quite sure of that, except it be liable to valuation.

2358. I mean, supposing that a herd's house was valued at 7 s. or 8 s. a year, the farmer on whose holding it was would be entitled to make a vote for that house?
I am not sure about that point, because it might be returned in the gross valuation of his farm.

2359. Under the new decision I think he would be entitled to make a note of it; formerly it was aggregated. Those then are your two objections to the proxy vote?
Those are my two objections to the proxy vote. With regard to some questions which have arisen with regard to proxy votes being allowed, and a landlord not being able to vote in two places at the same time, the same thing will apply to tenants who hold farms in different unions. I myself hold a farm in Athy Union, and there are several other tenants who hold farms in different counties, Kilkenny, Meath, and other counties, and who reside in county Kildare. It would equally apply to them if they could not exercise their votes by personal attendance.

2360. Supposing that the proxy vote instead of being abolished were extended to occupiers, would that take away your objection to it?
So far, if other portions of the Bill were carried out, I would not make that a stumbling block; but the abolition of proxy voting would be one of the strongest features of this Bill, speaking from my own knowledge of the way in which in four divisions around me, there was not a proxy vote to be made out of the very pettiest interest that was not manufactured, brought up and recorded, even in cases which I never anticipated, and used against myself.

2361. By the use of the word "manufactured" there, you do not mean to say that it was falsely done, do you?
I am not in a position to prove it; but it has been used in cases in which I have never heard of the interests of the parties before. I am not going to insinuate for one moment that gentlemen, as a rule, will adopt that course; but I know one particular case where a man was put forward and was made the means

9th June 1883.] Mr. FENELON. [Continued.

means of so doing himself; he was nominally a land agent, but in reality merely the tool of another.

2362. But if the union clerk did his duty, it would not be very easy to make those false claims, would it?
The union clerk of the Naas Union, who is as respectable a man as is to be found, tells me that all claims are supposed to be *bonâ fide*, and that you have scarcely a right to make an inquiry into them. I insisted on seeing the register of all the proxy papers used against me; another guardian told me that he was refused the same privilege, and he was told that proxy votes were not to be questioned.

2363. Your argument, as I understand it, is directed more against the method by which the proxy vote is given and recorded, than against the proxy vote itself. If a means could be devised by which it would be extremely difficult for false claims to be brought forward, would not that meet your objection to the system?
No, it would not obviate my objection to proxy voting, because I hold that, following precedents in other cases, such as voting for Members of Parliament, it is better to substitute personal voting for proxy voting.

2364. When it is possible?
When it is possible; and then probably there might be some means devised of meeting the difficulty which has been raised in some questions put as to gentlemen recording their votes in other unions.

2365. Can you suggest any?
No, unless there was a different day appointed. At present it is the 19th and 20th of March on which those votes are generally recorded. I have not the slightest objection to property being fairly represented, but not with any preponderance.

2366. How do you mean "fairly;" taking the amount of rates paid by the parties as a criterion, do you mean?
There is a question about that; it is not looked upon by myself (and I will say as much on behalf of the parties I represent) that the theory laid down that landlords pay five-eighths of the rates is a fact; because in the first place the tenants have to make up for it, and that with the greatest possible difficulty in many instances; they often have to screw a point so as to get the rate ready, that they may be allowed a half of it in the November rents; and in addition to that they look upon themselves at present (and I am in a position to state that they do so with justice) as being over rented, and consequently over taxed from the difficulties that surround the farming interest at this moment; I know that as a practical farmer; and consequently in paying the rates, though they have to be refunded half of the rates, they still look upon themselves, practically, as paying the whole; so that I do not think it is correct to say that the landlords pay five-eighths of the rates.

2367. As a matter of fact, they do pay five-eighths, but your theory is that owing to the tenants paying higher rents than they ought, in reality it comes out of the pockets of the tenants?
Yes, I know that that is the case with myself.

2368. Viscount *Powerscourt*.] Are you not under a judicial rent?
In one case I am, in one farm out of three, or rather a statutory lease, not a judicial rent. I am very happy to say it is not a judicial lease, because then I would be bound for 31 years; I am delighted to say that I am not bound for one third of that time.

2369. Lord *Shute*.] Do I correctly understand you to say that you have a lease?
I have had a lease of each of three farms, and in one case, when times were good, I gave an increase of rent, and the landlord has been sensible enough to reduce that rent from the increased rent to the old rent, which is still, I think, between 40 and 50 per cent. over Griffiths' valuation; and I hold that land at present.

9th June 1885.]   Mr. FENELON.   [Continued.

present. The average quality of land in Ireland is not worth Griffiths' valuation at this moment; and when I say that, I know several counties; I know Kildare, Queen's County, a great deal of it, Carlow, Wicklow, and Kilkenny. I only just mention that; I do not care to raise the question here, but I mention it to give some sort of reason why we state that we are paying the whole of the rates, in fact.

2370. When you took your lease, I suppose you took into consideration the rates you would have to pay?
Yes, we knew it was a matter of fact. At the time that I took the lease, it was simply, "Take it, or the result will be another thing by and bye."

2371. Lord *De Vesci*.] Is it not the case that when the Commissioners fix the judicial rent, they take into consideration that the rates are divided, that the tenant only pays half?
I know that; but the rent judicially fixed, as you call it, was a private arrangement between myself and my landlord; it was a concession made to me.

2372. But it was ratified, was it not?
Not by the Commissioner, but by the county court judge.

2373. *Chairman*.] As a fact, the higher the poor rate is, the less the landlord's income?
Yes, when he has to pay half, his income is, of course, so far reduced.

2374. Have you anything more to say about the proxy vote?
I would rather leave myself in your Lordship's hands.

2375. You have no proposal to substitute for it?
No, I did not think it was exactly my place as a witness, to come up to suggest anything, but merely to read the Bill over as it has passed the House of Commons, and give my assent and my reasons for assenting to the Bill, taking it as a whole.

2376. But I understand you to say that you think property ought to be fairly represented?
I would say that property should be fairly represented, but I look upon property at this moment as over represented at our boards of guardians; in fact, I know it is.

2377. You are speaking now of the boards taking in *ex officios* as well?
Yes; I do not mean to say that at all the boards property is over represented, but I know, of my own knowledge, that in some of the boards it is over represented; that the elective guardians, in fact, have no power at all; that they are mere cyphers at the board.

2378. Lord *Shute*.] How is that?
They are so much in the minority that if they have any question to bring forward, it is overruled by the *ex officios* and their supporters as elective guardians.

2379. Then you have had a large attendance of *ex officios* at your board?
At my board there is a good attendance of *ex officios*. Whenever there is any appointment to be made, we have a very large attendance of *ex officios*; they come to a man. And then you are aware that a certain number of the elective guardians attend, more or less, in the landlord interest.

2380. *Chairman*.] I was not aware of that; if it is so, tell us?
I know it to be the case.

2381. What do you mean by saying that they attend in the landlord interest?
That they are returned through the interest of the landlords. I have an official list here from the clerk of the union as to the attendances (*handing in the same*).

2382. It is out of my power, I may say, to attend, and I am very anxious to have the power to resign given to me?
You have already the power to resign; I know, of my own knowledge, a case where

where a gentleman resigned his position as *ex-officio* guardian, in order that another might be substituted for him.

2383. Lord *Saltersford*.] Did he do it legally ?
I cannot say that; I asked him, "Why do you resign," and he said, " I have been called upon to do so, because I would not attend."

2384. Lord *Shute*.] Did you happen to attend to what the last witness said about the owners of property voting in person, and suggesting that, in order that they might do that, the days of election should be extended from two to four or five days?
I have already mentioned that to your Lordships, that if that could be done, if any system like that could be adopted, I would not have the slightest objection to it. I think it is only fair that property should be represented in that way.

2385. Lord *Saltersford*.] I happen to know a gentleman living in Wicklow, and having also property in Wexford, Carlow, Waterford, Kilkenny, and Sligo. By what possible machinery would you meet his case ?
I was not aware that landlords had their property separated so much ; but even though that may be the case in that instance, it would be one of very few.

2386. Viscount *Powerscourt*.] There are plenty of landlords who have property in four counties ?
There are tenants likewise holding farms in different counties. I know Kildare men that have farms in Meath and some in Kilkenny ; and, probably, if a balance was struck, the tenants would lose just as much by the fact of their not being able to record their votes in different unions, as the landlords would lose.

2387. Lord *Saltersford*.] You have spoken of the abuses of the proxy vote ; have you given any attention to Part II. of the Bill, dealing with Poor Law election petitions, whereby disputed elections can be tried before the chairman of quarter sessions ?
I have read that attentively.

2388. Do not you think that that would obviate, or go towards obviating, any abuse of the proxy vote ?
That is, assuming that the proxy vote is to be retained.

2389. Yes; do you not think that the machinery of going before the chairman of quarter sessions would bring up all these defects?
Assuming that the proxy vote is to be retained, I hold that it is a much better machinery to inquire into the justice of Poor Law elections before a county court judge, than say before the clerk of the union or a Local Government Board officer, because then you can have agents, or a counsel, or an attorney. In my own case, the clerk of the union would not allow me an attorney. I, for reasons, contested a division which I do not reside in, and I was most anxious to see what the feelings were in the matter, and I had to investigate it myself. However, I succeeded in showing that there was a different feeling in the division of Naas from what was expected or thought to be in it.

2390. *Chairman*.] I suppose from that answer you admit that Poor Law elections now turn upon political grounds ?
Not so much on political grounds as on the manner in which the guardians represent the interests of the parties who return them to the board.

2391. Do you mean by their interests their political interests ?
Probably there might be a feeling in that way, but not taking it as a whole the political interests. I opposed a Roman Catholic this year because of his non-attendance and carelessness, and I am a Roman Catholic myself. I ousted him from the board.

2392. Not on political grounds ?
No; but on account of his want of attendance at the board, and sympathy with the elective guardians, and carelessness.

2393. Were

2393. Were political grounds not mentioned in your election address?
No, I think not. I issued an address, and I am not aware that there was anything at all in it on political grounds.

[*The following is the Address referred to:—*]

POOR LAW ELECTIONS—NAAS UNION.

Fellow ratepayers.—The time has come when a determined effort should be made to assert the independence of the ratepayers of Naas Union, and of the electoral division of Naas in particular. All over the union the ratepayers are determined that their representatives at the board in future shall be men enjoying their confidence, and who will, on all occasions when their duty demands them, be present to counteract the votes of irresponsible *ex officios*.

For a considerable time gone by the electoral division of Naas has not been represented by guardians who either looked after our interests as they ought, or attended to their duties as other guardians have done. The result of their neglect or their opposition to schemes* put forward for the benefit of Naas would have been disastrous were it not for the watchfulness of other members of the board who took an interest in the welfare of the union generally, and of Naas in particular.

We, the undersigned, therefore now confidently call upon the independent ratepayers of Naas electoral division, and ask your votes and interest at the coming election.

Two of us are already members of the board, and we can confidently point to our actions at the board as a guarantee that in future your interests shall be safe in our hands. The other candidate who seeks election in conjunction with us is a townsman who may be trusted to carry out your wishes in the most independent manner.

In conclusion, we need only point to the system practised by the *ex officio* members of the board, who flock into the boardroom on all occasions when the rates are to be voted away either as salaries or in pensioning their friends in an extravagant manner.

Upon the part taken by the ratepayers of Naas electoral division depends whether the board is to be governed by a few irresponsible *ex officios*, or by the voice of the people.

(signed)   *Edward Doyle,*
            Michael Bagleton,
            Edward Fenelon.

* The expression, "Schemes put forward for the benefit of Naas, &c.," refers to the efforts of Doctor Smyth, Medical Officer of Naas, for the proper sanitation of the town of Naas, and which scheme was opposed by two of the then guardians, but was pressed forward by all the board except the guardians of Naas proper.

2394. You opposed him simply because he was not a good guardian?
One guardian had to retire, he was a Protestant, the other was a Roman Catholic; and I distinctly stated that my opposition was made more to the latter than to the former.

2395. I did not say, "on religious grounds;" I hope that we have nothing of that kind in our unions; but I said, "on political grounds"?
I could not know what politics the man had that I defeated; he lived within a mile of the workhouse, and was only 15 times a year there, and I put in 22 visits, and I have to drive nine miles. I have had repeatedly, in occupying the chair at Naas board of guardians, to adjourn the business of the Naas division for the want of the attendance of the guardians of the division, and that particularly upon out-door relief cases, where we would not have any local knowledge.

2396. Mr. Molloy told us, I think, that there are 30 electoral divisions in Naas Union?
Thirty-seven; and there are 33 elected guardians.

2397. How many of those guardians would you say were elected on political grounds?
That question would apply probably to them all.

2398. You think that both sides are elected upon political grounds; is that what you mean?
No, but if you apply it to one side you must apply it to the other. If you put to me how many are elected in the interests of landlords, I could answer that.

2399. How many are elected in the interests of the National League?
I am not quite sure that that would be a fair way of putting it. I do not think the National League was exactly the programme upon which guardians were elected; at the same time I do not want to repudiate the influences which the League have, and should have, over the election of guardians; but there are 33 elected guardians, and there are four of these 33 who throw their interest with the landlord party.

2400. That is to say, they vote against the National League; that is what you mean?
Yes.

2401. And

9th June 1885.]   Mr. FENELON.   [Continued.

2401. And that the landlords are also opposed to the National League?
I believe Protestants and Catholics go together; I never had the luck to find myself in the same lobby with an *ex-officio* guardian, whether Protestants or Catholics.

2402. Then, I take it, it is only where political questions come in that you have these differences?
I will mention one case in which I moved that some of the Church Surplus Fund, which was going a begging, should be set apart for educational purposes.

2403. Have you the power to do that?
We petitioned Parliament for it; it was opposed by a Roman Catholic *ex-officio* guardian most ardently.

2404. On what ground?
He did not state that; he voted against me.

2405. Did he oppose it on the ground that it was not germane to the business of the Poor Law Board?
He never mentioned why. I may tell you that our *ex officios* on those occasions are more or less reticent; they do not give very many reasons for their vote, but vote as they like, and they have a right to do so.

2406. Out of these 33 elective guardians, how many represent the National League programme, I will call it. I know it is the case in some instances, and I believe it is so in many instances, that the candidates have stated that they were there as representatives more or less of the National League principles?
I am not aware that that was ever stated publicly to our Board.

2407. No, but at the election, I mean?
I am not aware that it has been stated at the elections; but those parties being known to the ratepayers, and their political leanings being known, I am quite sure that if a man with National League principles stood for a division, and a man opposed him, the man with National League principles would be supported.

2408. On that ground?
Yes.

2409. Irrespective of whether he would be a good guardian?
I am sure that if a man did not promise well to be an eligible and good guardian, the fact of his being a National Leaguer would not get him returned.

2410. Lord *Monk-Bretton*.] They would not return a National Leaguer who was not likely to make a good guardian rather than an anti-National Leaguer who was likely to make a good guardian; will you go as far as that?
I would not exactly say that.

2411. *Chairman*.] We will come now to Clause 10, " Lists of voters to be prepared; " have you anything to say as to that?
I would say that those lists when prepared should be published in some central place. The Bill states at some convenient place; it is not mentioned where. I would suggest in the centre of the division, some public place, so that every ratepayer could see whether his name was properly returned or not.

2412. It leaves it to the Local Government Board?
Yes, and I think the sixth clause leaves a great deal in their hands.

2413. With regard to Clause 12, which is the next one, I think you wish to call our attention to providing that the register of voters shall be prepared; what do you wish to say about that?
There is very little to be said about it, beyond the trivial point of the remuneration to the clerk of the union for furnishing a copy of the register to the voter, so that he can see whether the names are properly filled in.

2414. Some of the Poor Law clerks rather object to the remuneration proposed in this Bill as too low, and they have suggested, some of them, that the

9th June 1885.] Mr. FENRLON. [Continued.

register should be printed, so that the ratepayer who requires a copy should be allowed to make a copy of it himself?

All the ratepayers?

2415. Any one who wishes for it?
Probably not one out of 20 ratepayers would call for it. For instance, in the case of the Representation of the People Act there have been dozens of parties that have waited upon me to have their forms filled in; and I presume in this case some central person that would be supposed to have a little more knowledge than the average, would be called upon to see whether their names were properly returned. The only objection I would raise to this clause is that they should have to pay a shilling at all; it should be gratis; but I will not press that objection.

2416. You do not think that a shilling is too little?
No, not for a hundred names.

2417. Now, turning to Part II., Clause 16, which is "As to the manner of trying election petitions," that provides that the election petitions shall be tried at quarter sessions without a jury after the expiration of 21 days?
Yes, I would strongly approve of that clause in the Bill, because it enables a party when he feels himself aggrieved to bring the matter before the county court judge; I think that that is the most suitable place to have the inquiry.

2418. It has been suggested by one witness that the county court judge should be the revising officer instead of the clerk of the union; what is your opinion on that?
Probably it would not be necessary to have that; as the clerk of the union would know that the matter would be subsequently inquired into, probably it would not be required that it should be handed over to the county court judge. I think, in that case, the clerk of the union could be trusted, when he would know perfectly well that there was a power in one of the clauses afterwards to make amendments in the matter.

2419. Turning to Part III., Clause 25, do you agree with Mr. Machan that the property of a minor or a lunatic should be disfranchised?
I have considered that question, and in one way I dissent from that view; I dissent from the view likewise that no person not being of age should vote; I hold that every person paying rates should have a vote as they have at present, except there are some stronger grounds than I can see against it; with regard to lunatics, I am very happy to say that they are very rare in the country, at least, where I am; but if minors could be trusted to understand those things (I speak now of ratepayers, and then, of course, it would apply likewise to owners of property), I would have no objection that minors, no matter whether men or women, should have that right to vote, and record their votes as at present; I do not think, however, it would materially affect either party.

2420. To vote, of course, through their next friend?
That would still revert to proxy voting.

2421. Not necessarily, because the next friend might be compelled to vote personally?
It would be a second edition of proxy voting still.

2422. You could not expect a baby in arms to vote?
No. As to any case like that, having already expressed myself with regard to property being fairly represented, I may say that if there could be a fair way seen through the matter, to allow property to have its fair number of votes, I would not object, provided it was hedged about, and guarded against anything in the shape of irregularity.

2423. Viscount *Powerscourt*.] How would a minor or a lunatic vote?
A minor might be 17 or 18 years of age, and he could vote; he might be 20.

2424. You must draw some limit; a baby of two months old is equally a minor with a person aged 20?
That is very true.

2425. How

9th June 1885.]	Mr. FENELON.	[Continued.

2425. How would you deal with that?
I have not considered that matter. I stated in the commencement that I was prepared to take the Bill as a whole, without offering any suggestions of any amendments upon it, because, not knowing very much about the procedure in those cases, I considered it was not a thing which I was called upon to do.

2426. Do you mean that you take the Bill as a whole without considering its details?
I have gone through the clauses and given my reasons, and any questions which his Lordship in the chair, or any nobleman asks me, I shall be prepared to answer. I stated that I would have no objection to have property fairly represented by having the votes recorded if some safe way could be found in which those votes would be given with the same intention, or in the same manner, in which the minor or lunatic would give them, if capable of voting.

2427. Lord *Shute*.] Surely you would have to change the whole of the law if you gave minors a vote?
No, not in the Poor Law; a little girl of 10 years can pay rates; any one in Ireland who pays rates can vote, no matter what he is; whether or not that has been allowed in other unions, if he or she pay rates their votes are allowed in our union; whether it be legal or not I am not going to say.

2428. At all events under this Bill it is provided that no minor is to vote, and if a minor is not to vote how is his property to be represented?
It is for those who carry all the brains of the country, and for those who meet here in the House of Commons and the House of Lords to suggest the plan, not for me.

2429. *Chairman*.] I think the next point you wish to say something about is fixing the qualification for Poor Law guardians at 12 *l.*?
I am strongly in favour of that; I have known a division where there was a very great difficulty in finding a man valued at 25 *l.* to become a candidate, and there were men valued at 20 *l.* and under who would have been much more eligible than a man at 25 *l.* or 30 *l.* It does not always follow that a man valued at 100 *l.* or 200 *l.* is the more eligible man. Sometimes men valued very low would be far better guardians than one valued high.

2430. Particularly in the urban districts?
Yes.

2431. But you are aware, I suppose, that the Local Government Board have the power, if they think fit, to reduce the qualification in any union?
They have the power, so I am informed, but we would never think of moving the Local Government Board to exercise that power because we have at this moment the greatest possible difficulty in getting the Local Government Board to transact the business that they have the power to do, and which they should transact regularly. Now, when I state that, I had better give the reason. The division which I formerly represented for some 9 or 10 years has been vacant now for three months, and it was only when I had a question put in the House of Commons through our representative, Mr. Leahy, that the Local Government Board consented to state that they would issue an order for the election. There was already a resolution of our Board forwarded to the Local Government Board and acknowledged by them, and it remained a dead letter for two months, and it was only when a question was put in the House to the Chief Secretary, that the order for the election was announced; but it will only come off in three months; and that Naas Division is meantime disfranchised for the want of a guardian, and when we find that that happens in a matter in which we ought to look upon the Local Government Board as being most anxious to see the proper number of guardians in every division, we would never think of asking them to alter the rules as to the qualification of guardians or dispensary committees.

2432. The qualification for dispensary committees, as I understand, is fixed by statute; the qualification for the Poor Law guardian is arbitrarily fixed by the Local Government Board, and we have been told that in poor unions they have reduced it to as low as 10 *l.*?
Thirty pounds, you are aware, is the qualification for a dispensary committee.

(0.1.)	E E	4233. That

2433. That is fixed by statute!
But 25 l. in the Naas Union, is the qualification for Poor Law guardians.

2434. And it would seem rather an anomaly that the qualification for the board should be 10 l., and yet that its deputed committee should require a qualification of 30 l.?
That is very true; and speaking about committees, I quite appreciate the observation which I think your Lordship made, that in this Bill there has been no mention made of dispensary committees at all. Probably it is not necessary to go into that, but it is somewhat strange that when the Poor Law Guardians Bill was taken up, dispensary committees should have been left out altogether. Now, in the dispensary district in which I live, all the members of the dispensary district are *ex-officio* members of it, *ex-officio* guardians, and elective guardians; some of the very largest ratepayers in those four divisions that comprise the dispensary district are shut out, and some *ex-officio* guardians of no property except what is nominal, have a vote, being *ex-officio* members of the board of guardians.

2435. But do you mean that they are not ratepayers?
They are small ratepayers.

2436. What is the rule in the appointment of dispensary committees?
The rule in all dispensary districts, the rule carried out at Naas Union, at all events, is, that all *ex-officio* guardians residing within the dispensary districts, and all elected guardians representing that district or the whole of the property in the district, will be on the dispensary committee. I am not in a position to say if that is more than the number allowed, in what way it will be pared down, whether it will be from the *ex-officio* guardians or from the elective guardians; but in my division there are 17 of our dispensary committee, 12 being magistrates and five elective guardians.

2437. I know that in many dispensary districts (and in my own it is the case), many of the members of the dispensary committees, and I think the majority, are not Poor Law guardians?
In some cases magistrates do not reside in the district in the number needed to compose the committees. The committee is generally composed of an odd number, and consists of all the guardians representing the divisions in that dispensary district, and all the magistrates who are *ex-officio* guardians in that district, and then the balance is elected on the first meeting of the new board from those who may be put forward by the Divisions.

2438. Lord *Saltersford*.] That is to say elected by the board of guardians?
Yes.

2439. *Chairman*.] "Selected," rather?
Yes, and probably, too, elected; because, probably it goes to a contest; one will be proposed by one gentleman, and another by another.

2440. Lord *Inchiquin*.] Is it not the case that at the first meeting of every board, the board select the members of every dispensary committee; it is a matter of selection, in fact?
Not at all. In some cases it is already selected by the fact of the certain number of magistrates in addition to the elective guardians, residing in the dispensary district.

2441. I have been chairman of a board of guardians for some years, and every year a list is put before me, and the members are actually selected. I can remember a case that only occurred the other day where it was a question about an *ex officio* being put on in preference to somebody said to be likely to be a more constant attendant?
I must stand by what I have stated. In the dispensary district of Kilcullen, there are 12 magistrates residing in the dispensary district, or rather one of them does not reside in the dispensary district; he only holds property in it; there are 12 magistrates and five elective guardians, and they compose the dispensary committee; there is no election whatever.

2442. Have

2442. Have you persons called wardens?
We have wardens in certain portions of our district where guardians or ex-officio guardians do not reside at places convenient for the purpose of issuing tickets.

2443. *Lord Saltersford.*] But they are not members of the committee?
Not at all.

2444. *Chairman.*] Now the last point which you wish to call attention to, I believe, is the proposal for reducing the number of *ex officios*?
Yes, I go for that too. Taking the Bill as a whole, I support it, and I support it in the detail of reducing the number of *ex officios* to one-half the number of elected guardians.

2445. On what ground do you advocate that alteration?
The ground upon which I advocate that, in preference to the present system, is simply this: in several unions, to my own knowledge, the *ex officio* element, together with the elected element, preponderate; so that a great many people have no voice whatever, and in consequence do not attend the Boards. I could name Boards where that is the case.

2446. Let us confine ourselves to Naas?
As far as Naas goes, probably there is as little cause of complaint in that as in any union. Still I have facts to show that the elected guardians are better custodians of the property of the ratepayers, and have managed the business of the union better than the *ex officios* have done.

2447. Will you give us an instance of that?
I will take this for example. The salaries of both master and matron were increased when the present master was appointed, and that too without any notice having been given by any guardian, and the Local Government Board approved of it because the appointment was a fresh one.

2448. Do you mean to say that those salaries were increased by the *ex officios*?
With an *ex officio* in the chair, and an *ex officio*, I believe, was the party who proposed it; and when I challenged the matter afterwards with the Local Government Board, they said it was perfectly legal to do so. I am quite sure I speak the feelings of the elective guardians when I say that they were completely dissatisfied over that.

2449. Did they vote against it?
I cannot say; there was a very small Board there. No notice was given; it was a complete surprise that the increased salary was given. I do not say that all the *ex officios* would have done it; there was a small Board, only 12 on that day, I believe, out of the 66.

2450. Were they bound to give notice?
The Local Government Board said not in a case where the appointment was a fresh one; but in a case where we have an officer already, no matter who he may be, we cannot either increase or decrease his salary one shilling without a fortnight's notice of motion. But in this case the master had resigned or gone away, and there was an advertisement in the paper to say, " Master and matron of Naas Union required at a salary " of so-and-so.

2451. Was the salary stated in the advertisement?
Yes, and the guardians outside were bound by that. I strongly opposed it, and the Local Government Board's reply was that it was legal.

2452. *Lord Monk-Bretton.*] The increased salary was advertised, was it?
Yes, without any notice to the Board that it would be done beyond the notice that they had from the absconding of the other master. The Board took upon itself to advertise for a master, and they increased the salary of the master by 10 *l.*, and of the matron by 5 *l.* As Vice Chairman of the Board, and carrying with me the feelings of a great many others, I always looked upon that as a very wrong thing.

(O.1.) E E 2 2453. Lord

9th June 1885.]   Mr. FENELON.   [Continued.

2453. Lord *Saltersford*.] Why could you not give notice for the reduction of the salary?
We must show very good cause for any such reduction, such as the want of any business capacity. The *ex officios* very lately out-voted the elective guardians in giving a retiring allowance to a medical officer, far in excess of what the committee of management recommended.

2454. *Chairman*.] That was Dr. Hayes, was it not?
Dr. Hayes.

2455. How many years had Dr. Hayes been medical officer?
Thirty-two.

2456. What was his age?
I could not say; he was a very old man, I believe; I think he must be over 80 years of age.

2457. And what was the superannuation allowance given to him?
The superannuation allowance given to him by the Board, a very small majority of the Board, was 60 *l*.

2458. Is that in excess of the superannuation allowances that were previously granted to your retiring officers?
I am not aware of any other dispensary officer being superannuated.

2459. Dr. Robinson; was not he superannuated?
Not in my time.

2460. It was not very long ago, I think?
I cannot call to mind that.

2461. You have had your chaplains superannuated, have you not?
In the case of the late chaplain, though there was a notice of motion given, and that by a Protestant, to give a retiring allowance, the Roman Catholics would not give it to him. There are grounds upon which the elective guardians opposed giving Dr. Hayes this sum of 60 *l*., which they thought more or less excessive. In the first place, Dr. Hayes, in addition to being medical officer (strictly speaking he could not be elected medical officer now; he was only an apothecary originally), was coroner for the northern portion of the county, and he carried on his coronership, his medical hall business, and his dispensary office business as a *ulo* employment; and we looked upon him as a man who had retired with a large fortune, and we thought that the ratepayers ought not to be called upon to supplement that, and the dispensary committee by nine votes to two recommended that he should be allowed 40 *l*., and we thought 60 *l*. was an extreme sum.

2462. He had had a quarrel with this dispensary committee, had he not?
No, I do not know that he had, because he brought forward several strong recommendations from the dispensary committee with regard to the manner in which he had done his duty.

2463. Was there not a feeling against him on the part of some of the elective guardians for having given a vote, as a magistrate, at the Presentment Sessions?
There was some remark about that, and one of his committee, I think the chairman, stated that, to his own knowledge, he attended as a magistrate at Naas at the very time that he should have been attending to his dispensary duties at Kill.

2464. It is also the fact, as I have stated, is it not, that he had given a vote as a magistrate at the Presentment Sessions, which was not popular with some of the elective guardians?
I think that had no influence whatever with the dispensary committee.

2465. Had it any influence with the board of guardians?
I could not say that it had.

2466. Could you say that it had not?
I could not. I looked upon him as a dispensary officer who was outstepping his

9th June 1885.]   Mr. FENELON.   [Continued.

his position in coming, as a magistrate, to record his vote against the rate-payers; and that, too, when he should be attending his dispensary duties.

2467. I want to have this clearly, because I am only speaking from hearsay myself; not being able to attend regularly, I did not attend on the occasion referred to myself; but I want to know, was the superannuation allowance granted to him as large as that granted on similar occasions to other officers of the union who had not had the same length of service?
I am not aware of any case, to my own knowledge, except the one you mentioned, Dr. Robinson, and that has escaped my memory.

2468. With regard to the chaplains?
No chaplain has had it, except an old man that has died.

2469. What did he get?
I cannot say.

2470. Can you give any other instance?
I will just cite some instances, showing that the elective guardians, as a rule, have been more economical, and saved the union in disbursing the money, more than the *ex officios*. The elective guardians successfully opposed the increase which was proposed by an *ex officio* for the out nursing of pauper children, and this saved the union the considerable sum of over 60 *l.* annually.

2471. Who advocated it?
The *ex-officios*.

2472. In a body; were the *ex officios* on one side, do you mean, and the elective guardians on the other?
It was proposed by an *ex-officio* guardian, and I proposed an amendment, and the proposal fell to the ground. I demolished his case, I believe. One *ex officio* proposed it, and another *ex officio* stated this, " I came forward here to second this, but from the statement made by So-and-so, and from something that has appeared, I shall not vote for it now."

2473. Viscount *Powerscourt.*] That is very much in favour of the *ex officios*, is it not?
Not when it was proposed by one of them. I had the whole of the elective guardians at my back to oppose it.

2474. Lord *Saltersford.*] Do I rightly understand you to say that the *ex officios* all voted one way, and the elective guardians the other?
There was no vote; it collapsed.

2475. But in Dr. Hayes' case, did all the elected guardians vote one way and all the *ex officios* the other?
All the *ex officios*, with two or three elective guardians who were in the interest of the *ex officios*, voted one way, and all those representing the people voted another way. Now, then, the next instance is this: the elective guardians succeeded in reducing the salary of the cattle inspector and veterinary surgeon from 100*l.* a year to 65*l.* a year. I was the means of doing that. I was opposed by all or a considerable number of the *ex officios*. My amendment was carried in opposition to an *ex officio's* proposal; and I think the *ex officios*, as I stated before, as a rule, generally vote together; it is very seldom that they dissent from each other.

2476. Viscount *Powerscourt.*] The others vote together too, do they not?
Certainly not always. I should be only too glad if we were as well organised. Then, further, the elective guardians reduced the salary of the clerk to the local authority from 4*l.* to 1*l.* per month; that was against the will of the *ex-officio* guardians. Then, too, the elected guardians totally abolished the clerk's salary to the Burial Board, in consequence of nearly all the graveyards being enclosed. I gave notice of motion for that, and carried it. Then the next instance is this: the elected guardians opposed an increase of 8*l.* per year to a relieving officer's salary, which the clerk of the union added without the consent or knowledge of the Board, and I having reported the matter to the Local Government Board, upon investigation the addition was cancelled and the clerk reprimanded. That

9th June 1885.] Mr. FENELON. [Continued.

was a case in which the salary was advertised; and the clerk of the union took upon himself to add 8 l. a year to the advertised salary, for the simple reason that this man was previously sanitary sub-officer, and he did not wish that he should lose any of the salary he held before; and, therefore, he added some of that to his salary as relieving officer to make the whole sum 35 l. It was reduced by 8 l. on my representation to the Local Government Board; I give them credit for that. It is most important to show you that the elective guardians on the Board take a proper interest in the management and disbursement of the funds. The elected guardians succeeded also in having a fifth relieving officer appointed at a saving of 18 l. per year less than the Local Government Board and ex officios granted to four officers; and that, too, in the face of the chairman's opposition. So that at present we have five relieving officers at 18 l. per year less than both the Local Government Board and the ex officios granted to four relieving officers. That is an extraordinary thing to find that we have at present five officers to whom we are paying 18 l. less per year than the Local Government Board and ex officios granted to four relieving officers.

2477. *Chairman.*] Your five, you mean, are paid less than the four by 18 l. a year?
Yes; how it arose was this: there was a sanitary sub-officer in the district who had very little to do, and I prevailed upon him to resign his appointment as sanitary sub-officer, and I had him appointed as relieving officer and sanitary sub-officer in addition. The man being a Protestant, the chairman of the Board counselled him not to attempt to do it, that we only wanted to perpetuate a job to shut him out. The result was that we re-appointed this man, or appointed him, in the first instance, to be relieving officer; and then he had one-fourth of the salary in addition for the sanitary sub-officership He had but 18 l., and he has now 30 l.; and the Local Government Board were giving 30 l. a year to four officers in excess of what they had, to discharge the duty; and there are now five doing it at 18 l. a year less. I am just mentioning this to show that the elective guardians can look after the business of the union. Some of us attend at serious inconvenience to ourselves for that purpose.

2478. Lord *Saltersford.*] You have mentioned several instances in which you reduced the salaries; how is it that you could do that in those cases, and not in the cases of the master and matron to whom you have alluded?
They were appointed at a salary advertised, and the Local Government Board would not allow that to be reduced. The clerk to the Burial Board was still drawing a salary for being clerk to a board that had no existence; I can explain every item of them. But speaking about the clerk's salary that has been reduced so much, I may say that he holds still something like 230 l. or 240 l. a year, notwithstanding all the reductions.

2479. *Chairman.*] Do you wish to say anything more on the question of reducing the number of ex officios?
No, beyond this, that I think that between having the one-third of the membership of the board and the numbers that they would be capable of returning as elective guardians by their influence, they would have at least a half of the guardians. For instance, in Naas they are capable of returning three or four; in Baltinglass they are capable of returning more than half the board; in Carlow they are likewise capable of doing it; in Edenderry they are capable of doing it; in Rathdown Union they are capable of doing it. Of seven unions there are only two in which there is anything like a fair representation of the people.

2480. You mean that the National League candidates are not returned?
The tenant farmer need not be a National Leaguer, and still he may be a ratepayer. For instance, I met men in my district who completely dissented from giving the large retiring allowance to Dr. Hayes; they are not National Leaguers, but belong to the Protestant Church.

2481. Viscount *Powerscourt.*] I did not quite understand what you said all these unions were capable of doing?

Of

9th *June* 1885.] Mr. FENELON. [*Continued.*

Of returning more than half, or at least a half, of the guardians in the interest of the *ex officios*.

2482. I am the chairman of the Rathdown Union, and I do not think that is the case there?
I would ask your Lordship if there has been any elected guardian chairman of the union?

2483. The vice-chairman is an elected guardian?
In Baltinglass, in Carlow, and Edenderry and South Dublin, they are all *ex officios*; and they were all *ex officios* at Naas till two or three years ago.

2484. *Chairman.*] There was no feeling against them till two or three years ago, on the ground that they were *ex officios*, was there?
None; but what caused the feeling at the commencement was this; that they would not allow one word to be said except about in-door or out-door relief; some six or eight years ago I gave notice to have certain questions discussed; fixity of tenure, fair rent, and so on, and the result was that the three chairmen walked out of the board; they would not have it discussed; but the chairman of that board afterwards wrote to me from England, quite approving of those principles in a year or two years afterwards.

2485. Then you think that one of the great advantages of getting rid of the *ex officios* as chairmen, will be that you will be able to bring in political questions, and to have them discussed at the Poor Law Board?
Not so much that, as that the people would not be sat down upon, whenever they wished to express themselves. Now there was a resolution moved at our board of guardians, expressing sympathy with the family of a deceased brother guardian, and the chairman would not put it; he drew his pen across it.

2486. He did put the resolution, did he not, but struck out a word which he thought brought in political matters; that is to say, a word to express that this deceased guardian held Nationalist views?
The words in the resolution were "a good Irishman and Nationalist."

2487. And he struck out "Nationalist" only?
He struck out "a good Irishman and Nationalist." In calling the attention of the committee to that, I put it in this way, that supposing I occupied the chair, and any of the guardians who differed from me politically wished to express their sympathy with the families of their deceased friends, if they put in their resolution that the deceased person was a strong Constitutionalist, I would no more think of erasing that, than of offering an offence to any nobleman before me.

2488. Lord *Saltersford.*] In these unions which you have referred to, in which more than half the guardians are in the *ex-officio* interest, you will not say, will you, but what there is a considerable number of ratepayers whose feelings are in accordance with those of the *ex-officio* guardians?
It may be in some cases. But, for instance, Mr. Meehan, who was here a moment ago. A guardian in Carlow Union complained to me that it was completely inexplicable to him how he was defeated; it was from the number of proxy votes registered out of the smallest possible holdings, holdings of a few pounds, and that was the means of turning him out of the place. He was almost unanimously voted for by the ratepayers. That is a case in which the landlord's interest predominates, and in which the ratepayer's interest is not represented at all.

The Witness is directed to withdraw.

(O.I.) E E 4

9th June 1885.

COLONEL H. D. CARDEN, having been called in; is Examined, as follows:

2489. *Chairman.*] I THINK you are a Magistrate of the Queen's County?
Yes.

2490. And an *ex-officio* guardian on the Mountmellick Board?
Yes.

2491. That, I believe, is one of the largest unions in Ireland?
Yes.

2492. Were you chairman of the Board?
I was chairman for 9 or 10 years.

2493. Up to when?
Up to this present year. There was one year during that 9 or 10 years that I was not chairman; I was turned out by reason of some of the *ex-officio* guardians not attending in time, and by an accident I was not elected.

2494. You were not elected at the last election?
No.

2495. Mr. Meehan, who has given evidence to-day, was elected in your place?
Mr. Meehan was elected in my place.

2496. How is your board constituted?
There are 44 elected guardians, and 37 *ex officio*.

2497. How many of those *ex officios* are resident?
There are, I may say, about 24 resident.

2498. How do the *ex officios*, as a rule, attend?
I may say very badly; there are, perhaps, five or six, or six or seven, that do attend.

2499. With regard to the Bill itself, do you approve of triennial elections, and vote by ballot?
I approve of both of them.

2500. What do you say to the proposed abolition of the proxy vote?
I am very strongly against the abolition of proxy voting. The owners of property who represent a very large portion of the property in the union would have little or no voice at all if the proxy votes were abolished.

2501. What effect has the proxy vote upon your union, as a rule?
Without the proxy vote, I may say that no Loyalist (I have heard the name used here, and therefore I will use it) would be returned at all in the union.

2502. You mean by that, no one who was not a Nationalist?
Nobody who was not a Nationalist would be returned at all.

2503. Nobody who was not a National Leaguer would be returned without the assistance of the proxy vote?
That is so.

2504. Take the electoral division of Mountmellick; can you give us any instances?
Mountmellick returns two guardians, and in the last election one, Mr. Baily, got occupation votes,—that is, votes of occupiers, 115; proxy votes, 120; making a total of 235. He was opposed by Mr. Foran, and he got 174 occupation votes and 44 proxy votes, making a total of 218; so that in that case the former guardian, who was not a Nationalist, remained in. In the other case, it was Mr. Shannon who was the former guardian; he got 111 occupation votes and 120 proxy votes, making 231; he was opposed by a person of the name

9th June 1885.]   Colonel CARDEN.   [Continued.

name of Carhury, who got 185 occupation votes and 231 proxy votes, which made the tie which was alluded to by Mr. Meehan.

2505. And Mr. Meehan has told us that the result of it was that, owing to the delay on the part of the Local Government Board, no guardian has been elected for Mountmellick?
There has been some correspondence going on between the Local Government Board and the Board of Guardians in Mountmellick on that subject. I saw a letter myself the other day from them inquiring into some questions which they wanted to get some information on before they granted the inquiry. That correspondence has been slow, undoubtedly, but still they are at work.

2506. They are doing something?
They are doing something.

2507. Have you any other electoral division which you would like to mention?
Borris; that is a division we also heard named to-day, and one in which I am very much interested myself. The former guardian was Mr. Onions. He had occupation votes 35, proxy votes 33, making a total of 68. He was opposed by a man of the name of Dunne, who had 53 occupations votes, and four proxy votes, making a total of 57. In that case the former guardian, who was not a Nationalist, remained in by a small majority. Then there is the Division of Maryborough in much the same way. Mr. Doran, who was a publican in the town, had occupation votes 243, proxy votes 79. Mr. Meehan had occupation votes 244, proxy votes 69, making a total of 313. He also is a publican. Mr. Jessop contested that division against those two, and he had occupation votes 115, and proxy votes 150, making a total of 265.

2508. Lord *Monk Bretton.*] What is Mr. Jessop's occupation?
He is a farmer, I believe.

2509. *Chairman.*] About what proportion do the rates paid by the owners and those who voted for the non-league candidates bear to the rates paid by those who voted for them?
Taking the division of Borris, and the valuation of property in that division, the sum is 1,363 *l.* which the owners pay on that, against 675 *l.* paid by the occupiers, tenants. Shall I give another division?

2510. I suppose it is all much the same?
It is all much the same; it bears much about that proportion.

2511. And yet, as you have shown us, they are only able, by the aid of the proxy votes, to return in two instances their candidate, and in the other they cannot return any candidate?
They cannot return him even with proxy voting.

2512. Passing to Section 10 of the Bill, with regard to the suggestion that the rates should be paid sometime before the election, what do you think of that suggestion?
The rates certainly should be paid sometime before the election; I cannot exactly say what time.

2513. Why do you say so?
I think it requires a little time, but I am not very clear about any particular time there.

2514. It was suggested by Mr. Robinson that they should be paid some two months before?
I think it would be advisable to give some time.

2515. With regard to Part II. on the election petitions, what do you say about that, and the suggestion with regard to the security for the costs of the petition?
I think, certainly, there ought to be security given. We might say that

(O.1.)   F F   whoever

9th June 1885.]	Colonel CARDEN.	[Continued.

whoever petitions should lodge 50 l. before anything is done; and if it is a frivolous petition he should lose it, and it should not come off the rates.

2516. Turning now to Part III., what do you say as to the provision that minors should be enabled to vote through their guardians or trustees?
I think minors and lunatics ought certainly to have powers of voting in that way.

2517. Can you tell us whether they vote now; Mr. Fenelon said that in his district it is the case that minors vote now?
I never heard that point raised; I cannot say.

2518. What do you say to the proposal to reduce the qualification for elected guardians to 12 l.?
I am strongly against it. As is well known, the Local Government Board can, if they wish, alter it; and I think in some unions it is as low as 6 l. I will just make one remark on what Mr. Meehan said, that there was a general complaint that the 20 l. was too high: I have been a guardian for certainly 30 years at Mountmellick, in constant attendance, and chairman for nine or ten years, and I have never yet heard a single complaint on the subject.

2519. I think I passed over, accidentally, a very important clause, the one which provides for the abolition of the proxy vote. I did not ask you your opinion upon that?
You put the proxy votes and the ballot together, I think, in your question just now.

2520. Going back for one moment to that subject, do you see any hardship to the body of ratepayers in the existence of the proxy vote?
I think none whatever.

2521. Can you suggest any other means by which non-resident owners of property should not be disfranchised?
No, I can suggest nothing.

2522. Can you tell us anything about one of Mr. Meehan's objections to it; that it is the cause of false claims frequently being made?
I have never heard of it myself. It may, of course, have occurred, but I never heard of it.

2523. You have never heard any complaint of that?
I never heard any complaint of it.

2524. In your judgment, does it seem to be easier to make a false claim to a right to a proxy vote than to an occupation vote?
I do not see that it could be.

2525. So far as you know these votes are not manufactured in your district?
I do not think so. Now, in regard to one case that Mr. Meehan also alluded to, about a legal gentleman; I know those legal gentlemen, and I am quite sure they would no more do it than you or I would do anything of the kind; such a thing would never enter their heads.

2526. Then it is not your experience that these things take place?
Certainly, speaking from my experience or my knowledge, I never heard of them.

2527. Lord *De Vesci*.] No case of the kind has ever been brought before a board at which you have been present?
Never. I never recollect such a case coming before the board during my time or after it.

2528. Lord *Shute*.] Do you think that the adoption of the suggestion made by the first witness about the owners of property voting in person, and then extending the number of days for the election, would have any effect in regard to property being represented?
I think

I think not; it would be an impossibility, no matter how long the time extended, almost with some owners of property to vote; they have property in different parts of Ireland, north and south. I know in my own county different owners having property in different counties, and it would be an impossibility, even if they had three or four days to do it in, for them to vote in all of them in person.

2529. It would not be possible, you think?
I do not think it would.

2530. Not in four or five days?
I do not think so, unless they were travelling from morning to night.

2531. Lord *Inchiquin*.] The occupier is always on the spot, and the proprietor is not?
Yes; there may be exceptions, as Mr. Fenelon has mentioned, of occupiers having farms in different counties, but that is rare.

2532. Lord *Monk-Bretton*.] You would have no objection to extending the privilege of proxy voting to occupiers?
No.

2533. *Chairman*.] It has been spoken of as a kind of privilege; do you think that we might fairly call the right to give a proxy vote a necessity. It has been represented as being odious, and in the nature of a privilege; I put it to you whether you think it is not also a necessity?
I think it is most decidedly a necessity.

2534. If non-resident owners are to retain their voting power, that is to say?
Most decidedly; they would have no power whatever otherwise.

2535. You see no other system that could be substituted for it consistently with the ballot?
No, I see nothing else. The valuation which the owners pay rates on in Mountmellick Union is 64,957 *l.* out of 102,865 *l.*?

2536. The total valuation of your union is 102,865 *l.*?
Yes; and the valuation on which owners pay out of that is 64,957 *l.* In that 64,957 *l.* I may say there is included what the railway and canal companies hold.

2537. They, of course, could not vote without the proxy?
No.

2538. Then we pass now to the proposed reduction of *ex-officios*; what do you say to that?
There is one note that I took of Mr. Meehan's evidence, relative to Clause No. 5, in Part I., if I may refer to that before we go away from the ballot. It was about the influence of parties. In the Division of Borris a case was mentioned by Mr. Meehan, where a certain landlord told his bog ranger, that is, his bailiff, that he would expel him from his employment if he did not vote; I may say that I am that person; at least I presume that Mr. Meehan meant me; now that is not the case. That man voted against me, at least against the candidate that I had proposed, and that I had nominated. He voted against me, and has been in my employment ever since, and is now in my employment. I only want to put the thing before your Lordships in the proper light; and on that occasion, and on the same occasion every year since, and in this year, two priests have gone round steadily to these people and have forced them to vote in opposition to this man who has been nominated by me for a number of years. I only mention that in contradiction of what has been already said.

2539. You think that there is a great deal of intimidation on the other side?
Most undoubtedly; if people were left to themselves, there would be very little doubt as to how elections would turn in many cases.

2540. What is the question upon which the elections turn; is it the fitness of the candidate for the position of Poor Law guardian or his political views?
I think entirely his political, and, I am sorry to say, religious views.

2541. What do you say with regard to the proposed reduction of *ex-officios*?
I am very strongly against the reduction. It is shown already that even with the supposed number of *ex-officios* they never can carry, I may say, anything at the board.

2542. When you say "carry anything," will you kindly explain what you mean by that?
Any measures that they may consider fit or proper. They can be at any time outvoted, and they always are outvoted, because they are always in a very small majority, even with the equal numbers of *ex-officios* and elected guardians.

2543. Are those questions to which you allude questions relating to the administration of the Poor Law or extraneous matters?
Both. We have but eight elected guardians in the union instead of 10, as Mr. Meehan supposed; I mean that in the Mountmellick Union there are only eight elected guardians on the side that are not Nationalists.

2544. Some witnesses have said "non-political."
I cannot go as far as that.

2545. At any rate Non-league people?
Yes; and with respect to the *ex-officios* granting higher pensions, that is quite an imagination. The *ex-officio* guardians are always anxious to grant what they consider a fair salary, and also a fair pension to a man who has served them a certain number of years; but as for granting anything extraordinary, they certainly do nothing of the sort.

2546. That is not your experience in your union?
Certainly it is not.

2547. If proxy votes were abolished, what would be the result in your union, broadly speaking?
If the proxy vote were abolished, the elected guardians would be, first of all, all Nationalists or Leaguers, or by whatever name you might like to call them; but if it were retained and the *ex-officios* reduced, the result would be that there would be 22 *ex officio* and seven elected Loyalists, if they may be so called.

2548. They have been called Loyalist candidates?
They have been called so, and that is the reason I made use of the name. That shows a total of 29 against 37 National Leaguers. If proxy votes were abolished all the elected guardians would be National Leaguers; but even supposing they were retained, and the *ex-officio* guardians reduced, the result would be, as I have stated, that they could only have 29 against 37 of the National League.

2549. In order to retain a preponderating vote for what has been called the Loyalist party, or I will say the party that pays five-eighths of the rates, it would be necessary that both the *ex-officios* and the proxy vote should be retained?
Exactly so.

2550. I believe you have some instances where elected guardians have been chosen on the ground simply of their political views?
I think that as a rule the guardians that are selected are generally chosen for that.

2551. I want to ask you this: is that the reason that is put forward in the addresses issued, if there are any addresses issued, or in the newspapers of the party; is that the reason given for electing the candidates?
In answer to that question I will read to your Lordships what I took out of one of the county papers, which will give some idea of what are considered to be the qualifications of the guardians. This is talking of the National party on the boards: "This work the National League has set itself to achieve, and it behoves every Irishman to aid it by every means in his power. When, therefore, the people realise the importance attached by the leaders of the popular movement

movement to Nationalist representations within the Poor Law boards, their duty is plain and simple. No matter how their personal sympathies go; no matter how eligible a candidate may be in other respects, they are bound to support alone those who subscribe to and advocate the broad and comprehensive programme of the National League; in fact, to put it plainly, a man should vote against his brother if he is not a National Leaguer. It will, therefore, be seen that the people, if they have the slightest regard for the principles of the League, cannot support any man whose name is not on the roll of membership, and least of all can they support any who appeal to their suffrages from within the sphere or influences of landlordism.

2552. What are you reading from?
A paper called the "Leinster Leader," of the 7th of March 1885.

2553. That is the local organ of the Land League?
Yes.

2554. Lord *Monk-Bretton*.] Is that a newspaper article?
Yes.

2555. It is an editorial article?
Yes, it is an editorial.

2556. *Chairman.*] But it is the organ of the League, is it not; is it supported by them?
Yes.

2557. I want to ask you now a question which Mr. Meehan has suggested about the bog-ranger just now referred to. Was he ever suspended from his employment in consequence of any dispute as to whether he had voted, or not voted?
Never, not for one hour; he has been in my employment for 20 years.

2558. Can you give any instances as to whether there is, or not, jobbery in regard to contracts in your union?
There is very great jobbery; and I will quote also from the papers about some of the contracts that are taken, to show that the lowest tender, no matter what the quality of the different goods may be, is very frequently not taken. In September 1882 there were two tenders for frieze; there was one tender from Mr. John M'Mahon, of Mountmellick, at 6 s. per yard, and there was another from Mr. James Moyles, Abbeyleix, at 5 s. 7 d. per yard. "Mr. Atkinson" (who was one of the guardians) "said that both samples were exactly the same, and manufactured by the same party. Mr. Corcoran proposed, and Mr. Meehan seconded, that the tender at 6 s. per yard be accepted. Mr. Byrne asked who the contractors were. The clerk replied, Mr. James Moyles and Mr. John M'Mahon A division was then taken, the result of which was that Mr. Atkinson and Mr. T. Cobbe were the only supporters of Mr. Moyles' tender. Mr. M'Mahon was accordingly declared contractor." Mr. M'Mahon is, I believe, a National League man.

2559. And the quality was the same in both cases, was it?
Those who understand frieze said that it was cut off the same piece. It was for the same kind of frieze, and there is a factory there for making the frieze; and it came off the same piece.

2560. Will you proceed?
Then, in September 1883, in knitting worsted there were two tenders. Mr. J. Pim at 1 s. 4 d. and Mr. M'Mahon, 1 s. 7 d. On a division the latter was accepted, Mr. M'Mahon again being the National Leaguer.

2561. What was the quality in that case; was there any allegation that one was a better article?
There was no remark made at all about it.

2562. Is it the fact that, as far as you know, these tenders have been given to the highest instead of the lowest bidder, on other grounds than that they were better articles?

(O.1.)   F F 3   Yes;

9th June 1885.] Colonel CARDEN. [Continued.

Yes; there was a tender for medicines last March. There were two contractors, Messrs. Leslie & Co., of Dublin, and Messrs. Hunt & Co.; and after some of the guardians had calculated, totted up the list to see which was the cheapest, there was not any very great difference. But Mr. Meehan "added that another thing that influenced him was that the people who owned Messrs. Hunt and Company's establishment were more in accord with the National spirit of the country, and Messrs. Leslie were opposed to it. That was why he stood there to propose that Messrs. Hunt's tender be accepted."

2563. There was not a word about its being the better article?
The articles, I believe, are both very good as far as that goes; there is no doubt about that, and I have numerous other cases of higher tenders being taken.

2564. You have got a great many more instances of that character?
I have numbers of them here.

2565. What do you say about political resolutions being brought forward?
That a great deal of the time is taken up at the board from political and all kinds of resolutions being put before the chair and being discussed, and in fact the business of the board very greatly interfered with and neglected. I have several of them here. One was passed the other day at the time the Prince of Wales was over. It was proposed by Mr. Gallagher: "That as Ireland has received nothing from English rule and its institutions but cold indifference and injustice, her people when they demanded their just rights handed over to the system of Castle tyranny and landlord felony, we, therefore, the members of this National Democratic board, have no sympathy with the Prince of Wales' visit to Ireland, and we call on all Nationalists to shun shows and ballrooms given in his honour. God save Ireland."

2566. Lord *Monk-Bretton*.] Was that proposed and carried?
It was proposed and carried, Mr. Meehan being in the chair.

2567. *Chairman*.] With regard to the appointment of dispensary committees, is there any political element there?
In the same way, in the case of dispensary committees, whenever an opportunity arises, at the first meeting of the board, those who are not Nationalists are struck off, and I could name four or five that were on one committee this year that were struck off in that way.

2568. Lord *Saltersford*.] The number of those that are appointed on dispensary committees are very few?
There may be some six, or seven, or more besides the *ex-officios*.

2569. *Chairman*.] Are *ex-officios* treated respectfully or the reverse when they attend your board?
I think that is one of the causes why *ex-officios* do not attend the boards, the disrespect that is shown to them, and very often offensive language is used, and it has been used to me, most offensive sometimes.

2570. Is there any system in that, do you think, or is it simply an accidental circumstance?
I think it is a practice that seems to have unfortunately sprung up of late, that they take that opportunity of saying unpleasant things. The board-room is a kind of place where people speak and say what they like, and they take that opportunity of saying what is very disagreeable.

2571. And you think that has something to do with lessening the attendance of *ex-officio* guardians?
Yes.

2572. Have there been any instances of excessive out-door relief in Mountmellick Union?
I can instance one, and that is in the division of Maryborough. The outdoor relief in the year 1880 was 282 *l.*; in 1881, 336 *l.*; in 1882, 349 *l.*; in 1883, 372 *l.*; and in 1884, 403 *l.* The expenditure had increased in those years

9th June 1885.]   Colonel CARDEN.   [*Continued.*

years from 1880 to 1884, from 283 *l.* to 400 *l.* odd in out-door relief. And the rate on that division in the year 1880, when two Loyalist guardians represented that division, was 2 *s.* in the pound, and it has gone on increasing from 2 *s.* to 2 *s.* 1 *d.* in 1881; 2 *s.* 4 *d.* in 1882; 2 *s.* 9 *d.* in 1883; 3 *s.* 2 *d.* in 1884; and 3 *s.* 5 *d.* in 1885.

2573. That is, from 1880 to 1885, it has gone up from 2 *s.* to 3 *s.* 5 *d.*?
Yes; and I can only account for it by the fact of two publicans being guardians for that division; that the out-door relief has been expended too liberally. It is very well known that a great deal of the money that is distributed in out-door relief goes into public houses.

2574. Lord *Monk-Bretton.*] Do you attribute that increase exclusively to the change in representation; had the circumstances of the year nothing to do with it?
No, I do not think the circumstances of the year bad. It did not change in other divisions; in fact the general out-door relief of the whole of the union has not increased in our union from the year 1880 to the present time.

2575. *Chairman.*] Is there anything else you would like to say about this Bill?
There is one thing, that the guardians should not have the power to alter the rate books. At present, under the Parliamentary Voters Act, if a claim is put before the guardians, and the person is qualified, that person can be put by them on the rate book; if he produces his receipts, and satisfies the Board, he can be put on the rate book. That is open to very great abuse; and to give you an instance of that, I may say that the other day, when I was in the chair, just before I left the chair, Mr. Meehan produced to the board a large number of claims for the nuns of the convent, in Maryborough, to be put on the rate book. It was naturally for the purpose of voting at the coming election of guardians. Under the Parliamentary Voters Act people could only vote when on the list, and of course it was only intended for the franchise; but probably, had I not been in the chair, because every other guardian of the National party who was present was acting in support of Mr. Meehan and the nuns (I think there were eight or ten), a large number of them would have been put on the rate book, quite illegally; and therefore I think that it should not be left to the board of guardians to have the power of doing things of that kind.

2576. Is there any other point you wish to mention?
I do not think so.

2577. Lord *Monk-Bretton.*] Do I understand that it is in the power of the board of guardians to put ratepayers on?
Yes, I will read the words in the Act; it is the 13th & 14th Vict. c. 69, s. 110, and I will just read you that part of it: "And be it enacted that it shall be lawful for any person who shall occupy any lands tenements or hereditaments rated under the Acts for the more effectual relief of the destitute poor in Ireland at a net annual value of twelve pounds or upwards in any electoral division in any county, or eight pounds or upwards in any city, town, or borough in Ireland, in which there shall be a rate for the relief of the destitute poor, and whose name shall have been omitted from such rate, to present to the guardians of the union a claim to be rated in respect of such premises, and such claim shall be in writing and signed with his name, and upon such occupier so claiming and actually paying or tendering the full amount of the rate or rates (if any) then due in respect of such premises, the guardians of the union shall insert the name of such occupier in such rate in respect of such premises as aforesaid." That is the provision in that part of the Act. So that it is open to very great abuse.

The Witness is directed to withdraw.

Ordered, That this Committee be adjourned to Friday next,
at Twelve o'clock.

INDEX.

TABLE OF PRINCIPAL HEADINGS.

	PAGE		PAGE
Acts of Parliament	235	Lunatics	253
Agents	235	Magistrates	254
Ballot	236	Minors	255
Beneficial Interest	237	Occupiers	257
Boards of Guardians	237	Officials	258
Chairman	239	Out-door Relief	258
Claims to Vote	239	Owners	259
Clerk of Union	239	Pensions	260
Contested Elections	240	Polling Officers	260
Cumulative Vote	240	Polling Places	260
Dispensary Committee	241	Property Guardians	261
Elections	242	Proxies	262
Election Petitions	242	Railways	264
Elective Guardians	243	Rates	264
Ex Officios	244	Register	264
Immediate Lessors	251	Returning Officer	265
Inspectors	251	Revision	266
Intimidation	251	Salaries	267
Jurors	251	Vacancies	270
Land League	252	Vice Guardians	270
List of Voters	252	Voters	270
Local Government Board	253	Voting Papers	270

INDEX.

A.

Abbeyleix Union. Qualification of elective guardians 30 *l.*, *Meehan* 2227.

Acts of Parliament:
    43 Eliz. c. 2. See *Poor Relief Act*, 1601.
    1 & 2 Vic. c. 56. See *Poor Relief (Ireland) Act*, 1838.
    6 & 7 Vic. c. 92. See *Poor Relief (Ireland) Act*, 1843.
    10 & 11 Vic. c. 31. See *Poor Relief (Ireland)* Act, 1847.
    11 & 12 Vic. c. 47. See *Evicted Destitute Poor (Ireland) Act*, 1848.
    12 & 13 Vic. c. 104. See *Poor Relief (Ireland) Act*, 1849.
    13 & 14 Vic. c. 69. See *Parliamentary Voters (Ireland) Act*, 1850.
    14 & 15 Vic. c. 68. See *Medical Charities (Ireland) Act*, 1851.
    25 & 26 Vic. c. 83. See *Poor Relief (Ireland) Act*, 1862.
    35 & 36 Vic. c. 33. See *Ballot Act*, 1872.
    43 Vic. c. 4. See *Relief of Distress (Ireland) Act*, 1880.
    44 Vic. c. 4. See *Protection of Person and Property (Ireland) Act*, 1881.
    48 Vic. c. 3. See *Representation of the People Act*, 1884.

Agents often magistrates, *Malloy* 1739——Can he *ex officio*, *Morris* 569,—if rated justices, *Walsh* 2099-2101——Are not necessarily ratepayers, *Molloy* 1740——Jealousy of them as *ex officios*, *McCann* 1850——Doubt whether they should be so, *Bagwell* 903—— Might be so only to represent owner who cannot attend, *Walsh* 2099——Should vote on behalf of owners for property guardians, *Smyth* 1336. *See also* PROXIES. INTIMIDATION.

Aggregation of Votes. See CUMULATIVE VOTE.

Aghadoe Electoral Division. Case of intimidation, *Bagwell* 941.

Appeal Court. Decision as to cumulative vote. See *Cumulative Vote*.

"*Application and Report Book*" tampered with, *Bourke* 347-53.

Askeaton referred to, *Hewson* 1408.

Assistant Overseers appointed from Land League, *Molloy* 1700-3.

Athy Union. *Ex-officio* element weak, *Ringwood* 1552-4; *Molloy* 1700——Political jobbery in appointments, *Ringwood* 1551; *Molloy* 1700-3.

Atkinson, Mr., referred to, *Carden* 2558.

Auditors. See OUT-DOOR RELIEF.

B.

BAGWELL, MR. RICHARD, Deputy Lieutenant of Tipperary, and *ex-officio* guardian of Clonmel and Clogheen (850-2).

    Analysis of his Evidence (850-947).

    Triennial elections an improvement, but yearly election of one-third of Board better still, 854, 932, 944-7.

    Ballot an improvement, 855;—to prevent existing intimidation, 938-43——Voting by registered letter recommended, 860.

    Proxies should not be abolished, unless property were represented by property guardians, 856-9;—as owners would be disfranchised, 860——Many proxies in same hands objectionable, 925-6——Might be valid only for one election, 927-37.

Report, 1885—continued.

BAGWELL, MR., RICHARD. (Analysis of his Evidence)—continued.
 Cumulative Vote: Maximum should be raised for owners, 860.
 Property guardians, elected by owners, suggested to replace ex officio, 858-64, 919 ;—the rest being elected exclusively by occupiers, 861.
 Ex officio: Number increased to one-half of Board when more rates were thrown on owners, 865-8——Reasons for this still hold good, 866——Reduction would leave property under-represented, 916-21 ;—and produce worse chairman, 897-8——Should be ratepayers, 877-9——Should not comprise all resident magistrates, 877-9——Questionable whether agents should be so, 903——Attend badly, 898 ;—partly from non-residence, 899-901, 922 ;—and partly from introduction of politics, 882-4 ;—which could be obacked by Local Government Board, 885-91 ;—but not by chairman, 886-7——Should be elected by brother magistrates, 901-2 ;—instead of being selected by rateability, 870, 875-6——Should have power to resign in favour of non-residents, 889-74, 924——Are better administrators than electives, and a check on jobbery, 880-1, 892-5.
 Owners, voting power small, 862 ;—are under-represented, 916-9.
 Elective Guardians: Reduction of qualification not desired by real public, 906——Would swamp substantial men, 904-5.
 Election Petitions: Trial before County Court Judge approved, 907 ;—but costs should fall on parties, 907-15 ;—and security for costs should be given, 915.

Baily, Mr., referred to, Carden 2504.

Ballaghaseau and Esker Electoral Division. Statistics of election, Tyrrell 970-4.

Ballina Union, poor, Bourke 276-7.

BALLOT:
 Approved, Robinson 33; Bourke 283-4; Morris 441-2; Spaight 649; Bagwell 855; Tyrrell 954; Gray 1147-9, 1156; Smyth 1177, 1197; Hewson 1375; Molloy 1605; Fox 1901; Walsh 2042; Meehan 2126-31, 2133, 2144; Fenelon 2345; Carden 2499—but not till lately, Smyth, 1197, 1215; McCann, 1793——No difficulty in it, McCann 1799.
 Approved for residents only, Ringwood 1522-4——Would disfranchise non-resident occupiers, ib. 1523-30,—and some women and infirm people, ib. 1530; Molloy 1614, 1620.
 Women would not shrink from voting, McCann 1800-1.
 Would prevent existing intimidation, Robinson 34; Bagwell 938-43, Tyrrell 954; Gray 1151-6; Fenelon 2343,—by landlords, Morris 621; Bagwell 940; Meehan 2126-30, 2135, 2318-24——On popular side, Smyth 1195-8, 1206-16——On both sides, McCann 1793-8; Meehan 2126. See also INTIMIDATION.
 Would ensure economical guardians, Bourke 384-6——Would make no difference, Robinson 104, 115, 200.
 Secrecy should be strictly observed, Robinson 53; Smyth 1194, 1199 ;—though owners need it least, Robinson 69; Bagwell 860——Present system as good, if secrecy observed, Molloy 1605-7 ;—which is sometimes the case, Gray 1134, 1148, 1151, 1153-6; Fenelon 2346, 2362.
 Proxies inconsistent with it, Meehan 2144.
 Votes guaranteed by scrutiny, Robinson 23, 94-5, 97-9; Molloy 1607.
 Procedure with regard to ballot papers, Robinson 98-9. See also VOTING PAPERS.
 Has long been contemplated, Robinson 35.
 Used at election of Town Commissioners, McCann 1799-1800.
 Would increase expense, Smyth 1174-80; Molloy 1614; McCann 1828; Meehan 2133. See also POLLING PLACES.
 Polling officers under, see POLLING OFFICERS.

Ballot Act, 1872. Provision for polling places under, Robinson 68——For sealing up counterfoils, ib. 95——Penal provisions of, should be incorporated in Bill, ib. 54-5; Morris 560.

Ballot Papers. See VOTING PAPERS.

Ballyburly Electoral Division. Statistics of election, Tyrrell 977-81.

Ballydurn Electoral Division. Proxies used at election, Walsh 2047.

Ballymahon Union. Valuation of owners and tenants, Fox 1953——Rates, ib. 1917-41, 1954-6——Out-door relief, ib. 1986-93, 2019-20——Attendance of ex officios, ib. 2021-2——Qualification of elective guardians, 20 l., ib. 1899——Seventeen Nationalists out of twenty, ib. 2027-8——Statistics of contests, ib. 191826, 1936-45, 1958-60.

Baltinglas

Baltinglass Union. Strong property vote, *Fenelon* 2479-83.

Banks can vote by proxy, *Morris* 455 ; *Spaight* 819——Seldom do so, *Morris* 454——Manager sometimes rated, *ib.* 456.

Bantry Union. Out-door relief seldom given, *Spaight* 761——Effort to oust *ex-officio* chairman, *ib.* 825.

Beneficial Interest gives additional vote, *Robinson* 4, 229-31 ; *Smyth* 1305 ; *Meehan* 2166-74——False claims of vote for, *ib.* 2145-52 ; *Fenelon* 2347.

Benefit Societies, few, *Spaight* 811——Might be a good thing if practicable, *ib.* 811-5.

Bessborough, Lord, referred to, *Walsh* 2075.

BOARDS OF GUARDIANS :

Composed equally of elective and *ex-officio* guardians, *Robinson* 7. *See also* EX OFFICIOS (1).

Good result anticipated, *ib.* 162——Should be entirely elective, *Meehan* 2262, 2264, 2331——Should be composed of elective property and occupancy guardians. See PROPERTY GUARDIANS.

Return of numbers of each Board, *Robinson* 176-7.

Anomaly from two classes being appointed at different dates, *Hewson* 1643 ; *Fox* 1906.

Good attendance of both classes salutary, *Robinson* 165——Returns of such attendance, *ib.* 176-8 ; *Fenelon* 2381 ;—which is equal. *Spaight* 830 ;—nearly so, *Walsh* 2076 ;—is good at election of officers, *Robinson* 179. *See also* EX OFFICIOS (5) ; ELECTIVE GUARDIANS (5).

Chief duty to keep down rates, *Smyth* 1249.

Should not have power to put persons on ratebook, *Carden* 2575-7.

Can be dissolved, *Bourke* 360 ; *Bagwell* 886, 889 ; *Molloy* 1702——Boards dissolved, *Spaight* 734 ; *Bagwell* 887 ; *Walsh* 2060, 2111-2——This expensive, *Smyth* 13246.

Meetings weekly, *Walsh* 2075——Order of procedure regulated by Local Government Board, *Morris* 580 ; *Walsh* 2089-90 ;—effectually, *ib.* 2092 ;—ineffectually, *Morris* 581——Tendency to introduce politics, *Molloy* 1767 ; *Carden* 2565-6 ;—which causes maladministration, *Spaight* 783-6 ; *Gray* 1117-22 ;—and should be suppressed, *Bourke* 432 ; *Meehan* 2291-——This possible, *Bagwell* 885, 888 ;—but difficult, *ib.* 889 ; —in practice, *ib.* 886-7 ; *Hewson* 1452-3——No disorder at meetings, *Molloy* 1782 ——Reporters present, *Ringwood* 1590-1.

See also EX OFFICIOS (5) (d).

Two classes agree in some unions, *Bourke* 326. *See also* EX OFFICIOS (5) (a).

Bond, Mr. James, referred to, *McCann* 1852.

Boolyglass Electoral Division. Proxies used at election, *Walsh* 2047.

Borris Electoral Division. Rates of owners and occupiers, *Carden* 2509——Election turned by proxies, *ib.* 2507——Intimidation by landlord, *Meehan* 2126-30——This contradicted, *Carden* 2528, 2557.

BOURKE, RICHARD, Poor Law Inspector since 1847, appointed under English Commission, transferred in 1860 from Mayo to Clare, Limerick, and Tipperary (269-280.)

Analysis of his Evidence (269-433.)

Triennial elections an improvement, 282.

Ballot desirable, 283-4——Would tend to election of economical guardians, 384-6. Proxies more largely used lately, 429, 430.

Proxies : Abolition of, would partly disfranchise owners, 285-6, 369, 371, 379-381 ;—but would not materially affect elections, 287-294, 369-378, 381, 411, 422-3, 428, 431 ;—or popularise the whole system, 422-3.

Proxies lately become unpopular for political reasons, 295-6 ;—especially where many held by one man, 398, 401, 421——Limiting the number one man may hold would diminish unpopularity, 398-404.

Elective Guardians : Fixed qualification not desirable, 303-6——Sometimes careless of economy, 391-7.

(130—IND.) G G 3 *Ex-officio*

Report, 1885—continued.

BOURKE, RICHARD. (*Analysis of his Evidence*)—continued.
Ex-officio guardians better administrators than elective, 329-331, 334, 364, 383, 406;—and less given to jobbery, 383, 424-7——Have influence when they attend, 409, 410;—but attend badly, 308, 312-4, 316, 318, 328, 336, 408;—partly through non-residence, 320-1;—but lately from political causes, 318-9, 327-6, 406-6, 432——Political discussions should be repressed, 432.

Ex-officio guardians, if selected by magistrates, even in smaller proportions, would attend better, 307-8, 312-7, 414-6;—but reduction in number would be unfair in principle, 311, 314, 412, 415-6;—property being inadequately represented, 287-294, 309-311, 344, 369, 376, 381, 387-396, 415——Maintenance of present numbers no hardship on elective guardians, 413;—nor considered so by public, 433.

Ex-officio guardians attend best at election of chairmen, 417——This disapproved, 417-420.

Chairman: Importance of good, 322——Magistrates less often selected than formerly, 324-5, 365;—but choice not entirely dependent on votes of *ex officios*, 323, 365-8.

Election petitions should be tried by county court, 297-8.——Costs should be borne by parties, 299;—who should give security, 300.

Out-door relief excessive lately to evicted tenants, 332-4,—even when not destitute, 333, 346——Case of Tulla Union quoted, 334-353, 359-364, 405-7.

Political feeling: Effect of, in appointments, 354-8.

Trustees of minors and lunatics should vote for them, 302.

Butler, Mr., of Waterville, referred to, *Spaight* 700, 726-30.

C.

Cahirciveen Union under *ex-officio* management, *Spaight* 681-2——Out-door relief, *ib.* 698-9, 701-3—applied for by guardian, *ib.* 726-30.

Canal Companies would be disfranchised by abolition of proxies, *Carden* 2536-7. *See also Railways.*

Carbury, Mr., referred to, *Carden* 2504.

CARDEN, Colonel, H. D., Magistrate of Queen's County, and *ex-officio* chairman of Mountmellick Union for last ten years, except one year, when Mr. Meehan was elected (2489 95.)

Analysis of his Evidence (2489-2577)

Ex officio attend very badly, 2496-8;—partly because they are insulted, 2569-71 ——Are already out-voted, and should not be reduced, 2541-4, 2547-9——Do not job in pensions and salaries, 2545-6.

Elective guardians should not have a lower qualification, 2518——Elected on political and religious grounds, 2540, 2550-6——Introduce politics at board, 2565-6—— Job in contracts, 2558-64——Out-door relief increased, and spent in drink, where guardians are publicans, 2572-4.

Elections should be triennial, 2499.

Ballot approved, 2499——Intimidation by popular party, 2539——Alleged intimidation by landlord denied, 2538, 2557.

Proxies should be maintained, 2500;—else owners would have no voice in elections, 2500-8, 2521, 2533 4, 2547-8,—even if elections spread over four or five days, 2528-30, 2535-7:—though owners pay two-thirds of rate, 2509-11, 2535-6——Proxies no hardship, 2520——Might be extended to occupiers, 2532——Do not cause false claims, 2522-7.

Minors and lunatics should vote through trustees, 2516-7.

Election Petitions: 50*l.* security for costs should be lodged, 2515.

Rates should be paid some time before polling day, 2512-4.

Guardians should not have power to alter ratebooks, 2575-7.

Carlow Union. Strong property vote, *Fenelon* 2479 83——Proxies abused, *Meehan* 2174; *Fenelon* 2488——More magistrates than *ex officios*, *Bagwell* 870, 900-1—— *Ex officios* attend well, *ib.* 898, 899-902.

Carnalway Electoral Division. Many owners, *Molloy* 1636—— Statistics of election, *ib.* 1634-5. *See also Naas Union.*

Carrick-on-Suir

Report, 1885—*continued*.

Carrick-on-Suir Union. For three counties, *Walsh* 2038*.—Number of guardians, *ib.* 2050——Seven Loyalist electives, *ib.* 2051, 2065——Proxies and occupation votes, *ib.* 2048——Meetings weekly, *ib.* 2075——Finances, *ib.* 2110—— Outdoor relief, *Ib.* 2110——Board dissolved, *ib.* 2060, 2111-2. *See also Ballyduran and Boolyglass Electoral Divisions.*

Cassin, Mr. Referred to, *Ringwood* 1549.

Castle Island. Circular from, *Spaight* 722-4.

Castletown Electoral Division. Value of property vote, *Hewson* 1456-64. *See also Rathkeale Union.*

CHAIRMAN:

Importance of good chairman, *Robinson* 180-1; *Bourke* 322; *Morris* 492, 571, 624-5; *Spaight* 738-45, 749, 783-6, 827; *Bagwell* 897; *Smyth* 1253, 1288, 1318; *Hewson* 1448; *Meehan* 2270-1,—who has great personal influence, *Morris* 624-5,—but no casting vote, *Tyrrell* 1047-8.

Can repress politics. *Ringwood* 1588-9; *Fenelon* 2485-7,—and irrelevant discussion, *ib.* 2484-5; *Morris* 496-7—Has difficulty in doing so, *Bagwell* 886-7; *Smyth* 1319-26; *Hewson* 1446-53; *Walsh* 2059-62——Can only refuse to put the question, *Hewson* 1447-51; *Walsh* 2059-61, 2087——Can leave the chair, *Smyth* 1322; *Fenelon* 2484 ——Should be backed up by clerk, *Hewson* 1449——Shrinks from dissolving Board, *Bagwell* 887; *Smyth* 1324-6——Nationalist, does not repress politics, *Carden* 2565-6. *See also* EX OFFICIOS (5) (d).

Bad chairman would discourage attendance of *ex officios*, *Smyth* 1255.

Good chairman less probable if *ex-officios* reduced. See EX OFFICIOS (2).

Ex-officio chairmen, *Morris* 624; *Spaight* 695, 700, 718-20, 823-4; *Gray* 1123; *McCann* 1852; *Fenelon* 2482-3; *Carden* 2495——Salutary influence of such, *Spaight* 672-5, 682——Ex officio, not necessarily the best, *Robinson* 261-2; *Meehan* 2298-2300 ——Disliked, as being intolerant of Nationalist feeling, *Meehan* 2279; *Fenelon* 2485-7.

Formerly almost always *ex officios*, *Robinson* 259; *Bourke* 365; *Morris* 496; *McCann* 1856; *Fenelon* 2483——These now opposed, *Robinson* 259; *Bourke* 324, 365; *Spaight* 823-6, 829; *Fenelon* 2483-4,—and rightly so, *Meehan* 2294,—for political reasons, *Robinson* 260; *Bourke* 365; *Spaight* 823-5; *Fenelon* 2485-7——This denied, *Meehan* 2293, 2296,—and condemned, *ib.* 2270, 2292, 2296——Opposed from preference for electives, *Bourke* 325——Opposed as repressive of irrelevant discussions, *Morris* 496-7; *Fenelon* 2484-7.

Elective guardians, chairmen, *Spaight* 683, 714——Loyalist, *Walsh* 2059—— Nationalist, *Tyrrell* 1025-7; *Smyth* 1171-2; *Meehan* 2115-20, 2159-63, 2293; *Carden* 2493-5 ——Such elected through bad attendance of *ex officios*, *Tyrrell* 1031-2, 1039-40.

Good attendance at election of, *Robinson* 179. *See also* EX OFFICIOS (5).

Election of good chairman depends on goodness of Board, *Bagwell* 897;—on *ex officios*, *ib.* 898; *Smyth* 1292-3;—not on *ex officios*, *Bourke* 323, 365-8; *Meehan* 2271.

Church Surplus Fund. Petition to apply it to education, *Fenelon* 2402-5.

Claims to Vote. See also Register. *Revision of Register.*

Due one month before polling day, *Robinson* 56; *Fenelon* 2349——Should be two months, *Robinson* 56-7; *Morris* 458-9; *Spaight* 655; *Tyrrell* 990-1,—or register should be signed a good while before polling day, *Morris* 5612.

Objection to, now difficult, *Gray* 1160; *Meehan* 2153-4; *Fenelon* 2346, 2349, 2362.

Hearing of, should be from ten to five o'clock, *Molloy* 1647.

Fraudulent claims. See PROXIES.

Clare. Referred to, *Bourke* 276, 280.

Class Feeling between owners and occupiers, *Smyth* 1343-9. *See also* CHAIRMAN EX OFFICIOS (5) (e).

Cleary, Thomas. Referred to, *Ringwood* 1551.

Clerk of Union. Good attendance at election of, *Robinson* 179——Examined by inspector, *Spaight* 647——Chief returning officer. *Smyth* 1177, 1364; *Meehan* 2133—— Must ascertain qualification of candidate, *Molloy* 1685——Should support chairman, *Hewson* 1449——Selects non-resident *ex officios*, *Smyth* 1361-4; *Hewson* 1437; *Walsh* 2061——Should prepare Voting List, *Meehan* 2133. *See also* LIST OF VOTERS. *Officials. Returning Officer.*

(130—IRD.)   G G 4   *Clogheen*

Report, 1885—continued.

Cloghern Union. See Evidence of *Bagwell.*

Clonbulloque Electoral Division. Statistics of election, *Tyrrell* 975-6. *See* also *Edenderry Union.*

Clonmel Union referred to, *Walsh* 2081——Attendance of *ex officios, Bagwell* 896. *See* also Evidence of *Bagwell, passim.*

Cobbe, Mr. T., referred to, *Carden* 2558.

Codd, Mr., referred to, *Ringwood* 1549.

Committee of 1878. Evidence of intimidation, *Robinson* 34-6.

Constituencies of Poor Law Elections wider than Parliamentary, *Fox* 1972-5.

CONTESTED ELECTIONS. Number of, *Robinson* 121, 130; *Molloy* 1648-9; *Meehan* 2123——Especially numerous of late, *Robinson* 120; *Morris* 464; *Molloy* 1649,—but not universal over one union, *ib.* 1753——Fewer formerly, *Morris* 464, 509; *Molloy* 1649——· Keen, *Robinson* 74; *Gray* 1079——Close, *Tyrrell* 969,—where proxies used, *Molloy* 1633. *See* also PROXIES.

Grounds recently political, *Tyrrell* 982; *Hewson* 1457-71; *Ringwood* 1541-4; *Fenelon* 2397-8, 2406-10; *Carden* 2540, 2550-6,—and religious, *ib.* 2540; *Robinson* 121——Not entirely political, *Meehan* 2248-51; *Fenelon* 2391, 2399,—or religious, *ib.* 2389-95——Grounded upon wish for better attendance, *Fenelon* 2389-95.

Cost of, *McCann* 1827——Thrown on rates, *ib.* 1827, 1829; *Meehan* 2124——Partly of division, *Robinson* 146——This probably best, *Hewson* 1385; *McCann* 1830——Should be paid by defeated candidate, *ib.* 1830; *Smyth* 1174, 1176——Now no expense on rates, *ib.* 1175. *See* also ELECTIONS. POLLING PLACES.

Encouraged by returning officer being the revising officer, *McCann* 1822-6, 1830, 1890——Would be discouraged by county court judge revising lists, *ib.* 1824-6, 1828,—and by printing all the lists, *ib.* 1833-4. *See* also *Revision.*

Contracts. Increasing economy in, *Smyth* 1313. *See* also ELECTIVE GUARDIANS (4). EX OFFICIO (5) (6).

Corboy Electoral Division. Owners can out-vote occupiers, *McCann* 1868-9, 1871. *See* also *Longford Union.*

Corcoran, Mr., referred to, *Carden* 2558.

Corporations. Vote through officer not a proxy vote, *Morris* 549-50—— Contrary evidence, *Spaight* 819. *See* also PROXIES.

Counting of votes at workhouse, *Robinson* 66, 99.

County Cess paid by tenant, *Fox* 2025-6.

County Court Judge. Determination of election petitions by; see ELECTION PETITIONS.——Should revise lists, *McCann* 1824-6, 1828. *See* also REVISION.

Crofton, Lord, an elective guardian, *Smyth* 1261-2.

Croom Union. Dishonest collectors, *Hewson* 1440.

CUMULATIVE VOTE. Used for Galway Town Commissioners, *Robinson* 34,—only, *Morris* 444-5, 548——Not in municipal elections, *ib.* 501-3.

Should be retained for guardians, *Bagwell* 860; *Meehan* 2328-32——Scale of, *Robinson* 4, 229-31——Additional vote for beneficial interest, see *Beneficial Interest.*

Maximum for each qualification, six votes for 200 *l.* and upwards, *Robinson* 4, 169-70. 229-31; *Bourke* 376; *Bagwell* 860; *Smyth* 1230; *Hewson* 1391, 1494; *Walsh* 2107-8 ——Curtails voting power, *Bourke* 389-90 — Should be raised, *Tyrrell* 1049; *Walsh* 2107,- for owners, *Bagwell* 860,—to twenty or twenty-five votes, *Smyth* 1230—— Should be raised for both owners and occupiers, *Hewson* 1387-9, 1488,—over 200*l.,* one vote being given for each 100*l., ib.* 1489-91,—for each 50*l., Walsh* 2107——This would be limited by extent of electoral division, *Hewson* 1490-1,—and would seldom amount to thirty votes, *ib.* 1493; *Molloy* 1745-6.

Maximum for all qualifications, thirty votes, *Robinson* 4-6, 28, 228-9, 232; *Spaight* 750; *Tyrrell* 1051, 1055-6; *Hewson* 1492; *Molloy* 1743; *Fox* 2030-1,—though not yet put in practice, *Robinson* 228-9——Was eighteen until 1884, *ib.* 6, 223-5, 228, 230-1; *Morris* 499; *Tyrrell* 1052; *McCann* 1874,—but then declared to be thirty by legal decision, *Robinson* 6, 233, 225-9; *Morris* 498, 547; *Tyrrell* 1056-7; *Molloy* 1743, 1745, 1764-5——Maximum of thirty seldom reached, *Molloy* 1745-6—— Eighteen not exceeded, *Hewson* 1494-5——Maximum of thirty-six theoretically possible, *McCann* 1869-70, 1872-3, 1877——Contrary opinion, *Fox* 2031.

Maximum

Report, 1885—*continued.*

CUMULATIVE VOTE—continued.

Maximum for all qualifications limited to eighteen by Bill, *Robinson* 28, 229 —This approved, *ib.* 228; *Tyrrell* 1053-4; *Molloy* 1743; *McCann* 1874,—if proxies and *ex officios* retained, *Morris* 500——Apportionment of reduction between different qualifications should be made by owner of votes, *Robinson* 229, 234-5,—failing which, should be pro rata, *ib.* 229, 233-6——Formerly occupation and immediate lessor votes aggregated, *ib.* 230-1; *Tyrrell* 1055-7; *Walsh* 2108,— and carried twelve votes maximum, *Walsh* 2108——This might be reverted to, *Robinson* 233; *Tyrrell* 1054-7; *Molloy* 1743-4; *Walsh* 2108,—but not so good, *Robinson* 234-5——Difficulty should be settled by Committee, *ib.* 232-3——Draft clause proposed, *ib.* 235.

Should be unlimited, if proxies and *ex officios* abolished, *Meehan* 2335-7—--Otherwise maximum of thirty should be retained, *ib.* 2337.

Amount of maximum immaterial if plan of property guardians adopted, *McCann* 1875-7. *See also* PROPERTY GUARDIANS.

Number of votes on each voting paper. See VOTING PAPERS.

D.

Dames, Capt. Longworth, D.L., referred to, *Tyrrell* 1024-5.

Dempsey, Daniel, referred to, *Ringwood* 1549.

Dingle Union. A poor district, *Speight* 694——Well managed, *ib.* 695, 836;—by *ex-officios, ib.* 681-2——Attendance, *ib.* 830, 835-8——Out-door relief, *ib.* 695-7, 703.

DISPENSARY COMMITTEE. Consists of guardians in district, *ex-officio* and elective, *Hewson* 1436; *Fenelon* 2434-7, 2440-1;—who are not selected, *ib.* 2440-1;—and non-guardian members elected by Board, *Hewson* 1435; *Meehan* 2235-7; *Fenelon* 2437-9; *Carden* 2568——When guardians deficient, *Fenelon* 2437, 2441.

Numbers of, *Fenelon* 2436, 2441; *Carden* 2568.

Composition objectionable, *Fenelon* 2434——Non-guardian members selected on political grounds, *Carden* 2567 :—and to secure election of particular doctor, *Hewson* 1435-6——Such members should be abolished, *ib.* 1441-2;—or only allowed to issue tickets, *ib.* 1443-4;—which, where there are no guardians, are issued by wardens, *Fenelon* 2442-3.

Struck on 25th March, *Hewson* 1434-6——Inconvenience from *ex-officios* being appointed later, *ib.* 1436.

Qualification retained at 30 *l., Gray* 1092-3, 1100-1; *Meehan* 2233-4; *Fenelon* 2432;—by Act, *Molloy* 1674-7——Anomaly if qualification of guardians lowered, *Gray* 1094; *Molloy* 1674-7; *Fenelon* 2434——30 *l.* ratepayers not difficult to find, *Gray* 1095——Qualification should be lowered, *Meehan* 2234, 2238. *See also* ELECTIVE GUARDIANS.

Dispensary Districts as polling districts. See POLLING PLACES.

Doran, Mr., referred to, *Carden* 2507.

Drogheda, Lord, referred to, *Ringwood* 1553.

Drumdaff referred to, *Smyth* 1260-1.

Dublin Unions. Revision of Lists, *Robinson* 64——Proxies much used, *ib.* 110——Elective guardians' qualification 30 *l., Gray* 1097——Magistrates many, *Smyth* 1359-60.

Dublin Union, North. Number of voters, *Robinson* 23, 73——Contests keen, *ib.* 74.

Dublin Union, South. Number of voters, *Robinson* 73, 102——*Ex-officio* chairman, *Fenelon* 2483.

Dungarvan Union. Embarrassed finances, *Morris* 636-8.

Dunne, Mr., referred to, *Carden* 2507.

E.

Edenderry Union:

Rates of owners and Loyalists, *Tyrrell* 1011-5——Strong property vote, *Fenelon* 2479-83——Strong Nationalist feeling, *Tyrrell* 983-7, 1028——Number of guardians, *ib.* 1016-9——Attendance, *ib.* 988-9, 1021-3, 1029-30, 1062——Qualification of electives, *ib.* 1007——Chairmen, *ib.* 1024-7——Magistrates enough for Board, *ib.* 1059 Finances, *ib.* 1033-9——Jobbery in contracts, *ib.* 1043-4. *See also Ballaghassan, Ballyburly,* and *Clonbullogue Electoral Divisions,* and Evidence of *Tyrrell,* passim.

(130—IND.) H H ELECTIONS:

Report, 1886—*continued.*

ELECTIONS:

Annual, *Robinson* 22, 124, 126;—on 25 March, *Hewson* 1436; *Fox* 1904; *Walsh* 2112——Should he in August, to tally with striking of rate, *Fox* 1902-3, 1907-8. See also *RATE*——No advantage in this, *Walsh* 2110 ——Are all on one day, *ib.* 2056-7; —on two days, *Meehan* 2179, *Fenelon* 2365——More time might be allowed for owners, if proxies abolished, *Meehan* 2189; *Fenelon* 2384——This would not meet objection, *Carden* 2528-31——Different polling days suggested, *Fenelon* 2364-5;—but would not meet difficulty, *Robinson* 43, 71-2;—and would be impracticable, *ib.* 43, 71; *Bourke* 286; *Morris* 448; *Spaight* 791;—and inconvenient, *Robinson* 71.

Interval of a year cannot be extended by Local Government Board, *Robinson* 123-4.

Should be triennial, *Robinson* 21; *Bourke* 282; *Morris* 440; *Spaight* 648; *Bagwell* 814, 932; *Tyrrell* 952-3; *Gray* 1157-9; *Smyth* 1174, 1237; *Ringwood* 1521; *Molloy* 1603-4; *McCann* 1788-9, 1792; *Walsh* 2041; *Meehan* 2122-5, 2209-10; *Fenelon* 2343-4; *Carden* 2499,—which would save cost and trouble, *Meehan* 2123-5, 2133;—diminish ferment, *Gray* 1157-9; *Meehan* 2124;—produce efficient guardians, *ib.* 2124;—and give time to make out lists, *ib.* 2125——But expense should not be increased, *Smyth* 1174.

Should not be triennial at present, *Fox* 1894-1900, 2034.

Annual renewal of one-third of board even better, *Bagwell* 854, 932, 944-7;—conducing to impartiality, *ib.* 854;—retiring members being re-eligible, *ib.* 947—— This plan has some advantages, but is costly, *Meehan* 2209 ——Is objectionable, *Gray* 1159 ——Good in theory, but of no great use in practice, *McCann* 1790-2;—retiring guardians being often re-elected, *Robinson* 125; *McCann* 1790-2.

Cost charged partly on rates of union, *Robinson* 146. *See also* CONTESTED ELECTIONS.

Not necessarily void by mistakes on register, *Robinson* 148——Fresh election, after avoidance, should be compulsory, as in Bill, *ib.* 154. *See also Vacancies.*

ELECTION PETITIONS:

Number of, *Robinson* 130; *Morris* 461——Few formerly, *ib* 461 —— Frivolous, *Robinson* 130; *Morris* 461-2, 464; *Spaight* 657; *Gray* 1082——Grounds of, *Robinson* 131, 133-4;—generally alleged mistake in register, *ib.* 131, 135, 145; *McCann* 1830, 1835——Grounds given in Bill quite right, *Robinson* 145.

Should be presented only by candidate or nominators, *Tyrrell* 996——Now dealt with by Local Government Board, *Robinson* 129; *Morris* 462; *Molloy* 1611;—usually in the office, *Bourke* 301;— unjustly, as Leaguers think, *Meehan* 2158-63, 2180.

Should be transferred to county court judge, *Robinson* 132, 145; *Bourke* 297-8; *Morris* 461-2; *Spaight* 656; *Bagwell* 907; *Tyrrell* 996; *Smyth* 1231-3; *Hewson* 1395; *Fenelon* 2389, 2417,—of county where workhouse is, *Gray* 1083;—as being more competent, *Smyth* 1231-3;—as counsel would be allowed, *Fenelon* 2389.

Liability for costs would discourage frivolous petitions, *Robinson* 132, 135; *Bourke* 300; *Morris* 462; *Spaight* 660; *Bagwell* 908, 912; *Smyth* 1236; *McCann* 1837; *Meehan* 2215.

Costs should be not on rates, but on parties, *Bourke* 299; *Spaight* 658-9; *Bagwell* 907-11, 913, 915, *Tyrrell* 997-9; *Smyth* 1233-5; *Molloy* 1664, 1667; *McCann* 1839-40; *Meehan* 2210-7; *Carden* 2515;—to discourage frivolous appeals, *Bagwell* 908, 912; *Smyth* 1236——Should be at discretion of judge, *Morris* 464, 466; *McCann* 1841-2 ——Should not be on Consolidated Fund, *Bagwell* 910——Under Bill, costs of returning officers, unless seriously blameable, thrown on rates, *Robinson* 137; *Molloy* 1662, 1665——This approved, *Bagwell* 914-5; *Tyrrell* 1000; *Molloy* 1662, 1666; *McCann* 1842——Costs should be thrown on division concerned, *Robinson* 139; *Gray* 1067-- Returning officers should pay costs if seriously blameable, *Spaight* 658-9; *Tyrrell* 999; *McCann* 1841;—and are willing to do so, *Spaight* 803——But in that case they should be otherwise dealt with, *Robinson* 139; *Morris* 465—— Costs trifling, *McCann* 1838 ——No great objection to their being on rates, *Morris* 466.

Security for costs desirable, *Robinson* 136, 138, 140-3, *Bourke* 300; *Morris* 463-4, 467; *Spaight* 600; *Bagwell* 915; *Tyrrell* 990; *Gray* 1082; *Hewson* 1390-7; *Molloy* 1663; *McCann* 1836; *Fox* 1963; *Meehan* 2214-5; *Carden* 2515.

Recognizance to prosecute desirable, *Gray* 1082, 1084-5.

Would be discouraged if lists revised by county court judge, *McCann* 1835. *See also Revision.*

Success of, does not necessarily make election void, *Robinson* 148. *See also* ELECTIONS.

ELECTIVE

ELECTIVE GUARDIANS. 243

Report, 1885—*continued.*

ELECTIVE GUARDIANS. *See also* BOARDS OF GUARDIANS, EX-OFFICIOS.
(1.) *Number and Class.*
(2.) *Qualification.*
(3.) *Efficiency.*
(4.) *Jobbery.*
(5.) *Attendance.*

(1.) *Number and Class :*
Total number 3894, *Robinson* 8—— Reduction of number not advocated, *Morris* 642.
Class of, low, *Smyth* 1291, 1319-20 ;—at present, *Fox* 1895-8, 1900——Will improve, *ib.* 1900——By ballot, *Bourke* 384-6——Not affected by ballot, *Robinson* 104, 115——Would be worse if *ex-officios* reduced, *Walsh* 2071 ;—if plan of property guardians adopted, *ib.* 2098.
Some are owners, *Morris* 623, 626-7——Very few are so, *Spaight* 847-9——Not owners, *Molloy* 1750-1——Owners unlikely to be elected now, *Spaight* 849——Some are *ex-officios*, *Morris* 437, 544-6, 622-3.
Some represent owners, *Gray* 1131-3 ; *Meehan* 2195-6, 2246 ; *Fenelon* 2379-81, 2390-2, 2399-400, 2445, 2475, 2479. *See also* OWNERS.
Do not represent owners, *Gray* 1131-3 ; *Molloy* 1695-6 ; *Meehan* 2195-6.
Now generally Leaguers, *Hewson* 1506-11——Cases of this, *Tyrrell* 1028-30 ; *Walsh* 2059-64, 2082-5 ; *Meehan* 2306——Proportion of Loyalists to Leaguers, *Smyth* 1221-2 ; *Molloy* 1644-5 ; *Fox* 2027-8 ; *Walsh* 2050-1, 2065 ; *Fenelon* 2399-400 ; *Carden* 2543-5.
Publicans sometimes elected, *Spaight* 667——Should be disqualified, *ib.* 668-7, 787-90.

(2.) *Qualification :*
Qualification can be fixed by Local Government Board, at or under 30 *l*, *Robinson* 159, 161 ; *Bourke* 306 ; *Morris* 476-7 ; *Spaight* 664 ; *Bagwell* 904-5 ; *Gray* 1095, 1099 ; *Molloy* 1671-4 ; *Fenelon* 2431 ; *Carden* 2518——Fixed at 30 *L*, *Bagwell* 904 ; *Gray* 1097 ; *Meehan* 2227. —at 20 *l.* or 25 *L*, *Bagwell* 904 ; *Tyrrell* 1007 ; *Gray* 1088, 1097 ; *Smyth* 1246 ; *Molloy* 1672, 1685 ; *Fox* 1899 ; *Meehan* 2227 ;—at 10 *L*, *Robinson* 161 ; *Bagwell* 904 ; *Gray* 1097-8 ; *Molloy* 1671 ;—as low as 6 *l.*, *Robinson* 161 ; *Bourke* 306 ; *Morris* 476 ; *Carden* 2518.
Limited by Bill to 12 *l.*, *Bourke* 303——Meaning of Bill should be made clear, *Robinson* 185-8——Qualification should be fixed by statute, *Meehan* 2232 ; *Fenelon* 2431——Contrary opinion, *Robinson* 160, 189 ; *Bourke* 303, 304 ; *Morris* 474, 478 ; *Bagwell* 904——Present arrangement satisfactory, *Robinson* 160 ; *Bourke* 304 ; *Morris* 474, 478 ; *Spaight* 664-5 ; *Bagwell* 904 ;—not complained of, *Walsh* 2066.
Reduction of qualification deprecated, *Tyrrell* 1006 : *Gray* 1088-91, 1150 ; *Smyth* 1246, 1247-9 ; *Molloy* 1671, 1693 ; *Fox* 1976 ; *Walsh* 2058, 2066 ; *Carden* 2518 ;—which would bring in less economical guardians, *Morris* 474 ; *Smyth* 1248-9 ; *Walsh* 2066 ;—of lower status, *Molloy* 1691 ; *Walsh* 2066 ;—and more stupid, *Molloy* 1678-80, 1690 ; *Fox* 1977——Contrary opinion, especially as to towns, *Fenelon* 2429-30—Reduction would increase contests, *Molloy* 1691 ;—promote jobbery, *Morris* 475 ;—and discourage attendance, *ib.* 474, 574——Not really desired by public, *Bagwell* 904, 906 ; *Tyrrell* 1008 ; *Molloy* 1682-4 ; *Carden* 2518——Qualification too low, *Molloy* 1672 ;—12 *L* too low, *ib.* 1671——Should be rather raised, *Gray* 1089-91 ; *Walsh* 2058——Post of guardian not coveted, *Molloy* 1692.
Qualification too high, *Meehan* 2225-9, 2238 ; *Fenelon* 2429 ;—in some places, *Smyth* 1247 ;—but Local Government Board not petitioned to lower it, *Meehan* 2230.
Qualification should be abolished, *Hewson* 1400-2, 1454-5—— Contrary opinion, *Molloy* 1678-80, 1693—— Abolition would not bring in non-local candidates, *ib.* 1681 ;—would encourage politics, *ib.* 1694.
Qualification never questioned, *Molloy* 1682-4 ;—must be ascertained by clerk, *ib.* 1685——Want of it invalidates nomination, *ib.* 1686-7——Guardians sometimes not ratepayers, though on ratebook, *Smyth* 1248.
Anomaly with regard to Dispensary Committee. *See Dispensary Committee.*

(3.) *Efficiency :*
Are careful guardians, *Fenelon* 2470-7 ;—better than *ex-officios*, *ib.* 2446 ;—sometimes good, *Morris* 629, 633, 639-40 ; *Spaight* 751 ; *Bagwell* 892 ;—generally honest, *Morris* 484 ; *Meehan* 2195-6 ;—wish to be economical, *Bourke* 331, 382-3 ; *Spaight* 751 ; *Fox* 2008-12 ;—as a rule, *Bourke* 395-6——Work well, *Meehan* 2265 ;—when politics excluded, *Walsh* 2078-9.
Economical in salaries, *Fenelon* 2475-9. *See* also *EX-OFFICIOS.*

(130—IND.)   H H 2   Unbusinesslike,

ELE   EX-O

Report, 1885 - continued.

ELECTIVE GUARDIANS—continued.

(3.) *Efficiency*—continued.

Unbusinesslike, *Bourke* 331, 334, 382-3; *Bagwell* 892; *Ringwood* 1584 ——Inconsistent in policy, *Robinson* 162; *Morris* 634;—though same men often re-elected, *Robinson* 125; *Bagwell* 947; *McCann* 1790-2——Careless, *Bourke* 395-7——Bad administrators, *Spaight* 733-6;—especially the Leaguers, *Tyrrell* 1033-4, 1038; *Hewson* 1440;—Loyalists better, *Tyrrell* 1036-8; *Ringwood* 1532, 1575, 1596; *Walsh* 2064-5 —— Irrelevant proposals by Loyalists, *Fenelon* 2402-5——Business hindered by politics introduced by Leaguers, *Bourke* 318-9, 327-8, 406, 432; *Morris* 580; *Spaight* 785-6; *Bagwell* 884; *Hewson* 1438-9, 1445-6; *Walsh* 2059-64, 2086-8, 2091; *Carden* 2565-6;—but this less probable under new rules, *Walsh* 2089-92. See also DISPENSARY COMMITTEE.

Petty tyranny with regard to boycotted farms, *Hewson* 1430.

Not economical, *Bourke* 321, 334, 382-3; *Morris* 635-8; *Bagwell* 892; *Smyth* 1311-4; *Hewson* 1406-14; *Fox* 1986-7——Have little interest in economy, *Bourke* 391-4; *Morris* 474, 629-31; *Spaight* 725, 731-2; *Smyth* 1336, 1314; *Hewson* 1405-6; *Fox* 2023-6 —— Think increased rates will reduce rent, *Spaight* 731-2——But occupiers not indifferent to rates, *Morris* 632, 634——Economical guardians overruled by Board, *Spaight* 725; *Smyth* 1261——All should have an interest in whole union, *Fox* 2034.

Timid in striking rate, *Bourke* 359, 364; *Morris* 637-8, 641; *Tyrrell* 1035.

(4.) *Jobbery*:

Jobbery by, *Morris* 596; *Spaight* 736, 752, 798-9;—in contracts, *Bourke* 383, 424-7; *Morris* 563-5; *Bagwell* 893-5; *Tyrrell* 1042-3; *Smyth* 1261, 1290-1; *Fox* 2014-8; *Carden* 2558-64;—on political grounds, *Tyrrell* 1044; *Ringwood* 1555-7; *Carden* 2558, 2560, 2562-3——Such jobbery difficult, *Smyth* 1287-9;—illegal in the case of guardians, *Spaight* 801;—but not in the case of others, ib. 802.

No jobbery in contracts, *Meehan* 2306-16.

Jobbery in election of officials, on political ground, *Spaight* 716-7, 722-4; *Hewson* 1435-6; *Ringwood* 1648-54; *Molloy* 1700-3——Partly controlled by Local Government Board, *Spaight* 800; *Molloy* 1700-3——Dispensary committee selected on political grounds, *Carden* 2567.

Jobbery in giving out-door relief, *Hewson* 1414-20; *Fox* 2032-3; *Carden* 2573-4; ——Do not understand extravagance of it, *Bagwell* 892; *Ringwood* 1584——Too ready to give it to evicted tenants, *Ringwood* 1580, 1584-5; *Fox* 1986-9, 2014; *Walsh* 2082-5——Not more so than *ex-officios*, *Meehan* 2301-2——Less able to resist pressure in that respect, *Morris* 484-9, 539 40; *Spaight* 761; *Smyth* 1261-3; *Ringwood* 1585-7; *Walsh* 2085.

Application by guardian for out-door relief, *Spaight* 726-30.

(5.) *Attendance*:

Attendance about one-third, *Morris* 591;—better than that of *ex-officios*, ib. 592; *Fox* 1986——Facilitated by meetings on market days, ib. 575-7——Loyalists attend better than Leaguers, *Tyrrell* 988-9, 1022——Contrary evidence, *Fenelon* 2391-3, 2395——Leaguers attend worse than *ex-officios*, ib. 1022-3——Sometimes swamped by *ex-officios*, *Fenelon* 2377-8, 2476. See also EX-OFFICIOS (5).

Electoral Districts differ from Electoral Divisions, *Molloy* 1748.

Electoral Divisions. Present, approved, *Meehan* 2138——Dispensary districts as electoral divisions, see POLLING PLACES.

Enniscorthy Union an agricultural district, *Ringwood* 1579——*Ex-officios* weak, ib. 1575——Rates, ib. 1574-5——Corrupt contract, ib. 1555-7.

Essex, Lord, referred to, *Smyth* 1340, 1351.

Evicted Destitute Poor (Ireland) Act, 1848. Relief of evicted tenants under, *Robinson* 190; *Morris* 484-5.

Evicted Tenants restored on payment of rent, *Bourke* 346——Out-door relief to, see OUT-DOOR RELIEF.

EX-OFFICIOS. See also *Agents*. GUARDIANS. OWNERS.	BOARDS OF GUARDIANS.	ELECTIVE
(1.) *Number.*	(7.) *Qualification.*	
(2.) *Reduction.*	(8.) *Value.*	
(3.) *Abolition.*	(9.) *Power.*	
(4.) *Increase.*	(10.) *Representativeness.*	
(5.) *Attendance.*	(11.) *Feeling concerning them.*	
(6.) *Appointment.*		(1.) *Number*:

Report, 1885—continued.

EX-OFFICIOS—continued.

(1.) *Number:*
Whole number in Ireland, *Robinson* 8.
In 1838, were one-third of elective guardians, *Robinson*, 162, 182, 194-5, 238, 255; *Morris* 480; *Gray* 1111; *Bagwell* 865——Sir G. Nicholls' Report, *Robinson* 162.
One-half of Board since 1847, *Robinson* 7, 9, 162, 239, 254; *Morris* 480, 597, 626; *Bagwell* 866-8; *Tyrrell* 1016-7; *Gray* 1110; *Smyth* 1294; *Ringwood* 1563; *McCann* 1820;—but never more, *Robinson* 19, 162;—where number of magistrates sufficient, *ib.* 7;—which is often not so, *ib.* 7-9, 158; *Morris* 480; *Spaight* 711-2——This proportion adopted because of burden of rates on owners, *Robinson* 162; *Morris* 480; *Bagwell* 800, 808——Not considered a grievance by public, *Bourke* 422; *Walsh* 2067-8——No hardship if maintained, *Bourke* 413——A sufficient protection to property, *McCann* 1819-20——Sir G. Grey's speech, *Robinson* 162——This limit fixed, magistrates being more numerous than in England, *Morris* 613. *See also MAGISTRATES.*

Proportion of *ex-officios* to elective guardians, *Carden* 2496——Resident *ex-officios* few, *Walsh* 2096,—in poor districts, *Spaight* 839-44——Proportion of residents to elective guardians, *ib.* 831-4, 945-6; *Tyrrell* 1018-9;—to non-residents, *Carden* 2497.

(2.) *Reduction:*
Reduction to one-half of elective guardians proposed by Bill, *Robinson* 194-6, 238 ——Proposal approved, *Meehan* 2273; *Fenelon* 2444 —— Would give owners fair representation, *ib.* 2479.
Reduction immaterial, if the remainder attend, *Bourke* 307-8, 312-7, 414-20; *Smyth* 1250; *McCann* 1852, 1865——Immaterial, as they do not attend, *ib.* 1861, 1864-5.
Reduction disapproved, *Robinson* 162-4, 171, 238-41; *Morris* 479, 481-2, 523; *Spaight* 668-70, 713, 792-3; *Tyrrell* 1009; *Gray* 1102-3; *Smyth* 1253-6; *Hewson* 1403; *Ringwood* 1569, 1571-3; *Molloy* 1695-6; *Fox* 1978; *Walsh* 2067; *Carden* 2541, 2549;—if present system retained, *Bagwell* 864-5——None but political reasons alleged for it, *Spaight* 821-2 —— Occupiers not uniformly against *ex-officios*, *Fenelon* 2488. *See also* (11.)
Reduction would leave property under-represented, *Robinson* 162, 169-71, 182, 197-9, 239-40; *Bourke* 309, 311, 314, 381, 412, 415-6; *Morris* 481-2; *Spaight* 714; *Bagwell* 866, 918, 922; *Hewson* 1403-4; *Molloy* 1695; *Fox* 1979; *Walsh* 2071—— Would swamp *ex-officios*, *Spaight* 669-70, 740, 748; *Carden* 2547-8;—who are already outvoted, *Morris* 580; *Spaight* 676, 747, 776-9; *Fox* 1987; *Meehan* 2241; *Carden* 2541-3 —— Would produce worse chairmen, *Morris* 495; *Spaight* 748, 827; *Bagwell* 898; *Tyrrell* 1031-2, 1039-40; *Smyth* 1254-6, 1292-3; *Walsh* 2050;—but not necessarily, *Bourke* 323, 365-8; *Meehan* 2271, 2279 (*see* also *CHAIRMAN*);—and worse elective guardians, *Walsh* 2071;—and would discourage attendance, *ib.* 2072; *Smyth* 1255——Would encourage politics at meetings, *Molloy* 1766-7; *Walsh* 2078;—and irrelevant motions, *Fenelon* 2403-5. *See also* (5) (d).
Reduction would increase rates, *Robinson* 200-7, 220-2; *Morris* 483-4; *Spaight* 708, 737, 794-6, 820; *Smyth* 1237, 1252, 1258; *Hewson* 1405; *Ringwood* 1547; *Fox* 1985-6; *Walsh* 2072—— Would result in less strict administration, *Molloy* 1768—— Contrary evidence, *Meehan* 2298-2300——Would not necessarily increase outdoor relief, *Molloy* 1769. *See also* (8).

(3.) *Abolition:*
Should be abolished, *Meehan* 2193, 2213, 2225, 2262, 2320, 2331, 2327-8, 2330-3;— as they only attend at elections, *ib.* 2268-9, 2274, 2333——But should be retained rather than proxies, *ib.* 2339.
Should be replaced by guardians elected by owners, *Bagwell* 863-4, 919; *Hewson* 1496-7, 1500-4——Contrary opinion, *Molloy* 1727-31. *See also PROPERTY GUARDIANS.*
System good, except as to attendance, *McCann* 1821. *See also* (5).

(4.) *Increase:*
Should be increased rather than reduced, *Molloy* 1695-6; *Fox* 1983-4·——Should not be increased, *ib.* 1979.
All magistrates should not be *ex-officios*, *Morris* 598, 613; *Bagwell* 919;—which would over-represent property, *ib.* 877;—but less so now, *Spaight* 804-7. *See* also *MAGISTRATES.*

(130—IND.) H H 3 (5.) *Attendance:*

Report, 1885—continued.

EX-OFFICIOS—continued.

(5.) *Attendance:*
Proportion who attend, *Gray* 1115; *Molloy* 1777; *Meehan* 2276; *Carden* 2498.

Attendance bad, *Robinson* 164, 172-3, 182-4, 256; *Bourke* 308, 311-2, 314, 316, 318, 336, 405-8; *Morris* 588, 583; *Spaight* 673 8, 682, 806, 810; *Bagwell* 896; *Tyrrell* 1021, 1029; *Smyth* 1250, 1253, 1258-9, 1295, 1297, 1327-8; *Ringwood* 1552-3; *McCann* 1821, 1852, 1861, 1864 6; *Fox* 1986, 2004, 2021-2; *Meehan* 2268-9, 2274-8, 2300, 2302-3, 2333; *Fenelon* 2393; *Carden* 2498;—which is unfortunate, *Robinson* 172; *Bourke* 336, 407, 419; *Spaight* 709——Need not be so bad, *Robinson* 173, 256; *Bourke* 328, 408; *Morris* 566, 578; *Spaight* 778, 778-9; *Bagwell* 922; *Tyrrell* 1040.

Worse than that of elective guardians, *Morris* 592; *Fox* 1986. *See* also *ELECTIVE GUARDIANS* (5).

Bad attendance points rather to increase than decrease, *Fox* 1983-4.

Reasons for bad attendance:—

(a.) Non-residence, *Robinson* 173, 248, 251; *Bourke* 320-1; *Morris* 523, 543, 579; *Spaight* 783-4; *Bagwell* 899-901, 922; *Tyrrell* 1020-1; *Smyth* 1298; *Ringwood* 1564; *Molloy* 1717, 1719-——Enough residents difficult to find *Walsh* 2096;—in poor districts, *Spaight* 839-4——Proportion of residents, *ib.* 831-4, 845-6; *Tyrrell* 1018-9; *Carden* 2497-——Physical incapacity, *Tyrrell* 1058, 1061——Selection by rateability, *Bourke* 311-2; *Bagwell* 876. *See* also (6)——Not non-residence, *McCann* 1854——Non-residents sometimes attend well, *Tyrrell* 1061-2——Attendance would be improved by *ex-officios* being elected, *Robinson* 182-3; *Bourke* 307-8, 312-5, 317, 414 6; *Spaight* 710, 808; *Bagwell* 901-2; *Walsh* 2092-5;—but only slightly, *Morris* 523, 527-30, 541. *See* also (6); *PROPERTY GUARDIANS.*

(b.) Want of interest, *Meehan* 2277——This contradicted, *Molloy* 1728——Want of sense of obligation, *Bagwell* 883; *Hewson* 1501——Confidence in elective guardians, *McCann* 1852-——Other occupations, *Morris* 567-70; *Ringwood* 1565;—which applies equally to elective guardians, *Morris* 572-3.

(c.) Want of weight, *Robinson* 172; *Bourke* 406-8; *Morris* 580; *Spaight* 676, 747, 776-9; *Fox* 1987; *Walsh* 2071; *Meehan* 2241; *Carden* 2541-3;—especially since agitation, *Robinson* 174-5; *Bourke* 318-9, 406——*Ex-officios* have weight, *ib.* 410; when they attend, *Robinson* 172; *Bourke* 409-10. *See* also (9).

(d.) Political discussions at Board, *Bourke* 318-9, 328, 432; *Spaight* 783-6, 830, 837-8; *Bagwell* 884; *Hewson* 1438-9, 1445; *Molloy* 1767; *Walsh* 2061; *Carden* 2565-6,—and irrelevant discussions, *Morris* 580, 582; *Bagwell* 884;—which are less when Inspector present, *ib.* 890-1——These should be repressed, *Bourke* 432; *Meehan* 2291——Could be so, by Local Government Board, *Bagwell* 885, 888;—though this difficult in practice, *ib.* 886-7, 889; *Hewson* 1452-3——Attempt of Local Government Board to repress them useless, *Morris* 580; *Bagwell* 886, 888; not futile, *Walsh* 2089-90, 2092. *See* also *BOARDS OF GUARDIANS*; *CHAIRMAN.*

(e.) Class feeling, *Smyth* 1344 6; *Fenelon* 2485-7——Opposition of elective guardians, *Molloy* 1780; *Meehan* 2250-2, 2279, 2305; *Fenelon* 2401-5, 2475——Contrary evidence, *Bourke* 326; *McCann* 1857; *Meehan* 2274, 2278——*Ex-officios* would not be complained of if they attended, *ib.* 2274, 2333. *See* also (11).

(f.) Sectarian spirit, *Hewson* 1485-7——Contrary evidence, *Fenelon* 2391, 2394, 2401-5.

(g.) Intimidation by mob, *Smyth* 1317. *See* also *Intimidation.*——Insults from elective guardians, *Bourke* 327-8, 406; *Morris* 566; *Smyth* 1252, 1258-9, 1317-20, 1323; *Carden* 2569-71——Uncourteous treatment, *Spaight* 720-1, 828; *Bagwell* 882-4; *Tyrrell* 1028-30; *Molloy* 1779-82——*Ex-officios* not insulted, *ib.* 1781-2; *McCann* 1857;—well treated where politics excluded, *Walsh* 2079;—and where they attend and work, *Meehan* 2274, 2333——*Ex-officios* contemptuous towards elective guardians, *ib.* 2274-——Intolerant of Nationalist feeling, *Meehan* 2279; *Fenelon* 2485-7.

(h.) Other reasons suggested, *Robinson* 257-8; *Bourke* 327——No reason given, *McCann* 1855.

Bad attendance leaves property under-represented, *Bourke* 311-2; *Bagwell* 922; *McCann* 1866. *See* also (10).- -Has probably increased rates, *Smyth* 1252, 1258;—but is not the sole cause of this, *Spaight* 783-6. *See* also (8).

Better attendance would swamp Leaguers, *Smyth* 1298. *See* also (9)——Would discourage politics, *Walsh* 2078. *See* also (8), and above (d).

Attendance good, *Molloy* 1704, 1776-8——Better near town, *Morris* 585, 590——Same as of elective guardians where no agitation, *Spaight* 830, 835-8——Nearly so, *Walsh* 2073-7——Some attend regularly, *Bourke* 316; *Walsh* 2039, 2073-5——Residents attend as well as elective guardians, *Tyrrell* 1021;—better than Nationalists, *ib.* 1022;—

Report, 1885—*continued.*

Ex Officios—continued.

(5.) *Attendance*—continued.

1022;—fairly, *Ringwood* 1559, 1564;—as do some non-residents, *Tyrrell* 1061-2; *Molloy* 1719——Sometimes swamp electives, *Walsh* 2065; *Meehan* 2240-1, 2265-9; *Fenelon* 2377-8, 2445. *See* also (9).

Improved lately, *Smyth* 1259, 1295;—and likely to improve, *ib.* 1331-2, 1353-4.

Good at election of officers, *Robinson* 179; *Bourke* 417; *Morris* 493-4, 594; *Spaight* 676, 716, 784, 827; *Gray* 1115; *Smyth* 1252, 1296, 1298; *Ringwood* 1565; *McCann* 1855; *Walsh* 2050; *Fenelon* 2379, 2393;—which secures good chairman, *Morris* 494, 571; *Spaight* 676, 827; *Tyrrell* 1031-2, 1039-40; *Carden* 2493——Good only at elections, *Meehan* 2268-9, 2274, 2333;—which is objectionable, *ib.* 2265-9, 2275, 2278-9, 2300, 2333; *Bourke* 417-20——Jobbery suggested, *Morris* 595——Such attendance no better than that of elective guardians, *Robinson* 179; *Hewske* 420; *Morris* 491, 594; *Spaight* 716;—who can whip up larger numbers, *Bourke* 413. *See* also *Chairman*.

Good at giving of contracts, *Ringwood* 1565; *Molloy* 1705.

Ex-officios cannot attend more easily than elective guardians, *Morris* 575-7.

Attendance discouraged by bad chairman, *Smyth* 1255; and by reduction of *ex-officios, ib.* 1255; *Walsh* 2072——Would not be improved by substituting non-magistrates, *Molloy* 323.

Good attendance salutary, *see* (8).

(6.) *Appointment:*

Appointed on 29th September, *Hewson* 1436; *Fox* 1905——Should be so in March, *Hewson* 1436——Should be so at same time as elective guardians, *Fox* 1906.

Where residents too few, highest rated of non residents selected, *Robinson* 14, 18; *Bourke* 308; *Morris* 523; *Spaight* 710; *Bagwell* 875; *Tyrrell* 1059-60; *Smyth* 1355; *Hewson* 1436-7; *Walsh* 2094;—by clerk, *Smyth* 1361-4; *Hewson* 1437; *Walsh* 2081 ——Doubt whether this applies to residents, *Smyth* 1355, 1358-63——This a bad plan, *Robinson* 182-4, 252; *Bourke* 308, 311; *Molloy* 1710, 1710——Does not secure good attendance, *Bourke* 311-2; *Bagwell* 876——Is retained in Bill, *Molloy* 1734-8.

Ex-officios should be elected by brother magistrates *Robinson* 182-4, 242-3, 252-3; *Bourke* 307-8, 312-7, 414-20; *Morris* 523-7; *Spaight* 710-3, 807-9; *Bagwell* 901-2; *Smyth* 1353-7, 1365; *Molloy* 1711-24, 1732; *Walsh* 2093-6; as in 1838, *Robinson* 182, 243, 255;—which would improve attendance, *see* (5) (a);—but would be disliked by popular party, *Smyth* 1357.

Magistrates cannot refuse to serve, unless number excessive, *Bagwell* 870; *Molloy* 1707;—which is rare, *Bagwell* 870——Non-residents can refuse, *Hewson* 1437——*Ex-officios* cannot resign, *Bagwell* 870; *Hewson* 1437; *Molloy* 1707-8——Contrary evidence, *Fenelon* 2382-3——Perhaps not legally, *ib* 2388——Should have that power, *Bagwell* 869, 871-3, 923-4; *Tyrrell* 1058; *Smyth* 1327-30, 1366; *Molloy* 1709-10; to make room for useful local men, *Smyth* 1330, 1365-6;—and non-residents, *Bagwell* 871-4; *Tyrrell* 1058-62; *Molloy* 1718-9; *Walsh* 2099.

(7.) *Qualification:*

Property qualification necessary, *Molloy* 1741——Scandals from want of it, *Smyth* 1242-4, 1251. *See* also *Magistrates.*

Ex-officios must be magistrates residing or having a 50 *l.* rental in union, *Robinson* 7, 10-1, 16, 156, 249, 250, 255; *Bourke* 308; *Morris* 585-7; *Bagwell* 873; *Walsh* 2094—— Not stipendiary magistrates, *Robinson* 13;—nor borough magistrates, *Morris* 588—— Residence the primary qualification, *Smyth* 1331; *Walsh* 2094——Qualification of being a magistrate should be abolished, *Molloy* 1670;—but this would not improve attendance, *ib.* 1727-31.

Ex-officios need not be on rate-book, *Robinson* 15-8, 156; *Bagwell* 877-8——View of Local Government Board that they must be rated directly, *Walsh* 2094, 2102-5 ——Should be qualified if rated directly or indirectly, *ib.* 2106——Should be ratepayers, *Robinson* 157; *Smyth* 1242-4; *Ringwood* 1566-70, 1572; *Molloy* 1670, 1713, 1739-41; *Walsh* 2099; *Meehan* 2224——Are sometimes not so, *Smyth* 1261; *McCann* 1851; *Meehan* 2263;—but seldom, *Robinson* 245-7; *McCann* 1846——Complaints of their not being so, *Smyth* 1251; *Molloy* 1742; *Meehan* 2262-3——Contrary evidence, *McCann* 1850—— Very small ratepayers sometimes, *Fenelon* 2434-5——Law need not be altered, *McCann* 1846, 1849.

Report, 1885—*continued.*

EX-OFFICIOS—continued.

(8.) *Value*:

Have personal influence, *Morris* 624–5 ; *Spaight* 738–45, 749, 783–6 ; *Bagwell* 880 ; *Smyth* 1250; *Hewson* 1516 ;—and leaven the Board, *Robinson* 162; *Smyth* 1250.
Attendance of, salutary, *Robinson* 162, 165, 172, 184; *Bourke* 316, 330–1, 334, 364, 382–3, 405 ; *Morris* 479 ; *Spaight* 671–5, 682, 718–20, 779 ; *Bagwell* 880–1, 894–5 ; *Walsh* 2067, 2078 ; *Molloy* 1705 ;—promotes good feeling, *ib.* 1705.
Absence of, not entirely the cause of maladministration, *Spaight* 783–6.
Are more businesslike than elective guardians, *Morris* 479 ; *Bagwell* 881 ; *Gray* 1101–14 ; *Smyth* 1250; *Molloy* 1768 ;—and their administration is better, *Gray* 1103–14——Are more ready to strike rate, *Morris* 641. *See also* ELECTIVE GUARDIANS (3).

Take an interest in the work, *Molloy* 1728. *See also* (5)(b).

Discourage politics, *Molloy* 1766–7 ; *Walsh* 2078 ; *Fenelon* 2485–7 ;—and check irrelevant discussions, *Morris* 496–7 ; *Fenelon* 2403–5, 2484–7. *See also* (5) (d).

Keep down rates, *Morris* 484 ; *Gray* 1116–7 ; *Smyth* 1252, 1258–9 ; *Ringwood* 1574–80——Are economical, *Molloy* 1728 ;—more so than electives, *Fox* 1986, 2013 ;—less so, *Fenelon* 2470–7——Administer rates no more fairly than electives, *Meehan* 2195–6.

Understand better than electives the extravagance of out-door relief, *Bagwell* 892; —and are more capable of refusing it, *Morris* 479, 540 ; *Gray* 1124 ; *Smyth* 1261 ; *Ringwood* 1582——Administer it better, *Spaight* 672–705——Contrary evidence, *Meehan* 2301–2——Give it on political grounds in spite of electives, *ib.* 2303–5——Keep it down, *Gray* 1124–7 ;—but give it when required, *Ringwood* 1582 ;—and then only, *Spaight* 708 ; *Gray* 1124——But reduction of *ex-officius* would not necessarily increase it, *Molloy* 1769.

Resist jobbery by elective guardians, *Morris* 563–5 ; *Spaight* 748, 827 ; *Bagwell* 894–5—— Give extravagant pensions, *Meehan* 2249–61, 2267 ; *Fenelon* 2393, 2453–7, 2475 ;—and salaries, *ib.* 2393, 2447–52, 2475–6 ;—in spite of elective guardians, *Meehan* 2250–2 ; *Fenelon* 2448–52, 2462–6, 2475——Give fair pensions and salaries, *Carden* 2545–6 ——Are accused of jobbery at election of officials, *Morris* 595. *See also* (5.) Less given to jobbery in contracts than elective guardians, *Bourke* 383, 424–7 ; *Morris* 563–5. *See also* ELECTIVE GUARDIANS (4.)

(9.) *Power*:

Preponderance on boards, *Meehan* 2240–1, 2265–9 ; *Fenelon* 2377–8 ;—in conjunction with Loyalist guardians, *Walsh* 2065 ; *Fenelon* 2445 ;—discourages attendance of other elective guardians, *Meehan* 2265 ; *Fenelon* 2445.

Preponderance, if attendance better, *Smyth* 1299 ; *Walsh* 2078.

Preponderance of, in voting pensions and salaries, see (8) ;—in elections, see (5).

Double power, as guardians and as voters, complained of, *Meehan* 2263, 2320, 2331. *See also* OWNERS.

Personal influence, see (8): CHAIRMEN.

Are outvoted on boards, *Robinson* 172, 174–5 ; *Bourke* 318–9, 406–8 ; *Morris* 580 ; *Spaight* 676, 747, 776–9 ; *Fox* 1987 ; *Meehan* 2241 ; *Carden* 2541–3. *See also* (5) (c).

Effect of reduction on, see (2).

(10.) *Representativeness*:

Objection to, as being not representative, *Hewson* 1497–9, 1501, 1515–6 ;—not elected, *Meehan* 2262, 2264, 2330–1. *See also* PROPERTY GUARDIANS.

Represent property, *Smyth* 1332–4 ;—best, *Bourke* 381 ; *Molloy* 1729–30——Present proportion sufficiently, *McCann* 1819–20 ;—not excessively, *Ringwood* 1571——Contrary opinion, *Fenelon* 2479——Are the only representation, *Spaight* 714 ; *Molloy* 1695——Understood to represent loyalty, *Smyth* 1333——Present proportion, with proxies and cumulative vote, are sufficient representation of property, *Morris* 599. *See also* (2) ; OWNERS.

(11.) *Feeling concerning them*:

Value of, recognised by small ratepayers, *Hewson* 1512–6 ; *Walsh* 2067–70 ; *Fenelon* 2488——Are sometimes elected guardians, *Morris* 437, 644, 632 ;—but not often, *ib.* 623——Agitation against them by large farmers chiefly, *Hewson* 1512——Would not be complained of if they attended, *Meehan* 2274, 2333.

Feeling of elective guardians, *see* (5) (e), (f), (g).

Report, 1885—*continued.*

F.

FENELON, MR. EDWARD, Farmer and Elective Guardian, and Vice-Chairman of Naas Union (2341-2, 2359, 2368-9, 2395). His election address (2393).

Analysis of his Evidence (2341-2488).
Triennial elections approved, 2343-4.
Ballot approved as preventing intimidation, 2345.
Proxies should be abolished, 2346, 2360, 2363-4——System open to manufacture of false votes, 2346-52, 2361,—and votes on very small rating, 2346-7, 2353, 2359-60, 2485,—which can also be given by occupiers, 2354-8——Detection hindered by clerk, 2346-7, 2362——Might be extended to occupiers, 2360——Disfranchisement of owners by abolition applies to tenants also, 2359-2386,—and might be obviated by having different polling days, 2364-5, 2384-5.
Owners should be fairly represented, 2365, 2376, 2384; but bulk of rates paid by over-rented tenants, 2365-74——Owners are over-represented at boards, 2376-8, 2479, 2481-3, 2488——Would be fairly represented by the men they return and one-third of board *ex-officios*, 2479.
Ex-officios, supported by some electives, preponderate on board, 2377-81, 2445——Should be reduced to one-third, 2444, 2479,—being more extravagant than electives in salaries, 2446-53, 2475-8,—and pensions, 2453-69, 2475,—and less economical than electives, 2470-7——Are opposed as being irresponsible, 2393,—but may, in some cases, be supported by ratepayers, 2488——Can resign, 2382-3—— *Ex-officio* chairmen unpopular as being a check on Nationalist resolutions, 2483-7.
Contests not entirely political, but on the ground of attention to business, 2389-2410.
Election petitions tried by County Court Judge an improvement, 2387-9, 2417-—Revision of lists by County Court Judge probably unnecessary, 2418.
Lists should be published in central place, and copies of register might be supplied gratis, 2411-6.
Minors and lunatics should have votes if possible, 2419-28.
Elective Guardians: Qualification should be fixed at 12 *l.*, 2429-30——Local Government Board discretion nugatory, 2431—— Anomaly from dispensary committee qualification remaining at 30 *l.*, 2432-4,—and from small ratepayers being upon it *ex-officio*, 2434-41——Wardens for issuing tickets, 2442-3.

Fitzwilliam, Earl, v. *Shillelagh Union*, settling maximum of cumulative vote. See CUMULATIVE VOTE.

Foran, Mr., referred to, *Carden* 2504.

Forgney Electoral Division. Statistics of election, Fox 1936-45, 1958-60. *See also Ballymahon Union.*

FOX, MR. RICHARD EDWARD, *ex-officio* deputy vice-chairman of Ballymahon Union, (1891-3).

Analysis of his Evidence (1891-2034).
Triennial elections would at present stereotype had class of guardians, 1894-1900 ——Elections should be in August, so that guardians who strike rate should administer it, 1902-8——Should be by ballot, 1901.
Proxies not objectionable, 1912——Abolition would disfranchise owners, 1909-11, 1913-6, 1942-6, 1950-60;—whose voting power is already too small, 1917-49, 2027-9; and who are otherwise under-represented, 1978-82—— Proxies should last from one general election to another, 1961-2.
Ex-officios should not be reduced, 1978;—which would increase rates, 1985-7——Non-attendance an argument rather for increase, 1983-4, 2021-2.
Elective Guardians: Lower qualification would bring in unfit men, 1976-7——Are less economical than *ex-officios* in out-door relief, 1986-2014, 2019-20;—when charge can be thrown on landlords, 2023-6;—and are given to jobbery in contracts, 2014-8 ——Acquiesce mutually in each other's extravagance, 2032-3.
Cumulative Vote: Maximum thirty, 2030-1.
Election Petitions: Security for costs should be given, 1063.
List of Voters might be made out at the same time as Parliamentary list, but constituency wider, 1969-75——Revision should not be by County Court Judge, 1964-7.
Bill inopportune, 2034.

Friendly Societies. See *Benefit Societies.*
(130—IND.)   I I

Report, 1885—*continued.*

G.

Gallagher, Mr., referred to, *Carden* 2565.

Galway Town, a county of a town, *Morris* 586—— Cumulative voting there, *Robinson* 34; *Morris* 444 ;—by ballot, *ib.* 445.

Galway Union. Owners not strong, *Morris* 615-9—— Proxies few, *ib.* 614—— Number of guardians, *ib.* 624-5—— Chairman, *ib.* 624—— Elective guardians owners, *ib.* 623, 626-7—— One an *ex-officio, ib.* 544-6, 822—— Attendance, *ib.* 585-90.

Gilltown Electoral Division. Statistics of election, *Molloy* 1638-40. *See also Naas Union.*

Glenties Union. No 12 *l.* occupiers, *Bourke* 304.

Gorey Union. Agricultural district, *Ringwood* 1579—— Little League spirit, *ib.* 1558, 1596—— Few contests, *ib.* 1534—— Number of guardians, *ib.* 1560-5——Attendance, *ib.* 1559, 1564, 1575——Rates, *ib.* 1574-5.

Government unpopular in Ireland, *Hewson* 1497-9.

Granard, Lord, referred to, *Spaight* 752 ; *McCann* 1852, 1855.

GRAY, MR. JAMES, for 36 years Clerk of Roscrea Union (1067-70).

 Analysis of his Evidence (1067-1162).

 Proxies not objected to, 1072, 1079*, 1081——Should be extended to property in owner's occupation, 1072-5, 1146——Abolition would disfranchise owners, 1071, 1075 —and women and infirm persons, 1076-7——But personation should be guarded against, 1077-9.

 Owners voting power small, 1125-44—— Representation would be further reduced by Bill, 1150.

 Ballot an advantage, 1147-9,—to protect voters, 1151-6—— Already acted upon by witnesses, 1134, 1151-6.

 Triennial elections would reduce ferment, 1157-9.

 List of voters open to inspection, essential under Ballot, 1160—— Arrears of rates should be paid before list made out, 1161-2.

 Ex-officios better administrators than elective guardians, 1103-14——Attend badly, except at election of officials, 1115——Should not be reduced, 1102.

 Elective Guardians : Qualification should be raised rather than lowered, 1088-91, 1150—— That for dispensary committee a fixed one, and not affected by Bill, 1092-3, 1100-1——Consequent anomaly, 1092-1101.

 Advantage of excluding politics from boards, 1116-23.

 Out-door relief increased lately, but resisted by guardians, 1124-7.

 Election petitions should be tried by County Court Judge of county where workhouse is situated, 1083—— Recognizance to prosecute and for costs should be entered into, 1082-5——Costs might fall on rates, 1087.

 Bill disapproved, 1145, 1149-50.

Grey, Sir George. His speech in 1847, on increase of *ex-officios, Robinson* 162.

Griffiths' Valuation too high now, *Fenelon* 2369.

H.

Hayes, Dr. His pension, *Fenelon* 2453-7, 2461-7, 2475, 2480.

Hennessy, Mrs. Case of improper out-door relief, *Meehan* 2303-5.

HEWSON, MR. JOHN B., elective and *ex-officio* guardian, and Vice Chairman of Rathkeale Union (1369-74).

 Analysis of his Evidence (1369-1516).

 Ballot approved, 1375——— Each voting paper should carry one vote, 1376-7——Polling places should be Petty Sessions Courts in dispensary districts, 1378-84, 1479-83;— which might be divided when too large, 1382, 1426-9——This would prevent mobbing, 1429, 1478——But elections would take two or three days, 1482-3——Cost should be on rates, 1385.

 Elective Guardians : Qualification should be abolished, as restricting choice of fit
men,

HEWSON, MR. JOHN B. (Analysis of his Evidence)—*continued.*

men, 1400-2, 1454-5——Their animus against landlords, 1430——Are unbusinesslike, 1406, 1438-40——Political discussions by, hard to repress, 1438-9, 1445-53——Give improper and excessive out-door relief, 1407-25, 1431-3, 1484, 1505-6——Are under influence of Land League, 1506-11.

Dispensary Committees manipulated with a view to election of doctor, 1434-6——Non-guardian members should only issue tickets, 1441-4——Anomaly from *ex-officios* and elective guardians not being appointed at same time, 1436.

Ex-officios: Reduction unfair, and would raise rates, 1403-6——Non-attendance due formerly to sectarian spirit, 1483 7——Unpopular only with large ratepayers, 1468-70, 1512-6——Not representative, 1497-9, 1501, 1515 6——Cannot legally resign, 1487——Should have no qualification, 1455, 1501.

Property guardians, to replace *ex-officios*, advocated, 1496-1504;—landlords voting also as occupiers, 1504——Would represent other property besides land, 1501.

Proxies should be extended to owners occupying, 1390-2——Abolition would disfranchise owners, 1386——Can turn elections, 1464-7——Owners, voting power inadequate, 1456-77.

Cumulative Vote should be unlimited, each 100 *l*, over 200 *l* carrying one vote, 1387-9, 1488-96.

Claims to vote should be established once for all, 1393-4.

Election Petitions should be heard by County Court Judge, 1395;—and security given for costs, 1396-7.

Minors should vote through guardians, 1398-9.

Hunt & Co. referred to, *Carden* 2562.

I.

Immediate Lessors have votes for holdings of 4 *l.* or under, for which they pay whole rate, *Robinson* 4; *Hewson* 1457-8; *Fenelon* 2354-9——May vote by proxy, *Robinson* 4——Do not use votes, *Fenelon* 2354-7——Such holdings not usually over 10 *s.*, *Hewson* 1496——Seldom give six votes, *ib.* 1494-6; *Molloy* 1745-6——Tenant farmers so qualified, *Hewson* 1457; *Fenelon* 2354-9——Aggregation of votes of, with occupancy votes, see *CUMULATIVE VOTE.*

Inspectors under English Commission before 1847, *Bourke* 270-4——Their duties, *Spaight* 646-7——Generally good officers, *Bagwell* 890——Check irrelevant discussions, *ib.* 890-1.

INTIMIDATION by Nationalist party, *Bagwell* 940 1; *Gray* 1151-6; *Smyth* 1197, 1206-10, 1214-6, 1261-4, 1280, 1317; *Walsh* 2070, 2085; *Meehan* 2126; *Carden* 2539——Diminishing, *Smyth* 1264——Would be diminished by multiplying polling places, *Hewson* 1429, 1478, 1482——Police powerless, *ib.* 1207, 1209. See also *LAND LEAGUE.*

By occupiers denied, *Meehan* 2128-9.

By priests, *Carden* 2538.

By landlord, *Bagwell* 940; *McCann* 1793-8; *Meehan* 2126-30; *Fenelon* 2345——Cases quoted, *McCann* 1795-6; *Meehan* 2126, 2129, 2135——Evidence contradicted, *Carden* 2528, 2557——By agents, *Bagwell* 940.

Undue influence by magistrates, *Meehan* 2239, 2318, 2323-6——Not much, *Morris* 620——Should be brought before Lord Chancellor, *Meehan* 2325-6.

Not much intimidation, *Molloy* 1613——Easy under present system, *McCann* 1796-7. See also *BALLOT.*

J.

Jephson, Mr., referred to, *Smyth* 1272.

Jessop, Mr., referred to, *Carden* 2507-8.

Joyce, Mr., referred to, *Morris* 624-5.

Judicial Rent onerous, *Fenelon* 2368——Division of rate considered in fixing it, *ib.* 2371.

Jurors. Special qualification in different counties, *Gray* 1096——Qualification raised again after being lowered, *ib.* 1089-90——Cost of Jurors' Lists, *Molloy* 1661.

Justices. See *MAGISTRATES.*

Report, 1885—continued.

K.

Kavanagh, Mr., referred to, *Molloy* 1703.
Kenmare Union under *ex-officio* management, *Spaight* 681-2——Outdoor relief, *ib.* 704.
Kerry. Outdoor relief in, *Spaight* 672-705.
Kilbride, Mr., referred to, *Ringwood* 1551.
Kilcolmanbane Electoral Division, referred to, *Meehan* 2167.
Kilcullen Dispensary District. Composition of committee, *Fenelon* 2436, 2441.
Kildysert Union, referred to, *Hewson* 1445.
Killarney Union managed by elective guardians, *Spaight* 678-9——Evicted tenant elected a relieving officer, *ib.* 722-4——Intimidation, *Bagwell* 941——Outdoor relief, *Spaight* 690. *See also Aghadoe Electoral Division.*
Kiltannon, owned chiefly by Major Molony, *Bourke* 338. *See also Tulla Union.*

L.

Lacka Electoral Division. Vacancy on Board, *Meehan* 2204.
LAND LEAGUE. See also ELECTIVE GUARDIANS.
 Class of Leaguers, *Smyth* 1291——Danger from it, *ib.* 1261-3. *See also* INTIMIDATION.
 Contribution by, of 1 *l.* a week to suspects, *Smyth* 1279; *Hewson* 1506.
 Influence over Boards, *Hewson* 1506, 1508-11——Proper influence over elections, *Fenelon* 2399, 2406-10——Interference in election of guardian, *Smyth* 1197; *Carden* 2550-6;—of official, *Spaight* 722; *Ringwood* 1551——Not for political reasons, *Meehan* 2293, 2296——Local secretaries of, appointed assistant overseers, *Molloy* 1700-3.
Landlords. See OWNERS.
Leahy, Mr., referred to, *Fenelon* 2431.
Lease, Statutory. Ratification of private arrangement, *Fenelon* 2371-2——Rent under it, *ib.* 2368-9.
Leinster, Duke of, referred to, *Tyrrell* 1021, 1032.
" *Leinster Leader.*" Extract from, *Carden* 2551-6.
Leslie & Co., referred to, *Carden* 2562.
Limerick County. Meeting of landowners, *Hewson* 1501.
Limerick Union. Proxies increased, *Bourke* 430-1.
LIST OF VOTERS;
 For preparation of register, *Robinson* 56;—necessary under ballot, *Gray* 1160;—only for contested divisions, *Molloy* 1647-8, 1650, 1656, 1659-61.
 Should be made out by clerk, *Meehan* 2133;—in July, *McCann* 1831;—in January, *Walsh* 2109;—triennially, *ib.* 2109; *Meehan* 2125;—not for each election, *Fox* 1969——At the same time as Parliamentary lists, *ib.* 1670-1;—though they would differ from these, *ib.* 1672-5.
 More time for, see CLAIMS TO VOTE.
 Not now printed, *Smyth* 1190; *Molloy* 1652-3, 1661——Should be so, *ib.* 1650-1; *McCann* 1831-4.
 Should be published in central place, *Fenelon* 2411-2——Notice that they are ready prescribed, *Molloy* 1648, 1653.
 Amendment of, see REGISTER.
 Appeal from, see ELECTION PETITIONS. REVISION.
 Lists for polling-places, *Robinson* 23, 41, 99——Cost of, *Smyth* 1186-8;—falls on candidate, *ib.* 1185-90.
Listowel Union. Number of guardians, *Spaight* 845-6——Formerly well managed, *ib.* 688,718-9——Now by elective guardians, *ib.* 677-9, 714——Jobbery in electing officials, *ib.* 717——Outdoor relief, *ib.* 684-7, 758.

LOCAL

Report, 1885—*continued.*

LOCAL GOVERNMENT BOARD;
Commissioner of, cannot be a guardian, *Morris* 584.
Powers of under Bill, as to cumulative vote, *Robinson* 23;——disapproved, *ib.* 23, 29——As to penal clauses of Ballot Act, *Robinson* 54;—disapproved, *ib.* 54-5——As to lists of voters, *ib.* 56——As to fresh elections, should be permissive, *ib.* 154-5——Too much left to, by Bill, *Fenelon* 2412.
Can alter areas, *Robinson* 112-3; *Spaight* 722-4; *Hewson* 1428——Decide election petitions, see ELECTION PETITIONS——Fix qualification of elective guardians, see ELECTIVE GUARDIANS (2)——Fix polling days, *Robinson* 43, 71-2;—but know little of how elections are worked, *Spaight* 752——Can control appointment of officers, *Spaight* 800; *Molloy* 1702——Ineffectual attempt to do so, *ib.* 1700-3——Can dissolve board, *Bagwell* 886, 889; *Molloy* 1702;—and send down vice guardians, *Bourke* 360;—but cannot extend its duration, *Robinson* 123-4——Could repress politics at Board meetings, *Bagwell* 885, 888;—though this difficult in practice, *ib.* 886-7, 889; *Hewson* 1452-3——Circular of, regulating business, ineffectual, *Morris* 580-1; *Bagwell* 886, 888;—not ineffectual, *Walsh* 2089-90, 2092. *See also* EX OFFICIOS (5) (d.)
Cannot check outdoor relief, *Spaight* 800;—unless illegal, *Smyth* 1261, 1271-2, 1290——Have sanctioned it, to suspects, *ib.* 1271-2, 1277-9, 1290;—for four weeks, *Hewson* 1420-2.
Laches of, in investigating complaints, *Meehan* 2200, 2203-8;—In exercising their powers, *Smyth* 1261; *Fenelon* 2346, 2431;—as to filling up vacancies, *Meehan* 2200, 2203; *Fenelon* 2431; *Carden* 2505-6;—as to outdoor relief, *Smyth* 1261——Action of, considered unjust by Leaguers, *Meehan* 2158-63, 2180——Consequent indisposition to apply to them, *ib.* 2197-9, 2200, 2211; *Fenelon* 2431.
Do not check extravagant salaries, *Fenelon* 2447-51, 2470——Contrary evidence, *ib.* 2476.

Local Government Board, ex parte Byrne and James. Decision as to maximum cumulative vote, *Morris* 547. *See also* CUMULATIVE VOTE.

Longford, Lord. Large voting power of, *McCann* 1870.

Longford Union. Part, very poor, *Fox* 2003——Strong property vote, *McCann* 1868-71——Electoral divisions, *ib.* 1853——Number of guardians, *ib.* 1853, 1858——Attendance, *ib.* 1852; *Fox* 2004——Revising officer, *McCann* 1890——Outdoor relief, *ib.* 1883-9; *Fox* 1995-2001.

Lough Rea Union, referred to, *Morris* 542-3.

Loughery, appointed rate collector for political reasons, *Bourke* 354-8.

Loyalists, as opposed to Nationalists, *Tyrrell* 972. *See also* ELECTIVE GUARDIANS (3). EX OFFICIOS (9). OCCUPIERS. OWNERS.

Lunatics. *See also* MINORS.
Cannot vote, *Hewson* 1399——Should have votes, if possible, *Fenelon* 2419, 2426——Guardians should vote for them, *Robinson* 237; *Bourke* 302; *Morris* 472, 607-10; *Spaight* 661-2; *Carden* 2516——Contrary opinion, *Meehan* 2218-21.

M.

McCANN, MR. HARRY, elective Guardian and Vice-Chairman of Longford Union, and formerly an *ex officio*, and a landowner (1783-6, 1811-3).
Analysis of his Evidence (1783-1890).
Triennial elections approved, 1788-92——No advantage in annual renewal of one-third of board, 1790-2.
Ballot necessary to prevent existing intimidation from both sides, 1793-8——Would not deter women, 1799-81——Would increase expense, 1828.
Proxies invidious, and should be extended to occupiers 1802-16, 1822, 1847-8——Abolition would partly disfranchise owners, 1817;—as for Parliamentary elections, 1806, 1818——But they are sufficiently represented by *ex officios*, 1819-21, 1866;—and by voting power, 1867-71.
Ex Officios: No jealousy of their not being ratepayers, 1846, 1849-51——Jealousy of agents being *ex officios*, 1850.
Ex officios' attendance bad, 1821, 1852, 1861, 1864-6;—except at election of chairman, 1855——Nothing else to complain of, 1821, 1865——Bad attendance not due to non-residence, 1854;—or to insults, 1857;—but to confidence in electives, 1852;—and want of responsibility, 1866——Reduction of number immaterial, 1865.

Report, 1885—*continued.*

McCann, Mr. Harry. (Analysis of his Evidence)—*continued.*

Ex officios should be replaced by guardians elected by owners not merely of land, 1858-63, 1878-81;—which would improve attendance, 1860, 1866——They need not be magistrates, 1862——The other guardians should be elected exclusively by occupiers. 1858, 1879——This plan would make maximum cumulative vote immaterial, 1875-7;—which is now 36; 1869-73;—and should be reduced to 18; 1874.

Lists of voters should be revised annually by County Court Judge, 1822-6, 1843; —which would save expense by discouraging contests and election petitions, 1824, 1826-30, 1833-5, 1842, 1890;—and should all be printed in July, 1831-2—— Costs of contests perhaps rightly on rates, 1829-30——Costs of election petitions should not be on rates, 1838-40;—but might be left to judge, 1841-2——Security for costs should be given, 1836-7.

Minors might vote through guardians, 1844-5——Voting papers should carry one vote each, 1882——Out-door relief, 1883-6;—not given to evicted tenants as such, 1887-9——So much as 1*l.* not given, 1886, 1888.

McMahon, Mr. John, referred to, *Carden* 2558-60.

MAGISTRATES:

Appointment by Lieutenant sometimes overruled by Lord Chancellor, *Bagwell* 879.

More numerous than in England, *Morris* 613;—but not so much so now, *Spaight* 804-6——Are being largely added to in Roscommon, *Smyth* 1331-2, 1353-4, 1367-8—— Number sometimes insufficient for *ex officios, Robinson* 7-9, 158; *Morris* 480; *Spaight* 711 2.

All should not necessarily be *ex officios, Morris* 598; *Bagwell* 877, 919.

If qualified, entitled to be *ex officios, Robinson* 9-18. *See also* EX OFFICIOS (7).—— Scandals from want of qualification, *Smyth* 1242-4, 1251——Substitution of non-magistrates as *ex officios* would not improve attendance, *Molloy* 1670, 1727-31.

Represent property, *Smyth* 1332-4,—best, *Molloy* 1727-31;—less so than formerly, *Spaight* 840-2; *Bagwell* 877-8; *Hewson* 1516. *See also* EX OFFICIOS (5)

Stipendiary magistrates not *ex officios, Robinson* 13——Nor are borough magistrates, *Morris* 589.

Are often agents, *Molloy* 1739.

Malcolmson, Mr., referred to, *Walsh* 2050, 2059.

Maryborough Convent referred to, *Carden* 2575.

Maryborough Dispensary Committee. Composition of, *Meehan* 2234-7.

Maryborough Dispensary District referred to, *Meehan* 2140-1.

Maryborough Electoral Division. Property vote strong, *Meehan* 2167-74; *Carden* 2507 ——Fraudulent proxies, *Meehan* 2145-54, 2164, 2202——Intimidation by landlord, *ib.* 2129——Mistakes in distribution of voting papers, *ib.* 2131——Outdoor relief, *Carden* 2572-3 *See also Mountmellick Union.*

Mayo referred to, *Bourke* 276-8; *Smyth* 1247.

Medical Charities Act, 1851, fixes qualification of Dispensary Committee, *Gray* 1093; *Molloy* 1675-6.

MEEHAN, MR. PATRICK A., grocer, a Nationalist, elected guardian of Mountmellick Union, and chairman since last April (2115-20, 2159-63).

Elected chairman at last election, *Carden* 2495——Defeated by excessive proxy vote, *ib.* 2507: *Fenelon* 2488——Supported jobbery in contracts, *Carden* 2558, 2562;—and Nationalist resolution, *ib* 2566—— Attempt of, to put Maryborough nuns on rate-book, *ib.* 2575.

Analysis of his Evidence (2115-2340).

Triennial elections approved, as saving expense and worry, and giving time for lists, 2122 5, 2133——Better than yearly renewal of one-third of Board, 2209-10.

Ballot approved, as preventing landlord intimidation and mistakes in issuing voting papers, 2126-33, 2135, 2318-28——No intimidation by occupiers, 2128——Courthouses, schools, or dispensaries, or rooms in farms should be the polling places, 2133-7 ——Present electoral divisions the best, 2138-42.

Proxies fraudulent, 2144-54, 2164-6;—but not brought before Local Government Board, 2197-2201, 2211-2,—owing to dilatoriness of that office, 2200-8—— Fraud can be prevented only by personal voting, 2155-7, 2189-91——Excessive vote for small property, 2167-76——System bad, 2177——Should be abolished, even though hardship might

Report, 1885—*continued*.

MEEHAN, MR. PATRICK A. (Analysis of his Evidence)—*continued*.
might result, 2178-84, 2188, 2329, 2332, 2338——Time for polling might be extended for owners, 2189.

Ex officio objectionable as too powerful, 2239-41, 2265-7——Attend badly except to elect chairman, 2267-79, 2333 ——Are not representative, 2262-4, 2330-1——Give extravagant pensions, 2248-61——Do not administer out-door relief better than electives, 2301-5——Should at least be ratepayers, 2224, 2262-3——Should be reduced, 2273;—if not abolished altogether, 2193, 2213, 2272, 2327, 2332;—but should be retained rather than proxies, 2339——Would not be so much objected to if they did the work, 2268, 2274, 2333.

Owners pay five-eighths of rates, 2183,—and should be fairly represented, 2193, 2197 ——Are so by voting power alone, 2184, 2187, 2192-6, 2242-6, 2317-8, 2327-34,— being in a minority, 2247, 2334——Rates press most heavily on occupiers, 2184-6.

Cumulative vote should be retained, 2328, 2331-2——Should be unlimited if *ex officios* abolished, 2335-7.

Chairman: Election of, should not be a party question, 2270, 2291-2, 2295-6—— *Ex officio* sometimes incompetent, 2271——Not in harmony with board, 2279—— Ousting of *ex officio* not the cause of maladministration, 2297-2300——Leaguer chairman not elected on political grounds, 2296.

Elective Guardians: Qualification should be lowered by Statute, 2225-32;—as also for Dispensary Committee, 2233-8——Administer rates fairly, 2195-6——Do not job in contracts, 2306-16.

Vacancies: Provision for, approved, 2223.
Minors should have no vote at all, 2218-22.
Election Petitions: Injustice of Local Government Board in dealing with them, 2158 ——Security for costs should be given, 2214-7.

MINORS. See also *Lunatics*.
Cannot vote, *Hewson* 1399,—by law, *Robinson* 151-2; *Morris* 608-9——Do so, *Fenelon* 2427.

Occupiers have no vote, *Tyrrell* 1002——Are allowed to vote, *Robinson* 153.
Owners allowed to vote through guardian, *Robinson* 149, 151-2; *Morris* 607; *Spaight* 662;—by proxy, *Tyrrell* 1003.

Should vote through guardian, by law, *Robinson* 149, 150, 153, 237; *Bourke* 302; *Morris* 471, 610; *Spaight* 661; *Tyrrell* 1001, 1004; *Smyth* 1239-41; *Hewson* 1398-9; *Molloy* 1668-9; *McCann* 1845, 1847; *Carden* 2516;—even when guardian a woman, *Tyrrell* 1005;—and age should be specified, *Robinson* 153.

Should vote, if possible, *Fenelon* 2419-28;—but not through others, *ib.* 2420-1; *Meehan* 2218-22.

Should not vote, *McCann* 1844.
Have no Parliamentary or Municipal vote. *Meehan* 2218, 2222.

Mohill Union. Outdoor relief improperly applied for, *Spaight* 752.

MOLLOY, MR. EBENEZER, for thirty-four years clerk of Naas Union, and president of Union Officers' Association, and deputed by them (1597-1601).

Analysis of his Evidence (1597-1782).

Triennial elections an improvement, 1603-4.
Ballot approved, as ensuring secrecy, 1605——Otherwise present system as good, 1605-11——No intimidation, 1612-3——Ballot hard for women and sick persons, 1614, 1620;—and costly, 1614——Polling should be at petty sessions courts in dispensary districts, 1615-9.

Proxies should not be extended to occupiers, 1621-5——Often turn elections, 1632-40——Abolition would disfranchise owners, 1627-31, 1646;—whose voting power is already inadequate, 1634-45, 1752-8——Complained of only by popular candidates, 1759-63.

Ex-officios should be ratepayers, but not necessarily magistrates, 1670, 1713, 1729, 1739-42——Should be increased rather than reduced, 1695——Owner's right to representation denied by popular party, 1695, 1700——Presence of *ex-officios* salutary, 1704-6, 1728, 1766-8, 1776-8; but not much politeness shown them, 1779-82—— Should have power to resign, 1707-10——Should be elected by magistrates, 1711-23, 1732-8.

Plan of property guardians would not secure better attendance, 1725-31, 1733.

Elective Guardians: lower qualification would produce stupid guardians, 1671-4, 1690-3;—and encourage politics, 1693———Qualification not complained of, 1688-9;—

MOLLOY, MR. EBENEZER. (Analysis of his Evidence)—*continued.*
nor evaded, 1682-7——Should not be abolished, 1678-81, 1694—— Electives not owners, 1749-51——Elect officials on political grounds, 1700-3.
Outdoor relief increased, though fairly administered, 1769-72.
Nominations should be twenty-one days before poll, 1647-50.
Returning officer should sit from ten to five, to hear claims, 1647 ; and should hear objections also, 1773.
List of Voters for contested divisions only should be printed, 1647-53, 1655-6, 1659-61—.—Objection before returning officer should precede appeal, 1653-5, 1775 ;— and register should be final after signature, 1653-5, 1774-5.
Election Petitions: security for costs needed, 1663——Costs should be borne by parties, 1662-7 ;—by rates if returning officer not seriously blamable, 1666.
Minors should vote through guardians, 1668-9.
Cumulative Vote: Maximum of eighteen, with old mode of aggregation, should be reverted to, 1743-7, 1764-5.

Molony, Major. Relief to his evicted tenants, *Bourke* 332-353.

Monastervan, referred to, *Ringwood* 1551.

MORRIS, MR. GEORGE, for five years Commissioner of Local Government Board, and formerly for 20 years elected and *ex-officio* guardian of three unions (Lough Rea, Galway, and another) in West of Ireland, and Vice Chairman of Galway Union (434-9, 479, 542-6, 584, 622), and for some years Chairman of Galway Town Commissioners (444-5); also large farmer and agent (451).

Analysis of his Evidence (434-642).
Triennial elections approved, 440.
Ballot an improvement, 441-2——Embodiment of Penal Clauses of Ballot Act in Bill should be absolute, 580.
Cumulative Vote: Maximum should be eighteen, proxies and *ex-officio* guardians remaining as they are, 498-500 — Is now thirty, 547——One voting paper for six votes convenient, 447 ;—though witness formerly in favour of one paper for each vote, as for Galway Town Commissioners, 443-7, 548.
Voting claims should be lodged two months before polling-day, 458 9 ;—and rates paid before list of voters made out, 460 ;—or register signed some days before election, 561-2——Revision of list should deal with objections as well as claims, 555—— Subject to appeal to county court judge, register should be conclusive, 556-8.
Election petitions often frivolous, 461-2 —— Should be tried by county court judge, 461——Petitioner should give security for costs, 463-4, 467——Costs should be at judge's discretion, 484-5——Might fairly fall on rates, 465-6.
Fresh election should be at discretion of Local Government Board, unless demanded by guardians, 473——Present system satisfactory, 473.
Elective Guardians: Qualification should remain discretionary, 474-8——If too low, would impair attendance, 474, 574 ;—and encourage corruption, 475,—and excessive outdoor relief, 539 —— Elective guardians more open to corrupt influence than *ex officios,* 563-5, 596—— A few are also owners, 622-3, 625-7—— Are often as good guardians as *ex officios,* 633, 640 ;—and thoroughly honest, 484 ;—but have not the same interest in economy, 629-31, 635-8 ;—and are more timid in striking rates, 635-8, 641—— Are inconsistent in their policy, 634——Should not be reduced in number, 642.
Elective guardians attend better than *ex officios,* 591-2 ;—and as well at election of officers, 593-4——Can do so more easily, 575-7.
Ex-officio guardians more business-like, 479, 540,—and keep down rates, 483-4—— Number should not be reduced, 479-84, 495, 523 ;— nor increased, 597-8, 613,— property being now fairly represented, 599-601 ;—though not unduly, 531, 611-2, 629-30 ;—landlords having little influence on elections, 614-21.
Ex officios attend badly, 523, 543 ;—owing to irrelevant political discussions at boards, 580-1 ;—owing to being slighted, 566 ;—and out-voted, 580 ;— owing to non-residence, 579,—and having other duties, 667-70,—which, however, applies also to elective guardians, 572-3.
Difficult to excuse them, 566, 578——Attended better before agitation, 583,— especially in Galway Union, 585-90—— May attend better when agitation over, 582 ——Should be elected by magistrates, 523-7,— which might slightly improve attendance, 527-30, 541—— Attend well at election of chairman, 491, 493-4 ;—and rightly so, 492, 571.

Proxies

Report, 1885—continued.

MORRIS, MR. GEORGE. (Analysis of his Evidence)—continued.
Proxies can only turn elections, 449-50, 531-8, 628——Give fair representation, 508 ——Abolition would partly disfranchise owners, 448-51;—which would be unfair in view of burdens on them, 451-3, 490, 611-2——Case of voting at municipal elections not parallel, 501-7——Banks and railways would be partly disfranchised, 454-7, 549-54——Voting by registered letter disapproved, 468-70, 517-22——Proxies not objectionable, 602——Dislike to them, recently, as checking patronage by people, 603-6.
Proxies: Use of, increasing, 509——Large number held by one person not objectionable, 510-1——But duration should be limited to three years, 512-6.
Chairmen: Importance of good, 402, 571, 624-5——Lately ousted for trying to prevent irrelevant discussions, 496-7.
Vice-guardians appointed when guardians shrink from their duty, 638.
Out-door relief given in excessive amount, 484-9,—for political purposes, 487 ;—to families of suspects not entitled to it, 484-6.
Minors and Lunatics: Trustees and guardians of, should vote for them by law, 471-2, 607-10.

Mountmellick Electoral Division. Statistics of election, *Carden* 2504——Result not yet determined by Local Government Board, *ib.* 2504-6; *Meehan* 2200, 2203. *See* also *Mountmellick Union.*

Mountmellick Union, large, *Carden* 2491 ;—in two counties, *Meehan* 2119——Valuation, *Carden* 2535-6——In hands of Leaguers, *Meehan* 2306——Contested elections, *ib.* 2123——Landlord intimidation, *ib.* 2126-30——Evidence contradicted, *Carden* 2528, 2557——Number of guardians, *Meehan* 2243-4, 2276 ; *Carden* 2496-7, 2543-5, 2547-8——Qualification, *Meehan* 2226-7——*Ex officio* not a ratepayer, *ib.* 2263—— Attendance of *ex officios* bad, *ib.* 2275-6——Outdoor relief, *ib.* 2280-90, 2303-5 ; *Carden* 2574——*See* also *Borris, Lacka, Maryborough,* and *Mountmellick Electoral Divisions.*

Moyles, Mr. *James*, referred to, *Carden* 2558.

Multiple Vote. See CUMULATIVE VOTE.

N.

Naas Union. Valuation, *Molloy* 1641-2——Electoral districts, *ib.* 1648, 1659, 1749—— Electoral divisions, *ib.* 1748; *Fenelon* 2396——Number of guardians, *ib.* 2396, 2399 ; *Molloy* 1750, 1752——Qualification, *ib.* 1672, 1685 ; *Fenelon* 2433——Property vote strong. *ib.* 2479——No intimidation, *Molloy* 1613, 1778——Attendance of *ex officios*, *ib.* 1704, 1776-7 ;—who are not much complained of, *Fenelon* 2446 ;—but electives better, *ib.* 2446, 2470, 2477-——Vacancy among guardians, *ib.* 2431——Chairmen, *ib.* 2483 ——Clerk, *Fenelon* 2382——Neglect of duty by guardian, *ib.* 2393-5——Salaries and pensions given, *ib.* 2447-69. *See* also *Curraulway* and *Gilltown Electoral Divisions.*

National League. See LAND LEAGUE.

New Ross Union, agricultural, *Ringwood* 1579——Rates, *ib.* 1574-5.

Nicholls, Sir *George.* His report on proxies quoted, *Robinson* 46-7——On *ex officios, ib.* 162.

Nomination of guardians, received on 4th March, *Robinson* 6; *Molloy* 1647-50——Invalidated by want of qualification, *ib.* 1686-7.

Nominator of guardian. See ELECTION PETITIONS.

Notice of Election issued on 25th February, *Robinson* 5——Publication charged on union, *ib.* 146.

Notices of Voters' Lists being ready, prescribed, *Molloy* 1648, 1653. *See* also LISTS OF VOTERS.

O.

OCCUPIERS:
Vote upon valuation, *Robinson* 4, 266;—by entering name in rate-book, *Hewson* 1394 ; —without a claim to vote, *ib.* 1393, *Robinson* 263, 266-7.
Must vote in person, *Robinson* 4, 76 ; *Ringwood* 1329——Rightly so, *Bagwell* 856—— Do not require proxies, *Robinson* 105——Extension of proxies to, see PROXIES—— Effect of abolition of Proxies on, see PROXIES (4).

(130—IND.) K K Proportion

Report, 1885—*continued.*

OCCUPIERS--continued.

Proportion of votes to persons, *Hewson* 1462-4, 1468;—to rateability, *Fox* 1917-35, 1939-41——Voting power curtailed by cumulative vote, *Bourke* 389;—but less than in case of owners, *ib.* 390.

Heavy burden of rates on, *Meehan* 2185-6; *Fenelon* 2366-9;--to some extent, *Bourke* 343-4; *Morris* 490; *Smyth* 1279, 1286——Have as great interest in economy as owners, *Meehan* 2184——Contrary opinion, *Robinson* 200-7. *See also* ELECTIVE GUARDIANS. EX OFFICIOS. OWNERS. PROXIES——Think increased rates will reduce rent, *Spaight* 731-2——Consider rate in lease, *Fenelon* 2370.

Readiness to take outdoor relief, *Smyth* 1315-6. *See also* OUTDOOR RELIEF.

Support League candidates, *Tyrrell* 973; *Fenelon* 2488;—but not necessarily so, *ib.* 2480, 2488—·-The larger generally do so, *Hewson* 1468. 1470, 1512;—but not the smaller, *ib.* 1468-9, 1512;—who would regret abolition of *ex officios*, *ib.* 1512-4——Class feeling between owners and occupiers, *Smyth* 1343-9.

Minor occupiers, see MINORS.

Officials appointed for political reasons, *Bourke* 354-8; *Spaight* 717, 722; *Ringwood* 1548-64; *Molloy* 1700 3——This condemned, *Meehan* 2370, 2292, 2295——Jobbery in election of, see ELECTIVE GUARDIANS (4); EX OFFICIOS (8)——Control of Local Government Board over appointment of. See LOCAL GOVERNMENT BOARD. *See also Salaries.*

Onions, *Mr.*, referred to, *Carden* 2507.

Orford, *Mr.*, referred to, *Molloy* 1703.

OUTDOOR RELIEF:

The chief item of expenditure, *Robinson* 207; *Bourke* 341-3; *Spaight* 706; *Bagwell* 892; *Ringwood* 1580——Thriftless, *Bagwell* 892; *Ringwood* 1580;—and difficult to check, *Spaight* 761, 775.

Burden of, on occupiers, *Bourke* 343; *Morris* 490——But chiefly thrown on landlord, *Bourke* 344; *Morris* 490; *Smyth* 1279, 1286.

Sometimes necessary, *Spaight* 775——Given by clerk on emergency, *Walsh* 2063.

Persons legally entitled to it, *Spaight* 769-72; *Molloy* 1771; *Fox* 2006——Widows with children should have it, *Molloy* 1771.

Evicted tenants legally entitled to it, *Robinson* 190, 193, 208-9; *Morris* 484-5; *Spaight* 752, 772; *Smyth* 1271-2, 1277-9——Law unaltered, *Spaight* 762-4 -·· Sometimes exceeded, *Robinson* 193; *Bourke* 339; *Morris* 486; *Spaight* 772——Such cases disallowed by auditors, *Robinson* 193, 208-9; *Bourke* 347-53; *Spaight* 773-4.

Excessive relief given to, *Robinson* 166-8, 191-2; *Bourke* 332-40; *Morris* 484-9, 539; *Spaight* 707, 752-3, 760, 765; *Smyth* 1260-1, 1265-82; *Hewson* 1420-5, 1431-2; *Fox* 1993-4; *Walsh* 2084-5; *Meehan* 2285;—even when not destitute, *Bourke* 333, 345; *Morris* 486; *Spaight* 752; *Smyth* 1261, 1265-6, 1269, 1272; *Hewson* 1420;—and not paying rent, *Smyth* 1270——Refused to such, *Walsh* 2088——Less now, *Robinson* 166; *Spaight* 766; *Smyth* 1264——Not less now, *Spaight* 755, 766.

1 *l.* a week given to suspects, *Robinson* 167, 101; *Morris* 488; *Spaight* 752-3; *Smyth* 1260-1, 1268, 1272, 1279; *Hewson* 1420, 1424-5, 1431-2, 1505;—to save Land League funds, *Smyth* 1279-80; *Hewson* 1506-7——More given, *Bourke* 340; *Morris* 488; *Spaight* 691; *Walsh* 2084——6 *s* a week despised, *Smyth* 1285——1 *l.* not given, *McCann* 1886-9; *Fox* 1991-2.

Usual amount given to others than suspects, *Robinson* 168; *Morris* 489; *Spaight* 760; *Smyth* 1266-7, 1284; *Hewson* 1420, 1433, 1505; *McCann* 1885-9; *Meehan* 2290, 2303-5.

Increase in, until 1884, *Robinson* 209-19; *Spaight* 757-9, 765-8; *Gray* 1124-5; *Smyth* 1258-9, 1311-4; *Hewson* 1407, 1411-3; *Molloy* 1769; *Fox* 1990, 1995, 2001, 2019-20; *Carden* 2572-3——Formerly very small, *Robinson* 210, 213; *Spaight* 756-8; *Hewson* 1412-3——Not increasing now, *Robinson* 218-9; *Molloy* 1769-——Increase not due to distress, *Spaight* 767-8; *Gray* 1124; *Smyth* 1258-9; *Carden* 2573-4——Only partly so, *Robinson* 215; *Fox* 2002-3.

No increase in, *Walsh* 2110.

Numbers receiving relief, *Robinson* 211, 214, 217——Small compared with England, *ib.* 212.

Kept down by *ex officios*, *Robinson* 183-4; *Morris* 540; *Spaight* 672-705, 708, 754 ——Given by them on political grounds, *Meehan* 2303-5——Excessive amounts given by Leaguers, *Ringwood* 1580; *Walsh* 2084——Given too readily by them, *Ringwood* 1580, 1584; *Fox* 1986-9, 2014——Improperly refused by them, *ib.* 2085——Administered equally fairly by both classes, *Meehan* 2282-7, 2301-2. *See also* ELECTIVE GUARDIANS (4); EX OFFICIOS (8).

Improperly

Report, 1885—continued.

OUTDOOR RELIEF—continued.
Improperly given, *Hewson* 1414-8; *Fox* 2006-7——Contrary evidence, *Molloy* 1770-2; *Fox* 1991-3——Not improperly refused, *Speight* 797——Applied for by evicted guardian, *ib.* 726-30 ——Intimidation with regard to it, *Smyth* 1261-4, 1280. *See also INTIMIDATION.*

House test enforced, *Ringwood* 1581-2; *Molloy* 1770——Very seldom by Leaguers, *Fox* 2006-11——Not more strictly by *ex officiis*, *Meehan* 2302——House refused by beggars, *Ringwood* 1582-4—— Workhouse training bad for children, *Molloy* 1771.

Should be in food and fuel, under Act, *Smyth* 1261, 1271-2, 1277-9, 1290 ;—which is difficult, *Hewson* 1484——Act evaded, *Smyth* 1261; *Hewson* 1424, 1484 ;—but charge disallowed, *Smyth* 1261, 1290.

Readily accepted, *Ringwood* 1580——Squandered by recipients, *Speight* 692-3; *Smyth* 1315-6.

Would be diminished by benefit societies, if these were practicable, *Speight* 811-5.

Relief list revised every month, *Gray* 1125-6.

Control of, by Local Government Board, see *LOCAL GOVERNMENT BOARD.*

OWNERS. *See also ELECTIVE GUARDIANS; EX OFFICIOS; MAGISTRATES; OCCUPIERS; PROXIES.*

Generally magistrates, *Molloy* 1722-4.

Vote in respect of rent, *Robinson* 4—— Right to vote troublesome to establish, *Hewson* 1393-4—— Most often not claimed, *ib.* 1471 —— Lapses after five years, *Robinson* 263-5; *Hewson* 1393——Might last three years, *Robinson* 264, 268——Should last for life, *Hewson* 1393-4. *See also PROXIES.*

Excessive vote out of small rating, *Meehan* 2167-76; *Fenelon* 2347, 2353, 2359-60, 2488.

May vote by proxy, *Robinson* 4 ;—and also in person, *Fox* 1946-7; *Meehan* 2170-2 ;—but not on same qualification in practice, *Fox* 1948-9——Proportion of non-residents, *ib.* 1913-5. *See also PROXIES.*

Heavy burden of rates on, *Bourke* 344; *Morris* 452-3, 504-5, 629-30; *Speight* 714; *Smyth* 1218; *Hewson* 1404, 1457-8, 1471; *Molloy* 1641-2; *Fenelon* 2373; *Carden* 2500——Pay about five-eighths, *Robinson* 45-6, 116-7, 162; *Bourke* 310; *Speight* 451, 629; *Speight* 714, 781; *Bagwell* 916; *Tyrrell* 1011; *Gray* 1128-30; *Smyth* 1218-9; *Molloy* 1695-6; *McCann* 1867; *Fox* 1917; *Walsh* 2053; *Meehan* 2183; *Carden* 2535-6 ;—and more, *Robinson* 47, 118-9, 162; *Bourke* 310; *Morris* 451; *Speight* 781; *Gray* 1135; *Hewson* 1458; *Molloy* 1636, 1640; *Fox* 1954-7; *Carden* 2509-10 ;—especially in poor districts, *Bourke* 391 ;—and especially if loyalist occupiers and long leaseholders are added, *Tyrrell* 1012-5——Practically do not pay five-eighths, *Fenelon* 2366-9.

Pay half of tenant's rate, *Robinson* 80, 117, 162; *Bourke* 343; *Morris* 452; *Speight* 781; *Bagwell* 856, 859; *Smyth* 1218, 1230; *Fox* 2025-6; *Fenelon* 2373 ;—but not in England, *Robinson* 80, 162——Pay whole rate on holdings under 4 *l.*, *ib.* 4, 116, 162; *Bourke* 290-2, 343; *Morris* 452; *Speight* 781; *Bagwell* 868; *Smyth* 1218; *Meehan* 2185. *See also Immediate Lessors.*

Desire to throw rates on owners, *Smyth* 1279-80, 1286; *Hewson* 1506-7—— Contrary evidence, *Speight* 783.

Have a right to be fairly represented, *Fenelon* 2376; *Meehan* 2183, 2187——Right sometimes denied, *Molloy* 1695-1700 ——Are fairly represented by being guardians and voters, *Morris* 599-601; *Gray* 1150; *Carden* 2547-9——Insufficiently so, *Bagwell* 916-7, 921; *Tyrrell* 1010; *Fox* 1979-82——Over-represented, *Meehan* 2183, 2192-4, 2246; *Fenelon* 2376-7.

Sufficiently represented by voting power alone, *Meehan* 2246, 2328-30, 2332-4, 2338; *Fenelon* 2384, 2422, 2426 ;—with unlimited cumulative vote, *Meehan* 2328-9, 2332, 2335-7 ;—with cumulative maximum, *McCann* 1869-71; being a minority, *ib.* 2247, 2334 —— Proportion of owners to occupiers, *Smyth* 1300-10; *Molloy* 1753-8 — Carry candidates, *Tyrrell* 977-81; *McCann* 1868-9; *Meehan* 2193, 2242-4, 2318; *Fenelon* 2479-81, 2488 ——Have more influence than tenants, *Bagwell* 940; *Meehan* 2239, 2245, 2318. *See also INTIMIDATION.*——Should not have too much, *Bagwell* 919—— Are represented by electives, *Gray* 1131-3; *Meehan* 2195-6, 2246; *Fenelon* 2379-81, 2390-2, 2390-400, 2445, 2475, 2479 ;—even if they do not carry candidates, *Meehan* 2246——Contrary evidence, *Gray* 1131-3; *Molloy* 1695-6; *Meehan* 2195-6.

Voting power insufficient representation, *Robinson* 169-70; *Bourke* 287-94, 369-78, 387-90, 411; *Morris* 531-7, 614-21; *Speight* 715, 750; *Bagwell* 862; *Tyrrell* 969-76, 984; *Gray* 1134-44; *Smyth* 1220-5, 1228; *Hewson* 1457-77; *Molloy* 1633-45; *Fox* 1918-34, 1937-41, 1958-60, 2029; *Meehan* 2317-8, 2333; *Carden* 2507-8, 2511 —— Can only turn an election, *Morris* 537-8; *Speight* 751; *Smyth* 1220-3; *Hewson* 1464.

(130—IND.)   K K 2   Proportion

Report, 1885—continued.

OWNERS—continued.
Proportion of votes to persons, *Hewson* 1459-61, 1468; *Molloy* 1753-8;—to rateability, *Tyrrell* 977-81; *Fox* 1918-34, 1937, 1958-60.
Representation of should not be reduced, *Bagwell* 916-9, 921;—by abolishing proxies, *Robinson* 42-7. *See also* PROXIES;—or by diminishing number of *ex officios*, *ib.* 171. *See also* EX OFFICIOS (2).—— Interest of, in good administration, permanent, *ib.* 162, 200-7; *Bourke* 320. *See also* EX OFFICIOS (8); ELECTIVE GUARDIANS (3), OCCUPIERS.—— Representation of, by *ex officios*, very important, *Bourke* 381. *See* also EX OFFICIOS (10).—— By proxies unimportant, *Bourke* 429; *Morris* 614; *Smyth* 1226-7.
Do not require protection of ballot, *Robinson* 69.
Representation of, by guardians elected by them exclusively. See PROPERTY GUARDIANS.
Not a homogeneous class, *Smyth* 1336-52——Real owners difficult to ascertain, *ib.* 1305,1340-1,1350-2——Consequent difficulty with Sanitary Acts, *ib.* 1341, 1350-2——Class feeling among, *ib.* 1343-7, 1349——No difficulty in ascertaining owners, *Hewson* 1500.
Vote for Loyalists, *Smyth* 1301; *Molloy* 1634, 1638; *Carden* 2504, 2507——Class feeling between owners and occupiers, *Smyth* 1343-9.

P.

Pallaskenry, referred to, *Hewson* 1406.
Pallaskenry Electoral Division. Property vote in, *Hewson* 1464-71. *See* also *Rathkeale Union*.
Parliamentary Voters (Ireland) Act, 1850. Qualified person can be put on rate-book by guardians, *Carden* 2575-7——This objectionable, *ib.* 2575-7——Assistant overseers under, *Molloy* 1703.
Parliamentary Voters' Lists, referred to, *Fox* 1970-5.
Paterson, Mr., referred to, *Tyrrell* 1026, 1021-2, 1039-40.
PENSIONS, to officials of Boards:
Fixed maximum, *Meehan* 2253-4, 2256-7——Subject to approval of Local Government Board, *ib.* 2255—— Should be left to guardians, *ib.* 2253, 2255——Case of maximum given, *ib.* 2252-61;—of excessive, given, *Fenelon* 2453-7, 2461-7——Refused to chaplain, *ib.* 2461, 2468-9.
Alleged extravagance in, by *ex officios*, see EX OFFICIOS (8).
See also SALARIES.
Petty Sessions Court Houses. See POLLING-PLACES.
Pim, Mr. J., referred to, *Carden* 2560.
Plurality of Votes. See CUMULATIVE VOTE.
Polling Booths. See POLLING-PLACES.
Polling Days. See ELECTIONS.
Polling Districts. See POLLING-PLACES.
POLLING OFFICERS. Assistant returning officers recommended, *Meehan* 2133——Should be constables of some education, *Smyth* 1191; *Molloy* 1614;—or local magistrates unconnected with division, *Smyth* 1193-4——Should make no charge, *ib.* 1191-2.
Lists of voters for, see LIST OF VOTERS.

POLLING-PLACES:
Provided by Ballot Act, *Robinson* 60——Present electoral divisions approved, *Meehan* 2138.
Polling booths would be required under ballot, *Smyth* 1176-80.
Should be the dispensary houses, *Hewson* 1378, 1380-3; *Meehan* 2133, 2136;—where they exist, *ib.* 2137, 2139;—which would save expense, *Hewson* 1384——Dispensary districts too large for electoral division, *Molloy* 1616-8; *Meehan* 2140-2;—but not often so, *Molloy* 1618-9——May be so in west, *Hewson* 1381—— Such might be divided, *ib.* 1382, 1426-9;—which would diminish power of mob, *ib.* 1429, 1478, 1482 ——Not very large in south, *ib.* 1381, 1383——Generally contain a court-house, *ib.* 1278, 1380, 1479-81——Are conterminous with several electoral divisions, *ib.* 1379-80.

Petty

Report, 1885—*continued.*

POLLING-PLACES—continued.

Petty Sessions Courts should be used, *Hewson* 1378, 1380, 1479-83; *Molloy* 1615; *Meehan* 2133-6;—which would save expense, *ib.* 2135;—but elections would take some days, *Hewson* 1482-3——These courts too sparse, *Smyth* 1178-9;—sometimes none, *Meehan* 2137;—generally one in each dispensary district, *Hewson* 1378, 1380, 1479-81.

School houses recommended, *Meehan* 2133, 2136;—failing which, a room in a farmhouse, *ib.* 2133, 2136-7——Schoolrooms probably not available, *Smyth* 1183.

Workhouses recommended as cheapest, *Smyth* 1181, 1184;—though distant, *ib.* 1182, 1184.

Poor Law. One administration for England and Ireland before 1847, *Bourke* 270-4——Little alteration needed in Ireland, *Gray* 1145, 1149.

Poor Law Commissioners settled area of unions, *Robinson* 112.

Poor Law Guardians (Ireland) Bill, 1884. Approved as a whole, *Fenelon* 2343——Introduction unseasonable, *Fox* 2034——Bill deprecated, *Gray* 1145, 1149-50.

Poor Relief Act, 1601, referred to, *Bagwell* 856.

Poor Relief (Ireland) Act, 1838, the original Irish Act, *Robinson* 47, 182; *Spaight* 804——One-third of Board elected by magistrates, *Robinson* 162, 182——Unpopular among landlords, *Bagwell* 865—— Aggregation of votes under, *Robinson* 231, 235——Scale of cumulative vote under, *ib.* 4.

Poor Relief (Ireland) Act, 1843, transferred rates of 4 *l.* holdings on landlords, *Bagwell* 868.

Poor Relief (Ireland) Act, 1847, increased number of *ex officios, Robinson* 162; *Bagwell* 868——Selection, when number excessive, *Molloy* 1737——Before it, no separate Irish administration, *Bourke* 270-4——Out-door relief to be in food and fuel, *Smyth* 1261.

Poor Relief (Ireland) Act, 1849, gives qualification of *ex officios, Robinson* 9, 16; *Walsh* 2094.

Poor Relief (Ireland) Act, 1862. Claim to vote under, should be two months before polling, *Robinson* 56——Aggregation of votes under, *ib.* 231, 235.

Poulett Thompson, Mr., referred to, *Bagwell* 865.

Power, Mr., of Bellevue, referred to, *Walsh* 2102-5.

Power, Pierce, case of, *Walsh* 2084-5.

Powerscourt, Lord, referred to, *Ringwood* 1565.

Property. See OWNERS.

PROPERTY GUARDIANS:

Half the Board should be property guardians elected by owners exclusively, *Bagwell* 858-61, 863; *McCann* 1858-60, 1880-1;—to replace *ex officios, Bagwell* 863-4, 919; *Hewson* 1496-7, 1500-4;—the other half being elected exclusively by occupiers, *McCann* 1858, 1876-9;—owners who are also occupiers choosing what capacity to vote under, *Bagwell* 862;—which would present some difficulty, *Smyth* 1348;—or voting in both capacities, *Bagwell* 862;—which some consider not unfair, *ib.* 862;—which is recommended, *Hewson* 1504——Owners would vote for property guardians, *Bagwell* 862.

Property guardians need not be magistrates, *McCann* 1862;—should have no qualification, *Hewson* 1455, 1500-1;—which would bring in others besides landlords, *ib.* 1500-1;—and would represent property of all kinds, *McCann* 1863.

Plan accepted by owners of Limerick, *Hewson* 1501——Fairer than present system in the abstract, *Smyth* 1338, 1340;—and would secure more careful guardians, *ib.* 1339;—attending better, *McCann* 1860, 1866——Would not give owners preponderating influence, *Bagwell* 919-20——Presents no difficulty as to proxies, *Hewson* 1510——Would make maximum of cumulative vote immaterial, *McCann* 1875-7.

Plan complicated, unless owners voted through agents, *Smyth* 1335-7, 1339-42;—owners not being a homogeneous class, and ownership being difficult to determine, *Smyth* 1336, 1339-42, 1350-2;—though they all have a landlord's interest, *ib.* 1349——Might embitter class animosity, *ib.* 1343-7——Contrary opinion, *Hewson* 1497——No difficulty in determining ownership, *ib.* 1500——Would end in deadlock, *Tyrrell* 1045-8——No advantage, *Molloy* 1723-8, 1733——Would not improve attendance, *ib.* 1728-31——Is disliked, *Walsh* 2097.

Occupiers' guardians would be entirely political, *Walsh* 2098.

(130—IND.) K K 3 Protection

Report, 1885—continued.

Protection of Person and Property (Ireland) Act, 1881. Relief to suspects under, *Smyth* 1279.

PROXIES. *See also* ELECTIVE GUARDIANS; OCCUPIERS; OWNERS.
(1.) *Appointment.*
(2.) *Value.*
(3.) *Objections.*
(4.) *Abolition.*
(5.) *Extension.*

(1.) *Appointment:*
Given only by owners and immediate lessors, *Robinson* 4, 78;—irrespective of residence, *ib.* 77-8;—not for land in owner's occupation, *Hewson* 1392——Can be used by owner in addition to personal vote, *Fox* 1946-7;—but not for same qualification, *ib.* 1948-9——Used almost entirely by non-residents, *Fox* 1945, 1951——In England entirely so, *Robinson* 49, 79-80——Can be given by railways and shareholders, *Morris* 455, 457, 551.
Not given in municipal elections, *Morris* 501-7.
Appointed a month before polling day, *Robinson* 37——Should be two months, *Tyrrell* 1066——Last five years, *ib.* 81-2, 263-5; *Morris* 513; *Bagwell* 927; *Tyrrell* 1064-5; *Meehan* 2165;—unless revoked, *Robinson* 87; *Tyrrell* 1064;—or owner dies, *Meehan* 2166——Formerly unlimited, *Robinson* 82——Five years perhaps too long, *Bagwell* 927——Should last three years, *Robinson* 82-4, 264, 268; *Morris* 512, 514-6; *Tyrrell* 1065-6; *Fox* 1961-2;—which would not make much difference, *Bagwell* 933, 937——Should not be renewed for each bye-election, *Morris* 515-6; *Fox* 1962;—but no objection to this except more trouble, *Bagwell* 927-30, 934-7——Is so in public companies, *ib.* 931.
Large number held by one person complained of, *Bourke* 398, 401, 403-4, 421;—objectionable, *Bagwell*, 925-6;—unobjectionable, *Morris* 510-1;—might be limited, *Bourke* 399-402——Is limited, *ib.* 400; *Bagwell* 925;—to twenty proxy appointments, except in case of agents, *Robinson* 84; *Tyrrell* 1063; who generally hold them, *Bagwell* 926.—The same person should hold all one owner's proxies, *Robinson* 85.

(2.) *Value:*
Number used, *Robinson* 23, 73, 110; *Bourke* 374; *Smyth* 1300-2; *Fox* 1932, 1938; *Walsh* 2046-8——General return could be obtained, *Robinson* 73, 75-6, 107-9, 111——Proportions in favour of loyalists and of Leaguers, *Smyth* 1301; *Molloy* 1634, 1638——Little used, *Bourke* 429; *Morris* 614; *Smyth* 1226-7——Owners careless, *ib.* 1227; *Ringwood* 1534; *McCann* 1813-4——Use of, increasing, *Bourke* 430; *Morris* 509——Much used, *Robinson* 75-6; *Spaight* 752;—in contests, *Robinson* 74, 106; *Gray* 1079; *Hewson* 1465-7, especially in towns, *Robinson* 110;—but question whether for political reasons, *Robinson* 122——Used to utmost extent, *Fenelon* 2360. *See also* CONTESTED ELECTIONS.
Could not swamp occupation votes, *Morris* 628; *Tyrrell* 963-5; *Ringwood* 1534;—but can turn elections, *Morris* 449-50, 537-8; *Spaight* 653-4, 818; *Tyrrell* 966-8, 983-7, 1041; *Smyth* 1221-5, 1228; *Hewson* 1466-7; *Molloy* 1632-40; *Walsh* 2049 54, 2064; *Carden* 2504, 2507, 2511;—in some cases, *ib.* 2507-8, 2511.
Are useful, *Spaight* 653-4——A protection to property, *Robinson* 197-9;—in principle, *Bourke* 285, 369, 371;—but of little value practically, *ib.* 287-94, 369-78, 381, 411, 422-3, 428-31; *Morris* 614-8——The only real protection to property, *Bagwell* 856; *Tyrrell* 958; *Walsh* 2043;—and a just one, *Morris* 506, 611-2; *Bagwell* 856——Not used in municipal elections, landlord paying much less of rate, *Morris* 501-7.
No substitute for, known, *Spaight* 819; *Meehan* 2182; *Carden* 2521, 2535. *See also* (4.)——Are a necessity, *Carden* 2533-4——A privilege, *Morris* 519-21.

(3.) *Objections:*
Bad in principle, *Bagwell* 858, 925-6; *Meehan* 2177, 2183-4, 2188; *Fenelon* 2363-4——Contrary opinion, *McCann* 1847——An invidious privilege, *ib.* 1802-8, 1810, 1815-6, 1822, 1848; *Morris* 519-21.
Complained of, *Tyrrell* 960; *Molloy* 1759-60;—recently, *Bourke* 295; *Morris* 603;—by leaguers, *Tyrrell* 961; *Ringwood* 1535-44; *Walsh* 2045;—by popular candidates, *Molloy* 1761, 1763——On political grounds, *Bourke* 296——Contrary evidence, *Morris* 605; *McCann* 1822——On ground of too many in same hands, *Bourke* 398, 401, 421——As swamping occupiers, *Tyrrell* 962, *See* also (2.)——Owing to desire for patronage, *Morris* 604-6——No objection to, *Morris* 602; *Spaight* 816-7; *Tyrrell* 959; *Gray* 1072, 1079, 1081; *Fox* 1912;—not complained of, *Smyth* 1229;—by public, *Molloy*, 1762; *Walsh* 2045——No hardship in retaining them, *Bourke* 411; *Spaight* 817; *Walsh* 2044; *Carden* 2520.

Fraudulent

Report, 1885—continued.

PROXIES—continued.
(3.) *Objections*—continued.
Fraudulent votes, *Meehan* 2144-5, 2154, 2339; *Fearlon* 2346, 2361——Instances given, *Meehan* 2145-54, 2164. 2166, 2202: *Fenelon* 2349-52——Easily manufactured, *ib.* 2346-8, 2359——Difficult to detect, *ib.* 2346, 2349, 2362;—except by clerk, *Meehan* 2153-4; who hinders detection, *Fenelon* 2346-7, 2362——Not brought before Local Government Board, owing to its dilatoriness, *Meehan* 2197-2200, 2211; *Fenelon* 2346 Should be punishable by courts of law, *Meehan* 2180;--but can be prevented only by abolition of proxies, *ib.* 2155-7, 2188-91; *Fenelon* 2348.
No fraudulent votes, *Carden* 2522-3, 2525-7——Such not easier with proxies, *ib.* 2524.
Excessive votes out of small rating, *Meehan* 2174-6; *Fenelon* 2347, 2353, 2359-60, 2488—— This also the case with occupation vote, *ib.* 2354-9.

(4.) *Abolition:*
Abolition desirable, *Meehan* 2144, 2181, 2329, 2332, 2338-9; *Fenelon* 2346, 2360, 2479;--rather than *ex officio*, *Meehan* 2339—— This alone would prevent fraudulent votes, *ib.* 2155-7, 2188-91.
Abolition would partly disfranchise owners, *Robinson* 42-5, 52, 86, 197-9; *Bourke* 285, 369, 379-80; *Morris* 448, 451; *Spaight* 650-2, 791; *Gray* 1071; *Smyth* 1218-9, 1244; *Hewson* 1386; *Ringwood* 1545-6; *Molloy* 1628-30, 1631, 1646; *McCann* 1817; *Fox* 1910-1, 1913 6, 1932, 1935, 1941-6, 1950-1, 1958-9; *Walsh* 2043; *Carden* 2500, 2528-31, 2534——Contrary opinion, *McCann* 1819; *Meehan* 2178-9; except in some cases, *ib.* 2180; *Fenelon* 2385——Objection insufficient, *McCann* 1805-7, 1817-9—— Would disfranchise tenants equally, *Fenelon* 2359, 2386——Such cases rare, *Carden* 2531——Would disfranchise railways and canals, *Morris* 454-7, 551-4; *Carden* 2536-7; —but would not take away vote through officer of a corporation, *Morris* 549-50. See also OWNERS.
Abolition would perhaps bring in worse guardians, *Robinson* 127-8, 200-7, 220-2; *Tyrrell* 983-7; *Ringwood* 1531-3, 1596; *Walsh* 2050-2, 2064; *Carden* 2500-3, 2547-8; —until this checked by ratepayers, *Robinson* 207, 222——Contrary evidence, *Bourke* 431——Would not allay discontent, *ib.* 422-3.
Difficulty might be met by extending time for owners to vote in person, *Meehan* 2199: *Fenelon* 2364-5, 2384—— Contrary opinion, *Robinson* 43, 71-2; *Carden* 2528 31 —— This would be impracticable, *Robinson* 43, 71; *Bourke* 286; *Morris* 448; *Spaight* 791;—and inconvenient, *Robinson* 71——Might be met by voting by registered letters, *Bagwell* 860——Contrary opinion, *Robinson* 50; *Morris* 468-70, 517; *Gray* 1080—— Secrecy could not be ensured, *Robinson* 50-1, 53, 88-103; *Morris* 469-70, 518-22; *Gray* 1080;—though this not always material, *Robinson* 53; *Bagwell* 860;—and proxies are a privilege, *Morris* 519-21——Secrecy could be ensured, *Bagwell* 860——Would involve large correspondence, *Robinson* 102.
Should be retained, *Robinson* 45-8; *Spaight* 650; *Gray* 1071; *Molloy* 1627; *Fox* 1909; *Carden* 2500, 2549;—under present system, *Bagwell* 856-8;—but not if property guardians adopted it, *ib.* 858-9—— Contrary opinion, *Hewson* 1500——If retained, ballot would not affect class of guardians, *Robinson* 104. 115, 200;—and would cause no difficulty, *ib.* 37-41——Would cause difficulty, *Meehan* 2144;—unless proxies extended to occupying owners, *Gray* 1072-7, 1146; *Ringwood* 1522-30.

(5.) *Extension:*
Should be extended to all, *McCann* 1806-12, 1815-6, 1848; *Fenelon* 2360; *Carden* 2532——Contrary opinion, *Robinson* 105; *Molloy* 1621-5——Should be extended to owners when occupiers, *Hewson* 1390-2;—if ballot adopted, *Gray* 1072-6, 1146; otherwise many would be disfranchised, *Gray* 1076 7; *Ringwood* 1522-30;—but personation must be guarded against, *Gray* 1077-9.

Publicans. See ELECTIVE GUARDIANS (1).

Q.

Qualification. See DISPENSARY COMMITTEE; ELECTIVE GUARDIANS; EX OFFICIOS.

Queen's Bench:
Decision as to cumulative vote, reversed on appeal, *Robinson* 6——Decision as to aggregating occupation and immediate lessor votes, *ib.* 231——Litigation as to improper outrelief, *Smyth* 1261, 1271-3.

(130—IND.) K K 4

Report, 1885—continued.

R.

Railways can vote by proxy, *Morris* 455, 551——Seldom do so, *ib.* 454——Have occupation votes. *ib.* 552;—not owner's votes, *ib.* 553——Would be partly disfranchised by abolition of proxies, *ib.* 551-4; *Carden* 2536-7——Shareholders vote by proxy, *Morris* 457.

RATES:

Half of tenants' paid by owner, *Robinson* 80, 117, 162; *Bourke* 343; *Morris* 452; *Spaight* 781; *Bagwell* 856, 859; *Smyth* 1218, 1230; *Fox* 2025-6; *Fenelon* 2373,—but not in England, *Robinson* 80, 162.

Of holdings of 4 *l.* or under paid wholly by immediate lessor, *Robinson* 4, 116, 162; *Bourke* 290-2, 343; *Morris* 452; *Spaight* 781; *Smyth* 1218; *Meehan* 2185;—under Act of 1847, *Bagwell* 868.

Struck in July, *Walsh* 2109-10——In September, *Fox* 1903——Should be administered by persons striking, *ib.* 1903, 1907-8——Should be collected before 1st July, *McCann* 1831.

Increase of, *Spaight* 756-9; *Smyth* 1311-2; *Hewson* 1407, 1410;—not due to increased contracts. *Smyth* 1313-4; nor increased poor population, *Hewson* 1409-10. *See also* ELECTIVE GUARDIANS (3); OUTDOOR RELIEF.

Considered by tenant in taking a lease, *Fenelon* 2370——Saddled with costs of litigation, *Smyth* 1272——For other charges on, see under respective headings.

No time prescribed for payment of arrears to entitle ratepayers to vote, *Robinson* 57-60; *Tyrrell* 993-5——This impracticable under ballot, *Robinson* 57——Should be some time before polling-day, *Carden* 2512-4;—two months before, *Robinson* 57-8; *Tyrrell* 992-5——Should be before list made out, *Morris* 460; *Tyrrell* 992-5; *Gray* 1161-2; *McCann* 1831;—one or two months before, *Walsh* 2109;—and register should be signed a good while before polling-day, *Morris* 561-2.

County cess paid by tenant, *Fox* 2025-6.

Rate Collector. Duties of, under Franchise Act, *Molloy* 1700-2;—transferred to other persons, *ib.* 1700-3——Case of appointment from political motives, *Bourke* 354-8—— Of dishonesty by, *Hewson* 1440.

Rate-book should not be altered by guardians, *Carden* 2575-7.

Rathdown Union, referred to, *Robinson,*73 ——Strong property vote in, *Fenelon* 2479-82.

Rathkeale Union contains several towns, *Hewson* 1408, 1476-7 ——Valuation, *ib.* 1471 ——Proxies, *Bourke* 374——Managed by electives since 1862, *Hewson* 1407, 1485-7 ——Rates and out-door relief. *ib.* 1407——Decrease in labouring population, *ib.* 1409. *See also Castletown* and *Pallaskenry Electoral Divisions.*

REGISTER. *See also* ELECTION PETITIONS; LIST OF VOTERS; REVISION.

Preparation of, *Robinson* 37, 56.

Appeal from, *Robinson* 131, 133-5;—essential, *ib.* 145; *Molloy* 1653-5;—to county court judge, *Morris* 556-7;—after objection before returning officer, *Molloy* 1653-5, 1775. *See also* ELECTION PETITIONS.

Should be conclusive, subject to appeal, *Morris* 558;—after signature, *ib.* 561; *Molloy* 1653-5, 1774; *McCann* 1824——Contrary opinion, *Walsh* 2113——After revision by revising barrister, *Walsh* 2114.

Should be signed a good while before polling day, *Morris* 561-2.

Revision of, see REVISION.

Copies should perhaps be procurable gratis, *Fenelon* 2413-6—— Small demand for them, *ib.* 2414-5.

Registered Letters. See PROXIES (4).

Relief of Distress (Ireland) Act, 1880, referred to, *Spaight* 762-3.

Relieving Officer. See OFFICIALS.

Rental:

The title of owners to vote for guardians, *Robinson* 4—— Not affected by rates, *Bourke* 397——Contrary opinion, *Fenelon* 2370. *See also* ELECTIVE GUARDIANS (3).

Representation of the People Act, 1884, referred to, *Molloy* 1700-1; *Fenelon* 2413.

Return of elections made on 25th March, *Robinson* 6. *See also* ELECTIONS.

Returning

Report, 1885—*continued*.

Returning Officer. His salary charged on union, *Robinson* 146——His costs on election petitions, see ELECTION PETITIONS.—— Should sit from ten to five to hear claims to vote, *Molloy* 1647——Should not be the revising officer, *McCann* 1822-3, 1842, 1890 - —No objection to this, *Walsh* 2113—— Has discretion as to publishing votes, *Gray* 1134, 1148, 1151, 1153, 1160; *Molloy* 1608-10; *Fenelon* 2346-7, 2362. *See also* PROXIES (3). REVISION; *Clerk*.

REVISION. *See also* LIST OF VOTERS; REGISTER.

Of List of Voters. No law for, at present, but done in practice, *Robinson* 62-3——Should include objections as well as claims, *ib*. 61, 64; *Morris* 555; *Molloy* 1773-4.

Time for, too short, *Robinson* 56; *McCann* 1824——Not regulated in Bill, *Morris* 559-60— —Triennial elections would give more time, *Mechan* 2125 — Triennial in Bill, *Robinson* 64——Should be annual, *ib*. 64-5; *McCann* 1825, 1843;—in August, *ib*. 1831;—half yearly, *Molloy* 1657-8.

Should not be by returning officer, *McCann* 1822-3, 1842, 1890——No complaint of this, *Walsh* 2113.

Should be by county court judge, *McCann* 1824, 1826, 1835;—which would save expense, *ib*. 1824, 1826;—by discouraging contests. *ib*. 1826, 1828, 1890;—and election petitions, *ib*. 1835, 1842——Great importance of this, *ib*. 1824-5, 1890.——Unwise and scarcely practicable, *Fox* 1964;—and probably unnecessary, *Fenelon* 2418;—if judge is to hear appeals, *Fox* 1965-7; *Fenelon* 2418.

By revising barrister, might be final, *Walsh* 2114;—but this would throw too much work upon him, *ib*. 2113.

Right to Vote. See OCCUPIERS; OWNERS; CLAIMS TO VOTE.

RINGWOOD, MR. HENRY: elective vice-chairman of Gorey Union (1517-9, 1592-5).

Analysis of his Evidence (1517-96).

Triennial elections approved, 1521.

Ballot might disfranchise women and infirm persons, 1522-30.

Proxies unpopular among Leaguers, 1535-44——Have not much weight in elections, 1534;- -but bring in best guardians, 1531-3——Abolition would disfranchise non-resident owners, 1531, 1545-6.

Ex officios: Reduction of, would raise rates, 1547-57, 1574-80, 1596——Attend well when there is business, 1563——Non-attendance caused by non-residence and other occupations, 1552, 1559-65——Should not be reduced, 1566, 1569, 1571, 1573;—but should be ratepayers, 1566-73.

Elective guardians elected by proxy vote the best, 1532-3, 1548-9, 1575——Jobbery by leaguers in electing officials, 1548-54;—in contracts, 1555-7——More extravagant than *ex officios* in giving outdoor relief, 1580-7.

Chairman can repress politics at meetings, 1588-91.

Robinson, Dr., referred to, *Fenelon* 2459-60, 2467.

ROBINSON, MR. HENRY, C.B., Vice President of Irish Local Government Board, and previously an Inspector, and also Assistant Under Secretary for Ireland (1-3).

Analysis of his Evidence (1-268).

Unions: Area originally settled by Commissioners, but may be altered by Local Government Board, 112-3.

Boards of guardians composed equally of elective and *ex-officio* members, 7, 19;—but number of magistrates sometimes insufficient, 7-9, 158, 252 —— Where number excessive, the highest rated selected, 14, 15, 182, 252;—should not be so, but *ex officios* should be elected by magistrates, as before 1838, 182-4, 242-3, 252-3, 255——Return of respective numbers referred to, 177.

Ex-officio members are magistrates residing or having a 50 *l*. rental in union, 7, 10, 16, 156;—but not stipendiary magistrates, 13——Non-residents must be magistrates of the county where they reside, 11-2, 249, 250;—but not necessarily on rate book of union, 15-8—— Residents need not be ratepayers, 15, 156 ——Should be so, 157——Rarely not so, 245-7.

Ex officios useful on board, 165, 172, 184;—and carry weight where they attend, 172;—but attend badly, 164, 172-3, 184, 256-8;—which is partly accounted for by non-residence, 173, 248, 251——Complain of want of respect, 174-5.

Guardians of both classes attend well to elect chairman or clerk, 179. 81.

Return of attendance of guardians referred to, 176-8.

[130—IND.] L L *Ex officios*

Report, 1885—*continued.*

ROBINSON, MR. HENRY, C.B.—(Analysis of his Evidence)—*continued.*

Ex-officios one-fourth of board in 1938, 162, 182, 194-6, 238, 265——Increased to one-half in 1847, 162, 254—— Proposal of Bill to reduce them to one-third, 194-6, 238;—disapproved, 162-4, 182-3, 238-241—— They represent property not represented by voting power of owners, 169, 170, 198-9, 239, 240;—who pay greater part of poor rate, 4, 45-7, 114-9, 116-9, 162;—whose interest in economy is permanent, 162;—and whose voting power would be reduced by Bill, 171——Sir G. Nicholl's Report on the subject quoted, 162—— No opinion as to other means of representing property, 244.

Elective Guardians: Qualification may be fixed by Local Government Board at any sum below 30 *l.*, 159-161——Is often 10 *l.*, 161——Uniform qualification inexpedient, 160, 189—— Doubtful whether uniform or maximum qualification of 12 *l.* intended in Bill, 185-8——Doubt should be removed, 185, 188.

Mode of election described, 4-6—— Elections annual, on 25th March, 22, 56, 124, 126——Interval cannot be extended by Local Government Board, 123-4:—but individuals are returned again, 125——Elections should be triennial, 21, 264.

Elections to fill up vacancies should not be compulsorily held, unless demanded by guardians, 154-5.

Contested elections increasing in number, owing to political and religious reasons, 120-1—— Expenses partly on union, and partly on division concerned, 146.

Voters, three classes: Occupiers, owners, and immediate lessors, 4——Owner's right to vote lapses after five years, 263-5;—which might be reduced to three years, 264, 268——Occupier's right does not lapse, 263, 266-7.

Claims to vote made one month before polling day, 37, 56——Should be two months, 56;—as also with regard to payment of arrears of rate as a qualification to vote, 57-8; —which can now be paid on day of voting, 59-60——This impracticable with ballot, 57.

List of voters to be prepared at time prescribed by Local Government Board, 50—— Lists of voters in district for use of polling clerk, 23, 41.

Revision of List and Register: Objections as well as claims should be heard, 61, 64 ——No law for this at present, 62-3;—but it is done in practice, 63—— Revision should be annual, not triennial, as proposed. 64-5.

Cumulative Vote: Scale, 4—Additional vote for beneficial interest, 4——Maximum of votes, thirty, 4-6, 28, 228-9——Increased from eighteen by legal decision, 6, 223-9—— Reduction to eighteen by Bill, 18 ;—approved, 223;—but person appointing proxy should determine to what voting qualification the reduction should apply, 229-236;—failing which, reduction should be distributed equally, 233, 235——Occupation and immediate lessor votes formerly aggregated, 230-1.

Proxies can be used only by owners and immediate lessors, 6, 37;—irrespective of residence, 77-8——No reason for extending use to occupiers, 105——Are used in England, 49, 80;—though not by residents, 79;—but owner does not pay half the tenant's rate, 80.

Proxies appointed one month before polling day, 37 ;—and last for five years, unless revoked, 81-2, 87——Duration formerly unlimited, 82———Should be restricted to three years, 82-4, 268.

Proxies: only twenty can be held by one person, unless an agent, 84——Same person should be appointed in respect of both voting qualifications, 85.

Proxies: Statistics of number of, imperfect, 23, 73, 75, 107, 111 ;—but might be ascertained, 76, 108-9——Proxies much used, 76, 110;—more during contests, 74, 106, 122——Are compatible with ballot, 37-41.

Abolition of proxies would partly disfranchise owners, 42-4, 52, 86, 197-9 ;—and would let in guardians with less interest in economy, 197, 200-3, 206, 220-2:—which is peculiarly the interest of the owners, 201-7——But ratepayers might ultimately check extravagance, 222—— Sir G. Nicholl's Report quoted, 46-7—— Proxies should be retained, 45, 48——But their effect on good administration not ascertained by witness, 127-8—— Different polling days difficult to arrange, and would not meet objection, 43, 71-2——Voting by registered letter would endanger secrecy, 50-1, 53 ;—though that sometimes immaterial, 53, 67-9 ;—and would cause large correspondence, 102—— Point not fully considered by witness, 103.

Voting papers now used, 4, 6, 37.

Ballot has long been under consideration, 35 ——Would be an improvement, 33—— Would prevent intimidation, 34-6 ;—secrecy being secured by sealing up counterfoils, 95-9 :—but would not affect class of persons elected, 200 ;—if proxies retained, 104, 115.

Difficulty,

Report, 1885—*continued*.

ROBINSON, MR. HENRY, C.B.—(Analysis of his Evidence)—*continued*.
Difficulty, under ballot, with regard to cumulative vote, 23;—should be dealt with in Bill, 23, 29——Separate ballot paper for each vote cumbrous, 23, 25, 67——Whole of votes on one paper recommended, 23, 26–9;—but might endanger secrecy, 24, 27; —though this often immaterial, 53, 67-9——Six votes on one paper preferable, 30-2, 70.
Penal clauses of Ballot Act should be expressly enacted in Bill, 54-5.
Polling places in electoral divisions provided for by Ballot Act, 66.
Election petitions now determined by Local Government Board, 129, 133–4, 145 ———Are many and frivolous, 130——Usual grounds of objection described, 131, 133-4 ——Proposal to try them before county court an improvement, 130, 135, 145 ; as frivolous objections would be discouraged by liability for costs, 132, 135——Security for costs perhaps advisable, 136, 138, 140–3——Returning officer's costs thrown on poor rate, 137——He would not be mulcted for error of judgment, 137——Misconduct should be otherwise dealt with, 139——If costs thrown on rate, should be on division concerned, 147.
Election not necessarily affected by annulling of votes, 148;—but, if made void, a fresh election should be compulsory, 154.
Minors: Trustees of, should vote for him, 149, 150——Do so now, but not under statute, 149-152——Definite right should be given by statute, 153——Minor occupiers may vote, 153.
Lunatics should be treated like minors, 237.
Chairman of Board: Importance of, 180-1——Generally a magistrate formerly, but not of late, 259;—owing to political reasons, 260——A magistrate not necessarily the best, 261-2.
Out-door relief, the main item in which careful or careless expenditure consists, 207 ——Excessive at one time, 166–8——Not so much so now, 166, 218-9;—but increasing every year, 209-211, 213-7——Given in excessive sums to evicted tenants, 190-3;— but not illegally, 190, 193, 208-9——Kept down by *ex-officios*, 184——Numbers relieved, 211, 214, 217;—small compared with England, 212.

Roscommon referred to, *Bourke* 278——Increase of magistrates in, *Smyth* 1331-2, 1353-4, 1367-8.

Roscommon Union in two counties, *Smyth* 1363——Number of guardians, *ib.* 1220, 1294 ——Qualification, *ib.* 1246——Rates and out-door relief, *ib.* 1258-9, 1266, 1284—— Litigation as to out-door relief, *ib.* 1261, 1271-5——Chairman, *ib.* 1288, 1292—— Voting power in town, *ib.* 1300-1, 1303-4.

Roscrea Union. Number of guardians, *Gray* 1110-1——Attendance, *ib.* 1115——Better administration since 1847, *ib.* 1103-22——Chairman, *ib.* 1123——Rates, *ib.* 1116, 1122 ——Out-door relief, *ib.* 1124-7 ——Last contest in, *ib.* 1134-44, 1151-5.

Rosse, Earl of, referred to, *Tyrrell* 1021, 1032.

"*Rossmorite*," *Smyth* 1323.

Rowan, Colonel, referred to, *Spaight* 823-4, 829.

Russell, Lord John, brought in Bill of 1847, *Bagwell* 868.

Ryan, Mr., referred to, *Ringwood* 1549.

S.

Salaries of old officials cannot be altered without notice, *Fenelon* 2450——Of new, can be fixed without notice, *ib.* 2449-50——Reduction difficult, *ib.* 2453, 2478——Extravagance of *ex officiis* in, *ib.* 2393, 2447-52, 2475–6——Contrary evidence, *Carden* 2545-6—— Economy of elective guardians in, *Fenelon* 2448-52, 2475-9. *See also Pensions*.

Sandes, Mr., *ex-officio* chairman of Listowel Union, *Spaight* 718-20, 823-8.

Sanitary work. Difficulty in, from multiplicity of ownership titles, *Smyth* 1341, 1350–2 ——Neglect of, by guardian, *Fenelon* 2393.

Shannon, Mr. referred to, *Carden* 2504.

(130—IND.)   L L 2   *Shillelagh*

Report, 1885—*continued.*

Shillelagh Union nearly all one man's property, *Robinson* 247*———*Election at, deciding maximum of cumulative vote, *ib.* 6. *See* also CUMULATIVE VOTE.

Sligo, referred to, *Bourke* 278.

SMYTH, MR. HENRY, tenant farmer, magistrate, and elective and *ex-officio* guardian and vice chairman till replaced by a suspect. At one time under police protection (1163-70, 1261).

 Analysis of his Evidence (1163-1368).
 Triennial elections approved, 1174, 1237.

 Ballot necessary, to prevent existing League intimidation, 1177, 1194-8, 1206-16, 1261-4———But increased expense should not fall on rates, 1174-7———Polling booths would be necessary, 1177-80;—or election might be at workhouse, 1181-4———Constables or local magistrates should be polling clerks, 1191-4———Lists of voters charged to candidates, 1185-90———Voting papers should carry only one vote each, 1194, 1199-1205.

 Proxies: Abolition of, would disfranchise many owners, 1218, 1234 ;—whose voting power is already too small, 1218-23, 1225, 1228———Owners careless in exercising voting power, 1226-7———Proportion of persons to votes difficult to ascertain, 1300-10 ———No complaint of proxies, 1229.

 Cumulative vote: After six votes for 200*l*, each 100*l*. should confer two votes, up to twenty or twenty-five votes, 1230.

 Election Petitions: Decision of, by county court judge approved, with security for costs to be paid by parties, 1231-6.

 Minors should vote through guardians, 1239-41.

 Ex officios should be ratepayers, 1242-4. 1251———Presence at board salutary, 1250———Reduction of, would raise rates, 1252, 1257-9 ;—and produce worse chairmen, 1253-6, 1292-3———Attendance bad, owing to insults from electives, 1250-2, 1258-9, 1262, 1294-9, 1317;—and mobbing, 1317———Chairman cannot enforce order easily, 1318-26 ———Increased magistracy will improve attendance, 1331-4, 1353-4-—Election of *ex officios,* instead of selection by rateability, good, but unpopular with Leaguers, 1354-65———Power to resign needed, 1327-30, 1363-8.

 Elective guardians lately extravagant, 1311-4———Qualification should not be lowered, 1245-9.

 Outdoor relief greatly increased, owing to illegal and excessive amounts given to suspects, 1258-86, 1290, 1314-6———Laches of Local Government Board in connection with it, 1261.

 No jobbery in contracts, 1287-91.

 Plan of property guardians, though good in principle, impracticable owing to difficulty in ascertaining ownership title, and would intensify class feeling, 1335-53.

SPAIGHT, COL. GEORGE CAMPBELL, a Poor Law Inspector (643-5, 733).

 Analysis of his Evidence (643-849).
 Duties of inspector, 646-7.
 Triennial elections approved, 648.
 Ballot approved, 649.

 Proxies can turn election, 603-4, 751-2———Abolition would disfranchise owners, 650-2———Difficulty could not be met by elections on different days, 791 ;—or in any other way, 819-— Proxies no hardship, 816-7———Should not be abolished, 818——— Owners' voting power already insufficient, 750, 781.

 Claims to vote should be made two months before poll, 655.

 Election petitions should be tried by county court judge, 656-7 ;— and security given for costs to be paid by parties, 658-60, 803.

 Minors and lunatics should vote through trustees, 661-2.

 Fresh elections should remain optional, 663.

 Elective Guardians : Qualification should remain at discretion of Local Government Board, 664-5, 727———Publicans should be disqualified, 666-7, 787-90———Electives are seldom owners, 847-8——— Have little interest in economy, 794, 730-2 ;—are bad administrators, 733-6 ;—but less so where politics excluded, 785-6 ;—prone to give improper outdoor relief, 752, 761 ;—and to political jobbery in electing officials, 716-7, 722-4———Local Government Board can control this, but not jobbery in contracts, 800-2.

                     Ex officios :

Report, 1885—*continued.*

SPAIGHT, COL. GEORGE CAMPBELL. (Analysis of his Evidence)—*continued.*

Ex officios: Administration of, good, 671 —— Better than that by electives, 672-708, 797 —— Attendance bad. 673, 676-8, 783-4 ;—as being swamped, 676, 747, 776-9 ;— and discourteously treated, 718-21 —— Bad attendance owing in some degree to non-residence, 830-46 —— Attend well at election of chairman, 716, 748, 783-6 —— Are about the only representation of property, 714 —— Reduction disapproved, as it would swamp them, 668-70, 713, 737, 792-8 ;—and produce worse chairman, 823-9 —— Advocated only on political grounds, 820-2 —— Their value rather personal than numerical, except at election of chairman, 738-49 —— Should be elected by brother magistrates, 709-13, 804-10.

Outdoor relief: Great increase in lately, owing to improper grants to evicted tenants rather than to distress, 720-30, 752-75, 798-9 —— Might be relieved by friendly societies if practicable, 811-5 —— Not improperly refused by *ex officios*, 797.

Owners: No attempt to throw all poor rate on them, 780-2 —— Unlikely to be elected guardians at present, 849.

T.

Tipperary, referred to, *Bourke* 280; *Smyth* 1358.

Town Commissioners. See *BALLOT.*

Tralee Union managed by elective guardians, *Spaight* 678-9 —— Outdoor relief, *ib.* 689-90.

Trench, Mr. Townsend, referred to, *Spaight* 705.

Tulla Union. Embarrassed finances of, *Bourke* 359-64, 405 —— Excessive outdoor relief, *ib.* 332 —— Records tampered with, *ib.* 347-53. *See also Killannon.*

TYRRELL, MR. GARRETT C., Ex-officio Deputy Vice Chairman of Edenderry Union (948-51).

Analysis of his Evidence (948-1066).
Triennial elections approved, 952-3.
Ballot will prevent intimidation, 954 —— Voting papers should carry one vote each, 955-7.

Proxies cannot swamp occupation votes, 959-65 ;—but can turn election, 968-74, 1041 —— Should be renewed every three years, 1063-6 —— Abolition would disfranchise owners, 958, 963-4 ;—whose voting power is already too small, 969-87, 1010-15.

Elective Guardians: Qualification not complained of, 1008 —— Should not be lowered, 1006-7 —— Loyalists attend better than Leaguers, 988-9, 1022-3 ; - who are given to jobbery in contracts, 1042-4.

Ex officios should not be reduced, property being already under-represented, 1009-15 —— Bad attendance, 1024-32, 1039 ;—owing to action of Leaguers, 1030, 1040 ;—cause of increased rates, 1033-5 —— Residents attend as well as electives, 1016-21 ;—but non-residents can sometimes attend as well, 1060-2 —— Should have power to resign, 1058-60.

Plan of property guardians would end in deadlock, 1045-8.

Claims to vote should be made two months before poll, 990-1, 994 ;—and non-payment of arrears of rate should disqualify, 992-5.

Election petitions should be tried by county court judge, 996 ;—security for costs being given, to be paid by parties, 996-9 —— But to be on rates, if returning officer's default venial, 1000 —— Should be presented only by candidate or nominator, 996.

Cumulative Vote: Maximum of six insufficient, 1049-50 —— If maximum be again eighteen, lessor and occupancy votes should be aggregated, 1051-7.

Minors should vote through guardians, 1001-5 —— Only proxies allowed at present, 1003.

U.

Unions. Settlement of area, *Robinson* 112 3 —— Number, *Morris* 480.

Union Officers' Association described, *Molloy* 1601.

(130—IND) L L 3

Report, 1885—*continued.*

V.

Vacancies on Board: Fresh elections for, prescribed by Bill, *Robinson* 154——This approved, *Meehan* 2223——Elections should be permissive, unless demanded by guardians, *Robinson* 154-5; *Morris* 473; *Spaight* 663——Some not filled up, *Meehan* 2200, 2203-4, 2207-8; *Fenelon* 2431; *Carden* 2505-6.

Valuation gives occupancy vote, *Robinson* 4.

Vaughan, Mr. W. P. H. L., referred to, *Gray* 1123.

Ventry, Lord, Chairman of Dingle Union, *Spaight* 695——Return of guardians obtained by him, *Robinson* 176-7.

Vice Chairman. See CHAIRMAN.

Vice Guardians. Their duties, *Morris* 638; *Smyth* 1325-6——Appointment of, threatened, *Bourke* 360; *Morris* 637-8——Appointed, *Spaight* 734; *Bagwell* 887; *Walsh* 2060, 2111-2. See also BOARDS OF GUARDIANS.——One made a magistrate, *Spaight* 840-2.

Void Elections. See *Vacancies.*

Voters. Three classes of ratepayers, *Robinson* 4——All ratepayers have votes, rightly. *Fenelon* 2419, 2427;—including women, *Tyrrell* 1005; *Fox* 1975; *Fenelon* 2348;—and minors, see MINORS——Many do not vote, *Smyth* 1308-10——Number of voters, *Robinson* 23; *Molloy* 1754;—difficult to ascertain, *Smyth* 1300-7——Voters disfranchised by non-striking of rate, *Walsh* 2064;—by non-payment of rate, see RATES. See also OWNERS.——Voting qualification, see below.——Constituency for Poor Law wider than for Parliament, *Fox* 1972-5.

Voting qualification, low. *Tyrrell* 1050; *Hewson* 1457-8. See also PROXIES.——Maximum, see CUMULATIVE VOTE.

VOTING PAPERS:
Under present system, *Robinson* 4, 6——Issue and collection of, *ib.* 6; *Fenelon* 2365——Publication of, at discretion of returning officer, *Gray* 1134, 1148, 1151, 1153; *Molloy* 1608-10; *Fenelon* 2348-7——Refused by him, *ib.* 2346——Right of candidate to inspect, *ib.* 2346——Votes known, *Smyth* 1213; *Molloy* 1612——System peculiarly open to intimidation, *McCann* 1796-7. See also INTIMIDATION.——Causes mistakes and trouble, *Meehan* 2131-3, 2157.
Counterfoil, *Robinson* 23, 94-5, 97-9. Scrutiny, *Molloy* 1607.
Under ballot, one for each voter should be prescribed in Bill, *Robinson* 23, 26, 28-9; but secrecy might be thus endangered, *ib.* 24, 27, 32, 67-9; *Smyth* 1194, 1199, 1203-4 Six votes on one paper perhaps best, *Robinson* 30-2, 70; *Morris* 447——One for each vote recommended, *Tyrrell* 965; *Smyth* 1200-3, 1205; *Hewson* 1376-7; *McCann* 1682; —with a book with blocks, *Hewson* 1376;—to ensure secrecy, *Tyrrell* 956-7——Extra expense small, *Smyth* 1201-2——One for each vote cumbrous, *Robinson* 23, 25, 67: *Morris* 445-7—— Procedure, *Robinson* 98-9. See also BALLOT.

W.

Wales, Prince of. His visit to Ireland referred to, *Carden* 2565.

WALSH, MR. PETER, *ex-officio* Guardian of Carrick-on-Suir Union, owner and tenant farmer (2035-9, 2055, 2080).

Analysis of his Evidence (2035-2114).
Elections should be triennial, 2041——Date of, need not be altered, 2110.
Ballot approved, 2042.
Proxies not complained of by public, 2044-5——Can turn election, 2046-50—— Abolition would disfranchise owners, 2043, 2055-7.
Elective Guardians: Qualification should be raised rather than lowered, 2058, 2066 ——Obstruct business by political discussion, 2059-65, 2079, 2086-8——Procedure now regulated by Local Government Board, 2089-92——Do business fairly when politics excluded, 2078——Leagues give excessive out-door relief, 2082-5.

Ex officio

Walsh, Mr. Peter. (Analysis of his Evidence)—*continued.*

Ex officio trusted by poor, 2067-70.——Reduction deprecated, 2067——Would increase rates, diminish attendance, and discourage good candidates, 2071-2——Attend fairly, 2073-7, 2110;—and are well treated by electives, 2079——Should be elected by magistrates, 2093-4;—which would perhaps improve attendance, 2095-6——Should pay rates, directly or indirectly, 2094, 2099, 2102-6——Should have power to resign, 2099——Agent might serve on board in owner's absence, 2099-2101.

Plan of property guardians would make electives all Leaguers, 2097-8.

Cumulative Vote: Every 50*l.* over 200*l.* should give one vote, 2107——If maximum reduced, lessor and occupancy votes should be aggregated, 2108.

List of voters should last three years, 2109,—non-payment of rates disqualifying, *ib.* — Register should admit of appeal, 2113 — Might be final if revised by revising barrister, 2113-4.

Wexford Union agricultural, *Ringwood* 1579——*Ex officios* weak, *ib.* 1551, 1575——Jobbery in electing official, *ib.* 1548-50——Rates, *ib.* 1574-5.

Whelan. Case of improper application for relief, *Walsh* 2085.

Workhouse. Votes counted at, *Robinson* 66, 99——The cheapest polling place, *Smyth* 1181-4. See also *POLLING PLACES.*

www.ingramcontent.com/pod-product-compliance
Lightning Source LLC
Chambersburg PA
CBHW032120230426
43672CB00009B/1810